URBAN SOCIOLOGY

RAJENDRA K. SHARMA

ATLANTIC
PUBLISHERS & DISTRIBUTORS

Published by
ATLANTIC PUBLISHERS AND DISTRIBUTORS
B-2, Vishal Enclave, Opp. Rajouri Garden, New Delhi-110027
Phones : 25413460, 25429987, 25466842

Sales Office
7/22, Ansari Road, Darya Ganj, New Delhi-110002
Phones : 23273880, 23275880, 23280451
Fax : 91-11-23285873
web : www.atlanticbooks.com
e-mail : info@atlanticbooks.com

Printed in India at
Rashtriya Printers, Delhi

Preface

This book covers university syllabi of Urban Sociology in India. Besides introduction to urban sociology it deals with : Urbanization and Urban Growth; Urbanism, Urban Ecology and Urban Personality; Theories of Urbanization; Types of Cities; Rural Urban Contrast; The Urban Family; Urban Culture; Urban Society; Urban Politics; Industrialization, Disorganisation and Corruption in Public Life. It discusses the Urban Problem of Over-Crowding, Housing, Crime, Juvenile Delinquency, White Collar Crime, Prostitution, Alcoholism and Drug Addiction, Suicide, Beggary, Poverty, Unemployment and Labour Problems. It analyses Urban outlook and Social Change, Planning and Slums. Finally, it describes the Welfare of Urban Backward Classes in India.

With analytical method of presentation and holistic outlook, coupled with a language free from technical jargon, along with statistical data from Indian Urban Scene, this book seeks to serve the needs of students as an ideal text-book and a reference book for teachers.

Suggestions from readers are invited for future improvements.

RAJENDRA K. SHARMA

Contents

1

Introduction to Urban Sociology

All the settlements, habitats of men and their creation can only be understood in terms of human ecology i.e., the relation between man and environment. Ecology in relation to plants and animals refers to a direct relation between the two, since plants and animals adapt themselves to their environment. However, there also we find peculiarities. A relation of symbiosis involves a relation of inter-dependence between two unlike beings. Thus the nitrogen fixing bacteria depend upon plants for their sustenance while they absorb the nitrogen from the air and supply it to the plant in a palatable form.

The relation between man and his environment is thus one of divergence and essential dependence. Thus the food gatherers and hunters depend fully upon their environment for sustenance. But man is a being which has the power to intelligently modify his nature to subserve his purposes. This relation of an essential symbiosis between man and Nature begins to emerge in the agricultural societies where man cultivates the crops. Thus while man is essentially dependent upon Nature he can at the same time modify it, this relation advances as there are advancces in technology and cultivation. Technology takes man away from Nature while technology develops using the basic components of nature.

The urban area represents the development of this relation of symbiosis in its extreme form. The city is an artefact of steel and stone. It represents a fully developed artificial environment which mocks at the vagaries of nature. Thus we have artificial air conditioning, water supply etc. But all these have their essential sources in a thorough study of such occurrences in nature and depending upon the relative qualities of the nature in which an urban area is located. Further, a site of an urban area depends upon its amenability for city construction without any natural obstacles like slopes, steep gradients etc. Urban transportation depends upon nature for its formulation. Further, an urban area thrives in the midst of a rich rural hinterland, not otherwise. Thus an urban area can only develop with an essential dependence and at the same time a total isolation from the necessities of a suitable and inevitable natural location.

Thus human ecology represents an essential relation of symbiosis.

FACTORS OF URBAN ECOLOGY

Urban settlements form distinct regular patterns. A city is a clearly distinguished spatial order of Urban activities.

The sectional difference within a city arises out of social consideration which creates for each part a different evaluation and different function.

A city is a multifunctional settlement. The functional assignment is the result of social forces and processes; which, in turn, are conditioned by institutional values; by traditions and customs of a specific culture. There are three factors which decide the ecological structure of a city. These are: (1) differentiation of functions, (2) class separation, and (3) cultural segregation.

1. Differentiation of Functions. In cities areas are differentiated according to the functions they perform. This is because of the complexity and specialization of city culture, for example, business district, factory area, residential zone etc. In these functional areas there are further specialised sub-divisions. For example, cloth shops all flock in a particular street of the lower middle class residential zone, upper class residential area etc. In cities each function occupies its most favourable location. Thus, while the business district is situated at its centre, residential areas expand towards the out skirts of the city.

2. Class Separation. In the cities of antiquity and medieval cities there was a clearly discernible partition of living quarters according to classes. In modern cities we have structures according to classes. In modern cities we have structural differentiation on class lines. The ecological patterns of housing are based on several criteria such as location, type, size of the house, quality and state of repair and accession etc.

3. Cultural Segregation. The ecological importance of cultural segregation lies in the fact of the importance of their separate cultural values to the separate cultural groups and their treatment by the majority groups. However, in India the caste system does not operate so rigidly in cities and towns.

Structured changes result from a rise in the urban population which alters its class structure and hence the housing pattern of lower class increases at a greater rate. The neo rich tend to encroach upon established families by moving into their quarters. Populations also increase due to immigration. This results in the pushing up of the upper class residential areas to city outskirts. The prevailing one family houses in the so described areas are converted into multi family dwellings and the area is converted into zone in transition.

VALUE OF ECOLOGY

The ecological approach to the study of urban community decides its most favourable location after a careful analysis of the geo-physical factors of a particular area, the nature of hinterland facilities available, the climatic factors of a city, the structural and functional significance of the surrounding area, availability of necessary population both in the quality and quantity etc. Further, the ecological approach which gives a thorough analysis of the geological factors of an area, helps in planning the internal structure of city. The internal structure of a complex community like a city must be so organised that each specialised function such as business, industry, housing, etc., gets its most favoured location. The ecological approach helps us in detecting the most favoured location for each function. Further, the ecological approach decides the pattern of streets and transportation routes in a city which forms the vital arteries of communication and the connection and other geological factors of a city. Further, the ecological approach, coupled with an understanding of the socio-cultural qualities of the people of an urban community decides the housing pattern and the nature and character of houses. Finally, it is ecology which once again alerts the city planner to make room for open spaces with trees which give fresh air and sooth the eye of the city dweller i.e., the creation of beauty spots and parks and to the concept of city beautification.

Ecological Processes

Thus, ecological approach to the study of urban community provides valuable material about its physical and structural aspects which form the base of social planning. Encouraged by this the urban sociologists have tried to evolve five ecological processes of the growth of a city. These are :

1. Concentration. According to which functions and people tend to flock towards areas of common attraction, for example, business concentrates in city centre.

2. Centralisation. This refers to the concentration of similar functions and people in common area, for example wholesale business, factories etc. Excessive centralisation leads to decentralisation. This process explains the gradual movement of retail trade to city suburbs in an expanding city.

3. Segregation. This refers to the isolation of specific functions and people to particular areas such as business centre, factories at the outskirts etc.

4. Invasion. This refers to the process of expansion of a particular function, say, business to a neighbouring area, as much as the surrounding zone of light industry due to overcrowding.

5. Succession. This refers to the establishment of the function say business which has encroached upon the neighbouring zone permanently. This explains the growth of the zone in transition.

Advantages of Ecological Approach

Depending on this theoretical background now let us examine some of the practical benefits of the ecological approach of study of an urban community.

1. Location. With regard to location even though it is said that a city can be located anywhere in practice, the city planners must take into consideration the geo-physical advantages of particular area and its suitability for the construction of a city, its amenability for expansion etc. The city planner must examine the availability for expansion etc. The city planner must examine the availability of a rich hinterland which can provide adequate food and raw materials to city dwellers and industries and which may provide customers for the products and services of a city. Further, the location of a city also decides its nature and function *i.e.*, whether it must be an industrial city or an administrative or cultural centre etc. Thus, an industrial city requires a constant supply of basic raw materials while an administrative centre must form the nucleus of a state or other aggregate. A health resort town must be built around pleasant and healthy natural surroundings.

2. Internal Structure. The location, nature and functions of a city decides its internal structure. With regard to this, the theories stated above give certain basic clues to a common pattern of urban growth which can be noticed in a flexible way in each and every city. Thus, wholesale business, shops of retail trade, major administrative offices and commercial establishments, eating places, places of entertainment and other materials of essential services are usually located at the centre of a big city which form the area of convergence. Light and ancillary industries form the immediate fringe of the business area and form the zone in transition, an area of flocking of all the vices and filth of a city such as slums. Immediately, after we have the area of workingmen's residence, an area of tenement houses and multifamily dwellings. Workers occupy this area because of its cheapness and proximity to the place of work. The middle class suburbs lie a little apart from this. It is an area of small one family dwellings of clean and well laid out streets and comparative peace and calm. The suburban retail shopping complex usually caters to the daily needs of these suburban dwellers. A little apart from this we have the commuter's zone, an area of spacious bungalows of upper middle class and rich people who usually own their own vehicles. Attached to this we have in some cities a fringe agricultural zone which grows vegetables and carries on dairying catering to the city's needs. The big factories of an industrial city usually lie at the outskirts near routes of heavy transportation because of its requirements of space and easy transportability of raw materials and bulk products. The schools, colleges and other cultural centres lie in the various suburbs of the city depending upon necessity and patronage. Ecology decides upon the areas of segregation of particular cultural groups in certain cities, for example, negro community in U.S. cities.

3. Routes. Ecology determines the street pattern of a city upon which depends the location of various functions in various areas of a city. Usually the routes of heavy transportation lie around the city while smaller routes converge upon the city centre from all other zones. Further, it is the street pattern which decides upon the patterning of particular functional zones.

4. Beauty Spots. Ecology points out areas in a city for the construction of parks and other centres of natural beauty and gives ideas of city beautification.

Thus, the study of the ecological plan and structure of a city is a basic prerequisite for its social planning. It provides relevant clues to the contemporary city planner in the planning of new cities and suburbs and city expansion and in rectifying the anomalies of unplanned cities, with its development in precision and as a thorough scientific subject.

URBAN SOCIOLOGY

Urban sociology is an important discipline under the general discipline of sociology. It is a branch of sociology. In urban sociology, as in general sociology, we study social relations though to a limited extent and in shorter context. The kind of social relations studied in urban sociology is evident from the name. These are the relations which occur in an urban society. Thus, urban sociology is a study of urban society. The urban society is studied and investigated according to sociological methods and techniques, these techniques, of course, are scientific. The study of urban society can be general as well as specific. In every city we find certain features which are to be found in every urban society and are, therefore, to be regarded as general. These are distinct from the features of a rural society. For example, in cities, the relations among individuals are impersonal. Besides, the general features which are common to all metropolises, there are certain specific features peculiar to one or more towns but inappliable to others. Urban sociology studies both general and specific features.

THE ORIGIN OF URBAN SOCIOLOGY

Sociology is not an ancient study. Indeed it began its career as a science in the last century only. Urban sociology, being a branch of sociology, is naturally much less old than the parent study. As a matter of fact, the systematic discipline of urban sociology came into being in 20th century only. As in the case of rural sociology, maximum work in the field of urban sociology has also been done in the United States of America. In the 20th century, much intensive work has been done in the specialized fields of urban sociology. For example, many books have appeared on classification of towns, citizenship, development of towns, urban environment, social disorganization in cities, demographical trends, community life and its impact upon personality, family, marriage and divorce in cities etc. Besides, a good deal of work has also been done on reform and development of urban life. In this connection special mention needs be made of intensive research into the mechanism of social welfare, proper use of leisure, religious, cultural and educational institutions in cities and town planning and rehabilitation. But, however, it is a matter of regret that little work has been done in India on the above mentioned aspects of urban life.

DEFINITION OF A CITY

City forms the central point of urban sociology. It marks the highest watermark of human civilization. Now, what is a city? From 17th century onwards city has become a subject of scientific research of various social scientists. Like many other sociological categories, the city is an abstraction composed of concrete entities like residences and shops and an assortment of many functions.

The city has been defined according to several points of view. A place is legally made a city by a declaration by a competent authority. Attempts to define a city statistically, have failed due to the absence of a representative measure. Others have defined a city as a place which has become so large that people no longer know each other. Since the quest for a single definition has met with little success, some authors, notably Sorokin and Zimmerman, Maurier and Sombart hold that a proper definition must consist of a combination of factors, multiple or 'compound' definitions. Sorokin and Zimmerman enumerate eight characteristics in which the urban world differs from the rural world. These are (1) occupation (2) environment (3) size of community (4) density of population (5) heterogeneity (6) social differentiation and stratification (7) mobility and (8) system of interactions. As occupation forms the main basis for other social activities, we call a city an 'agglomeration' where people are engaged in other than agricultural occupations. According to some scholars the difference between village and urban society is merely one of structure, the largeness and smallness of it. Though it is a fact that villages are small and cities are big, it is not proper to consider the size of the structure to be the difference between a city and a village since it varies from country to country. In U.S.A. a place having population of 2,500 or more is considered to be a city. In France this limit is still less, that is only 2,000 whereas in Belgium it is twice more, that is, 5,000. In Egypt, on the other hand, places with a population of 11,000 or more alone are considered cities. Thus, it is quite clear that a number of Egyptian villages would be cities according to French, American or Belgian standards and that a number of cities in these countries would be villages according to Egyptian standards. Some scholars make a distinction between a village and a city on the basis of community life. This criterion is preferable to the size criterion. However, the differences in community cannot account for the basic distinguishing characteristics of rural and urban life. In some cities we find elements of villages outlying their borders. Similarly, in villages adjacent to cities we find many urban characteristics. Again, it will be wrong to distinguish between a village and a city on the basis of nature and temperament of people residing in its jurisdiction. We can easily find people with same nature and temperament both in cities and villages. Had there been some fundamental difference between a village and a city, there must not be men of same temperament and nature in both villages and cities. For example, the persons of religious temperament are peculiar neither to cities nor to villages but are to be found both in villages and towns.

Thus, it is extremely difficult to so define the city as to contradistinguish it from the village. Therefore, the following observations of Gist and Halbert are very apt: "Thus the familiar dichotomy between 'Rural' and 'Urban' is more of a theoretical concept than a division based upon the facts of community life." And in the opinion of E.E. Bergel, "Everybody seems to know what a city is but no one has given a satisfactory definition." There are many things which are quite obvious and easily recognizable but which defy definition and the concepts of city and village are one of these. Following are the difficulties in defining and distinguishing a city from a village:

1. There are no universally acceptable definitions of village and city.

2. The distinction between a village and a city is one of degree merely. There are no fundamental or qualitative differences.

3. Both villages and cities undergo changes. Thus, it is no easy task to distinguish between a village and a city and almost impossible to formulate the distinction in words. However, modern sociologists have tried to distinguish the city from the village on the basis of professions, environment, size of the population and social interaction. In social organization, we can perceive difference in regard to family, marriage institution, the role of women, neighbourhood, the feelings of belongingness, heterogeneity of groups and classes between rural and urban societies. In rural and urban societies, there is usually a marked difference between quality and extent of social control. Obviously, it is lose in cities and strong in villages. Moreover, there are differences of orientation with regard to attitudes towards progress, political life, destiny, fate, artificiality and social disorganization. There are also quite clear differences in regard to social and economic structures. The distinction between village and city will be discussed in detail a little later. Meanwhile, we shall describe the characteristics of urban community life. An urban community may be defined as a group of people having a certain minimum population or number and also possessing certain specialized economic, political and social structures with some recognizable characteristics. In the above definition of an urban community, the social characteristic is the most distinguishing and vital. The following are the special or distinctive features of urban community:

(1) Social heterogeneity; (2) moderate social contracts; (3) social tolerance; (4) moderate control; (5) social dynamism; (6) voluntary association; (7) impersonality; (8) lack of communal feeling; (9) loss of morals; (10) unbalanced individuals; (11) prevalance of crimes; (12) dynamic life; (13) rapid change and (14) artificiality in life. The urban sociology is a study of the communities having above mentioned characteristics.

Urban Social Actions

Urban social actions guided by urban social relationships are secondary and specific in nature. They are segmentary in character and mainly aim at the fulfilment of a single function of an urbanite's life. Thus, while in rural areas imitation of one's father's work is work and education combined in one, in urban centres specialized and general education paves the way for one's career in a technical job.

Urban Social Relations

Urban social relations are many and diverse and formal in character.

Urban Social institutions based on these are again specialized agencies which serve particular functions, say education through schools, law enforcement by the city government etc. Elaborate procedure is laid down to guide the activities of these institutions and membership is through necessity and availability of the service. Thus size, density and heterogeneity and specialization are the typical urban characteristics. Urban sociology studies human social life in relation to these factors.

Urban Problems

On the other side of the coin we have the novel and peculiar urban problems which are a necessary concommitant of urbanization, such as housing, sanitation, slums, provisions and recreation, pollution of all types, fluidity of the law and order situation, increase in crime, vice and deviance, various physical and mental disorders, increasing suicides and divorces, traffic problems, zoning anomalies etc. The study of all these forms is an important corollary of the study of urban sociology. Thus urban sociology is a study of all aspects related to man's modification of environment to subserve his varied purposes with all its implications.

SCOPE OF URBAN SOCIOLOGY

If we carefully glance at the various characteristics and special features of urban sociology mentioned above, we will become aware of the nature and scope of the subject. Indeed, the above mentioned features make quite evident and plain the scope of urban sociology. The scope of urban sociology is vast. Under it, besides the study of the general principles of urban sociology, development of towns, social disorganization, we also study the problems of urban life and town planning. It also makes a study of the interaction between the urban environment and the development of human personality, it also studies the structure of family, role of family and permanent and changing elements of a family. Similarly, it studies the institution of marriage in urban context, the fundamentals and trends in marriage. In urban sociology we study factors responsible for family disorganization. The urban sociology also studies class structure and class struggle in urban societies. It also studies such features of social disorganization as crimes, juvenile delinquency, prostitution, beggary, unemployment, disease, pollution, slums, gambling dens, recreation centres, bars and clubs and the night life. In urban sociology we also study the factors and causes of social and personal disorganization and the remedies thereof. It also undertakes an investigation of industries and industrial relations, the causes of dis-harmony between labour and management and the ways and means of bringing about the harmony and peaceful constructive relations. The urban sociology studies not only the facts of urban life but also evaluates the facts in order to understand their causes and means of improvement. It also undertakes the study of social tensions in order to learn the real causes behind them. If we know exactly the cause of a disability, its solution automatically presents itself to us. Thus urban sociology is not merely a theoretical study but a practice as well.

Thus, we see that the scope of urban sociology is very vast because although urban sociology is a recent science, urbanism forms a major part of contemporary life patterns which is slowly encroaching upon and engulfing the existing forms of rural life. To say in nutshell, urban sociology studies the nature and characteristics of a city, its size, density and characters of its people, its spatial pattern and changes thereon; the peculiar type of relations and social interaction found in the urban milieu, the nature of primary social institutions such as family in an urban setting, the novel institutions of commercial recreation, education etc. Moreover it studies all the implications and complexities and consequences of urban social problems, the various urban social groupings including deviant groups and the various aspects of urban social attitudes. In short, urban sociology is a developing science which studies all aspects of urban life.

Urban sociology studies all aspects of a city life such as its size, density of population, social organization, problems etc. It is a specialized discipline which has been recently developing. Urban sociology exclusively deals with an analysis of urban problems. Urban problems occupy the major attention of urban sociologists today because of their complexity and their craving for an immediate solution. They arise at an instant such as unanticipated increase in traffic at a place in a single day becomes a problem.

Hence, urban problems lie beyond the comprehension of even an intelligent planner. These require handy solutions, for example, a traffic jam or excessive traffic must be diverted to other areas immediately to prevent accidents. Thus urban studies aim at a detailed and satisfactory analysis of the observable urban problems as a means of providing clues to understanding many other immediate and instantaneous problems.

STUDY OF URBAN SOCIOLOGY OF INDIA

As in the 1960s, urbanization in India has maintained an upward trend during the 1970s, showing not only an increase in the proportion of urban population but also an increase in the number of cities. The growth in the number of cities is spectacular so far as the bigger cities are concerned. With this spectacular growth in the number of bigger cities, certain consequential changes are brought about in the urban social structure which should draw the attention of sociologists and other social scientists. We may inquire into the extent to which sociologists and other social scientists have shown interest in the study of the various facets of the urban phenomenon and the major findings they have arrived at. For this purpose we shall focus our attention on such studies which pertain to the 1970s, with a backdrop of studies done during the 1950s and the 1960s.

At the outset, it is pertinent to take account of some of the basic facts of urban life in India as can be gathered from the 1971 census. This represents the changes in the urban population during the 1961-71 decade, and this may provide us with an idea as to the future trends. It may be mentioned in passing that the chief source of information about urban population and the urbanization process in India is the decennial census record. Bearing this in mind, we may take account of some of the basic information about the Indian urban life as can be gathered from the 1971 census.

HISTORICAL BACKGROUND

Though India had a distinct urban culture even earliest times, even a cursory review of sociological literature on Indian society would show that a more abiding interest is shown by scholars in the study of rural community and its various institutions, rather than the study of urban life and its changing manifestations. Some of the sociologists tend to view the distinction between 'rural' and 'urban' in the Indian context as somewhat different from the context of western societies because the dominance of rural life in India would not warrant a strong interest in the Indian urban situation as is true of the urban situation in the west. However, a closer look at some of the Indian cities and towns would show that the interplay of caste, family and kinship is quite evident in the urban areas (Ross 1973; Vatuk 1972; Singer 1968). Thus the traditional elements of caste and kinship are as strongly entrenched in the structure of urban community as in the rural community.

The dissociation of the process of industrialization and the urbanization process has led scholars to realise the weak economic base of the city with the accompanying manifestation of urban poverty and the proliferation of slums. (Venkatarayappa 1972; Misra 1972; Desai and Pillai 1970).

N.S.S. Reports

A study of urban stratification was taken up as part of the sample design adopted by the National Sample Survey sponsored by the Government of India from its third round onwards. Under the auspices of this programme of study, the urban areas were divided into ninetyfour strata which were grouped into clusters of three or sometimes four categories. The N.S.S. Reports provided data on a large number of topics which had been omitted by the censuses, such as labour force participation, household expenditure, income, unemployment, etc. (Bose 1970 : 26). But, as Ashish Bose remarks: "...surprisingly, very little use has been made of NSS data in urban studies."

Town Planning Laws

In the 1960s the enactment of Laws concerning town planning brought forth a wealth of information pertaining to Indian cities. Various governments set up directorates of town planning under which Outline Development Plans of major cities were drawn within the jurisdiction of each State. On the basis of these Outline Development Plans, the final draft of Master Plans were prepared. The School of Planning and Architecture at Delhi has taken up studies of several cities in the country with main emphasis on identifying areas for suitable development.

Demographic Studies (1960s)

The 1960s were particularly marked by a number of urban demographic studies. The Institute of Economic Growth located in Delhi initiated a series of long-term researches on urbanization by establishing an urban research section in the Demographic Research Centre. The immediate support to this new venture of urban demography came through the decennial national censuses undertaken since 1872. One of the significant achievements of the Indian Census undertaking has been the attempt to establish the distinction between 'rural' and 'urban', which it did on the basis of a set of demographic and economic criteria. Though the definition of 'urban' has been modified in successive censuses the very concept of 'urban' has assumed certain definite characteristics which have enabled the identification of the 'urban' and has facilitated research activities in the 'urban' field.

Prior to 1951, no distinction was established between a 'town' and 'a group of towns adjoining one another closely' so as to form a single locality. The 1951 census defined the 'town group' as a distinct concept. Further refinements of the concept of 'city' and 'town' were made in the 1961 Census Report, which could facilitate proper analysis of urban phenomena. The census authorities also published several monographs on city surveys, thus making a useful addition to urban studies.

During the 1960s the impact of urbanization on social institutions was the subject of study by a few scholars. Gore (1960) studied the changing characteristics of family in Bombay; Aileen Ross's (1973) study of the Hindu Family in its Urban Setting; and I.P. Desai's (1964) study of Family Life in Mahuva are some of the more representative studies in this direction.

Contributions by Geographers

Significant contributions have been made by urban geographers. In this connection, special mention may be made of a unique study made by Sinha (1970) of Sirsi town in North Kanara district of Karnataka. Sinha makes extensive use of certain statistical formulas in the analysis and interpretation of data pertaining to the town. He seeks to provide a more precise understanding of the growth patterns of the town. National Geographical Journal of India published a number of papers pertaining to the evolving urban patterns in India.

The 1970s

During the 1950s and the 1960s the sociological literature partaining to urban life in India had an impressive start principally with the basic orientations being drawn by the Indian Census, and with the sponsorship of research organizations provided for studies in different regions of the country. As a consequence of these factors a more positive approach to the study of urban process and urban institutions developed.

The studies undertaken during the 1970s were no more cumulative as they were based on diverse interests. The interest of the government in seeking out definite areas of investigation in the field of urbanization and the consequent problems posed by the process seem to dominate most of the studies. The 1971 census draw the outlines of the pattern of urbanization in India by pointing out that the bigger cities were growing at a faster rate than the smaller cities and towns. The bigger cities were able to spend more money on civic amenities as the civic interests were better articulated there than in smaller cities and towns. Thus the bigger cities attracted more of the migrant population than the smaller cities could attract. As the migrant population with very few skills and with little formal education increased in the bigger cities, it led to an aggravated form of overcrowding and the growth of slums. Thus slum development has been very closely associated with migration. The bigger cities are faced with the problem of slum development and slum improvement. The city governments have not been able to meet such an aggravated condition of slum growth. They are seeking out assistance from the governments in implementing programmes of low-cost housing, especially meant for slum-dwellers. Venkatarayapaa (1972) Wiebe (1975) Desai and Pillai (1972) have brought out in their studies the aggravated situation of the slums in the Indian cities.

Under conditions of rapid urban and industrial growth, the Government of India had become keenly aware of the problem of overcrowding in the Indian cities. Seminars were held in Delhi and Bombay to suggest suitable remedial measures. As an urban manifestation the slum has come to be defined in more specific terms as a consequence of such open discussions.

Between 1961-1971, four new cities in the million-range were added to the existing million-cities, giving rise to eleven million-cities in 1971. In his edited work, R.P. Misra (1978) brought together in a single volume the studies on each of these eleven cities.

Alfred de Souza's (1978) edited work on Indian cities covered a wide range of topics such as nutrition, slums and urban housing, city-hinterland relationship, and issues pertaining to migration. R.C. Sarikwal (1978) tried to highlight some of the problems which the growing industrial town of Ghaziabad near Delhi faced. This study provided an understanding of the growth patterns of the industrial township.

Historical Studies

Historical studies of individual towns and cities provide an insight into the process of urbanization in a historical perspective. Several such urban studies taken up in the 1970s and the earlier decades have evoked interest in the historical and comparative perspective. Crane (1955) and Ghurye's (1962) works were, pioneering studies in this direction. Crane's work provided an insight into the growth of cities during the pre-British period in the light of which the growth of cities during British rule is discussed. Ghurye, in his work, compared urban growth in the colonial setting with urban growth since Independence.

In his study of Ahmedabad, Kenneth Gillion (1968), analysed the colonial situation under the British as it prevailed on the West coast. The British succeeded in minimizing the influence of many of the age-old customs and traditions in this city which had been the traditional stronghold of the Gujarati trading community. Ahmedabad was thus transformed into a leading centre of textile manufacturing.

In her study of Bombay in mid-nineteenth century Christine Dobbins (1972) brought to light the speed and variability with which different local communities which were generally receptive to the new ideas introduced by the British took advantage of the new opportunities. This had been done by identifying the merging elites in Bombay in the mid-nineteenth century. Bayly (1975) referred to the emergence of the urban elite in the city of Allahabad. The new elite gave the much needed leadership to the nascent nationalist sentiments. Their members were instrumental in shaping the early policies of the Congress Party.

Pradip Sinha (1978) traced the growth of the metropolitan city of Calcutta from a cluster of villages during the times of Job Charnock to the period when it assumed the status of the capital city of India. In this study, Sinha highlighted the emergence of the urban middle class and also the class of Western-oriented wealthy residents who had the benefit of Western Education.

In the Serampore study by Pranabranjan Ray (1971) took account of the colonial situation, first under the Danish settlers, and then under the British rule, Ray pointed to the fact that the trading communities of Serampore flourished under alien rule, leading to its establishment as a prosperous commercial town.

In his study of Indian society Milton Singer (1972) stressed the process of transition of an older culture, which he designated as the Great Tradition, to a complex modern culture (the little Tradition). In his study of Madras City, Singer observed the emergence of a new culture as a result of the contact with the West. He pointed out that the demands of the modern professions pursued in urban areas are of such a nature that even the most orthodox among the urban residents are not completely free from such influences.

Among the recent works which tried to take account of the varied aspects of the urban phenomenon in its Indian context is the one edited by M.S.A. Rao (1974). It took account of the theoretical issues, historical aspects, and the impact of urban influences on rural life.

FIELD OF URBAN STUDIES

The emerging field of urban studies presents several paradoxes to any one in understanding its scope and context because much of its subject matter is problem oriented. It is concerned with the phenomena known as urban troubles, urban problems or urban crises. However, the label of problem-oriented is an over-simplification since the various elements of urbanism are interwoven. The intellectual roots of urban studies lie in both traditional academic disciplines and less orthodox fields. Urban studies have evolved from aspects of city planning, sociology, economics and also from black and ethnic studies, social welfare and interdisciplinary social services.

Thus, it is a unique discipline which aims at problem solving generally through the creation of viable policies. The frame of reference of urban studies is the city i.e., an existing city and its complexes. Urban studies relate to the 'Here and now'. They relate to several disciplines like sociology, economics, etc. in an understanding and analysis of contemporary issues such as class, caste, race relations, violence in slums, the efficiency of town planning and social welfare measures. Hence the scope of urban studies is very vast, as wide as urban society itself. Problems are recurrent. The nature of urban problems is such that unless they are solved, the equilibrium in urban life will be destroyed. Hence urban study is a continuously developing and active discipline which provides an understanding of the main area of urban society which is very necessary in the contemporary context. As urban studies aim at providing immediate solutions to instaneous issues, they cannot hope to tackle long standing social problems.

METHODS OF URBAN STUDIES

Most of the urban problems are relative of an area or a context. Hence urban studies need a set of handy tools which, while providing a sufficiently satisfactory analysis of the problem gives us a clear cut picture about it. Hence, urban studies use the social survey method, for example, take the problem of housing. How to house people of different races in a single area requires a specific hypothesis. The survey depends upon an admixture of stratified random sampling to select its units such as the representatives of rows. The survey mostly relies upon statistical data as they are clear and handy for analysis. It prepares a set of computerised questionnaires which are studied to the maximum extent. It is administered to the population. Interviews are conducted on its basis by trained workers. The collected data is classified, categorised and quantified. The qualitative aspects are subsumed under the quantified categories and results or solutions are declared on the basis of the quantified picture such as a graph or a table. Many a time a general framework of methods is used to study connected problems by slight modifications. Sometimes a follow up study is undertaken in a problem area on the basis of the original level to ascertain the value and success of the ameliorative measures.

VALUE OF URBAN SOCIOLOGY

The foregoing discussion makes amply clear the value and importance of urban sociology. The metropolises of today in advanced countries are standard bearers of revolutionary changes in social, political, economic and cultural movements. The process of urbanisation has been greatly hastened in advanced countries due to industrialization and technological change. This urbanisation has also given rise to a number of economic, social and cultural problems. As a result of urbanization there is change in personal tendencies and trends, the norms and standards of marriage and family have undergone sea-change and there has been considerable rise in corruption and disorganization. It has also given rise to grave problems of health, psychological as well as physical. In order to understand and remedy this sorry state of affairs we need a systematic study. And as the problems are grave and crucial, governments are closely attentive to these. It is in this connextion that the need of urban sociology is felt. An urban sociologist is a social doctor or engineer and like doctors and engineers he is concerned with the organization and disorganization of urban society. Therefore, without his services urban problems cannot be effectively solved. This is why the services of urban sociologists are in high demand. In order to reconstruct towns, the services of urban sociologists are indispensable.

QUESTIONS FOR EXERCISE

1. Define urban sociology and discuss its nature and scope
2. Define city and describe the characteristics of urban life.
3. Trace the history of urban studies in India.
4. Discuss the methods of study and value of urban sociology.

2

Urbanization and Urban Growth

Urbanisation has been often used to denote the level of population concentration in an urban area. Hope Tisdale, treats urbanisation as a process of population concentration and identifies two elements in the process : (1) the multiplication of points of concentration, and (2) the increase in the size of individual concentrations. Urbanisation can occur only when the rate of growth of the urban population is greater than the rate of growth of the non-urban population in a country.

MEASUREMENT OF URBANIZATION

The most important source of data concerning urbanisation is the population census. The process of urbanization can be measured in terms of four demographic aspects or dimensions : (1) The degree of urbanisation; (2) The tempo of urbanization; (3) The concentration and dispersion of population; and (4) The components of urban growth. The most important measures of urbanisation are: (1) Percentage of population in urban areas; (2) Ratio of urban rural population; (3) Size of locality of residences of the medium inhabitation; (4) Tempo of urbanisation. These will now be discussed in more detail.

1. Percentage of Population in Urban Areas. This is the simplest and the most common measure of urbanisation. It is calcualted as follows:

$$PU = \frac{U}{P} \times 100$$

where :

PU is the percentage of urban population;

U is the urban population; and

P is the total population.

According to 1971 Census of India :

The urban population = 109,094,309

Total population = 548,159,652

Therefore,

the percentage of Urban population in India

$$PU = \frac{109,094,309}{548,159,625} \times 100$$

$$= 19.90.$$

Thus, the measure is easy to calculate and interpret. The data for this are also easily available. However, it suffers from several weaknesses. Firstly, the definition of an urban area differs from country to country, and also within the same country at different times. Secondly, it does not give us any indication of the percentage of population living in different types of towns.

2. Ratio of Urban-Rural Population. This is also a popular measure adopted in census surveys in India. It is calculated as follows:

$$UR = \frac{U}{R}$$

where:

UR is the urban-rural ratio;

U is the urban population; and

R is the rural population.

Ratio of urban-rural population indicates the tempo of urbanisation. Therefore, it is useful for historical comparisons.

3. Size of Locality or Residence of the Median Inhabitant. This measure follows the principles of median age. It is calculated by the following formula:

$$MI = Q_i + (Q_{i+1} - Q_1)\frac{50 - PP_1}{PP_{i+1} - PP_1}$$

where:

MI is the median inhabitant;

PP_1 is the cumulative per cent of the population for the locality size just under 50 per cent;

PP_{i+1} is the cumulative per cent of the next locality size category;

Q_i is the upper limit of the locality size *i*; and

Q_{i+1} is the upper limit of locality size *i*+1.

For example in 1960 in Mexico the five categories of locality had the population shown below :

Total	3,49,23,129
Less than 1,000	1,22,22,347
1,000-2,499	49,95,644
2,500-4,999	29,59,460
5,000-99,999	82,33,426
10,00,000 and over	65,12,232

On the basis of the above data the following calculation is made : Size of locality or residence of the median inhabitant;

$$MI = Q_i + (Q_{i+1} - Q_1)\frac{50 - PP_1}{PP_{i+1} - PP_1}$$

$$= 2{,}499 + (4{,}99 - 2{,}499)\frac{50.00 - 49.30}{57.78 - 49.30}$$

$$= 2{,}705.$$

4. Tempo of Urbanisation. Tempo of urbanisation shows the rate of change brought about by urbanization. It is calculated on the basis of annual population growth rates. In it the demographer tries to find out how the urban changes had occurred and whether it was linear, geometric, exponential or hyperbolic.

Besides the above mentioned measures of urbanisation certain other aspects have been of interest to the researchers in this field. For example, researches have been made in urban population growth in terms of the various components such as the different localities or the demographic components with these localities.

TRENDS OF WORLD URBANISATION

The United Nations has gathered data about trends of world urbanisation. In 1965, approximately 35% of the world's population lived in urban areas. Within this the percentage of the developed regions was 61 and for the developing countries it was only 32. The lowest level of urbanisation is found in Africa. while for the total continent it is 20% the break-up for different regions is as follows : Eastern Africa 8, Middle Africa 14, Western Africa 18, Northern Africa 32, and Southern Africa 44%. The next in line is Asia with 22% urban population. On the other hand, the percentage of urban population in developed countries is very high such as North America 72, Oceania 67, Europe 61, USSR 53 and Latin America 52. The highest level of urbanization in 1965 was in Australia and New Zealand, 82%. It was followed by Northern Europe 72%, Temperate South America 73% and Western Europe 72%. It may be noted here that though the level of urbanisation in Asia is very low, it being the largest continent, with China and India covering 2/3 of the total world population, it constitute a little more than 1/3 of the urban population of the world. Most of the less developed countries have a very low percentage of urban population. For example, the urban population percentage in the following countries : India 19.9, Indonesia 17.4, Kenya 9.9, the Philippines 31.7, Sri Lanka 22.4, Thailand 13.2 and Uganda 7.7. The number of cities over 1,00,000 in these countries is very small and yet a very high percentage of urban population lives in these cities. For example, the percentage of urban population living in cities with 1,00,000 population in some developing countries is : Egypt, 72.9, Kenya 70.04, Indonesia 65.98 Mexico 62.68, and India 48.47.

Large Cities

The existence of large cities is found in the world since ancient times. Babylon had a population of 3,50,000 in 6th century BC. Some other big cities in ancient times were Patliputra 5,00,000 in 400 BC, Alexandria 7,00,000 in 100 BC, Rome 11,00,000 in 200 AD, Bagdad 7,50,000 in 900 AD and Ankhor 10,00,000 in 10th or 11th century. Upto the 18th century Asia had more urbanisation than Europe. However, Europe gradually led in urbanisation due to economic reasons. The Western urban centres were mainly commercial. Other factors which led to the emergence of urban centres are sea and river, merchantile trade and industrial revolution. During the period 1800-1950 the percentage of urban population rose from 3.0 to 29.8. The percentage of inhabitants in urban centres with more than 1,00,000 rose from 1.7 to 13.1. In 1920 the world total population of agglomerations of 20,000 or more inhabitants for major areas of the world was 266.4 million. This population developed in succeeding decades as follows : 1930–338.2, 1940–431.5, 1950–533.0, 1960–760.3. The percentage of this urban population to the total population of the world was : 14.3 in 1920, 16.3 in 1930, 18.2 in 1940, 21.2 in 1950, 25.4 in 1960. The percentage of urban population in developing regions was 15.4 in 1960, while in more developed regions it was 46.0. The average annual rates of growth of urban population for the world for developing regions and more developed regions during the period 1920-1960 will be clear from the following table :

	Agglomerations of 20,000 or more inhabitants		*Cities of 1,00,000 or more inhabitants*	
	1920-1960	1950-1960	1920-1960	1950-60
World	2.6	3.6	2.9	3.6
Developing Regions	2.7	4.9	4.7	5.7
More Developed Regions	2.1	2.7	2.2	3.9

GROWTH OF URBAN POPULATION IN INDIA

Some urban centres in India flourished from time to time though the country has always been predominently rural in character. For example, Varanasi and Prayag were great centres of learning for so many centuries. In 19th and early 20th century Bombay and Calcutta were famous industrial centres. The process of urbanisation however has particularly grown in the twentieth century. The definition of an urban unit was fixed first of all in 1961, according to which the term included all municipalities with 5,000 or more inhabitants. A place with less than 5,000 inhabitants could also be considered urban if the Census Superintendent believed it to be so. Since the 1961 Census the criteria for urban localities are : (i) Urban density of not less than 1,000 per square mile, (ii) at least three-fourth of the working population should be engaged in non-agricultural activities. However, all the localities with the municipal local self-government were included in urban class irrespective of the fact whether they fulfilled the above criteria or not.

India's population, as on 1 March 1991 stood at 844.32 million (437.80 million males and 406.52 million females). This includes the projected population of 7.72 million in Jammu and Kashmir. The second largest populous country, India is the home of 16 per cent of the world's population. The country, however, accounts for 2.42 per cent of the total world area.

The population of India as recorded at each decenial census from 1901 has grown steadily except for a decrease during the decade 1911-21. In absolute terms the country's population has increased by 160.99 million during the decade 1981-91. This is ten times the population of Australia and is more than the population of Japan.

An encouraging feature revealed by the provisional results is the decline in growth rate of the population in the last decade compared to 1971-81. It marginally decreased from 24.66 per cent recorded in 1971-81 to 23.50 per cent during 1981-91.

In most states the growth rate declined during the decade. However, Andhra Pradesh, Arunachal Pradesh, Madhya Pradesh, Maharashtra, Nagaland, Tripura, West Bengal, Daman and Diu, Lakshadweep and Pondicherry which account for one third of the country's population, recorded increase in growth rate. Nagaland registered the highest growth rate of 56.86 per cent while Kerala the lowest of 13.98 per cent.

Most Populous

Uttar Pradesh continued to be the largest state population-wise with 16.47 percent people of the country living there (139,031,130), followed by Bihar with 10.23 percent (86,338,853) and Maharashtra with 9.33 percent (78,748,215), West Bengal occupied fourth place accounting for 8.05 percent (67,982,732) of the country's population followed by Andhra Pradesh with 7.86 per cent (66,354,559). Ranking of the states and union territories according to population size is in table on the next page.

Bombay metropolis continued to be the most populated city of the country with urban population of 12.57 million, Calcutta taking the second place having 10.92 million. Delhi ranks third with a population (urban) of 8.38 million followed by Madras 5.36 million.

Population Density

One of the important indices of population concentration is the density of population. It is defined as the number of persons per square kilometer. The population density has gone up from 216 in 1981 to 267 persons in 1991. In 1901, it was 77 persons. Density is the highest in Delhi (6,319) followed by Chandigarh (5,620). Lakshadweep which has the smallest population size is the third most densely populated area with a density of 1,615 persons per square kilometer. Pondicherry ranks fourth (1,605)) followed by Daman and Diu (906).

Arunachal Pradesh is the most sparsely populated area of the country with 10 persons per square kilometer.

The ten heavily populated districts of the country are Calcutta, Madras, Greater Bombay, Hyderabad, Delhi, Chandigarh, Mahe, Haora, Kanpur and Bangalore. All of them have density of above 2,000 persons per square kilometer and 5.01 per cent of the country's population lives in these districts. The average density of these 10 districts is 5,791.

Sex Ratio

In any study of the population, analysis of the sex composition plays a vital role. The sex composition of the population is affected by the differentials in the mortality conditions of males and females, sex selective migration and the sex ratio at birth.

The sex ratio is defined as the number of females per 1000 males. In India it has generally been adverse to women. The ratio has also declined over the years except in 1981 when it slightly improved to 934 from 929. In 1991, there had been a fall by five points to 929 per thousand males. But Kerala represented a different spectrum. The state has a higher number of females than males 1,040 females for thousand males.

In the Indian context, a sex ratio of 950 and above can be considered as favourable to females. The states and union territories coming under this category are Himachal Pradesh (996), Andhra Pradesh (972), Goa (969), Karnataka (960), Manipur (961), Orissa (972), Tamil Nadu (972), Dadra and Nagar Haveli (953). Daman and Diu (972) and Pondicherry (982).

Chandigarh accounted for the lowest number of females per thousand males with 793.

Literacy

For the purpose of census, a person is deemed as literate if he or she can read and write any language with understanding. In the 1991 census, the question on literacy was canvased only for population aged seven years and above, unlike earlier censuses which took into account population of five years and above for this purpose.

The provisional results reveal that there has been an increase in literacy in the country. The literacy rate is 52.11 per cent (63.86 for males and 39.42 for females).

For the population aged seven years and above the literacy rate has increased by 8.55 percentage points. The increase in male and female literacy rates is of the order of 7.49 and 9.67 points respectively. Even though strict comparison with earlier decades may not be possible due to the changes in the age group to which they relate, it appears that increase in literacy rate observed during the decade 1981—91 is higher than the increase of 6.97 percentage points observed during the decade. During the decade 1961—71 literacy rate for population aged five and above had increased by 6.14 percentage points.

TABLE 2.1

Population 1901-91

Year	Population	Decade growth rate (per cent)	Average Annual exponential growth rate (per cent)	Progressive growth rate over 1901
1901	238,396,327	—	—	—
1911	252,093,390	5.75	0.56	+5.75
1921	251,321,213	—0.31	—0.03	+5.42
1931	278,977,238	+11.00	1.04	+17.02
1941	318,660,580	+14.22	1.33	+33.67
1951	361,088,090	+13.31	1.25	+51.47
1961	439,234,771	+21.51	1.96	+84.25
1971	548,159,652	+24.80	2.20	+129.94
1981	683,329,070	+24.66	2.22	+186.64
1991	844,324,222	+25.50	2.11	+254.00

Sourse: Census of India 1991. Provisional populalion Totals.

Notes: 1. In 1981, census was not conducted in Assam. Based on the 1971 census and the provisional results of the 1991 census the population of Assam as on 1 March 1981 has been interpolated.

2. As a consequence of the revised estimate for the year 1981, the total population of India as of 1981 has been estimated as 883,329,097 as against the earlier published figure of 685,184,692.

3. The 1991 census has not yet been conducted in Jammu and Kashmir. The provisional population figures for India include the population figure for Jammu and Kashmir projected by the Standing Committee of Experts on population projections.

Kerala retained its position by being on top with a 90.59 per cent literacy rate in the country. Bihar stood at the bottom with a literacy rate of 38.54 per cent, with Rajasthan being close to it having 38.81 percentage. But literacy among the women was lowest in Rajasthan with a percentage of 20.84 as compared to 55.07 among the males.

According to Census of 1981, Maharashtra had the maximum urban components of 35.03%, while Himachal Pradesh had the urban component at 7.71. Uttar Pradesh had an urban component of 18.01, a growth of 4.02% on 1971 Census.

TABLE 2. 2

Population of Million Plus Cities

City	Population 1'000s 1981	1951	Growth ratio 1981/1951	1981 Sex ratio	Literacy ratio
Calcutta	9,194	4,670	1.99	781	65
Greater Bombay	8,243	2,967	2.78	772	68
Delhi	5,729	1,437	3.99	808	63
Madras	4,289	1,542	2.78	930	67
Bangalore	2,922	786	3.72	896	64
Hyderabad	2,546	1,131	2.25	919	58
Ahmedabad	2,548	877	2.91	869	63
Kanpur	1,639	705	2.32	804	55
Pune	1,686	609	2.77	880	67
Nagpur	1,302	485	2.90	910	66
Lucknow	1,008	497	2.03	832	58
Jaipur	1,015	304	3.34	861	54

URBAN POPULATION GROWTH IN U.P.

According to 1981 Census, U. P. has a population of 111 million constituting one-sixth of India's population. About 91 million are in rural areas and 20 million in urban areas comprising 82% and 18% respectively.

Five districts of Lucknow, Dehra Dun, Kanpur, Agra and Jhansi are on the top. They have maintained their order in urbanisation during the decade. On the lowest rung stand Sultanpur, Tehri-Garhwal, Basti, Pratapgarh and Pithoragarh. In absolute terms the district of Basti has the largest rural population component (34,04,916) followed by Gorakhpur (33,94,809), Deoria (32,55,933), Azamgarh (3,215,334) and Allahabad (30,10,921). On the other hand, Kanpur district has the largest urban population (17,82,665) followed by Agra (11,10,364) and Lucknow (10,51,633).

Uttar Pradesh and Karnataka are the two states which have a higher growth rate of population than the all-India average though from 1901 to 1971 they had a lower growth rate than the all-India average. Since 1901 the population of Uttar Pradesh had more than doubled from mere 48.6 million to 111 million. The rural population of the state had also more than doubled from a mere 43.2 million to 91 million.

On the other hand, the urban population quadrupled from a mere 5.4 million during the last decade. While the rural population has gone up by 19.7% the urban population increased by 61.2%.

In all there are 704 towns in Uttar Pradesh which together comprise the urban area. They consist of seven municipal corporations, viz, Kanpur, Allahabad, Varanasi, Agra, Lucknow, Meerut, Bareilly. There are 187 municipal boards, 22 cantonment boards, 47 notified areas, 418 town areas and 25 census towns. In 1981 Uttar Pradesh equals Punjab and is higher than Haryana, Arunachal Pradesh, Nagaland and Sikkim in the sex ratio. The districts where the females outnumber males are Tehri-Garhwal, Almora, Pithoragarh, Chamoli, Azamgarh, Pratapgarh and Jaunpur.

Fastest urban growth in Kerala

Kerala has registered the fastest urban growth during 1981 to 1991. The decennial growth was around 61 per cent, a record of sort, as against the national average of 36.19 per cent for the same period. An analysis of the last census reveals this. However, the state has been dislodged from its long-held status of the country's densest state with West Bengal recording 766 density per sq. km as compared to 747 of Kerala.

The state's long stride from 106 towns in 1981 to 197 towns and 20 urban outgrowths in 1991 brings in its wake a mixed fare of some welcome and some ominous signs for the future. Demographic researchers and census officials perdict a more cramped state by the turn of the century but assures the population a better health care and other amenities.

The state, having the lowest birth rate (14 against an all-India average of 23) and highest literacy rate (over 90 per cent), is likely to stabilise around 10 to 12 by the end of this decade. But with its already high density of population, it faces an acute space problem. The land scarcity makes density higher and urbanisation faster, said Mr N.M. Samuel, state director, census operations.

Kerala has also reversed the national trend of growth in urban population. It experienced a marked increase in urban population growth from 3.19 in 1981 to 4.76 in 1991 whereas the all-India average declined from 3.83 to 2.09 for the same period.

Two main criteria for classifying an area as urban are: density of the population of 500 or above and 75 per cent male population involved in industrial activity. Civic amenities are another criterion. Though the state lacks large industrial units, the Kannur, Ernakulam and Thrissur districts have witnessed phenomenal growth of cottage and small industries, survey officials said. Kannur has emerged as a leader in *beedi* making while Thrissur has a mixture of small and cottage industries. Ernakulam-Kochi remains the state's industrial capital.

COMMERCIAL ACTIVITIES

Kerala is today a continuous ribbon of settlement and it is difficult to distinguish a village spread from an urban pattern. With commercial activity picking up, the state is emerging as one of the largest markets for consumer items.

According to the industry department studies, three of the 14 districts that have not gone all urban are the northern-most districts of Kasargod, Wynad and Pathanamthitta. In other districts, the number of census towns are swelling fast though the number of statutory towns lag behind more for political reasons. There are 131 census towns in Kerala today.

While faster urbanisation means better amenities, the state with its remittance economy will witness an abnormal rise in prices of real estates. Prices of prime land in cities like Thiruvananthapuram, Kochi and Thrissur have risen sharply. In the last decade, 1.87 lakh acres of paddy fields were converted into residential land.

With urbanisation, health care has considerably improved as is evident from the very low infant mortality rate and the lowest death rate (six per 1,000 against 11 at the national level).

If the state retains the prevailing urban growth, it would become an all-urban state in the near future. The state is obviously becoming more and more urban each year, observes Dr. Krishna Kumari, head of demography and population studies in Kerala University.

CAUSES OF GROWTH OF CITIES

It is very difficult to say as to when did the first city form or when did it originate. As Gist and Halbert have very aptly observed, "Like the origin of civilization itself the origin of the city lost in the obscurity of the past." The growth and development of cities is linked with two factors; on the one hand, it is dependent upon the growth of population, and, on the other, it is linked to the growth and development of industrialization. Industrialization results in increased population and the increased population, in turn, leads to division of labour. The produce has to be transported from one place to the other and put on the market. This requires means of transport, markets, godowns, shops etc. With industrialization there is not only increase in population but also in the growth of population. This is due to the fact that wherever there is industrialization, a big labour force is needed: besides we need enough supervisory staff. Moreover, in as much as industrialization involves new construction, creation of markets, shops and business premises, thousands of men would be absorbed in these works. Naturally, therefore, the population of an industrial centre would grow immensely. In response to various needs of the newly grown population, educational, cultural and other institutions and associations come into being. If the population of a place is large it is bound to be heterogeneous; and a heterogeneous people require large police contingents and other law enforcing agencies in order to maintain law and order. All these factors are instrumental to the development of cities. If a university, high court or medical college is established anywhere, there is great influx of population to that area. With the substantial increase in the population of a place, many shops, markets, hotels, restaurants, clubs and cinemas come into existence and thus the foundation of a city is well laid. The towns situated on sea coast easily turn into big cities as a result of industrialization. The industrialization implies increase both in import and export. Most of the goods entering a country or going out of it are carried by ships. If a coastal town has good harbour facilities, traffic through it is bound to increase with industrialization. The greater the traffic through a harbour, greater will be its population and greater would be the turn-over and handling of goods. All these things naturally help the rapid development of cities. Similarly, the hill resorts or towns situated on coast are liable to become cities if these command good views and the climate is salubrious. In short, wherever there is industrialization or good climate or government offices or scenic beauty and good climate or education and cultural institutions, such places are liable to develop into cities.

CAUSES OF DEVELOPMENT OF NEW CITIES

The above discussion makes it plain that there is no single factor or cause which can be held responsible for the development or origin of cities. It is not possible to define and enumerate the cause of the development of various towns. This is because, beside general causes of the origin and development of cities, every city has its personal history and certain causes for its origin and development are peculiar to it. For example, if and when a certain place is declared to be the capital of some state or country it is bound to become a city overnight. Broadly, following may be enumerated as the main causes of the development and origin of cities:–

(1) Industrial Revolution. The cities are business centres. The increase in business stimulates industrial activity. When large industrial complexes come into existence, big markets, housing and shopping complexes are a natural sequel to industrial activity. The places situated in the vicinity of large industries automatically become important business centres, and at a business centre there is a collection of a large number of people and when population of a place is big enough it naturally turns into a city.

(2) Business Revolution. Wherever there is large turnover of trade and business that place must in due course turn into a city. As N. L. Sims observes, "Trade is a necessary cause of the existence of a city as circulation of blood is a necessary cause for the life of an organism." A large business centre must naturally have big markets, marts, shopping complexes, housing colonies, educational and cultural associations, clubs, restaurants and hotels. All these things are *sine qua non* of a city and if some place has these it must be a city.

(3) Agricultural Revolution. The revolution in 20th century science has completely metamorphosed the entire structure and quality of agriculture. Today we possess highly sophisticated agricultural tools and implements and these help us to get far higher yield of crops than before with the help of very few hands. The revolution in agriculture has released a big labour force, who hunt for jobs. Labour being available cheap, the capitalist is induced to invest money into new factories in order to utilize cheap labour. When large labour force migrates to any place, that place grows and tends to develop into a city. In

West, agricultural revolution is an important factor in the development of cities.

(4) Increase in the Means of Transportation. In the development of cities, means of transport play a crucial role. Without the facilities of transportation and the easy availability of such means as trains, trucks, buses, taxies, scooters etc, no place can become a business centre. Previously, the chief means of transport available was the bullock cart and this means is expensive as well as time consuming. Today by means of rail, road or air we can transport goods from one place to the other very quickly and inexpensively. In big towns or metropolises, therefore, goods are brought from great distances by air, rail or road transport and they become business centres for national as well as international goods. One of the reasons for the quick growth of metropolises like Calcutta and Bombay is the easy availability of the various means of transport.

(5) Development of Communication. With the development of means of communication like postal, telegraph and wireless services etc., it has now become possible for the businessmen, away from each other by great distances, to establish contacts with each other. This in turn stimulates business and trade activity. The trade becomes international. The facilities of communication have helped greatly the growth and development of cities.

(6) Political Factors. Owing to political reasons certain places assume great importance; and consequently, become big cities. In almost all states the capitals have developed greatly and fast. For example, Chandigarh was an obscure village but when it was decided to make it the capital of Punjab it was metamorphosed and became a modern city. Similarly, the growth of London, Tokyo and Delhi can be traced to the fact that these are capitals of Great Britain, Japan and India respectively. Besides the reason of being capitals many towns develop fast into metropolises if some strategic importance is attached to these.

(7) Education Centres. The places which are centres of higher learning, soon become big cities. This is because students and teachers from far and wide assemble at such places and in order to cater to their needs shops, markets, hotels, restaurants and clubs come into existence. Thus, all the prerequisites of a city materialize and wherever there are big markets, shopping and housing complexes, a city is bound to come into existence.

(8) Growth of Population. It is an evident fact that whenever and wherever there is increase in the population all prerequisites of cities are bound to come into existence. Subsequent to independence of India and consequent blood bath of communal frenzy and rioting there was great influx of population from Pakistan to India, many a small town in India grew into cities. Thus, increase in the population is an important factor in the growth of cities.

(9) Security. A place which is vulnerable to external attack or which is subject to attack by some marauding tribes cannot grow into a city because no body would like to invest any money at such place. People would invest money and do business only at those places which are safe and secure and where life and property are not constantly threatened.

(10) Municipal Facilities and Means of Entertainment. In good cities there are schools, colleges, universities, music institutes, dance centres, medical colleges and industrial training institutes. People can avail of these facilities and enhance their abilities. In villages, in spite of plenty of money with people, there are no means of enjoyment and entertainment. On the other hand, in cities there are cinemas, music and dance clubs, theaters, night clubs, hotels and restaurants. In cities people can buy comfort and enjoyment by spending money. On account of easy availability of means of improving one's abilities and self culture and also easy availability of means of entertainment people are attracted from villages to cities.

As referred to above industrialization is a very important cause and factor in the origin and development of towns. But some sociologists regard industrialization to be the only cause of the development of cities. It will be in fitness of things to critically examine this view. It is a fact that in India most of the big cities have developed due to industrialization. In India, this is also true that population has increased much faster in those areas which are highly industrialized. Therefore, the number of cities is more in those states which are more industrialized than others. In India maximum number of cities is in Maharashtra which is the most industrialized state of India.

A comparative statistical analysis of growth of population in various states reveals that relative growth of population in descending order is as follows : Maharashtra, U.P., Mysore, West Bengal, Delhi etc. In these states the number of cities has also increased. Interestingly this growth in population corresponds to the growth of industrialization. Thus it can be safely assumed that the rapidity of the growth of population and increase in the population, in turn, leads to the development of towns and cities. Therefore, it is quite true that industrialization is the most important cause of this development of cities. But it would be an exaggeration to say that industrialization is the sole factor in the development of towns and cities. The singularity of industrialization as the cause of the coming into existence of cities is clearly contradicted by the example of Chandigarh. The coming into existence of Chandigarh is clearly a result of political decision and whatever industry we may find there is the result and not the cause of the political decision. Similarly, the present growth of Delhi is primarily due to large influx of refugees from Pakistan. Thus we can sum up by saying that though industrial revolution is the most important factor, it is, by no means, the sole factor in the origin and development of cities. All the factors enumerated above are indeed more or less important.

PAST FACTORS OF DEVELOPMENT OF CITIES

In the context of discussion about the development of cities, it shall be appropriate to discuss the causes of growth and development of cities in India in the past. In this connexion we may mention the following important factors:

(1) Holy Places. The religious life is the essence of Indian life; religion permeates every fibre of it. In past people visited certain towns considered holy as a matter of highest duty. The sacred places visited by the stream of pilgrims round the year soon develop into cities. The outstanding examples of such cities are: Prayag, Kashi, Hardwar, Mathura, Puri etc.

(2) Favourable Climate. The second biggest factor in the coming into existence of cities in India was the climatic factor. The favourable climatic conditions greatly helped the development of cities. That is why most of the Indian towns are situated on the banks of Ganga and Jamuna. Indeed, all over the world, majority of the cities are situated on the river banks. In favourable climatic, conditions are included adequate rainfall, temperate weather, good fertile soil etc. In deserts and hills we find very few big cities.

(3) Means of Communication. In the past modern sophisticated means of communication were not available and, therefore, most of the places were not easily accessible. Wherever, the facilities of communication were better, cities came into existence.

(4) Agricultural Facilities. Included in agricultural facilities are good irrigation, fertile soil and suitable climate. As in the past, there were no big industries, agricultural facilities were the main conditions which determined the establishment of cities.

(5) Cantonments. In old India, there were numerous small and big princely states. All princes and kings used to live in forts which were surrounded by military cantonments. In order to supply the goods to persons living in big numbers in forts and cantonments, towns and cities used to spring around these military centres. Thus, the city of Gwalior is situated on the outskirts of Gwalior fort. Similarly, old Delhi is nearby red fort. A large army needs food, clothing, shelter and many such things. In order to maintain supply we require big mandis, shopping complexes, cinemas, restaurants and other paraphernalia usually associated with cities.

(6) Capitals. Like cantonments all those places which are made the capitals of states soon turn out to be cities. This is natural. As a consequence of official patronage much money is invested in such places and all municipal facilities besides a guaranteed security made available.

(7) Cultural Centres. In India, culture is highly valued, therefore, cultural centres are fully protected by the official machinery. At these centres people gather from far and wide. Thus, these centres turn into cities.

(8) Educational Centres. In ancient India, there were many celebrated seats of learning. At these seats of learning students in large number from far and wide used to assemble. Therefore, these became cities. Nalanda and Taxila are examples of such centres.

(9) Art Centres. In all countries, there are certain places renowned for artistic manufacture. These places become big business centres and thus, turn into cities. In India, examples of such places are Kannauj, Bareilly, Kanpur, Moradabad etc.

(10) Business or Commercial Centres. For a variety of reasons some places become commercial centres. Usually, places situated on the river banks or sea coast become flourishing business centres. These places, too become cities.

URBAN GROWTH AT A SLOW PACE

The level of urbanisation in India has gone up from 23.34 per cent in 1981 to 25.72 per cent in 1991 — an increase of 2.38 percentage points over the whole decade, the annual rate of increase being 0.24 per cent only. During 1971-81, the average annual rate of increase in the level of urbanisation was 0.34 per cent — about one-third higher than recorded in the last decade. The pace of increase or what is demographically termed as the "Tempo of urbanisation" has thus considerably slowed down over the last ten years. This is an intriguing situation. As economic growth takes off, the level of urbanisation, being at a low level, should normally increase faster every decade and it is only when the level reaches sufficiently high that the slow-down takes place.

The urban rural growth differential (URGD) which was expected to go up has declined during the last decade. Besides, the rate of growth of rural population has actually gone up during the last decade. The annual growth rate of rural population which had declined from 1.96 per cent in 1961-71 to 1.78 in 1971-81 went up to 1.80 in 1981-91. Coupled with the sharp decline in the rate of growth of urban population, the increase in the rate of growth of rural population is one of the astonishing results of 1991 Census. The urban rural growth differential was 1.25, 2.05 and 1.29 per cent respectively in the last three decades.

A fall in the rural population growth rate is of fundamental importance for increasing the level of urbanisation and for the implied increase in the level of economic development. In the 15 major States which account for 97 per cent of the country's population, there has been an increase in the annual growth of rural population during the last decade. Bihar and Uttar Pradesh have the unique but dubious distinction of recording a continuous increase in the annual growth rate of their rural populations over the last three decades. The rural growth rate in Bihar went up from 1.76 to 2.03 while that of Uttar Pradesh increased from 1.67 to 2.02 during these three decades. Demographers, social scientists and policy planners must see as to what is happening in these two States.

When compared to the rest of the world, the level of urbanisation in India is very low. The world as a whole had a level of 45 per cent in 1990; the highest level being 84-85 per cent in Australia and New Zealand followed by 77 per cent in Japan, between 72 to 75 per cent in North America, South America, Latin America and Europe, 66 per cent in Central America and

USSR, and 34 per cent in Africa and Asia. Even Pakistan had an urbanisation level at 32 per cent.

There is nothing sacrosanct about a high level of urbanisation. But from the economic point of view the higher the level of urbanisation, the higher is the stage of economic development typified by a higher level of industrialisation and development of modern sectors of commerce, transport and services. Economic development is further typified by a shift in the structure of work-force from agricultural to non-agricultural activities which, in turn means a shift in population from the rural to urban areas, either by rural-urban migration or by the development of rural areas themselves into industrial and commercial areas. Economic development is also characterized by a rise in agricultural productivity which also leads to a shift of the surplus population from agricultural to non-agricultural activities as has happened in Punjab and Western Uttar Pradesh.

By definition, the Indian census treats those areas as urban which are either statutory towns or which have got a minimum population of 5,000 persons coupled with three-fourths of its male work-force being engaged in non-agricultural economic activities and a density of at least 400 persons per square kilometre. That is, even those areas which are classified as rural administratively would be treated as urban in census if they fulfil the above three criteria. Such urban areas are called "census towns". In 1991, there were 1,693 census towns out of a total of 4,689 towns in the country.

The levels of urbanisation differ very sharply from State to State. Among the fifteen major States of India, four States had levels about 30 per cent (Maharashtra-39, Gujarat and Tamil Nadu-34 and Karnataka-31), four States had levels between 25 and 30 per cent (Punjab-30, West Bengal and Andhra Pradesh-27 and Kerala-26); four States were between 20 to 25 per cent (Haryana-25, Madhya Pradesh and Rajasthan-23 and Uttar Pradesh-20), while three States had levels below 15 per cent (Orissa and Bihar-13 and Assam 11).

Comparing the decennial growth rates of urban population over last two decades, we find that the States which were less urbanised in 1971 had very high urban growth during 1971-81. During that decade, Orissa had a decadal urban growth of 68 per cent, Uttar Pradesh 61 per cent, Haryana 60 per cent, Rajasthan 59 per cent, Madhya Pradesh 56 per cent and Bihar 55 per cent. On the other hand, the States at higher levels of urbanisation such as Maharashtra, Tamil Nadu, West Bengal, Kerala, Gujarat and Punjab had relatively much lesser growth rates of urban population. During 1981-91, however, the picture is somewhat confusing. While Tamil Nadu, West Bengal, Karnataka, Punjab, Gujarat and Maharashtra (the more urbanised States) had relatively lesser rate of urban growth. States like Bihar, Orissa, Uttar Pradesh and Rajasthan (the less urbanised States) had also lesser growth rate of urban population.

The current state of India's urbanisation can thus be characterised by five major distinguishing features : (a) the level of urbanisation in India is relatively very low when compared to the rest of the world and that three-fourth of India's population continues to live in rural areas which are cesspools of poverty and social backwardness; (b) the pace of urbanisation which had started picking up during 1971-81 has slowed down substantially, the current annual gain in urban population being just 0.24 per cent; (c) there is a very wide disparity in both the levels of urbanisation as well as the pace of urbanisation among various States; (d) in some of the more urbanised States, the urban growth has been halted leading to stagnation in urbanisation (and the implied stagnation in economic development); and (e) even in less urbanised States, the rate of growth of urban population has been arrested.

OVER-URBANIZATION

What is Over-Urbanization?

Over urbanization refers to the increased exemplification of the characters of urbanization in a city or its surrounding rural area. It results due to the excessive development of urbanistic traits. Due to the expansion of the range of urban activities and occupations, greater influx of secondary functions like industry, increasing and widespread development of an intricate bureaucratic administrative network, the increased sophistication and mechanization of life and the influx of urban characters into the surrounding rural area, over urbanization gradually replaces the ruralistic and traditionalistic traits of a community.

Traits of Over-Urbanization

Over-urbanization manifests itself in a number of physical, personal and social problems like congestion, over-crowding, increased formality in relations and ways of life, increased occupational specialization, greater development of secondary organizations to satisfy various human needs, rush, tension, traffic jams, increased isolation and segmentation of personality, problem of housing and provision of other necessities, various physical and mental diseases of tension and of ennuity, break up of family life, absence of open spaces, multistoreyed buildings, greater mechanisation of life and slums etc.

Problem of Over-Urbanization

Over-urbanization is a problem for sociologists since it destroys the basic tenets of a happy, social life i.e., peace and intimacy. Over urbanization will completely destroy the essential nature of primary social institutions which are the bed rocks of life, unless these are replaced with a viable set of decent and healthy social relationships. The increased anonymity, lack of privacy and congestion destroys the mental calm of the urbanite while increased mechanisation destroys the core of his human nature.

Remedies to Over-Urbanization

The only plausible solution for protecing the remnant of human life from the ills of excessive urbanization rests in the development of real and relatively homogeneous and self contained spacious suburbs away from the city centre which provide to the residents all the basic essential services like schools, hospitals, libraries and playgrounds, etc. and thus pave the way for the development of a common culture and intimate neighbourly relations over a period of time among the inhabitants.

PUSH BACK FACTORS IN MIGRATION

Migration is known as a process of movement of people from their areas of residence to other areas in search of better living conditions. Usually rural-urban migration consists of migration of rural people to urban areas for education, employment and better conditions of life. This movement is prompted due to rural unemployment, attractions of city life and an opportunity of escaping from the rigid codes of conventional social life. However, we may note certain push back factors in migration which are recently being taken note of.

1. Distance. No one contradicts the fact that distance is the main push back factor in migration which restricts the impulse of the ruralite to migrate. Ravensten has argued that migration decreases in proportion to the distance of the city. However, with the increased development of quick and rapid means of transportation this factor has lost much of its significance as a push back factor. Push back factors either restrict or prevent the process of migration.

2. Family-Attachment. Family attachment acts as another push-back-factor of migration in traditionalistic societies. This factor also explains the partial migration of the ruralite to the cities. This factor restricts long distance migration and restricts migration to the nearby towns or cities.

3. Lack of Adjustment. Lack of adjustment with urban conditions and the feeling against foreigners also acts as push-back factor. Usually old people and people who cherish and take pride in their socio-cultural value refrain from migrating to the city at any cost. Some people, even though they migrate, find it difficult to adjust to the formality and technicality of urban social relations and its anonymity and turn back to their original home place in a short period of time.

4. Unemployment. Increased urban unemployment may also act as a push-back factor. The average village educated youth or the unskilled labourer who may find it difficult to secure a suitable job may return to his piece of land in the village to take out a meagre livelihood.

5. Higher Cost of Living. The higher cost of living in the cities and the absence of fresh natural vegetables, milk, etc. in their daily food, lack of fresh air and the restrictions of urban life and employment may send back a villager to his joint family fold.

6. Disillusion etc. The disenchantment with urban ways of life and its glamours may act as a push-back factor. The carving for primary social values, the inability to catch up with the urban educational and occupational system and the inability of securing jobs in a city without technical skill, the relatively high cost of living may all act as push-back factors. Age may also to some extent act as a push-back factor. Over urbanization, excessive congestion, the difficulty in procuring all the necessary products and services at a reasonable cost amidst excessive competition may also act as push-back factors in a great and expanding city. However, the operation of push back factors is more, or less, conditioned by the possession of a permanent rural base. These push-back factors come into operation during the later stages of migration. These factors act as a check to the rural exodus and may to some extent aggravate the rural unemployment problem while preserving the basic nature of rural social life.

QUESTIONS FOR EXERCISE

1. Describe the chief characteristics of the city.
2. What social problems according to you are typically urban? What precisely are the factors in the urban milieu that give rise to them ?

3

Some Related Concepts : Urbanism, Urban Ecology and Urban Personality

URBANISM

In 1915 Petrick Geddes wrote his *Report on Re-planning of Six Towns in Bombay Presidency*. In 1953 G.S. Ghurye wrote on the 'Cities of India' in the March issue of *Sociological Bulletin*.

The roots of urbanism go deep into Indian history. Any attempt to see the various forces in clear array must place them in the perspective of times since the social process in India over the past century or two has maintained a remarkable continuity. The historians of India's colonial urban centres have, contributed materially to our understanding of the contemporary setting. A discussion of materials as diverse as those for urban India has to delimit its broad contours as well as its analytic level.

Colonial Urbanism

In India the pre-colonial urban centres had tended to be political at the core. Their rise and fall was often closely linked to the sponsoring political regime, though the addition of commercial and religious activities would give the urban centre a certain immunity from political vicissitudes. The seventeenth and the eighteenth centuries saw the establishment of the European trading posts.

In 1974 Howard Spodek examined the urban centres in the Saurashtran peninsula towards the end of the eighteenth century. These centres were located at the far edge of the imperial formations, both Mughal and Maratha. These were city states, whose chiefs might be made to pay tribute to one or another imperial centre from time to time, but whose political and administrative autonomy was seldom questioned. The composition of these towns was built around the ruler and his kinsmen and followers, whose principal interests were centred on the agricultural activities in their vicinity and the surplus they could extract from these. Their interests tended to be localized. With their capital, or skills, or both, these groups enjoyed considerable mobility between the various city states. With this mobility would go a certain breadth of experiences and of networks. In the eighteenth century, these resources could be used to advantage for physical mobility would often cover occupational — and therefore economic and political mobility.

Eighteenth-century merchants played an important part in the emergence of the capitalist class of later times. In the areas of trade and banking their activities were remarkable for the range of territory covered, for the technical complexity of their operations, and for the use of the ties of kinship and caste for underwriting key commercial relationships. Much of this activity was oriented towards the royalty and the nobility. It included the provision of finance as well as supplies needed for prosecuting war fare. For European trading posts, the inland trading networks — aggregating inland manufactures for export and distributing the imports — were also built out of the prior trading links, practices and traditions. Indian traders often found it profitable to finance the operations of their European counterparts.

With their capital and the range of their operational networks, the merchants usually dominated their relationships with artisans in whose output they would trade. The artisans controlled little capital, and their occupational traditions gave them few of their own interlocal networks. The artisans were dependent upon the merchants for marketing their output. This dependence was so acute that, when on occasion the artisans tried to strike out on their own, the traders could bring them back in line. This relationship of assured dominance was also indexed in the four-fold varna division the menial Shudra artisan ranking clearly below the trading Vaishya.

The strength of these ties, and the measure of subordination entailed, varied from one region to another. It appears to have been rather more in Gujarat than in Tamil Nadu. Reporting on the Konku region in Tamil Nadu, Beck (1972) finds them heading a village faction as against the landowning caste. In the Punjab, from the artisan's viewpoint, 'the system of customary relations was stable, not the individuals and families that filled it. Physical mobility between villages in search of opportunity or of better terms was common for the Punjabi artisan, aligning him with the movable, rather than the landed, social groups; and this had implications for later developments. Yet, overall, the dominance of the merchants over the craftsmen was enough. The capitalist industrialism of later years was led and dominated by merchant capitalism, not by craftsmen.

If neighbourhoods had been united by caste membership in the pre-colonial urban centres, so were these in the trading posts established by the Europeans. The difference between the two kinds of towns lay, rather, in the locus of political control. As British power grew, Calcutta, Madras, and Bombay became the political centres, overshadowing both the native-controlled ports, like Surat and Calicut, and the native capitals, like Murshidabad, Poona, and Delhi.

During the nineteenth century physical changes in these urban centres were due to the administrative outposts for collecting land revenue and other work; the army facilities; the apparatus connected with the canals and the railways; courts and lawyers; a school or a college here, a hospital or a mission there. Centres where the colonial regime established its institutions would grow in a modest way, even as the countryside reeled under deindustrialization and the like. Urban initiatives depended, by and large, upon the overarching, exogenic processes rather than upon endogenic evolution and control. The subcontinent lay stunned under the colonial arms. After the brief Bengal Renaissance, only late in the nineteenth century would some sustained initiative pass into Indian hands, as with the founding of the Poona Sarvajanik Sabha and of the Arya Samaj in Lahore.

The social and cultural crosscurrents, however, were considerably more complex. The initial application of modern scholarship to India's languages and literatures revealed clusters, several of whose nodes were religious (Kopf 1969, Dobbin 1972). These gave cause for a certain pride in ancient glory, but the glory was sectoral.

WHAT IS URBANISM?

Urbanism is a special concept which inherits within itself all the characters connected with urbanization and the urban way of life. The concept was given its final shape by Louisworth. Urbanism is a category of relevant elements and term. It is a developing concept as the urban life pattern itself, as it appears, as a developing and constantly changing phenomenon. As such, there is no well defined theory of urbanism presenting in a systematic fashion all the available knowledge concerning the city as a social entity. However, we have a wealth of literature presenting insights of sociological relevance and also empirical studies offering detailed information on a variety of particular aspects of urban life. Thus, we may assume that the larger, the more densely populated and the more heterogeneous the community, the more accentuated and the more present are the characters of urbanism.

Features of Urbanism

There are a number of sociological propositions concerning the relationship between a habitat and (i) the size of population (ii) its density and (iii) heterogeneity as the important factors defining the characters of urban way of life. Now, let us examine them briefly as to their relevance.

1. Size of Population. Since, the time of Aristotle it has been recognized that increase in the number of inhabitants in a settlement beyond a certain limit will affect the relationship between people and habitat. Hence, it leads to competition over scarce resources and a search for alternatives and reduces intimacy and nearness of relations, while increasing the number of contacts and acquaintances. Large numbers involve a greater range of individual variation. Further, the greater the number of interacting individuals, the greater is the potential differentiation between them. The personal traits, occupations, the cultural life and the ideas and attitudes of members of an urban community may, therefore, be expected to range between widely separated poles, such give rise to the spatial segregation of individuals, according to colour, ethnic heritage, economic and social status, tastes and preference. The bonds of kinship, of neighbourliness and the sentiments arising out of living together for generations under a common folk tradition will be absent under such circumstances. Competition and formal control mechanisms provide the substitutes for bonds of solidarity. Personal and intimate contacts are reduced. Urbanites meet one another in highly segmental roles. They are dependant upon more and a variety of people for the satisfaction of variety of their life needs. The superficiality, anonymity and the transitory character of urban social relations consequent upon numbers, makes intelligible the sophistication and rationality of urbanites. Urban social relations are reversed, indifferent and formal. Occupational etiquette and professional codes guide city life and behaviour. Impersonal market as the place of exchange and distribution of goods and services is a typically urban character.

2. Density. Increase in the size of the population over a limited area increases its density. Increase in density produces differentiation and specialization as a necessary condition for survival. In denser areas while physical contacts will be close, social contacts are distant. Increase in size and density of population are the necessary concommitant of urbanization. Density increases diversification. We are exposed to glaring contrasts between splendour and squalor, riches and poverty, intelligence and ignorance, order and chaos. Competition for space is great. Place of work tends to become dissociated from place of residence. The juxtaposition of divergent personalities and modes of life tends to produce a relativist perspective and a sense of tolerance of difference. The living together and working together of individuals with no emotional ties foster a spirit of exploitation. Nervous tensions and frustrations are common. Moral controls no more work in a congested area and a degree of deviance and disorganization is thus a regular feature. Density itself produces a sort of mass culture whose values are transitory co-operation, group feeling, sort of commonality etc.

3. Heterogeneity. Heterogeneity is another concommitant of urbanization as urban areas are the reservoirs of people of a variety of cultural, ethnic and social backgrounds. Social interaction among a variety of personality types breaks down the rigidity of caste and complicates the class structure. The heightened individual mobility accepts instability and insecurity as a norm. The coming into contact and mixing up of a variety of cultural patterns inevitably leads to their assimilation and the creation of a sort of common mass culture in an urban agglomeration. This accounts for the sophistication and cosmopolitanism of the urbanite. Partly as a result of physical footlessness and social mobility the turnover in urban group membership is rapid. Urban people are a fluid mass and hence collective behaviour there is unpredictable. However, through its accommodation of differences, city makes up for a levelling influence.

Thus we see that increase in size, density and heterogeneity of population, which are the major elements in any society account for much of the character of the contemporary urban society as inevitable consequences.

THEORIES OF URBAN GROWTH

Many theories have been developed to explain the dynamics of city growth. All these theories are based upon the operation of five ecological processes of concentration, centralization, invasion and succession and observations based upon it about actual city growth in concrete situations. However, there is no all inclusive theory of an ideal pattern of urban dynamics as growth of particular cities depends upon many factors, the basic one being natural location of a city site. However, one can notice a set of common principles which govern city growth everywhere. Thus the areas in a city are divided according to the functions they serve as functional zones and each function chooses for itself the most convenient location e.g., the central business district, residential zone etc.

Theory of Burgess

Burgess is the pioneer and his theory on city dynamics provides the base for later theorists on the subject. Burgess set out to evolve a theory of dynamics but he arrived at a theory of patterns of city growth which applies to any stage of urban development.

The Urban Zones

According to Burgess, an urban area consists of five concentric zones. The zones represent areas of functional differentiation and expand rapidly from the business centre. The zones are:

(1) The loop.

(2) The zone in transition.

(3) The zone of working men's homes.

(4) The residential zone of high class apartment buildings.

(5) The commuter's zone.

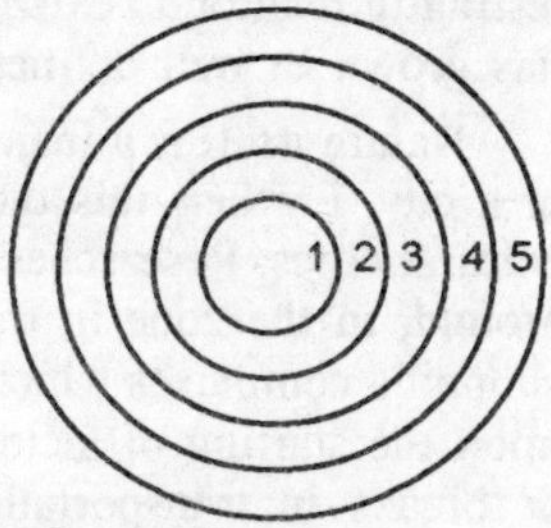

1. The loop or central business district. This is called as down town in American terminology. It is usually situated at the centre of the city. It is an area of business and official activity. Transportation routes from all parts of the city converge upon it. All the activities connected with business and service such as shops of various articles, departmental stores, restaurants, cinema houses, banks, main post offices and warehouses are all situated in and around the area at convenient places.

2. The zone in transition. This is the area which is situated in the immediate vicinity of the market district. It is a haphazard area of dilapidated buildings and slums. It is in the process of transition from a residential area into a business area. It develops out of over-concentration of business area and the consequent turnover of extra and weak units into less favourable neighbourhoods. It is an area of business and light industry. It is an area of squalor, regular vice and disorganization.

3. The zone of working men's homes. This is situated immediately after the zone in transition or the factory area as the workers usually prefer to live near the place of their work. This area is a near slum, congested with multifamily dwellings. It is inhabited by workers who have escaped from the influence of the area of deterioration.

4. The residential zone. The residential zone of high class apartment buildings or exclusive residential districts are usually situated at a reasonable distance from the city centre and consist of decent single family dwellings inhabited by middle and upper middle class professionals and executives. Well-planned roads, lounge spaces and beauty are the features of this area.

5. The commuter's zone. This lies at the outskirts of the city and is usually an area of the rural urban fringe. Hence this area reflects the characteristics of both types of habitats. This area is usually inhabited by people working in cities who also own land or by people who cannot find accommodation in cities. The inhabitants of this commuter's zone go daily to their place of work in the city through city transportation.

Criticism

Burgess himself was the first to point out that his proposition was not an actual description of patterns of city growth but an abstract scheme. This theory does not conform to the actual growth patterns of cities as proved by subsequent testing in relation to existing cities. It is very rare that we can find a city which has grown in well defined concentric cities.

Nature itself is a major limiting factor deciding the limitation in the shape of a city. Further, this theory does not explain the patterns of commercial or cultural cities. Researches have shown that excess business, instead of flocking around, in the zone in transition flows away to more remunerative suburban shopping complexes which is a novelty. The concept of industrialization insists upon the starting of factories along waterfronts or at the outskirts of the city or breaks in transportation as convenient sport on grounds of health and availability of raw material. The prominence of the loop has been greatly reduced due to the opening up of suburban shopping centres. The idea of the commuter's zone has been reduced in importance with the growth of twin cities. Contrary to expectation, new business and industry does not always flock towards the city centre or to the immediate area but move towards the convenient available area within the city for their location without touching the existing pattern. The theory does not account for the growth of satellite townships. However, the idea that residential zone lies away from the city centre and factory area nearby conforms to facts. The theory on the whole provides a ground work for the understanding of the growth patterns of contemporary cities.

FACTORS OF URBAN LOCATION

Cities differ in the most convenient spot of their location according to the functions they serve. Thus, while industrial towns are to be located near the places of extraction of their raw material or convenience of transportation, capital cities are to be located near the centre of a district or province.

The major factors which determine the location of any city are three, viz.

(1) Nature of the geographical properties of a site, (2) culture or the social organization, technological level and the economic system of a given society and (3) Function viz. the main purpose served by a particular city.

1. Nature. To some extent the city represents the endeavour of man to free himself from the domination of Nature but there are limits to this endeavour. Nature determines the available space for the creation of a city. Thus in U.S.A. people prefer low altitudes and plains to build cities. Deserts or hilly terrains are unsuitable for city location. The first cities were in certain river valleys like the Nile, Euphrates, Indus and also on seashores (e.g., in Indus valley cities, Egyptian cities etc.). Cities with commanding river and ocean positions have an advantage over inland cities in relation to transportation. Nature also determines city location as to the availability of raw materials. Thus mining and oil towns must be built around areas of mining and oil drilling. Recreation and health resort centres are built around spots of healthy climate. Spacious bathing beaches determine the location of Beach resorts. Thus natural spots of Urban centre include (1) where a country road meets a highway, (2) where a highway branches off into several main arteries, (3) at the crossroads of main communication lines, (4) at lake, sea-shore and river ports.

2. Culture. With exceptions, cities cannot break away from their rural hinterland as regards their culture and social organization.

Urban centres develop apart from a rural area if they serve an exclusive function, e.g., steel cities. The level of technological development of its immediate hinterland and the availability of entrepreneurical talent also determines the location of city many a time. For example, a militant nation will build its cities on locations which offer opportunities for domination e.g., Etrusean built hilltop fortresses in Damascus. Recreation can also have important implications for city location e.g., beach resorts like Kovalam, Gopalpur etc. Education can sometimes determine the location of cities, growth of a university town amidst a calm and relatively less educated rural hinterland e.g., Shanti Niketan, Roorkee etc. The cultural influence is particularly important if cities are intentionally founded because the choice of the location mirrors culturally conditioned preferences e.g. Ancient Alexandria.

3. Function. The location of city depends as much upon the function it performs as upon the availability of necessary opportunities. Although cities are usually a conglomeration of functions, many a time a single function dominates and defines a city e.g., Bokaro and Newcastle are steel cities. Sometimes a particular function can be performed effectively at a particular site. This factor explains the growth of mining towns, port towns, fishing towns, beach resorts etc. On the other hand, cultural cities, market centres and distribution and service cities offer many a wide variety of choice as to their location. Cities serving a complexity of functions such as administration, industry, service etc., develop at the most convenient central point to fulfil all its functions.

To sum up, there is no all inclusive principle determining the ideal location of a city. The factors discussed above jointly or in isolation determine the most favourable site for the construction or growth of a particular city.

ECOLOGICAL INTERPRETATION

Cities are always changing. As business expands, industries move in. There is growth in area and population changes in spatial arrangements and the social conditions which alter the city is the result. The changes take place in a definite order. For instance, there is a tendency towards centralization as well as decentralization with increasing economic activity. Land values go up. Taxes increase. Marginal businessman in the loop, no longer able to compete, moves out to cheaper outlying localities. Similarly, as the loop becomes unable to satisfy the needs of an increased population, subcentres and convenience stores spring up in outlying residential areas. In some cases business replaces residences and the residential areas are pushed to the periphery.

The fringe of the business area is most affected during expansions or contractions. An expanding business section causes flight from hitherto well organized residential areas. Land values adjacent to the new business area begin to decline and the whole border district deteriorates. Poor people may move into buildings hastily remodelled into cheap living quarters and a new slum arises. In a similar way population growth or decline changes the spatial pattern of a city. As residential areas become overcrowded, land values, taxes and rents rise. The result is a mass concentration and centralization of residential sections. But this process is accompanied by a process of decentralization. The upper class who find the area inconvenient to live in migrate. The poorest who could not pay the high rents and the mixed group of all those who could not find adequate accommodation move out. Different types of new residential areas develop such as high class sections with spacious home, middle class settlements and aggregations of hastily erected shabby houses for the lowest income group. Apartment houses predominate in the original section and one family sections move towards the outskirts of the city and beyond and the suburb is created. As this process is repeated, the spatial feature of the city changes. Fashionable suburbs become middle class sections and the upper class built on vacant land.

Thus in an expanding city the business centres tend to grow in size thereby dislocating residential areas.

At the same time residential areas show a centrifugal tendency by moving more and more towards the outskirts and beyond the city limits. Urban settlements form into distinct and regular ecological patterns. A city is a clearly distinguishable spatial order of urban activities. The sectional differences within a city arise out of social considerations which create for each part of a city a different evaluation and different functions. The ecological patterns of a city exhibit (1) differentiations of functions, (2) class separation, and (3) cultural segregation.

However, this explanation does not confirm to the actual growth of cities. It is rarely that we notice a deteriorated neighbourhood surrounding business district although there may be slums. Further, the growth of suburban shopping complexes has immensely reduced the prominence of central business district. Contrary to the explanation, housing districts are generally found in the midest of a city. The idea is to remove the factories and transfer zone to the outskirts of the city. Apartment houses sometimes exist amidst one family houses. However, the notion of congestion and relative land values is understandable. The explanation serves as an ideal construct which may provide a guideline to future city planners.

MIGRATION AND URBANIZATION

Migration in relation to urbanization includes Rural-urban exchange, i.e., migration from country to city and intracity migration. Ravenstein argued about a constant population shift in instalments. The migrants move as a rule, only a short distance from villages to smaller towns and from smaller towns to cities. Consequently, the urban population is constantly displaced and replaced. However, he also admitted the existence of long distance migration to industrial and trade centres. Generally, rural youths, adolescents and females migrate to city in search of jobs, education, amenities of city life and life partners.

Weber and others developed this theory and argued that the current migration is toward cities. Inhabitants of the immediately surrounding area flock to the city creating gaps in the rural population which are filled by persons from more remote districts. Trends in migration depend upon the selective principles such as age, sex, education etc.

The chief characteristics of the urban community are its size, density, heterogeneity, class structure and secularism. Urban population is larger in number and density, urban areas are generally congested. People are heterogeneous and diverse in their basic characters and cultural background. Total strangers belonging to the same class live side by side in a single neighbourhood. Position in the urban class hierarchy determines one's position in urban society. This in time is determined by education, economic and social status, wealth etc. The urban person is secular and cosmopolitan in outlook and tolerant towards all shades of opinions and religious practice. Low birth rate and death rate are both features of an urban community. The patterns of urban life demand lesser number of births and supporters. Urban death rate is reduced due to an effective control of diseases. Another demographic feature of an urban community is that near groups have a greater influence upon a person than family groups. In urban population all have to do something to promote their upkeep. Urban population thus exhibits the features of a degree of independence and self support and solitary relations.

Inter city migration refers to migration between different areas of a city in search of job or housing or a place of convenience. Usually, youths and small families move out of one area in a city. Thus, a low class family may move out of a middle class area due to its inability to pay high rents while a high class family may move out due to congestion. The city also witnesses both horizontal and vertical mobility between occupations and along the social scale.

STUDY OF HUMAN ECOLOGY

Urban aggregates form the top extreme of human adaptation to Nature, since cities are the artefacts of human ingenuity and reflect the almost total subordination of nature to subserve man's purposes. Human ecology in relation to urbanism makes an interesting reading. It occupies an important place in the study of urban sociology. It lays down the foundation for a study of the other aspects of urban society. Hence a study of urban ecology is a necessary preliminary to a study of urban sociology as a whole. Urban ecology is a special study of human ecology.

Human ecology first of all defines the spatial patterns of a city. We know that functional specialization of particular areas is a necessary factor of city growth. Human ecology defines the most favourable spot for the location of each function such as market, residential areas etc., of a city. Thus the most suitable location for the market is the central place of a city wherein transportation routes converge. Factories are to be situated along water fronts or breakers in transportation points or along the outskirts of the city. Hilloks, slopes etc. which come amidst the city are to be considered while locating areas. Residences must be situated in calm areas, a little away from the centre of the city. In contrast, in rural areas the situation of a habitat is decided by and confined to a restricted area near the cultivable fields.

Human ecology defines the characteristics of urban population i.e., its size, density and heterogeneity and accounts for it. It also decides the spread of urban population between areas and occupations.

Human ecology defines the location of cities. One cannot think of locating a city in a desert or an isolated spot. City is a conglomeration of varied elements. As such, a city can exist only admist a suitable rural hinterland which provides labour and basic materials to sustain it.

PROCESSES OF URBAN GROWTH

The most important contribution of human ecology to urban sociology is the study of the processes of urban growth which is an application of the laws of plant and animal ecology. These processes are:

1. Concentration. This refers to the flocking up or converging of people and functions around a main centre of attraction. Thus, all shops and traders flock around the central business districts.

2. Centralization. It is a further process of concentration wherein all the functions pertaining to a specific interest will be situated in a specific area. Thus, all shops and warehouses are in the centre while factories develop along the outskirts of city.

3. Decentralization. It is a further negative process of centralization which results from over or excessive centralization and congestion. It results in over population and consequent spill over of extra units to other suitable places. Thus, excessive congestion of shops in a place leads to cut-throat competition and small traders who fear extinction move away to suburban residential areas. This results in the creation of suburban shopping centres which provide for the immediate need of suburban dwellers.

4. Invasion. Invasion is a connected process of decentralisation. Decentralisation in one area or over centralization leads to the invasion of the neighbouring area by extra units. Thus, shops of the central loop spread over and push away the neighbouring housing district. Invasion leads to partial dislocation of the existing interests.

5. Succession. It is the final process wherein the new interest settles down in the newly invaded area. The zone of deterioration in several cities explains away this process.

All these processes explain the nature of city growth, spatial pattern and mobility, changes in city pattern etc. Another important area of human ecology is urban immigration and population mobility between areas and occupations.

PRINCIPLES OF URBAN ECOLOGY

In an urban structure are evident some special features. Certain localities of cities are centres of some special trade, profession or industry. For example, Chandni Chowk, Karol Bagh and Connaught Place are popular shopping centres and Sadar Bazar, a centre of whole-sale trade in Delhi. Some corners or squares of a city are famous for their hotels and restaurants while other centres may be renowned for their trade and commerce. There may even be some special places in a city notorious for gambling dens, brothels and all sorts of crimes. There are usually in cities dens of corruption notorious for bad characters. Sociologists have discovered close links between the social life of a city and its environs, that is, technically speaking, its ecology. As the Level of the ground is an important and influential factor for the growth and development of the life of flora and fauna, in the same way the level of a city and its distance from the centre affects the social life of a city. In the science of ecology we study the relationship between the topography and environs of a city and its social life.

The ecological factors affecting the social life of a city are not the same everywhere. In cities dominated by government servants the life is centred around government offices and buildings. In some towns the main centre of life is military cantonment while in others it might be air force complex. In the industrial cities big factories are the centre of life of that city. In big industrial towns we find, besides big factories, schools, colleges, university, courts, clubs, theatres, hotels, cinemas and wine centres. Slums are a usual feature of industrial cities. The large labour force working in various factories of city must per force stay in the city. It is usually not feasible to provide good houses to them. Therefore, they stay in temporary hutments, makeshift tenements which are without any municipal facility whatsoever. These shanties and huts make a slum. The rich in industrial cities stay at a respectable distance from the hub of the city in grand mansions and palatial buildings. Around the commercial and trade centres there are usually concentrations of population. The industrial cities are as a rule densely populated. In these cities we also find red-light areas gambling and wine dens and toddy houses. In small towns we do not find these things because labourers return to their homes after work. In such cities the population is not large and these cities are usually tilted toward villages. In small cities social organisation is stable and we also find a fair amount of social control in such cities. In big industrial cities life is full of conflicts and tensions. The incidence of crime is high. There are strikes, gheraos and bandhs. However, cultural life of these towns is very rich.

ECOLOGICAL ELEMENTS IN CITIES

An investigation into the ecological elements of cities shows that following are the important ecological elements:

1. Geographic Conditions. The topography and climate of a city affect the diet, the living conditions, the social, the cultural, the political and the economic life of its residents. The cities situated on the banks of a river are as a rule thickly populated. Adjacent to mining centres producing coal, cement, oil and other industrial raw materials, big industrial cities spring up. The hill towns are sleepy lagoons in winter, but, with the summer influx of tourists they spring into life and become centres of buzzing activity. In the city situated in the vicinity of jungles, wood industry is the main profession. In deserts the population is sparse and industry scanty. Thus we see clear influence of geographic conditions on the life in the cities. As far as diet is concerned, geographic conditions have much less influence on city than on villages. In cities like London and Calcutta we can find every kind of diet. However, it will be very difficult to get Indian food in small British cities. However, living conditions are clearly affected by geographic conditions. In Japan we will find few wooden houses in big cities. In Rajasthan houses are made mostly of chiselled stone. On account of technological advances the influence of geographic factor has been reduced in matters of clothing and other living conditions. On account of refrigeration facilities deserts have bloomed. The moral life in big towns is comparatively lax. There is little social control and people feel free to indulge in their whims and fancies. The political, social and cultural life in big cities, however, is varied and rich.

2. Means of Transport and Communication. The second important ecological element which influences urban life is the means of transport and communication. If the facilities of transport and communication are poor in a city, its population is bound to be small, trade and commerce below average and the cultural outlook of its residents narrow. In the absence of suitable facilities of transport and communication traditionalism and orthodoxy rule the minds of city-dwellers and the social life is slow and uneventful; the cultural and artistic activity is conspicuous by its absence. On the other hand, if the means of transport and communication are good, the population of the city is large, the trade and commerce flourishing, social and cultural life are highly dynamic. The economic, cultural, artistic and religious activity in such cities are very rich and varied. People in cities which are well connected by road, rail and air with other parts of the country and world are generally prosperous and have a broad catholic outlook.

3. Business and Industry. The business and industry also affect the life of a city. If a city is highly industrialised it will be full of contradictory things and pairs of opposites would exist side by side. On its one corner we shall find palatial buildings and grand multi-storeyed mansions and on the other side we shall find hutments and shanties totally devoid of any municipal facilities. Thus dirt and grandeur coexist in big cities. It will also have beautiful clubs, restaurants, hotels parks and playgrounds. Along with all this we shall find brothels and gambling dens. The life in cities which are centres of trade and commerce is very different from that of industrial cities.

4. Economic, Social and Cultural Organisations. Apart from the above mentioned factors, economic, social and cultural organisations between people are established. It is these elements which determine the diet, clothing and housing of city dwellers. If a city is prosperous and its citizens artistic minded, we shall find in that city good theatres, music halls, art gallaries and also decorative facades of buildings. If people are highly religious we may find in that city good temples, mosques, churches or synagogues etc.

MENTAL HEALTH OF URBAN COMMUNITY

Mental diseases and mental instability are a typically urban phenomenon as instability and insecurity of life and mental isolation are features of the urban community. Mental disorders result due to the lack of emotional satisfaction of a person. The main feature of urban life is tension, anxiety, isolation and insecurity. Intimate social relations are few in an urban society and it is those relations which provide mental satisfaction.

Cultural Factors

Some cultural factors representative of urban way of life affect the mental health of an urbanite. They are:

1. Urban Tensions. Urban life is characterised by many physical irritations such as excessive noise, the constant cacophony or mechanical sounds, incessant visual attacks on the eyes by glaring multi-coloured lights; mass congestion in public conveyances, restaurants, departmental stores and amusement places, and the strain caused by daily commuting. All these factors produce un-necessary anxiety and extra tension on the urbanite's mind which is beyond his mental capacity to endure and thus affect his mental health.

2. Strain from Competition. In rural areas a man's roles in life and society are fixed, well defined and assured. On the other hand, competitions on a large scale and to a greater extent are regular features of the urban life process. Thus, there is competition for jobs, for seats in educational institutions, for business orders, for customers, for patronage, for membership in clubs, for political office, for a cinema ticket, in short to secure anything and everything in life. As such, the loser in the game may put the blame on his own inability and thus develop an inferiority complex or become frustrated. Moreover, excessive competition itself puts an extra amount of strain on a person's mentality.

3. Conflicts. Large scale conflicts among different interests were rare in simple and homogenous societies. In contrast, conflicts are an inherent feature of city life which is complex and heterogeneous in people's outlooks, attitudes, interests etc. City life is also characteristic of numerous daily contacts, competition in all walks of life and a variety of economic, political and social interests. Hence a slight misunderstanding between two persons may result in a conflict. This further saps the mental energy of a human being. These conflicts may sometimes lead to riots, loss of jobs, family tragedies. Strikes and agitations are a constant feature of urban life. The equal importance given to conflicting interests and opposing points of view may create confusions in the urbanite's mind and complicate it.

4. Cultural Diversity. Cultural homogeneity provides a man with a stable note of values and a set pattern of life which reduces conflict and provides security to life. But urban centres are a reservoir of a variety of sub-cultures, institutionalized attitudes and contradictory set of moral values. Even deviant sub-cultures and value systems are present and demand equal attention from the urbanite. This cultural diversity tends to create confusions and tensions by presenting conflicting and sometimes contradictory set of values as to the right set of values to be followed to lead a successful life.

5. Insecurity. Suicides and other forms of personal disorganization are rare in rural societies where group life is well founded and the group looks after the physical and mental health of all of its members. But isolation and a sense of loneliness are the typical features of urbanism which breaks up cohesive group life by its very nature and leaves the individual bewildered. He admits a conglomeration of value systems and belief patterns without proper guidance as to their merit. Further, the urbanite has nothing to fall back upon in times of crisis. The constant competition and conflict of urban life may eliminate a person at a time if he shows signs of weakness.

QUESTIONS FOR EXERCISE

1. Human Ecology is the study of a symbolic relation between man and environment. Elucidate this statement.
2. Define ecological structure. What are the processes which bring about changes in the ecological structure?
3. Discuss the importance of ecological approach to study of urban community.
4. Explain the role of city government in solving the problems of rapid urban growth in India.
5. What is Urbanism? Discuss the salient features of urbanism.
6. Give a critical account of the concentric zone theory.
7. Briefly indicate the factors involved in the location of cities.
8. Critically examine the ecological interpretation and urban growth patterns.
9. Discuss migration in relation to urbanization. What are the chief demographic features of an urban community ?
10. What do you understand by Human Ecology? Indicate the contribution of ecological approach to urban sociology.
11. Describe some of the important principles which shape the ecological patterns of the city.
12. Analyse the factors that affect the mental health of the urban community.

4

Theories of Urbanization

CENTRAL PLACE LOCATION THEORY

Many years ago Sir Flinders Petree attitude that the only or main reason for the existence of a city is its function as a storage centre. Geographers still have a tendency to explain the location of urban sites in terms of their functions as service centres. An elaborate scheme of this type was offered by a German geographer Walter Christaller. His basic arsumption was that a given rural area supports an urban centre which in turn serves the surrounding countryside. Mackenzie was inclined to accept a similar view point when remarking that during this period of population dispersion the city was for the most part the child and servant of expanding rural settlement. Christaller's view has been introduced in America by Mann with modifications.

Evaluation

This theory, however, is patently at variance with facts. Whether we examine the distance between larger cities or the general distribution of urban settlements we find no regularity in spacing. Perhaps the theorists were mainly influenced by the fact of the growth of towns in the beginning as market centres.

Ulmann admits the vulnerability of the scheme for larger places. In highly industrialized areas the central place scheme is generally so distorted by industrial concentration in response to resources and transportation that it may be said to have little significance as an explanation for urban location and distribution. But he claims that the theoretical ideal appears to be most nearly approached in poor, thickly settled farm districts areas which are most nearly self contained. The central place hypothesis is the only existing theory which employs a single principle as a determinant of location of cities. However, growth of contemporary cities and their location depends upon a multiplicity of factors. Hence the central place location theory of cities fails to account for the location of contemporary cities.

SECTOR THEORY OF URBAN GROWTH

Several attempts have been made to find the principles which shape the ecological patterns of the city. To find rules which govern equally the spatial developments of all urban settlements regardless of time and location seems an ever continuing venture.

The Sector theory of Home Hoyt was developed two years after Burgess's theory was tested in relation to the growth of existing cities. According to Hoyt this theory was intended as a modification of Burgess's theory. Hoyt's theory was more dynamic in character than Burgess's proposition since constant changes, population movements, expansion of industries and their effects on spatial patterns were studied. Hoyt's main contentions were as follows :

1. Industrial areas do not develop around the central business district but along railroad lines and water fronts, or more recently near the outskirts of city. Industrial areas thus expand not in circles but string like patterns.

2. High-class areas are not located in the last concentric zone on the periphery but only in one or more sectors. As the city grows the upper classes keep moving from the centre, abandoning areas to the lower classes which extend their habitats from the centre towards the outskirts in areas of a triangular rather than circular shape.

3. High grade residential areas originate near the retail and office centre but tend to proceed along established lines of travel or towards another existing nucleus and buildings or trading centre preferably toward high ground or a lake, bay, river or ocean front.

4 The high priced residential neighbourhood tends to grow towards the homes of the leaders of the community.

Evaluation

As Hoyt's theory is also based on the study of a few cities it suffers from its own drawbacks. It cannot supply us any more with a universal pattern of the growth of cities. As Hoyt wrongly contends, high class residential areas do not proceed along transportation lines, as high class people prefer to live away from the din of urban traffic. Hoyt's theory docs not explain the growth of suburban or satellite townships. It also cannot account for the concept of "twin cities." Moreover city growth depends upon its location and one cannot expect every other city to be located near high grounds or a water front.

But the sector theory is definitely a welcome development over the concentric zone theory as it makes room for the modern concept of location of industries also for the growth of a variety of cities wherein the areas of the concentric zone are located along side in various sectors. Moreover, it gives importance to city growth around transportation lines which is akin to the modern concept of convenient location of ecological areas of a city.

FACTORS OF URBAN LOCATION

According to BERGEL the 3 factors which have a considerable influence on the location of cities are: (1) Nature (2) Culture (3) Function. The properties of a site are commonly referred to as the nature aspects: the social configurations as culture and the purpose as function. Each of these has an array of elements which are independently variable. No one city is the result of a few of these factors or all of them alone. All cities exhibit the influence of all these elements at different periods of time. Now, let us look at each of these in detail.

1. Nature. Geographical factors like mountains, terrains, rivers, lakes etc., have influenced the location of cities. With the growth of science and technology man has gained control over nature to a large extent, but not a total control, for the presence of lakes, polar regions, rapid unmanageable falls etc., limit the establishment and growth of cities. In India, vast desert in Rajasthan prohibits location of cities in the heart of the state. On the contrary Punjab, due to its affinity to the navigable Indus river, has become an important link with the North West Frontier Province as a "fence factor."

Important water fronts have led to the growth of cities all over the world because of the following factors.

(1) Building highways is a costly affair and has been usually the construct of forced labour. Water fronts are a bountiful supply of nature.

(2) Roads being extremely unsafe in winter, river boats are the alternative means of transport to the bulk of the city population dwelling close to water fronts.

(3) River transport is by far the fastest means of travel.

(4) Water transport is even today the cheapest for goods like coal, oil, wheat etc., which are "bulk" items.

(5) International trade relies largely on ocean routes like Panama and Suez canals.

Hence, many cities have sprung up on river banks and spread to the fringe areas sometimes across the river to meet the needs of the growing population. The growth of cities like Bombay has been obstructed because of the limit placed by the surrounding water. Calcutta, situated on the Hoogli is an important social, economic and political unit in our country because of the natural advantages. In view of a river bank it has proximity to areas abundant in cash crops like cotton, jute etc., and the fine communication and transport network it enjoys in rural and urban areas.

Good climate and pleasant scenery as elements of nature likewise determine the establishment of health resorts, beaches etc. which embellish existing towns and cities nearby. These would otherwise have remained unnoticed.

Bangalore and Mysore are typical examples of this factor of location wherein nature provides the means for man's progressive developments to follow.

2. Culture. The social organisation, the technological level and economic system are included under this category. Bergel analyses the most ancient times when mankind was directly and exclusively dependent on land as a factor of production.

(i) *Transport*. The increased means of transportation today have led to a diffusion in the agricultural economy with diverse uses of the land factor. It is today a market economy unlike the old self sufficient units of the past. Those places which link road to rail traffic or have different modes of transport become important cities .

(ii) *Market*. We witness a shift in importance of one city to another with changing market demands. The discovery of raw materials in new locations demands the establishment of mining centres closely with adequate link facilities too. Thus a shift in one steel centre in India and elsewhere is a common result of change in pattern of availability of raw materials, change in consumer demand etc.

(iii) *Recreation*. Recreation as an aspect of culture was originally confined to the place of stay or work. But with progress of civilisation, more and more people turn to ''outside'' locations for recreation activities, overnight scamps etc. Hence, where nature gives a plentiful supply of pleasant survey, salubrious climate and so on, resorts develop rapidly.

(iv) *Religion*. Religion as another element of culture determines the location of cities too. In India for example, Amritsar, Mathura, Badrinath, Madurai etc., have religious connotations and have grown into important centres of religious life.

3. Functions. When important cities and centres are analysed in terms of their respective functions, it stands out clearly that these functions cannot be performed effectively by any substitute centres. Examples of this phenomenon are service centres, local market centres, mining cities, shipping ports, fishing places etc. Hence, it would be most profitable to choose a manufacturing centre for car tyres closest to an automobile industry. Likewise, perishable commodities should be marketed immediately to ports speedily without delay; hence fishing for export is done closest to ports and not inland. Inland fishing is normally for domestic purposes. Marketing centres are generally situated centrally in relation to urban markets and rural areas so that the function is performed effectively and efficiently. Thus centres like Erode, Ougale etc. are important milk marketing boards in the South like Anand in the North Gujarat.

However, no single factor alone namely nature, culture and function, can determine the location of cities in any period of time and place. Nature does afford opportunities of city growth, but man has to make the final choice, depending on the standard of economic, cultural level and so on. It has hence been rightly pointed out that ''Topographical conditions are not so much disinct causes of particular ecological configurations as they are limiting factors to which some kind of ecological adjustment can be made''.

URBAN RENEWAL

Urban renewal is an aspect of urban planning and it refers to the renovation and rejuvenation of dilapidated areas of city and conscious planning for the future growth of a city. Urban renewal is an essential aspect of urban planning in India as Indian cities are mostly hapazard in their development and are the most neglected areas of development. Urban renewal aims at making the city a healthy and happy place to live in. Its purpose is to solve the burning spatial and social problems of a city. It aims at proper zoning, renovation, appropriate construction of transportation lines, lounge spaces and providing adequately for the necessities of the city population including housing and employment.

Renewal Problems

As urban renewal is a constructive and reformate process it is bound to face obstacles. The obstacles depend upon the nature of the city government, nature of the city, its location and population.

1. Economic. The major economic factor involved in urban renewal is the availability of funds with the city government. Further, it also depends upon the economic composition of city population. Hence, plans involve their favourable spatial location.

Further the removal and reconstruction of dilapidated areas is obstructed by vested interests and criminal gangs which have an interest in the area. Urban renewal plans must also take into account if possible future location of economic interests say factory and business.

2. Legal. The legal problems of urban renewal refer to zoning regulations. They play a very important role in the expansion of city. Zoning regulations of many cities require that equal areas must be provided for all types of functions in a city and this, while restricting the space available for housing and lounge space in residential areas sometimes also accounts for the adjacent location of residential areas near factory sites.

3. Administrative. The administrative problems involved refer again to the political pressure and pressure from interest groups in checking plans for urban renewal. The administrative problem also refers to the inability of the city government to control the growth of crime and vice in cities which act as hindrances for city growth and renewal. This problem also refers to capacity of the government for intelligent planning and control over future expansion of cities.

TRENDS IN RURAL-URBAN MIGRATION

There is no comprehensive theory of rural urban migration. Scholars have tried only to account for currents in rural urban migration and factors giving rise to it. Although we call it rural urban migration. In fact, it is mainly rural migration and urban immigration since it is the surplus unemployed ruralites who go to an urban centre in search of job or after the attractions of city life. Hence, the best way to study rural-urban migration is the study of migration trends and factors affecting it. The best way to find out trends in domestic migration is to study some of the selective principles of migration. These are as follows :

1. Age. The first selective principle of rural urban migration is age. It explains why people below 19 years and above the middle age stay behind in rural areas while adults and absolescents move away to urban areas. It also accounts for the high birth rate in cities.

2. Sex. The second selective principle usually mentioned is sex. Usually, males move away to cities in search of jobs. The influence of sex is less marked with regard to the factor which causes migration than to the goal of the migrant.

3. Character traits. The selective principles in general explain the main characters or features of people which favour migration in relation to opportunities and intent. There is still a controversy over the specific character traits which favour migration. Some stress on an inherited biological tendency to be adventurous among certain races such as in Poles, Sindhis etc. Others like Ross thought the most intelligent migrate leaving behind the farm to bull heads and suckers. Zimmerman argued that "the city attracts the extremes and the country retains the means". However, all these arguments are conjectural.

4. Intelligence. Numerous studies have been made to determine the role of intelligence as a selective factor with regard to migration. For instance, studies of rural areas of South U.S.A. indicate that the more intelligent people migrate and less intelligent remain behind. It is also argued that the feeble minded people also migrate to cities as they are thrown out of rural areas. However, all these arguments are debatable in the light of facts.

5. Moral Standard. The opposite is the case regarding selectivity according to moral standards. The habitual criminal, the individuals who do not like to work, the professional prostitute and similar anti-social characters leave the country. The country or village is thus apt to lose some of its best intellects and also worst characters.

6. Education. Another selective principle of migration is education and training but empirical data regarding this factor is scarce. In former times, the rural migrants were uneducated and untrained. Today, however, the conditions have changed. Both the best trained and the unqualified move to cities.

7. Physical fitness. Finally, we may mention the value of physical fitness as a selective factor. Empirical data about this factor are again scarce. Generally, rural migrants were strong and sturdy. But today, with mechanical sophistication, cities are attracting the weak and the constitutionally deficient persons also. Thus, health becomes more of a negative selective factor.

These are supposed to be some of the biological traits which are likely to determine either way the trends in domestic migration. However, the influence of much of these factors in selection has been reduced with successive urbanization. Today, rural urban migration is a complicated aspect which involves many factors.

QUESTIONS FOR EXERCISE

1. Define Urban place, Urban locality, Urban agglomeration and related terms in sociology.
2. How do you measure urbanization? explain with example ?
3. Show the present trend towards urbanization in the world.
4. Analyse the trends of urbanization in India since 1901.
5. Write short note on urban population growth in U.P.
6. Write short note on characteristics of urban population growth in India.
7. Do you agree with the view that the entire development of towns is due to industrialization? Discuss briefly the factors which were responsible for the development of town in the past.
8. Point out the causes of growth of cities in pre-industrial India.
9. Discuss the Central Place Location Theory of Cities.
10. Critically examine the Sector Theory of Urban Growth as enunciated by Hoyt.
11. Analyse the principal factors that govern the location and distribution of cities in India.
12. Discuss the Economic, Legal and Administrative Problems involved in Urban Renewal.
13. Discuss the selective principles of rural-urban migration.

5

Types of Cities

According to 1991 Census figures there were about 200 cities in India having population of more than one lakh, these statistics were tentative and final figures are not available. Besides big cities there are thousands of towns. No two of the cities are exactly alike. The geographical conditions, population make-up and differentiation and other features of each city are unique. Thus, whereas Delhi is the central capital, Kanpur is an industrial city, and whereas Bombay is an important harbour, Mussoorie is a summer resort. In spite of the unique character of every city there are also some common features, among various cities. For example, Agra, Kanpur, Calcutta, Ahmedabad, Bombay are all industrial cities. Therefore, the feature of industrialization is common to scores of Indian cities. We can thus classify the cities on the basis of some fundamental features shared by all cities of a class. All the cities mentioned above are industrial cities and, therefore, production centres. In these cities a variety of goods is produced and manufactured. However, it must be clearly borne in mind that though many cities share some fundamental features, each city is unique and there are features which are peculiar to it alone. For example, both Kanpur and Bombay are big industrial cities. Both are centres of cloth production having numerous textile mills; both are important rail junctions. But Bombay is a major port which Kanpur is not. Whereas Kanpur is a centre of leather technology, Bombay is an important centre of film production. Thus, the cities of one class also have numerous diverse features as well.

Types of Cities

On the basis of broad common features of the cities we can classify them into following types:

(1) Production centres

(2) Centres of Trade and Commerce

(3) Capitals

(4) Health and Recreation Centres

(5) Cultural Centres

(6) Diversified cities.

As we have mentioned earlier, there can be no absolute classification of cities, all classifications are relative. Many cities fit in more than one category mentioned above. For example, Delhi fits in with the first three categories. It is an important production centre, an equally important centre of trade and commerce and is, of course, a capital city. Bombay, on the other hand, satisfies the necessary conditions of first five categories listed above. It is an important production centre, an important centre of trade and commerce, capital of Maharashtra, a centre of health and recreation and also a cultural centre. Besides these, Bombay also has many other specilities. Being on the seacoast its climate is temperate and it is also the most important film-making centre. It is also world's renowned centre of entertainment and amusement. Bombay's importance lies not only in the fact that it is capital of Maharashtra but issues from the fact that it is a famous city. Not without reason it is called Gateway of India. Again, the importance of Bombay does not lie in its being a big centre of culture and entertainment but issues from the fact that it is a port through which import and export worth millions of rupees is made. Though Bombay is a centre of cloth production, it is more important as a centre of trade and commerce. Therefore, after taking into consideration everything we find that Bombay fits in with the second category most, that is it is a centre of trade and commerce. Thus, while classifying a city we have to see as to which of its features is most prominent. Therefore, though Delhi is an important production centre as well as the centre of trade and commerce its most important feature is that it is a capital city.

Types are not pure

It must be borne in mind that the above classification of types of cities has been done on the basis of the most fundamental or prominent features of city. If a city is a capital as well as big trade and commercial centre our classification will be determined by the fact whether the fact of being capital or being a commercial centre is more fundamental or prominent. To illustrate, Chandigarh is the capital of Punjab and it is also a commercial centre. But the fact of capital is more fundamental and important than the fact of being the commercial centre. On the contrary, of Bombay the fact of being commercial centre is far more important than that of its being the capital of Maharashtra. It is generally observed that once a city is made the capital of a state its importance and stature grows. Owing to official patronage, greater security and availability of easy loans etc., such cities become important production centres or centres of trade and commerce. On the other hand, some cities are high production centres naturally. In modern times it is difficult to find examples of pure types of cities. Some exceptions may of course be summer resort or hill towns. Some of these are purely centres of health and recreation. Below we shall discuss the types of cities in detail:

1. Production Centres. Generally, the more important cities of the world are industrial towns. The main reason for increasing urbanisation in modern times is the industrialisation. Consequent upon industrial revolution the urban population all over the world has increased considerably. In India, the majority of cities having population of one lakh or more are industrial towns. According to the kind of population, the population centres can be classified into following categories:

(A) *Primary Population Centres.* The primary population centres are those places where materials for industrial use are produced. For example, mining centres where oil, coal, iron etc. are produced are primary production centres. The population of such places is usually not very large. Generally, only those persons live at these centres who are directly or indirectly involved in the production of raw materials. By elaborate transport these centres are connected with places at which raw materials are further refined. Among such towns in India are Nellore, Masulipatnam, Ranchi, Gauhati, Mysore, Kolar, Dehradun Bareilly etc. In Dehradun and Bareilly the wood obtained from forest is sawed and packed on to secondary population centres. Bareilly is also known for its bamboo population. In Gauhati, we have oil wells, in Ranchi we have coal mines and in Kolar there are gold mines.

(B) *Secondary Production Centres.* Most of the centres of population are included in this category. In secondary production centres the raw materials obtained from primary population centres are used for manufacture of a variety of goods. At such places population is large and keeps growing. As the primary centres of population produce one or two items, the secondary population centres usually produce scores of items but are famous for one or two items. For example, Ferozabad is famous for its glass bangles, Kanpur for leather goods, Moradabad for brass-work, Gwalior for earthen wares, Aligarh for locks and scissors, Jamshedpur for steel and iron, Rampur for knives and scissors, Bareilly for furniture, Banaras for saris and brocade work, Bangalore for silk sarees. In these towns a major portion of population is involved in the production of goods specific to it. The industrial activity obviously affects greatly the economic and social life of the industrial town. In some cities some goods are produced. For example, Meerut and Aligarh both are famous for scissors. In some cities one type of goods is primarily produced. For example, in Moradabad brass wares industry is not only major but virtually the only industry. In some cities numerous things are produced. In Bombay not only there is cloth production but there is also production of electrical and engineering goods in a big way. If there are more than one industry in any city, the chances of unemployment due to economic recession in one industry are less. This is because if one industry faces recession and there is retrenchment, the retrenched men may find jobs in the other industry. Whereas, if the labour force of a place is employed in one industry and if there is no other industry, the economic recession in the industry would result in wholesale unemployment and the labour would be compelled to migrate.

2. The Centre of Trade and Commerce. Generally, the cities are production centres and centres of trade and commerce; but in some cities the trade and commerce is the dominant feature and production is secondary. For example, though Bombay is a major production centre, it is a far bigger centre of trade and commerce. Therefore, Bombay must be regarded primarily to be a centre of trade and commerce. Generally, the cities situated on the seacoast and those which are ports are centres of trade and commerce. Naturally through these ports large quantity of goods are sent to and received from foreign lands. More than 95% of trade and commerce transacted with foreign lands is made through sea. The major Indian ports : Porebandar, Surat, Kandla, Bombay, Marmogao, Manglore, Calicut, Cochin, Allepy, Quilon, Tuticorin, Dhanushkodi, Neggapattam, Karical, Cuddalore, Pondicherry, Madras, Masulipatnam, Kakinada, Vishakhapatnam and Calcutta. With the exception of Calcutta, Madras and Bombay all other ports are known exclusively for trade and commerce. Though Madras is primarily a centre of trade and commerce but it is also the capital of Tamilnadu. Bombay and Calcutta, however, are so diverse and vast that these virtually fit in every category mentioned above. While it is true that ports are usually the centres of trade and commerce, it is by no means the case that these are the only such centre. Indeed there are many inland towns which satisfy the condition of being centres of trade and commerce. For example, Meerut is a big mandi for gur : so is Muzaffarnagar. Dehradun is a mandi of rice. In mandi goods from far and wide are collected and therefrom distributed to retailers. New York, London, Calcutta, Delhi, Kanpur and Madras are big mandis where goods from great distance are collected.

3. Capital. All cities, world over, which happen to be the capitals of states have grown into bigness and shot into prominence. Their importance and eminence is not due to their industry or mandi but due to their being the capitals. Indeed, once a place is made the capital, business and industry are but sequel of the main fact of its being the capita. Prior to industrial revolution, capital cities generally were the most eminent cities of the world. The examples of Rome, Paris, London and Moscow amply bear this out. However, as mentioned before, on account of official policy and patronage the capitals tend to become centres of trade, commerce and production. London, New York, Delhi, Moscow, Berlin and Peking can be cited as examples. However, the chief importance of capitals is political rather than industrial or commercial. In the field of industry and commerce Kanpur is the foremost town of U.P. But the city of pride in U.P. is Lucknow and not Kanpur. This is because Lucknow is the capital of U.P. Some cities' importance lies only in the fact of their being capitals : Shillong, Bhubaneshwar, Chandigarh, Jaipur, Hyderabad, Trivendrum, Patna are few such examples. Bombay, Calcutta, Madras, Bangalore, Ahmedabad and Srinagar are capitals respectively of Maharashtra, Bengal, Tamilnadu, Mysore, Gujarat and Jammu and Kashmir. But the importance of these cities lies not mainly in the fact of their being capitals but in other factes.

Srinagar, for example, is a summer resort and health centre. Ahmedabad is an industrial city. Bangalore is famous for its aeronautic industry. Bombay, Calcutta and Madras are centres of trade and commerce.

4. Health Recreation Centres. Many towns have very salubrious and healthy climate owing to their peculiar geographic location and climatic conditions. Generally the towns situated on the seacoast have temperate climate throughout the year and, therefore, people go there to escape the extreme heat of summer and extreme cold of winter. Similarly, hill towns are cool in summer and their climate and water are beneficial to health. Therefore, people from plains flock in great number to such towns in summer months and also go there to watch snowfall in winter. In order to attract more tourists to such places, municipal and state authorities do everything possible to beautify such places and make available all amenities. Many cultural shows are arranged. Many health clubs are opened. Similarly, a number of amusement centre, dance clubs are opened and beauty shows are arranged. In almost every state of India there are one or more important hill resorts. In British days, these towns were made the summer capitals of governments. Simla used to be the summer capital of India as well as Punjab. Now this practice has been discontinued, but much official work, particularly conferences during summer days are arranged in these hill towns. The important summer resort in India are in Uttar Pradesh, Almora, Bhovali, Chakrauta, Lansdown, Mussoorie, Nainital and Ranikhet; in Mysore, Bangalore; in Assam, Cherrapoonji and Shillong; in Tamilnadu, Conoor, Kodaikanal and Octacommand; in Punjab, Dalhousie, and Kulu, in Bengal, Darjeeling and Kalimpong; in Maharashtra, Mahabaleswar; in Rajasthan, Mt. Abu; in Madhya Pradesh, Pachmarhi and in Bihar, Ranchi. At these places few people live permanently but most come in season. The livelihood of permanent residents of these places, depends upon tourist traffic. At these places diverse type of entertainment is available. There are big hotels where wine flows freely and cabarets and western dances are staged for the entertainment of the audience. Most of the tourists coming here hail from the rich affluent class and they spend lavishly. These places get their distinctive colour and personality as a result of the kind of tourists reaching these places. Some hill resorts are patronized by government and officialdom whereas others are patronized by rich industrialists. There are some where middle class tourists also go. Thus the personality of a hill resort is determined by the kind of tourists. Some health resorts have sanatoria and health clinics and these are visited mostly by the sick. In Bhovali there is sanatorium for tuberculosis and Ranchi has a hospital for the mentally sick. In Kasauli there is a Pasteur Institute.

5. Cultural Centres. In India where religious sentiment dominates, many towns have become famous and developed into big cities on account of their religious value and importance. All the towns situated on river banks have an aura of holiness attached to them. Besides, India is a multi-religious country and each religion has one or two places regarded holy by the followers of each religion. For example, Amritsar has a famous Sikh Gurudwara known as Golden Temple. Ajmer is a place of pilgrimage for the Moslems. Ayodhya, Hardwar, Rameshwaram, Prayag, Puri, Mathura etc., are holy cities of Hindus. Bodh Gaya and Sarnath are holy places of Buddhists. Pilgrims from far and near come to these places to obtain spiritual solace and earn the religious merit. There are a number of historic cities in India renowned for some monument, mausoleum or some other structure celebrating some historic event. Agra, for example, is well known world over for its historic monuments, Taj Mahal, in particular. Bijapur is known for its circular tower and Chittorgarh for its Victory tower. Delhi is famous for its Red Fort and Jama Masjid. Sanchi is famous for its *Stupas* : Nalanda and Taxila for their ancient universities now in ruins; Fatehpur Sikri for its *Buland Darwaza*. Many cities are famous for being centres of higher learning. Allahabad, Bombay, Calcutta, Delhi Lucknow, Meerut, Madras, Nagpur, Roorkee, Kurukshetra, Sagar, Tirupati, Cuttak, Dharwar, Ujjain, Shantiniketan, Jadavapur, Burdwan and many other towns are famous for their universities. Pondicherry is famous world over for its Aurobindo Ashram.

6. Diversified Cities. Besides the cities which fit into one or the other of the above mentioned categories, there are some towns which fit into none of the categories. They may be holy, but holiness is not the fundamental reason for their growth; they may have a university but this, too many be incidental. There are places which may be important equally as cultural centres, production centres and as capitals. Thus it would be unjustified to put them in any one category. Such towns are accordingly referred to as *diversified* towns. For example, Varanasi is a holy city of Hindus; it has a famous university also in which students and teachers of all nationalities get together. It is also a commercial centre. It is also famous for its gold work on saris. Thus in Varanasi we find intellectuals, merchants, mendicants, beggars and prostitutes. A man may go to Varanasi for business, pleasure, study or for learning merit or reaping spiritual solace. All these things add colour and charm to the town. It is the most appropriate example of a diversified town.

India is a vast country; the process of urbanization is progressing here continuously. Therefore a detailed description of its many cities would require many volumes. However, broadly speaking, all Indian cities fit into one or the other category listed above. Indeed, the cities of the whole world can be classified in the above mentioned categories.

PREREQUISITES OF A CITY

Since cities are the products of higher reaches of civilization and represent the peak of the socio-cultural aspects of any society, the prerequisites of emergence of any city are four. They are as follows :

(1) A favourable ecological basis since cities have to support a large population.

(2) An advanced technology in both the agricultural and non-agricultural spheres.

(3) A complex social organization since cities have to harmonize life patterns of a divergent population.

(4) A well developed power structure.

Hence, it is presumed that the first cities developed only under the metal age, which were permanent army camps established by the possessors of metal arms who vanquished the other neolithic peasants.

Some scholars hold that the first cities were primitive villages which developed gradually into urban centres.

Western Cities

1. Ancient. The ancient cities were usually sovereign political entities sometimes called as city-states. They consisted of the house of ruler, high priest and feudal lords and elite guard. However, when political stability was established the cities began to grow and assume additional functions. Palaces and temples were built. The nucleus of the city population became the palace, temples and houses for the people employed therein. Soon craftsmen were added who furnished weapons as well as civilian supplier. Once they were able to produce more than the city's requirements the city developed a market. As occupational specialization increased, the population of the cities became stratified into an aristocracy; secular and priestly and its staff, a class of merchants, a class of artisans and a class of the poor made up of free men without regular means of subsistence and slaves.

2. Medieval. With the breakup of the Roman empire the cities became static administrative centres of a highly centralized aristocracy. The cities rapidly decayed in their development of the other spheres of life. Hence cities were few in the middle ages since the feudal lords preferred life entrenched in their rustic oriented castles. However, cities developed once again at the end of the middle ages with the development of trade. From then on cities have been constantly developing in structure and diversifying their functions. The zenith of the growth of city culture can be witnessed in the modern industrial urbanized civilization. Hence, when we speak of medieval cities we can only speak of the late medieval or early modern pre-industrial cities, as medieval cities as such are nothing more than a developed village or an administrative centre.

3. Modern. Industrialization can be said to have commenced with the replacement of manual power to mechanical power and with the transformation of the guild economy into the factory economy. While ancient cities developed as political centres, the medieval cities developed as trade centres, modern cities developed as industrial and service centres.

The growth of the modern city can be said to have originated with the development of factory colony and has progressed there upon to the contemporary gigantic multi-industrial cosmopolitan centres.

DISTINCTION BETWEEN MODERN AND MEDIEVAL CITIES

Hence modern cities differ from medieval cities in all respects such as structure, functions, population composition, social interaction, problems and so on. All these differences found in the modern cities can be attributed to the greater expansion and complexity in life patterns and the development of a mass culture.

1. Size. Regarding size basically medieval cities were trade centres which developed only around 5-6 K.M. area from a seashore or so. Hence, their population was well defined and confined to the trading population and their ancillaries. One can only imagine the size of modern metropolitan cities which expand beyond the imagination of our city fathers within no time. Indeed one can set no limit to the expansion of modern cities, which expand to accommodate the multifarious functional requisites of citizens. Further, there was a set pattern for the growth of medieval cities. While prominent market places developed at the centre, godowns and warehouses developed near seaports. While traders lived in a prestigious locality, petty traders, craftsmen etc., lived in another less favoured locality and so on. One can set no limit to the development of modern city suburbs which grow in a haphazard manner. Sometimes middle class people live side by side with high class residents. With the development of multi-functional shopping complexes, the city markets have lost their strategic and functional significance. Even with regard to location, while medieval cities developed mainly near sea shores, the development of quick and efficient transportation has freed the modern city of its locational problems.

2. Population. The size of population and its density is large in modern cities. While a medieval city housed say 10,000 people or so as a whole, a modern suburb accommodates more than that number in a metropolis. Hence, rush and congestion are the bigger problems of modern cities. While the medieval cities consisted mainly people of local or regional origin, our contemporary cities are cosmopolitan and international in character.

The people of modern cities come from diverse even contradictory socio-cultural background. Another interesting feature of our modern cities is the existence of a huge chunk of floating population and commuters.

3. Occupations. Occupational specialization, sophistication and diversification can be said to be the basic features which differentiate a modern industrial city from all other types and which give rise to other differences. The medieval cities acted as centers of exchange and largely depended upon their rural hinterland for sustenance. With the development of transportation, the modern cities can be said to have been almost divorced from their rural hinterland. With agricultural occupation coupled with non-agricultural occupations in medieval cities, mainly industrial and commercial and service occupations predominate in our contemporary cities. Sophistication and complexity in the life structure has led to the diversification of the occupational base and greater technicalisation of occupations. Professionalism in occupations can be said to be the specific feature in the development of industrial cities.

4. Politics. In the political sphere while medieval cities were autocracies, industrial cities are mainly parts of a federal and national set up. The contemporary city government is mainly elected and acts as a specialized organization of city life. It formulates the code of conduct of life of city dwellers and looks after their day-to-day welfare. The functions and organization of a modern city government consisting of a bureaucracy are more complicated and diversified.

5. Society. In the social sphere once again we find a greater degree of difference. Social life in the medieval cities was more or less conventional and had a rustic tinge in it. Institutions like the family still enjoyed some value and informal relations among the citizens or a clique of them predominated. The population was less diversified and less cosmopolitan in character. Hence there were little problems and tensions. Usually traders occupied the top brass of a well defined social hierarchy. There was, however, relative mobility among the classes. Social life in the modern cities is more diversified and cosmopolitan. Secondary and formal relations predominate The primary institutions like family have lost their basic importance. Specialized organizations in every sphere, food, clothing, shelter, sex etc, cater to the needs of the city dweller. The norms of ordinary human decency are the only norms of our modern cities. Progress and change are the watchwords of a modern city. Rush, tension, anxiety are the regular features of our modern city. Modern cities have a more or less diffused social hierarchy. While the industrial magnates can be said to form the top brass of the hierarchy, there is considerable democratization and mobility in social classes. Late marriages, education and employment of women, free sex, co-education, are all concepts of the industrial social culture.

6. Culture. In the cultural sphere modern cities exhibit great strides in the development of education, technology and mass entertainment. While entertainment formed a specific and well organized aspect of medieval cities, entertainment in a modern city is a standardized and commercial occupation which caters to the unavoidable leisure time needs of a weary and tension-ridden multitude. Education is a common and necessary factor in our modern cities, while it was confined to certain categories, say traders and craftsmen in the medieval cities.

7. Problems. As with all other aspects of life, problems are many and varied in a modern city. While it was possible to order and plan a well patterned life process in a city of comprehensible size and population one can never say so today, the problems of our cities extend from provision and distribution of food, housing etc., to the various mental, physical and social problems of city dwellers. While vices like prostitution were confined to certain parts of medieval cities, social disorganization and vices have become a diffused factor in our cosmopolitan industrial culture.

Conclusion

Thus, one can notice vast differences in degree of organization and functioning of medieval and modern cities. Medieval cities can be said to form the necessary link between a conventional rustic and modern city culture, and which contained in embryo form all the needs of modern city culture.

The essential differences between the two types exist in the greater diversification and sophistication of occupations and life patterns and the consequent development of cosmopolitan mass culture. In modern cities we see the spreading up of the values of an essential city culture to all spheres of life, to their perfection.

ROLE OF MIGRATION IN URBAN GROWTH

Urbanization is a process which has taken place at a rapid scale in recent years in different countries due to the influence of a variety of causes of which industrialization is the key factor. Urban area is an outgrowth of the existing rural populace. Hence migration plays a key role in the growth of cities in any country. It is the chief factor which has helped urban growth in all countries in modern time. In fact, the cities could grow only because of the flocking of a large quantity of unskilled labourers to their centres from the villages. Usually, migration is from rural to urban centres and centres of lower culture to centres of higher culture. It takes place due to various reasons such as rural unemployment and attractions of the glamours of city life. In India cities existed throughout recorded history as capitals of the various empires. They were usually centres which attracted the flowers of the age to the royal courts and which enjoyed a flourishing trade.

TABLE 5.1

Increase in Urbanization due to extension of Town

	1901	1951	1961	1971	1981	1991
1	2	3	4	5	6	7
I 1,00,000	6,661	27,507	39,883	61,226	94,504	138,802
	(26.0)	(44.63)	(51.42)	(57.24)	(60.42)	(65.20)
II 50,000—99,999	2,892	6,137	8,713	11,680	18,190	23,309
	(11.29)	(9.96)	(11.23)	(10.92)	(11.63)	(10.95)
III 20,000—49,999	4,007	9,688	13,139	17,126	22,409	28,079
	(15.64)	(15.72)	(16.94)	(16.01)	(14.33)	(13.19)
IV 10,000—19,999	5,335	8,399	9,902	11,706	14,930	16,531
	(20.83)	(13.63)	(12.77)	(10.94)	(9.54)	(7.77)
V 5,000—9,999	5,159	7,993	5,329	4,756	5,603	5,532
	(20.14)	(12.97)	(6.87)	(4.45)	(3.58)	(2.60)
VI less than 5000	1,562	1,906	0,597	473	784	614
	(6.10)	(3.09)	(0.77)	(0.44)	(0.50)	(0.29)
All Class	25,616	61,630	77,562	106,967	156,420	212,867
	(100.00)	(100.00)	(100.00)	(100.00)	(100.00)	(100.00)
Percentage of Urban In Total Population	10.84	17.24	17.97	19.91	23.34	25.72

Cities, in the modern sense of the word, are only a century old. They developed as industrial and administrative centres rapidly during this century. Migration is the chief factor which contributed to the growth of modern cities in India. Besides the general factors, the specific factors which encouraged migration in India are the break up of the handicraft industry in the light of competition from machine made goods and the consequent surplus pressure of population on land and rural unemployment. However, the relatively less developed transportation system and the clinging to the traditional value structure had prevented migration for some time. This partly explains the relatively slow rate of urbanization in India. The causes of migration are as follows:

1. Unemployment. The increased migration of semistarved artisans and agricultural labourers provided a huge amount of supply of unskilled labourers to urban factories and thus paved the way for gradual urban growth. After independence, the process of urbanization has increased and migration in its various facets is playing an important role in this process. As a result of well developed transportation and constant urban contacts the ruralite today has given up many of its inhibitions and is ready for acquiring and enjoying the advantages of an urban society. Youths took the lead in this process. They usually revolt against the rigidity and staticity of rural life and migrate to the city where they hope to find a relatively prosperous job in a short time and to enjoy new comforts but end up in doing unskilled jobs. Thus, migration provides the needed youth population for the urban milieu.

2. Education. Another novel feature today is the rural migration for education. This process is helped by the growth of cities near villages. The landed aristocrats who are gradually coming to appreciate the value of urban education and employment are sending their children to cities. This has helped in further urban growth and widening of the urban base. Rural people who migrate to cities usually settle there, if they can find a job. Some people with poor means of livelihood make it a point to migrate permanently to the town or city once they can find a base there.

3. Marriage. Further, rural people today make it a matter of prestige to marry their girls to a city bred and city educated youth. This amounts in large scale female migration

4. Glamour of City. Today, the rich landlords are being attracted more and more by the glamour of city life. Hence they establish a house there and some of them have even gone to the extent of totally selling out their property and migrating to towns. This process is further encouraged by the recent land legislation.

Today long-distance migration between cities in search of education and employment has also increased and this adds to the growth of a particular city. Infact, most of the people of our urban middle class and clerical occupations have a rural base or come from a rural background.

BANGALORE

Ecology plays a leading role in determining the nature and structure of a city. According to Mackenzie cities develop through the processes of concentration, centralization, segregation, invasion and succession. Thus, the ecological structure of a multi-functional city like Bangalore exhibits the distribution of different areas to different functions according to necessity and convenience. Hence arises the necessity for an urban sociologist to understand the ecological structure of a city as a prerequisite to an analysis of its functions and social organization.

Bangalore is a typical multi-functional city which is, at present, the capital of Karnataka state. It is an industrial city set in the midst of mainly a rural region of which it is the commercial, educational, recreational, health and administrative centre. It is located in the centre of a table land with a few hills around it within a distance of 22 miles. It was established in 1537 A.D. by Kempegowda as a mud fort. It grew at first with the construction of temples of Vinayaka, Gavegangadharaswamy etc. The development of the town took place due mainly to Britishers. Besides, the modern methods of traffic, commercial education, and cultural interest all played their role in its development. Extensions developed and are developing even today to cater to the housing needs of the middle class and low income group people. Bangalore houses many industries like H.A.L., H.M.T., Binny Mills, B.E.L. etc., because of its locational and other advantages. Besides, it acts as an internal and international centre of exchange for various durable and perishable articles of trade from all over Karnataka and out-side, it is also a cosmopolitan cultural centre and centre of all main cultural activities of the state. It is also a university town.

Hence one wonders how the city has adjusted its functions into a structural pattern. For an onlooker, at first sight, Bangalore strikes as an area of confusion and chaos since it does not follow Burgess' contention or any other pattern of a city growth. Its functions were gradually added to it and it is not a planned city as the modern concept goes. But this confusion is more apparent than real since a careful analysis shows that there is its own peculiar order in the distribution of population, houses, educational and social institutions etc.

The specific factor employed in dividing ecological zones in Bangalore is the activity pattern, i.e., the nature and types of activities the people of the zones engage in. On this basis one finds definite clusters of a specific activity such as industrial or cultural spread over different parts of the city.

Activity Zones of Bangalore. Bangalore may be divided into 7 zones: (1) The business zone (2) The factory zone (3) The agricultural zone (4) The culture zone (5) The middle class residential zone (6) The retired people's residential zone (7) The military zone.

(1) The Business zone. The centre of dominance of commercial activities, communication and transport system converge on the city market and majestic areas. The other parts of the city include sub-urban shopping centres which are diffused today all over the city. Mention may be made of the recently developed Jayanagar shopping complex which is the supply centre of trade. In this zone lie the warehouses and establishments of big merchants, hardware stores, cloth shops, small workshops, machinery and utensil shops, a number of hotels and most of city's cinema houses. Business activity predominates here.

This zone has two areas — one is the city market majestic area which comprises — Arapept, Maniwarthapet, Blaepet, Sultanpet, Doddapet, Chikkapet, Kempegowda Road etc. The other is the cantonment market which comprises Tasker Town, Blackpilly, Russel market etc., and abounds in foreign goods.

(2) The factory zone. Employees of harbours and factories, slums, labourers and poor are inhabitants of this area. Huts and dilapidated houses around big factories are found in this region. Industrial production and activities connected with it are carried in this area. This zone comprises 7 areas in the city — Area 1 lies near Lal Bagh, Area 2 lies near city market, Area 3 lies near Magadi Road, Area 4 lies near Srirampuram, Area 5 lies near Tumkur Road, Area 6 is the Central factory area located at the heart of the city. Area 7 lies by the side of cantonment. In these areas are located the various factories and small scale industries and industrial estates of the city which developed in the location whichever they could find.

(3) Agriculture zone. Agricultural zone lies at the four extreme bounds of the city and is gradually pushed back due to the rapid development of suburbs. The inhabitants of Dumlur Duanalli, Appareddypalya in Bangalore east carry on agriculture and grow paddy. The inhabitants of Jogplya, Halsur, Kalenalli etc, in Bangalore north grow mainly vegetables. Besides this the residents of Munimaranapalya also grow casuriana trees in their fields. The people of Gavipur, Guttalli etc., grow vegetables in the vast stretches of land available to them. These people also carry on dairy farming and poultry.

(4) The culture zone. This zone comprises activities connected with education, social service and other cultural activities. As we know, Banglore is a centre of higher education and is the nerve centre of the cultural activities of the state. The various schools, colleges and cultural auditoriums and socio-cultural associations and institutions are spread in the different parts of the city. This zone comprises 6 areas. Area I lies near Basavanagudi and comprises the national college, Indian Institute of culture and Gokhale Institute of public affairs. Area 2 is near Lalbagh, Fort Road and comprises Lal Bagh and Victory Hall. Area 3 is near Visveswarapuram and comprises the Ashoktaposhakastabha and Arya Samaj. Area 4 is almost in the centre of the city and consists of Central College, Maharanis College, Mount Carmel College, Engineering College, Technological Institute. Y.M.C.A., Century club, Museum, Cubban park etc. Area 5 lies near Residency Road and consists of St. Joseph's college, Bishop Cotton Girl's school. The Indian Institute of culture arranges lectures and discussions. Lal Bagh is a pleasure garden. Town Hall and Ravindra Kalakshetra which come under area 4 are the main cultural auditoriums of the city. The Century club is a prestigious club.

(5) The Middle class Residential zone. This comprises the various suburbs in the city to some extent which are expanding day-by-day. The owners of small business, clerical and professional employees and some middle class people reside in this area. This zone has mainly four areas. The first area lies to the South of Mysore Road comprising Visveswarapuram, Upparalli, Chiokamavalli, Kalasipalya, Chamarajpet etc. Area 2 lies towards the north of Kempe Gowda Road and comprises Gandhinagar. Area 3 lies towards the east of Bellary Road and comprises Uppanalli, Benson town etc. Area 4 lies in cantonment and comprise MacIver town. These area abound in tenement houses.

(6) The Retired People's residential zone. This consists of the various suburbs in the city which are growing day-by-day. These areas abound in spacious one family dwelling and well decorated houses. The retired people and higher middle class people who want peace and quiet live here. It comprises four areas which are located in the four corners. Area 1 lies in the South West extremity and comprises Narasimharaja Colony, Basvanagudi, Sankarapurma, Hosahalli etc. Area 2 lies towards north east of Maharaja Mills and comprises Shesharajpuram, Malleswaram, Yeshwanthapur, Gokul etc. Area 3 lies towards the north of St. John Hill. Area 4 lies in the cantonment and contains MacIver town, Langford town etc. This zone comprises mainly of well planned and spacious one family dwellings, well-laid streets, lounge spaces etc., with the suburban shopping complex at its centre.

(7) The Military zone. It is a conductive zone in the city of Bangalore. It developed because the Britishers placed a garrison and made it a permanent military camp. Today our defence forces, defence training and supply units etc. use this area for their activities. However, even today this can be called a foreigners' locality. The entire cantonment area comprises this zone.

In summing up the social ecology of Bangalore city it may be stated that: (1) the business areas are mainly located in the centre of the city (2) The bulk of the factory areas are located towards the western border and outskirts (3) The agricultural area forms a green belt around the city (4) The cultural areas tend to be evenly distributed. The recreational services tend to concentrate near and around the culture areas (5) The retired people's area lies near the agricultural areas on three sides of the city (6) The middle class areas lie contiguous to the retired people's areas.

PRESENT CONDITION OF BANGALORE

According to a news item dated Jan. 19, 1996, once known as the "garden city", its salubrious climate attracting tourists and retired people alike,. this 450-year-old metropolis built by Magadi Kempegowda is today turning into a concrete jungle.

Even Winston Churchill, who lived here between 1896-98, described Bangalore as "the roses of Europe innumerable large pots attain the highest perfection of fragrance and colour. Flowering shrubs and creepers blossom in glorious profusion. Snipes and snakes abound in the marshes brilliant butterflies dance in the sunshine.''

But today, invasion by industries and multinational companies, who have descended on this burgeoning metropolis to cash in on its technical and scientific manpower and cheap labour has brought with it all the related ills.

Over the years Bangalore has shot into the limelight for being one of the fastest-growing metros in Asia and rapidly evolving as the new economic capital. Investor-friendly economic policies of the state government have further accentuated the influx of multinationals who ''fall in love with Bangalore at first sight,'' dotted as it is with beautiful parks, avenues and buildings, giving it the sobriquet ''garden city.''

The skyline of Bangalore has undergone a massive change during the past one decade, with builders from Bombay laying siege to this ''pensioners paradise'' and throwing out of gear all the infrastructure which was meant for a lower population level. There was a time when use of fans was banned in government offices as the climate did not necessitate them. Now room coolers and airconditioners are a common sight. With the population figure touching the five million mark, there is tremendous pressure not just on the traffic but on civic amenities like water supply, power and housing. Rents have skyrocketed, while power breakdowns have become the order of the day. Generators have not only added to the noise and atmospheric pollution but have also raised the city's temperature.

Bangalore faces another pressure from the industrial town at Hosur in Tamil Nadu, bordering Bangalore. In addition to drawing a huge chunk of manpower from Bangalore, other workers too have chosen to live in Bangalore and work in Hosur factories.

One redeemable feature is that the city has a number of trees, thanks to the vision of former chief minister Ramakrishna Hegde and his forest minister, B.A. Jivijaya, who had taken up planting of trees in 1983. Today, flying over Bangalore one can see a lush green canopy over a major portion of the city except in Chikpet and city market areas which are bereft of trees. Over the years, most of the civic amenity sites have been converted to residential areas by influential people. In 1931, Bangalore city had more than 114 tanks in the Bangalore Development Authority (BDA) area. It is now reduced to 10. Tanks in the heart of the city have been converted into business places, bus stands, and stadiums.

Situated on a ridge about 900 meters above sea level, between two river basins — the Arkavathi and the south Pennar — the city is solely dependant on Cauvery water, which has to be pumped from Torekadanahalli in Mandya district. This requires enormous power and fluctuation in voltage has seriously affected the water supply. The Vrishubhavathi river and the Challaghatta valley are both polluted by the sewage from Bangalore and have degraded the environment along Mysore road and Hal airport.

Taking the advice to "industrialise or perish" given by the visionary engineer and statesman, late Sir M. Visvesvaraya, who was the pioneer of public enterprise in the country, successive governments in Karnataka encouraged setting up of large and medium industries in Bangalore but forgot to visualise the load on the environment. With a flourishing trade and commerce and an increasing influx of people, Bangalore today is far from the idyllic city it once was.

KANPUR

Kanpur is the industrail metropolis of U.P. and a steel city. Hence its social structure clusters around industrial structure and the concentration of population, urban development, increase of the elite, mobility of labour, social pathology, cultural change, the extent of social services and the residues of social relations.

Kanpur has a population of more than five million. Industries are the chief source of employment. The number of women employees is insignificant due to a series of causes. Firstly, there is a paucity of residential accommodation and maternity benefits. Secondly the practice of purdah restricts women migrating to industrial suburbs. Thirdly, the absence of tribal people around this area accounts for smaller number of female labourers. The employment of child labour has declined in recent years. A picture of forced unemployment in the industiral sector is revealed by the number of lay offs and retrenchments. Unemployment is more acute among skilled, semi-skilled, unskilled and electrical workers. Unemployment among literates is also a common feature in this industrial belt. Majority of the population is composed of Hindu, Muslims, Sikhs, etc. The chief bulk is comprised of a Hindu group in addition to Scheduled Classes. A little over 3/4 of immigrants are ruralities who come here to seek jobs due to lack of land holdings. 4/5 Of the population belong to the sub-standard level of living and a skeleton of the population constitutes the upper class. As a concommitant of haphazard industrial city, a quarter of Kanpur population lives in slums. A major proportion of the families live in what are described as "general areas", with varying environmental patterns and differing standards of civic amenities. Only a small minority live in descent localities known as "civil areas" which have all the urban amenities. Educational facilities are very unevenly distributed. Industrial and service occupations constitute the main means of livelihood. The relative position of occupational categories is very near one another and relative poverty is a main factor. Usually, there is only one earning member for a family. Members of different classes and of the same class generally live side by side. There are no well established social organizations. Educational facilities and civic amenities are haphazardly distributed. Modern recreational facilities are actually developing.

QUESTIONS FOR EXERCISE

1. Discuss the types of cities. What kind of classification is possible according to functional point of view ?

2. Bring out the characteristic of pre-industrial cities. Draw a comparison between pre-industrial cities and modern industrial cities.
3. Compare and contrast the characteristic of medieval cities with modern industrial cities.
4. Explain the rural urban differences in Population Stratification and Social Interaction.
5. Examine the role of migration in India's urban growth.
6. Describe the internal structure of either Bangalore or Delhi.
7. Explain the social structure of Delhi or Kanpur.

6

Rural Urban Contrast

Rural and urban communities form the end points in the continuum of development of human habitats. In fact, one can say that the stabilization of human life on this earth which followed a linear pattern upto the development of peasant communities can be said to have taken a leap in the development of urban habitats. Although urban habitats developed out of the rural habitats, they show glaring differences in every aspect of life from its predecessor. Since urban communities everywhere developed out of the functional growth of multi-functional necessities of a society, they absorbed a multitudinous and diversified population from different villages. Since it developed as an artificial outgrowth consisting of a composite population one can presumably expect greater differences in the life pattern and organization of these two essentially different based modes of living. While village was a natural growth, city was an artificial outgrowth.

TABLE 6.1

Rural and Urban Population : 1901-1991

Census Year	Population (Million) Rural	Urban	Percentage of Total Population Rural	Urban
1	2	3	4	5
1901	213	26	89.2	10.8
1911	226	26	89.7	10.3
1921	223	28	88.8	11.2
1931	246	33	88.0	12.0
1941	275	44	86.1	13.9
1951	299	62	82.7	17.3
1961	360	79	82.0	18.0
1971	439	109	80.1	19.9
1981	524	159	76.7	23.3
1991	629	218	74.3	25.7

Hence rural-urban differences form a basic subject of study of urban sociology. An exhaustive analysis of rural-urban differences give us a clear-cut idea of the essential qualities and personality of the urban conglomeration. Rural-urban differences exist in every field of life, size of population, social interaction, stratification, etc. To get a basic idea of rural-urban differentials now let us analyse its character as regards the three chief factors, population, stratification and social interaction.

1. Population. After the size of a city the immediate striking feature is its population. The study of population includes size, density, composition, etc., usually a smaller number of people characterise the rural areas. Since agriculture is essentially a household occupation the rural areas were built originally as family clusters and continue to be so with little variation except through births and deaths. Usually the population of a typical village varies between 100/500. There are controversies regarding the size of a city population, we may call a group town if it has more than 1000 people. There is a further difference in the size of the population of a town and city or metropolis. The same can be said about the density of the population. The cities are relatively more dense than the village since the composition and spread of a rural population is more or less fixed according to its size at any time. Congestion is one of the basic problems of modern cities. Regarding composition, the urban population is more diversified and less homogeneous in all respects, because as already stated, cities developed out of the flocking of a multitude of rural populace. The urban people come from different socio-economic and cultural milieu and profess different values. Usually the urban population gets added up through migration of rural people for education and employment. Hence there exists a disparity in the population structure. Youths and males are usually larger in the number many a time. In villages one can hardly notice such disparities because of the operation of the balancing up process of Nature. The urban population replaces itself from time to time due to migration to other towns etc. Another specific character of urban population is the existence of a larger number of floating population at all times. Thus, while the rural population is static and homongeneous the urban population is diversified and dynamic.

2. Stratification. Stratification is the main factor in any community through which every society tries to adjust its different capabilities into a system of relative priorities and privileges dependent on its value structure. Hence one may search for essential difference in this aspect between the village and the city which profess different value systems. Rural societies usually profess a conventional value system which gives priority to entrenched villages and positions. Urban societies are progressive in outlook, place, personal achievement, as the criteria before their people is to achieve social standing. Hence people everywhere practise a sort of caste system, with population divided along an entrenched social hierarchy with relatively little mobility between the different strata of society.

The accord of priority depends on the quality valued in that society. For example, in earliest peasant societies the chieftain was a man of physical power and warriors enjoyed high social status. Indian society practises a caste system in which priests are accorded the highest social status. But usually, in a relatively well settled peasant community the land owning and agricultural classes form the top brass while the craftsmen and petty traders form the middle strata. The lower strata is occupied by agricultural labourers and slaves. A man's social position is fixed by his birth into a family of a particular strata. While the people of higher social strata enjoy all the privileges and advantages in society the lower strata are exploited and live a sub-human existence. In contrast, the urban people practise on open class system. In the urban social milieu these caste categories merge into the class categories. Economic factor is the chief differentiating factor of urban stratification. In it usually the upper class consists of the wealthy people, industrial magnates and owners of capital and big business. The middle class consists of executives, professionals, etc. The lower class consists of industrial labourers, clerks and other people of lower income. Technical qualifications, personal achievements and acquisition of wealth are the main factors of entry into these classes. Usually relative mobility and a sort of democracy exists between these classes and urban consumption patterns.

3. Social interaction. Social interaction is the basic prerequisite of social relationships and it decides the nature, structure and functioning of any society. There must be at least a minimal degree of difference in the mode of social interactions of urbanites and ruralites who are parts of different social milieu. These differences arise out of the relative simplicity or complexity of a society, the composition of its population and the number of its functions.

It is very difficult to compare rural and urban society, and this has prompted Gist and Halbert to write, "Thus the familiar dichotomy between 'Rural' and 'Urban' is more of a theoretical concept than a division based upon the facts of community life."[1] Generally, these difficulties are the following:

1. There is no Universal Definition of Village and Town. The major difficulty which confronts any comparison between the societies of village and town is that there is no universal definition which can clearly distinguish between a town and village one cannot say just where a village ends and a town begins. If a castle is constructed twenty miles away from Bombay, it could not be called in town. If the atmosphere of a village is created in the middle of a town, the town will not be called or thereby become a village. Even the criteria for designating the names village or town in any country are different in different contexts. Before a place can be called a town it must possess a population of 2000 in France, 2500 in America, 5000 in India and 30,000 in Japan. Secondly, any place is considered to be town not only on the basis of its population. There are many other factors but there is no universally recognised

1. Gist and Halbert, *Urban Society*, (1954), p.3.

definition of village and town. In the words of Bergel, "Every body seems to know what a city is but not one has given a satisfactory definition."[2]

2. There is a Difference of Degree Between Village and Town. Actually, the difference between town and village is merely one of degrees, as a result of which it is very difficult to make a clear distinction between the two. Every village possesses some elements of the town while every town exhibits certain features characteristic of the village. MacIver and Page are quite right when they say, "But between the two there is no sharp demarcation to tell where the city ends and country begins."[3]

3. The Environments of the City and Village are different. The environments of the village and the town are not the same. And, in the same town a variety of environments can be seen. Thus, how is one to compare villages and towns? Which of the mutually conflicting or contradicting environments is to be considered characteristic of a town and which not, and which of them is to be compared with the environment of the village?

4. Both Village and Town Change. Yet another obstacle in the comparison of village and town is the fact that both keep on changing. Each influences the other. Industrialisation has brought a complete change in the form of the village, and this change is continuing. Amidst this change it is difficult to decide how long it should be considered a village and when should it be allowed to pass into the category of towns. With the advent of new factors like electricity and education, to mention only two, the distinction between village and town is being steadily diminished. In respect of most of the characteristics of population, like birth-rate and family-size, both resemble each other.

DIFFERENCE BETWEEN RURAL AND URBAN SOCIETY

But, inspite of the existence of these difficulties, sociologists have shown distinction between village and town societies. The chief among them are the following.

Differences in Social Organisation

The biggest distinction between rural and urban society is that of social organisation. These exhibit differences in the following respects:-

1. Family. The families in the villages and towns exhibit the following differences: (a) In the villages the families are comparatively stronger than the families in the towns, where greater importance is attached to the individual than to the family. (b) In the villages the system of joint family is to be found in greater number than in the towns. (c) In the villages there is greater control, intimacy and organisation than in the families in towns. (d) In the towns, as compared with villages the functions of the family are more steadily decreasing.

---

2. Bergel, *Urban Sociology*, McGraw Hill Series (1955), p. 5.

3. McIver and Page, *Society*, p. 311.

2. Marriage. In respect of marriage there are the following differences in the societies of villages and towns (a) In the towns there is a preponderance of love marriages in comparison with the villages (b) In towns as compared to the villages, one finds a greater number of divorces. (c) In the towns rather than the village greater freedom is allowed in the selection of life partner.

3. Condition of Women. Generally, the women in the villages are not much, if at all educated and their social status also is low.

4. Neighbourhood. In the villages the neighbourhood has a greater importance than it has in the towns. In the towns sometimes people do not even know their neighbours.

5. 'We Feeling'. In the rural community the 'we feeling' is found to be far stronger than in the urban community. The influence of the community on the individual in the village is greater than in the towns.

6. Inequality of Classes. The inequality of classes is much more demarcated in the towns than in the villages and there are correspondingly more conflicts in the towns. In the words of Bogardus, "Class extremes characterize the city."[4]

Differences in Social Restrictions

A great difference is evident between the social control characteristic of the rural and urban societies. About the social control in the village, Biesanz and Biesanz write, "In the rural community custom is the king, the folkways and mores control most of behaviour."[5] On the other hand, the society does not exercise much control over the individuals in the urban society. In the crowds and the high velocity of life in the towns no one has time to look to another. In the words of Kingsley Davis, "He can escape the oppressive control of any primary group when he wishes simply by disappearing into the sea of strangers.'[6] But the control of police, law, court etc., is greater in the town than in the village.

Differences in Social Relationships

The following distinctions between the rural and urban populations in respect of their social relations are evident:

1. In comparison with the social relations found in the cities those in the villages are more personal. In the words of Gist and Halbert, "The city encourages impersonal rather than personal relationship."[7]

2. In the villages the relation of the individual is usually with primary

---

4. Bogardus, *Sociology*, p. 144.

5. Biesanz and Biesanz., *Modern Society*, p. 114.

6. Davis, *Human Society*, p. 331.

7. Gist and Halbert, *Urban Society*, p. 263.

groups, family, near relations etc. In the towns their relations tend more towards secondary groups.

Differences in social interactions

The social interactions peculiar to the rural and urban societies exhibit the following distinctions:

1. In comparison with towns the social relations in the villages are far smaller in number and those that do exist are personal. On the other hand, the social relations in the towns are numerous, of which most are indirect and impersonal.

2. In the towns, but not in the villages to quite the same extent, division of labour and specialization are found to exist. In this way the scope for social co-operation is far greater in the towns than in the villages.

3. The activity of competition has a far greater velocity in the town than in the villages.

4. The conflict in the villages is usually direct while the conflict is comparatively indirect in the urban context.

5. When compared to villages there is greater toleration in the towns and consequently a larger degree of accommodation.

6. The process of assimilation takes place rather slowly in the village as a result of a near absence of cultural difference. In the towns people of different cultures live side by side and thus the process of assimilation operates much faster.

Differences in Social viewpoint

The following differences are found in the social viewpoints in rural and urban society:

1. According to Newmeyer, "Rural culture tends to be conservative."[8] In the words of Ross, "The city is cosmopolitan whereas the country is nationalistic and patriotic."[9] In this way the village is more progressive than the town.

2. In the towns, more than the villages, people take interest and are active in polities.

3. In the villages greater importance is attached to religion and ritual than in the town. Whereas the religion of the rural people is based upon faith, the religion in the city is relatively based more upon reason.

4. The villagers are more fatalistic than the urban people because the lives of the villagers are affected to a very large extent by natural forces while the urban people are equipped with scientific knowledge and techniques in handling natural calamities and catastrophies.

---

8. Newmeyer, *Social Problems and the Changing Society*, D. Van Nostrand Co.; Inc., New York, p. 63.

9. Ross, E. A., *Principles of Sociology*, p. 77.

5. There is more artificiality in the urban people than in the villagers. Bogardus has correctly written, "Rural people are frank, open and genuine; they scorn the artificiality of many phases of city life."[10]

Differences in social mobility and stability

There is greater social disorganization in the towns than in the villages. To quote Sorokin and Zimmerman, "The rural community is similar to calm water in a pale and the urban community to boiling water in a kettle. Stability is the typical trait for the one, mobility is the typical for the other."[11] In this way, cities possess greater mobility than the villages.

Differences in Economic Life

There is great difference between the economic lives of the villages and towns. In this respect the major differences are the following:

1. "Two fundamentally different modes of getting a living set the rural and urban worlds apart." In the villages the major occupation is agriculture while in the towns the major occupations are of an industrial nature.

2. Standard of living in the villages is lower than that of the towns because the means of earning money are limited in the villages. Besides making more money, the urban people are more prodigal than the villagers. In the words of Ross, "Country life then suggests 'save'! city life suggests spend'!"[12] At the same time the villagers do not get much opportunity to spend whereas the man in the city is at his wits' end as to the means of making enough money to enable him to buy commodities displayed for consumption.

Difference in cultural life

The cultural lives of the city and the country exhibit the following distinctions:

1. Culture is more static in the villages than in the town.

2. In the village the basis of culture is caste and purity. In the towns it has a secular basis.

3. Traditions have a very important place in rural culture, while urban culture does not attach much importance to them.

URBAN INFLUENCE ON RURAL SOCIETIES

The foregoing distinction between the urban and rural societies is apparent only in those rural societies which are far removed from the cities and which have remained immune from the influences of the latter. In India the influence

10. Bogardus, *Sociology*, p. 133.

11. Sorokin and Zimmerman, *Principles of Rural Urban Sociology*, Henry Holt and Co., New York, 1929, p. 44.

12. Ross, *Principles of Sociology*, p. 76.

of urban life can clearly be seen in rural societies in the vicinity of large cities like Calcutta, Bombay, Delhi etc. This influence is evident in such unidentical aspects like social structure, family organization, food habits, standard of living, dress habits, cosmetics, religion, rituals, beliefs etc. A description of this influence will show those peculiarities of rural life which are in the process of transition:

1. Change in Social Life. The greatest influence of the city upon the social life of the villages has been upon the caste system. The relation between caste and profession is no longer necessary because the people are adopting new professions according to interest and profit, in place of the professions determined by the caste. Members of all castes have taken to shopkeeping. The work of a milkman is no longer confined to those who are traditionally connected with it. The business of food grains is now carried on by members of many castes, besides the one caste which had been set aside for this purpose. Members of the highest caste are seen working in many kinds of professions. The ancient mode of thinking in terms of untouchability does not prevail any longer. Inter-caste marriage is still the exception rather than the rule but the restrictions placed upon the various castes regarding the normal exchange of social contact have now been lifted. This is true at least about the Brahmin, Kshatriya and Vaishya castes. The social laws about untouchability have lost a good deal of their former sting due to buses, railways and other modern means of transportation. The untouchables are demanding all kinds of rights which have been legally given to them, though even then the villagers are as yet not prepared to give them equal rights in all respects.

2. Decrease in the influence of panchayats. Another effect of the city upon the social life of the village is evident in the way in which it has influenced the control of the panchayats in the village. The influence of the panchayats of the caste is gradually being lost because the punishment imposed by it is no longer considered obligatory while there is no fear of social extermination. Nevertheless the thoughts and conduct of the people in the village are still controlled to a certain degree by the family and the society. The form of the village panchayat has also undergone change because as a result of the influence of the city they are being disregarded.

3. Change in the family organization. The city has influenced the organization of the family in the rural community to a very large extent. In former times the families in the villages were well organized. The order of the elders was treated as a divine mandate. Tho elders arranged marriages. The family exercised significant control upon the conduct of the younger people. Whatever the context, the honour of the family was invariably the first consideration. Generally, the system of joint family prevailed in which near relatives from the paternal side lived in cooperation. Now this tradition of the joint family is slowly disappearing from the villages. The families are growing smaller and show distinct signs of disintegration. The younger generations when they return from the cities, treat their elders as conservative and do not tolerate their control. Not only in respect of marriage but even when it comes to thought and conduct, they consider the control of the elders as improper and despotic. The facilities and the comforts of the city like electricity, cinema, radio, newspapers; parks, clubs, hotels, libraries, post offices, colleges, etc., are not available in the villages, due to which the educated youngmen of the villages develop a hatred and scorn for the life of the village and deem it better to become clerks in the city than to engage in agriculture in the villages. This is leading towards a complete disintegration of the erstwhile organisation of the family. Any young lady who has spent a few months in the city becomes proficient in the use of cosmetics and considers herself superior to her sisters in the village. Consequently, the other young ladies of the village also take to imitating the superficial airs of model. Their conduct takes on a colorful and irresponsible attitude and they desire greater freedom in their daily routine. When the villagers return from the city they describe the incidents which they had witnessed in the city, thus creating a craving for similar ways in the minds of the uninitiated boys of the village. Due to the influence of the city the power of the rural families has been destroyed, the organisation has broken down, the standard of morality has fallen expensive habits have been acquired. Life has become more artificial and selfish. Individualistic, materialistic and atheistic tendencies are gaining ground.

4. Difference in means of transport and communications. As a result of the influence of the city the means of transportation in the village have undergone a radical change. Formerly, the people did not hesitate in walking twenty miles but now they spend hours waiting for a bus but they will not prefer to walk. The cycle is becoming extremely popular. The landlords and rich businessmen have started using cars. The roads are now repaired. People have also accepted rail travel. Along with the change in the means of transportation newer occupations have found their ways into the village life. Wheat grinding machine and the like are more or less a familiar sight in the villages. With the introduction of new agricultural implements the facilities for repairing them have also become available in the village. The blacksmiths, hair-dressers, goldsmiths, carpenters etc., of the village have adopted modern tools in their work in preference to the old ones. The use of new implements in agriculture is becoming popular.

5. Change in modes of recreation and other facilities. Due to the influence of the city the means of recreation in the villages are on the increase. Radios and gramophones are becoming popular. Younger people can be seen playing football and volleyball. Cards, chess and other such games are also popular. Besides the means of recreation, the other facilities of life are also increasing in the villages due to the influence of the city. One often finds a doctor in a big village, and one is not surprised at the presence of electricity either. Schools are being opened in the villages and arrangements made for bringing such modern innvoations as the open air. Newspapers have access to villages which are near the towns, the people of such villages being in the habit of visiting the city whenever they have need for seeing a cinema or doing any shopping.

6. Change in the mode of living. The city has great influence upon the living, dress and food habits etc, of the rural people. The young men in the villages have started using collared shirts, bush shirts, coat and pantaloon, shoes, etc. The ladies wear coloured saries and blouses with deep plunging necklines. The children are also outfitted with urban type of dress. Utensils made of glass, aluminium and china clay are also being used in the village. The city has made popular the use of tea, betel, tobacco, vegetable ghee, cigarette, etc. Wrist watches, sun-glasses, fountainpens, torches and safety razors are being commonly used in the villages.

On the other hand, rural districts are essentially homogenous. There is not much of social differentiation.

7. Social stratification. The principles of class and caste operate differently in rural societies from the way they operate in the urban world. There are four major differences between the social pyramids of rural and urban area.

(1) The rural society is not classless nevertheless the number of social classes is less in rural society than in urban society.

(2) The extremes of social pyramid are not so far apart in rural societies as in urban.

(3) It is not only that the range of social classes is less in rural society but that rural classes tend to be intermediate or ''Middle'' classes. The city is on the other hand not only the home of the millionaire but also that of pauper.

(4) The caste principles in city are not as rigid as in the rural society. Movement from one class to another is easier in the urban context than in rural societies.

7. Social Mobility. Sorokin and Zimmerman said, 'The rural community is similar to clam water in a pail and the urban community to boiling water in a kettle.'' In rural areas the members are more strongly attached to their social status which is ascribed. In the urban area they are shifted from one status to another more often and more easily. This applies to social mobility, physical mobility and also occupational mobility.

8. Social interaction. The rural system of social interaction differ from that of the urban system. There are qualitative and quantitative differences in the social contacts of rural and urban people. The number of contacts is much greater in the country than the city.

Sorokin and Zimmerman point out the important qualitative differences between rural and urban systems as follows:

(i) The area of contact of the ruralite is narrower and more limited than that of urban persons (ii) The totality of contacts by the rural persons consists more largely of personal and primary face to face contacts than those of the city dweller. They are more enduring.

9. Social Solidarity. There is a basic difference in the social solidarity and cohesion of rural and urban societies. The rural society has a unity based on similarities and informal and non-contractual relationships. Urban solidarity is based on differences and dissimilarities which arise out of division of labour and specialization and formal and contractual relations.

THE ROLE OF MIGRATION

Rural and urban societies form two ends of a continuum and they exist side by side and interact with one another in several ways.

Rural urban migration is a main form of rural urban contact which is promoted by the development of transportation and means of communication. There has been a great amount of migration of rural people to urban areas. The cause of migration mainly lies in rural unemployment. These rural migrants become exposed to city life in all its varied aspects. These rural migrants communicate their new experience to their rural relatives and friends and thus act as agents of contact between the rural and urban culture and social life. Rural urban migration has three types of impact as regards urban influence over the rural society.

(1) There are villages in which a sizeable number of people have sought employment in far off cities. They live there leaving the members of their family in villages. In Madhopur it was noted that 75% of the total migrants send money regularly. Further, 83% visit the village from 4-5 times a year to once in two years. Some migrants have invested the money they have earned in the city in building houses or buying land in the villages. In such villages urban employment often becomes a symbol of higher social prestige.

(2) Most of urban impact relates to the villages near industrial cities like Bhilai. When an industrial town comes up amidst several villages some villages are totally uprooted. The people who migrate to other villages create housing and adjustment problems. Thus, in the villages near an industrial town there is the problem of immigrants to the village.

(3) When a metropolis expands, it intrudes into some of the nearby villages.

Rural urban migration, if it increases the number of contacts between the two habitats, provides a channel for constant cultural contact and cultural exchanges. Temporary commuting by the vendors of the village or city people who live in rural suburbs keeps up the tempo of contact of the two habitats. Rural migration helps the urban areas with its necessary manual labour and the rural habitat gains in income. As the rural migrants travel small distances and keep up contact with their rural families they constantly travel between the two habitats.

Rural migrants spread the novel ideas of urban production processes like the use of machinery and the novelties of urban social world like the various fashions in dresses etc. Rural migrants, by their glamorous description create in the minds of the people who remain behind, a craze for urban ways of life. Thus, more and more people visit the city and bring back with them features of city life into the rural habitat. The migrants come into contact with diversified ideas about all aspects of life and become keen to adopt suitable ones to their native habitats so as to improve its condition. Thus, they learn and begin to use hybrid seeds, pumpsets to draw water, electric lights, radios etc, which bring the rural area a step nearer to an urban area. Further, migrants set in motion a process of continuous and constant migration. Migrants also act as agents of trade and transit for many rural products like fresh vegetables, fruits etc.

Thus, although transport provides the necessary channels of contact it is rural-urban migration which establishes and maintains constant contact between two forms of habitats.

ROLE OF TRANSPORT AND COMMUNICATION

Rural and urban habitats form the two halves of a continuum. While rural societies represent the natural aspects and its influence upon human life, the urban aggregates depict man's works of ingenuity and intelligence. Hence the relationship between them is in the essential spheres of life.

Transport and communication means form the main artery which establishes essential social relations between the two forms of habitats. While it brings about changes in the structure of rural society as isolated and self-sufficient units, it supplies to the urban area all its essentials of existence. It may not be difficult for an Indian to understand the implications of the introduction of a bus service to a village not more than 5 miles away from a town or city. Before the introduction of transportation and communication the town was totally ignorant of the existence of village so near it and vice versa. This influence is as follows:

1. The basic factor affected by means of transportation is that of surplus agricultural produce and urban market. As the urban area is usually incapable of producing its agricultural requirements it depends upon the village for its essential supplies of perishable products like fruits and vegetables etc. Thus, urban areas provide gainful markets to the surplus village produce. Many a time it acts as an inducement for commercial enterprise and introduction of cash crops. Thus, the people of villages around Mandya in Mysore took to sugarcane production on a large scale due to efficient roads and means of transport. It also gives additional occupation and provides more opportunities for employment in the fields of dairying, production of fruits and vegetables etc.

2. In the second instance, transportation supplies the much needed labour force to the urban needs while it reduces rural unemployment to a great extent.

3. The introduction of transportation creates the necessary relation between a village and the national government.

4. In the social sphere, it breaks up the essential framework of the rural social structure since youth essentially go out to urban areas in search of education and employment. It breaks up many of the essential prejudices of rural society. For example, people of all castes, even un-touchables, must sit beside each other during travel by bus. It introduces new attractions to the rural

people and breaks up the simplicity of rural social life. Rural people are attracted to urban cinemas, hotels and other novelties and gradually a visit to a city becomes an essential point of pride in the rural society. The hitherto accepted norms and ways of life appear obsolete to an urban influenced ruralite. In short, the impact of urbanization upon rural life takes place. The novelties of urban social life, say drinking coffee, wearing fashionable dresses, etc., enter into the rural social life. The generation gap in the rural society, which has remained hitherto un-noticed becomes a principal cause for tensions, clashes etc.

Folkways and mores loose their hold upon an urbanized rural life. Transportation introduces an element of rush into the placidity of rural society. Transport and communication increases the number of contacts between a village and a town and introduces the urban element of rush and time consciousness in the urban-connected ruralite life. Urban contacts increase the villager's knowledge about improvement of agriculture, animal husbandry etc. Contacts with a rural area also help in the shifting of ancillary industries to such areas.

Thus, while in developing countries transportation is a must and an essential part of any habitat since they depend upon technology and large scale production in every sphere of life, in traditional societies transportation forms a basic agent of rural-urban contact which introduces gradual changes in the social structure of economic framework. Rural urban contacts increase the monetization of rural economy and society and open up additional avenues of money supply into the rural society. Transportation breaks up the inhibitions and rigidity of rural life and makes it flexible and somewhat secular.

In short, transportation and communication results in successful rural-urban contacts. It reduces the hold of religion and folk beliefs upon rural people and introduces at least some aspects of the scientific attitude into the rural mentality.

QUESTIONS FOR EXERCISE

1. Distinguish between rural and urban communities.
2. Distinguish the rural and urban pattern of life.

7

The Urban Family

Urban family is nuclear, small, unstable and sometimes even disorganised. This may be seen from the growing number of divorces in Indian and Western urban areas.

Basic and Universal Functions of the Family

The following are the basic and universal functions of the family:

1. Biological Functions. The most fundamental biological functions are as follows:

(a) *Reproduction*. According to the Hindu scriptures procreation is the main function of the family. Commentators on the Hindu scriptures have written that the religious activities of man cannot be consummated unless he has a son and he cannot repay his ancestral debt. He has to suffer in hell if he has no son. In almost all societies of the world barren women are the objects of scorn and derision. In the words of Ogburn and Nimkoff, "The sex and parental functions are distinctive of the family."[1] And in some societies marriageability is attributed only to a woman who gives evidence of her fertility by conceiving a child before marriage. Hindu scriptures permit a second marriage if there is no issue from the first wife. The woman was permitted to conceive a child from another man through 'niyoga' if the husband is impotent or otherwise incapable of procreation. In most human societies of the world the child is believed to be the nucleus of the family. Procreation perpetuates the family. It increases the population of the country. Some Hindu thinkers have considered reproduction to be the sole aim of marriage. In the rituals of Hindu marriage the groom says to his bride that I accept you in order to obtain good progeny. To quote Sutherland and Woodward, "The basic biological function which the family has been performing, is a function absolutely essential to the survival of any human or animal society."[2]

---

1. Ogburn and Nimkoff, *A Handbook of Sociology*, p. 459.
2. Sutherland, R.L. and J.L. Woodward, *Introductory Sociology*, (1941), p. 610.

(b) *Provision of food, housing and clothing.* Food, housing and clothing are indispensable to the existence of human life. A major biological function of the family is the provision of these amenities for its members. The earning members of the family provide food and clothing for all the rest. Every family has a house to live in and the food for the family members is generally cooked at home. In the words of Dennis Chapman, "Each new family establishes an independent home as soon as possible after marriage, the new home reflecting the interest and the culture of both husband and wife."[3]

2. Psychological Function. The second fundamental and universal function of the family is psychological. Ogburn has included affectional functions in the necessary or vital functions of the family. According to Groves, it is the function of the family to provide opportunities for the establishment of intimate relations. Burgess and Locke have written, "Mutual affection is becoming the essential basis of marriage and the family."[4] The individual receives affection, sympathy, love and psychological security in the family. The relations between man and woman in the family are not exclusively physical. Profound conjugal affection for each other is generated in husband and wife by working together in the family and by sharing each other's joys and sorrows. In the absence of family love an all round development of the individual is not possible. The family plays an important part in the development of the child's personality. Ralph Linton has written that merely the satisfaction of bodily needs is not sufficient for the proper development of the infant. Children are in greater need of individual attention, love and satisfaction of response.

3. Satisfaction of sexual needs. A fundamental function of the family, according to Reed, is to regulate and gratify sexual needs. Manu accepts sexual satisfaction besides reproduction as the aim of family. Vatsyayan also looks upon sexual satisfaction as the primary objective of the family. In the modern age, the fulfilment of sexual needs is one of the primary functions of the family. When sexual needs remain unsatisfied in the family, it starts disintegrating. To quote Havelock Ellis, "With failure of sexual harmony, the marriage structure rests on shifting sand."[5]

4. Protection and care of the young. According to Groves the protection and care of the children is a necessary function of the family.[6] The human child is the most helpless and weak being. A family is needed in order to maintain its existence and to ensure its coordinated and balanced development. Its balanced development is achieved with difficulty without the care of the parents and other family members.

3. Dennis Chapman. *The Home and Social Status*, (1955), p. 39.
4. Burgess and Locke, *The Family from Institution to Companionship.*
5. Ellis, H., *Little Essays on Love and Marriage.*
6. "Home is the place where when you have to go there they have to take you in." Robert Frost, *The Death of the tired Man,* Complete Poems of Robert Frost, Henry Holt and Co. Inc., New York (1940), pp. 43-55.

Traditional Functions of the Family:

The following are the traditional functions of the family:

1. Economic functions. The family performs many economic functions some of which are the following:

(a) *Division of labour*. In the family, the work is divided among the members of the family according to their status and role. The male members generally do the work which means outdoor movement. The women generally take care of the domestic chores while the children undertake only such work as can assist in their development. While this division of labour prevents putting excessive burden on the shoulders of one individual, it ensures the systematic performance of the family activities. All people undertake responsibility and work co-operatively.

(b) *Arrangement for income*. Money is needed for such of the family requirements as food, cloth, habitation, etc. The family is the centre of economic activities, consumption, etc. The family makes arrangements for an income in an effort to fulfil the needs of the family members.

(c) *Organisation and care of property*. Most families possess some property in the form of a house, farm, jewellery, money etc. The family looks after this property and in case such a contingency arises it also equitably distributes it among the members. The family is the judge of what property an individual shall receive who shall look after the property and how, and other important questions.

2. Social functions. The social functions of the family are important since the family is the fundamental and primary unit of society. Among many social functions the following deserve mention:

(a) *To establish status*. An important function of the family is the determination of an individual's status in the society. The modes of earning wealth of an individual are also generally determined by the family.

(b) *Socialization*. The family imparts learning to the individual on all those subjects whereby he can become an ideal member of society. It carries out the socialization of individual and teaches the etiquettes of eating, conversing, coexisting etc.

(c) *Social control*. Another function of the family is to exercise social control over the individual. The prevalent moral norms are enforced upon the individuals and their conduct and thoughts are controlled so that the order in society may remain intact. In the family, the antisocial tendencies of the individual are watched.

(d) *The accumulation and transmission of social heritage*. The family keeps the social heritage intact and hands it over to the generation to come. As a result, the social traditions, customs and ideals etc., are transmitted continuously from one generation to the next.

(e) *Assistance in the choice of a life partner*. The family renders assistance to the individual in his choice of a life partner. Although, in the modern age, people have started preferring personal choice of a life partner yet in India even now in most cases the choice of the bride or the groom is still the province of the other family members.

3. Religious functions. In the Hindu scriptures family life has been considered the basis of the fulfilment of religious duties. The scriptures prescribe the wife as essential in the fulfilment of duty. The literal meaning of the Hindi equivalent of the word wife (patni) means the woman who accompanies the man in the performance of the religious rituals, which were considered complete in the absence of the wife. Besides this, the performance of religious activities also demanded the presence of a son. Thus in the ancient Hindu system the main function of the family was the fulfilment of duty. Living in the family the members fulfilled their religious duties. Now, the religious activities of the family have been materially reduced.

4. Cultural functions. The family keeps the culture of society alive. It moulds its members according to the social culture. The children are educated in the various aspects of culture from their infancy. The family creates such an environment for them that they learn to live and to behave in accordance with their culture. The senile members of the family impart education in matters of conduct, thinking, religion and ethics, etc., to the children.

5. Recreational functions. The family provides entertainment for its members. The love between husband and wife, the halting utterances of the children, the scoldings and preaching of the elders and other such occurrences serve to create an atmosphere in which every one can find an object which can interest him or her.

AGENCIES PERFORMING THE FUNCTIONS OF THE URBAN FAMILY

In the modern age the functions of the family are changing because other agencies are taking over its functions. The main agencies of this nature are: (i) Maternity hospitals, (ii) Women hospitals, (iii) Baby clinics, (iv) Creches, children parks and the kindergarten, (v) Baby sitters, (vi) Hotels and restaurants, (vii) Public aid to the family, (viii) Club, cinema and other means of recreation.

1. Maternity hospitals. Previously children were born at home and midwife was called in at the time of delivery. Now in the prosperous families this is done in the maternity hospitals. During pregnancy the women constantly consult doctors and are confined to the hospital some days in advance of the delivery. They remain for some time in the hospital after the child has been delivered. This system is very beneficial. In this the mother and the child are constantly in the care of expert physicians and can get any and every kind of medicine whenever required. Even if there is difficulty in the delivery, operations can be performed without delay. There can be neither the facility of medicine nor the arrangement for operation in the family house. This creates much travail and the lack of these facilities can even be a danger to the lives of the mother and child in certain cases. One cause of the increase in the use of maternity hospitals for child delivery is the disintegration of the joint family. In the modern societies the newly wedded people live separately from their families. At the time of delivery there is no old and experienced woman near them who could give them proper advice and could take the matter into her own hands. Secondly, the houses in the towns are so small that it becomes difficult to accommodate relatives. Under these conditions the easiest course to follow is to confine the pregnant woman to a maternity hospital or a delivery home to avoid all kind of worries and dangers.

2. Women hospitals. In the modern age of specialization there are specialists for every kind of disease. Now-a-days one can secure specialists in the peculiarly feminine diseases in all big towns and cities. Thus, it is they who treat the women for their diseases. Previously, this work was done in the family, being performed most incompetently and dangerously.

3. Baby clinics. Now-a-days, in addition to the treatment of women, there are doctors who specialise in the treatment of children. Previously the more common infantile diseases were treated at home but now this is done in the baby clinics. In this way much of the responsibility for the care and treatment of the diseased is on the doctors' shoulders. This, however, does not mean that this function has been completely taken away from the family.

4. Creches and children parks. Creches and children parks are being developed in modern progressive countries. Employed women who work in factories leave their boule feeding children at the creches where educated women look after them, feed them at the proper time, and keep them occupied with toys, etc. Institutions of this kind have developed very much in modern countries, particularly in the U.S.S.R.

Similarly, in the Western countries, Montessori schools, nurseries and children parks have been developed for children between three and six years of age. In these, every care is taken of the children. The number of nurseries and creches in India is very small.

5. Baby Sitters. In the Western countries much of the chores of caring for and upbringing children has been taken up by baby sitters, in addition to the creches and nurseries. These baby sitters are generally female. Their duty is to keep the children busy and for this they receive payment by the hour. In America when a woman has to go out of the house on an important mission on which it is inconvenient to take children, she leaves them with the baby sitters.

6. Public Aid. Previously, one of the fundamental functions of the family was caring for and assisting the old, the invalids and the unemployed. Now-a-days in many European countries the government undertakes to assist the old, helpless, unemployed people and orphaned children. There is a similar system in Canada and America also. Women who work in factories get paid leave along with free medical facilities. Everywhere the government assists the old people and the orphans through the media of pension and insurance. In many countries an extra allowance is paid by the government when the number of children increases. There is a special arrangement for this kind of assistance in Russia, Sweden, Germany and Italy.

In this way, many institutions render assistance to the family in the performance of its duties. Hotels and restaurants provide food and rest while the picture houses and clubs provide the recreation. In this way these institutions share much of the family's work. But these can never replace the family, they can only supplement its efforts.

CHANGES IN MODERN URBAN FAMILY

In the modern period, the institution of family is undergoing rapid change and modification. The main changes, in this connection, are the following:

1. Reduction in the Economic Functions of Family. In the modern age, many of the economic functions, which were previously being performed by the family, are now being performed by factories, government aid and other associations.

2. Reduction in other Activities of Family. Many of the other functions of the family have now been taken over by other agencies. The work of looking after and bringing up children is now being performed in creches, children parks, kindergarten schools and by baby sitters. Hospitals undertake the work of delivering children and of treatment. Restaurants provide food to thousands of families.

3. Increase in Family Recreation. With the invention of radio and television, and the advent of indoor games modern families have been transformed into centres of recreation.

4. Changes in the Relationship of Man and Woman. Now that the women have gained equal rights with men, their mutual relationships have undergone much change. Mowrer has correctly written, "The husband is no longer the head of the house-hold in many families, in spite of the fact that he still provides the family name as well as the Christian name which his wife uses upon more formal occasions. Within the family circle however he is no longer the autocrat whose word is law. In fact he is lucky if his children look upon him other than as a meddlesome outsider or as an alley to be catered to when support is needed in breaking down his wife's opposition to some programme of the children.

The wife on the other hand, finds herself equal to her husband in the family circle, if not superior. She rules the destiny of the family group with a sympathetic, but nonetheless determined hand. She is no longer the drudge and slave of the other days. So far as the children are concerned, her commands are even more to be taken into account than those of father."[7]

5. Laxity in Marital and Sex Relationships. The rigidity traditionally associated with marital and sexual relationships no longer characterises the modem family. To quote Sutherland and Woodward, "The family has been greatly affected by the changes in sex mores."[8]

6. Increase in the Importance of Children. In the modern family the importance of children has increased. They are now only rarely physically punished but are instead taught lovingly. The modern families tend to become child-centred families.[9]

7. Decrease in the Importance of Blood relationships. In the modern family there has been a continuous decrease in the importance of blood relationships. The family is now constituted of a husband, a wife and their children.

8. Disorganisation of Joint Family. The modern family is no longer joint. The joint family is rapidly being disorganised.

9. Smaller Family. Due to the prolific use of contraceptives and the tendency to regard children as an obstacle in the progress and enjoyment of life, the birth rate is continuously falling and the modern families are becoming smaller.[10]

10. Family Disorganisation. The process of disorganisation is quite apparent in the modern family. The number of divorces is on the increase. The control which the family exercises over the individual is being lessened.

11. Instability. The modern family is no longer a permanent association. It is precarious and can be rendered void at any time. Marriage has been reduced to a mere social contract which is not difficult to break in the event of even the slightest friction. In comparison with the ancient and medieval families the modern family is weak and unstable.

New Problems Confronting the Urban Family

In this way the modern family is beset with many new problems the major among which now follow:

1. Problem of adjustment of the husband-wife relationship. In the modern family the most difficult problem is that of the mutual adjustment of husband and wife. The educated and enlightened woman of today wants to be the equal

---

7. Mowrer, Earnest, R., *The Family* (1932), pp. 274-275.

8. Sutherland and Woodland, *Introductory Sociology*, p. 603.

9. "They in fact tend to dominate the scene, their wishes determining the policy of the family. Thus the trend seems to be toward the filiocentric family in which the child plays the dominant role."
—Earnest R. Mowrer, *The Family, University of Chicago Press,* (1932), p. 274.

10. "The two child family is now the prevailing social standard or ideal,"
—J.K. Folsom, *The Family and the Democratic Society*, p. 188.

of her husband in every sphere of life. But the husbands have not yet adjusted themselves to this situation. Hence a conflict between the two is inevitable. Laxity of sexual relations and the instability of marital relations also tend to create conflict between the husband and the wife and to spoil their relationship.

2. Problem of sexual adjustment. The modern family is also faced with the problem of sexual adjustment, it being the outcome of changes in sex values. D.H. Lawrence, among the Western authors, has presented a graphic and revealing sketch of this problem in his novels. Psychoanalytic literature has also adversely affected the ancient ideal of fidelity in sex relationship. Some scholars have gone so far as to declare variety in sex relationships not only desirable but also necessary. This tends to encourage pre-marital sex relationships. All the factors have the effect of creating sexual disharmony between husband and wife and as a result numerous families are disorganised.

3. Marriage based on romantic love. The third major problem that confronts the family is that of marriages being based on romantic love. After marriages of this nature when the dreams of the husband and wife do not materialise in the family they are seriously frustrated. They start blaming each other and either live out their life in a state of perpetual strife or break the ties of marriage. In their book Social Disorganisation, Elliott and Merrill have described divorces as the inevitable consequence of romantic marriages.

4. Problem of broken marriage. A major problem faced by the modern family is an increase in the number of broken marriages. Marriage has been reduced to a mere social contract. Materialism, individualism and rationalism are the causes of paucity of such feelings as benevolence, love, etc. Greater stress is laid on sexual pleasure. The laws of divorce are also not very stringent. All these causes have the cumulative affect of increasing the number of divorces.

5. Problems of working women. Now-a-days there are more women who are employed outside the precincts of the home. They consequently do not get sufficient time to look after their children. Returning exhausted from their work they do not have the energy left to attend to their husbands or their children. This hinders the development of children and increases conflict and misunderstanding between husband and wife.

6. Laxity in family control. A major problem has been created for the modern family by the decrease in the control exercised by the family over its members. This has undermined the administration of the family. Boy girl, husband wife, brother sister each wants to pursue his own course and does not relish any interference, be it advice or be it rebuke.

7. Family conflict and strife. Changes in the values of life and a reduction of the family control in the modern family have led to increased conflict between husband and wife as well as between parents and children. This conflict is usually not apparent but it does disturb the peace of the family, destroy the faith in one another and remove the sense of psychological security.

8. Lower birth rate. The birth rate is falling constantly due to late marriage, frequent use of contraceptives, and a tendency to consider children a burden. This tends to accentuate the instability of the family since the absence of children reduces the sense of responsibility in the husband and wife, besides preventing intimate family relations.

DISORGANISATION OF MODERN URBAN FAMILY

The modern family is gradually becoming increasingly disorganised. According to Elliott and Merrill, "In the broadest sense family disorganisation may be thought to include any sort of non harmonious functioning within any of several types of family."[11] Family disorganisation is the disruption of the harmony among family members. Some signs of this phenomenon can be seen in the following changes in the family:

1. Lack of family unity. Men, women, boys and girls each have their own ideals, their own plans, individual programmes and individual thoughts, in which they welcome no interference whatsoever. In this way, even while living together, eating and moving together, no one is concerned with another. The house becomes almost a hotel where the family members gather only to take food and rest. Where both the husband and wife are employed a similar distance is seen to exist between them.

2. Decrease in family control. In modern times, the control of the family over its members is continually decreasing. No one wants to be lectured by anyone else. The younger generation finds a bitterness in the wisdom of its predecessors. They do not want to be controlled by them in any sphere. They want to be separated from the family immediately after they start earning or after they are married. In this way, the disorganisation of the family is obvious.

3. Strife. The strife within the family is presently on the increase because of the absence of family control as well as the absence of a sense of unity among the members. Joint families are rapidly becoming disorganised. Violence, litigation, etc., are common enough occurrences. Faith in one another is decreasing. There are many separate families within one house. The disorganisation of the family is only too evident from this.

4. Laxity in marital bonds. The tie of marriage is the basis of family. Weakening of marital ties results in a weakening of family ties. Now-a-days marriage is no longer a religious ritual but merely a social contract which can easily be cancelled or annulled on grounds of boredom or some kind of misunderstanding. Consequently there is a constant increase in the number of divorce. A major cause of the weakening of marriage ties is the failure of men to adapt to a new circumstance created by the education of women. Previously, women were completely dependent upon their husbands. Now, being educated, they also earn as much as their husbands or at least possess the capacity to do so. They have come to recognise their rights. They want to be equal of the men

11. Elliott and Merrill, Social Disorganisation, p. 352.

in every aspect of life. They now demand the same fidelity which their men demand of them. When the men do not want to have women on a equal footing with themselves the result is a struggle due to which the family tends to become disorganised.

5. Conflict between parents and children. Now-a-days an important element indicative of family disorganisation is the conflict between parents and children. The control of the old people over young men and women is constantly decreasing. They do not want to be ordered by their parents in their behaviour, marriage, society, etc. Consequently, the misunderstanding between the two parties increases and the family becomes further disorganised.

6. Lack of security. As a result of conflict between husband and wife and parents and children, psychological security is being continually diminished due to which mutual trust is decreasing and the family organisation is being shattered.

7. Industrialism. In the modern industrial system women and children work in factories along with the men. This reduces the unity of the family and increases disorganisation.

8. Ideal of Romantic Love. Modern marriages are based on the ideals of romantic love. When the dreams of the two partners do not materialise, in the family hatred increases and is gradually transformed into conflict.

9. Less Social Protection in Family Crises. Previously conflicts between husband and wife were overcome by the constraining influence of the elders, kinsmen, social mores and traditions and the family was saved from disintegration, but with the existing loss of respect for these modes of social control the husband and wife are deprived of any guide or mediator and in a fit of temper or even vengeance they destroy the delicately and lovingly nurtured sapling which is the family no matter how much remorse they may experience when they have cooled down. Previously, being financially dependent upon the husband the wife silently bore much injustice and did not dare think in terms of a separation. Now, the women who are capable of earning their livelihood marry only for love and when that is not forthcoming there is almost nothing to deter them from dissolving their marriage. At some places extreme laxity of divorce laws has led to very great instability and impermanence of the family.

10. Replacement of domination by co-operation. The basis of husband-wife relationship in the modern family is no longer domination but co-operation. Previously, everywhere, be it in the East or in the West, the wife was dominated by the husband and hence the family stability survived despite the husband's dictatorship. But with the removal of this dominance, in the modern time, the stability of the family can be maintained only by benevolence, sympathy and co-operation. Normally, it is not easy to create these qualities. Hence, the instability of the modern family.

It is obvious from the above mentioned causes, that the family is being rapidly disorganised in the modern age. The families are becoming smaller.

The number of divorces is increasing. Mutual intimacy and faith are being reduced and their place has been taken by selfishness and frivolity.

FUTURE OF MODERN URBAN FAMILY

This has led some people to doubt whether the family will survive in the present crisis in the highly industrialised and mechanised societies of the West. Sorokin writes. "Accordingly contractual family, in the progress of its development has unexpectedly reached the point where it has lost most of its functions and prerogatives, even those it retains are often atrophied and poorly performed. It has shrunk in size. It has become increasingly unstable and fragile. Less and less does it furnish even pleasure and comfort, primary objects of the sensate contractual family. When any institution finds itself in such a situation it is in the process of decay. This is precisely the position of the contractual sensate family to-day."[12] Will the family survive to continue in the form of a primar association? What will be the future of the family? Actually, there can never be any doubts concerning the continued existence of the family since it is based upon the fundamental needs of human beings. It would be no exaggeration to say that the family will assuredly exist in whatever varied or transformed form, as long as the human society exists. The desire for procreation is a natural desire in men. Outside the family there can neither be any legal offspring nor any proper arrangement for its upbringing. Some or the other kind of marriage system and a family are needed to afford a permanent means for the gratification of the sexual impulses of men and women. The family satisfies not merely the physiological needs of the male and female but also their psychological needs, the desire to love and to be loved, the sense of psychological security, etc. The family exercises the control of society upon the individual. The family creates an environment in which the child can be brought up to develop his personality fully and to become an ideal citizen. Many studies have revealed that among people aged more than thirty, the death rate among the unmarried men and women is twice that of the married women and men. Among people who die as a result of tuberculosis, accidents, suicides, alcoholic indulgence and sexual diseases, the proportion of unmarried is greater than that of the married. Mutual affection of family members guards against many of the mental and physical difficulties of a complicated society. This is clearly indicative of the benefits which accrue to man from the institution of family. Actually, the family is a primary and fundamental unit of society. It is the foundation of all social life. It socializes the individual and assists him in the choice and selection of a life partner. It determines inheritance and procures property. It is difficult to describe all the direct and indirect benefits of the family. It is an inseparable part of human nature. It is the foundation of the social structure. Hence, one will agree with Burgess and Locke when they say "It seems safe to predict that the family will survive, both because of its long history of adaptability to changing condition and because of the importance of

---

12. Sorokin, P., *The Crisis of Our Age*, p. 192

its functions of affection-giving and receiving in personal satisfaction and in personality development."[13]

FAMILY WELFARE IN INDIA

One of the most crucial problems facing the nation today is the burgeoning population which has been growing at an alarming rate. By 1981, India's population had doubled itself since 1947 and has touched 8,463 lakh in 1991. It is increasing by about 170 lakh every year. Such a rapid increase in population has very serious repercussions on socio-economic development. Varying social customs and beliefs favour large family which impede the process of change and willing adoption of modern methods of contraception. A universal desire to have atleast one or two male children and the mean age of marriage of women at 18.3 years also become contributory factors to large families. Inspite of this, India is committed to attaining the twin goals of 'Health for All' and 'Net Reproduction Rate of Unity' by the year 2000.

In keeping with democratic traditions of the country, Family Welfare Programme seeks to promote on a voluntary basis, responsible and planned parenthood with two-child norm, male and female or both, through independent choice of family welfare methods best suited to the acceptors. Family welfare services are offered through total health-care delivery system. People's participation is sought through voluntary agencies, opinion leaders, people's representatives, government functionaries and various other structures and influential groups. Imaginative use of mass media and interpersonal communication is resorted to for explaining various methods of contraception and removing socio-cultural barriers. As a result, the number of acceptors of various family planning methods have started increasing over the years.

Implementation Machinery

These programmes are implemented through state governments with cent per cent Central assistance. In rural areas, it is being further extended through a network of primary health centres and sub-centres. During the Seventh Plan period 45,169 sub-centres were established in addition to 84,400 sub-centres already established upto the end of the Sixth Plan. Subsequently, 7,14,494 and six additional number of sub-centres were established during the years 1990-91, 1991-92 and 1992-93 (upto 1 March 1993) respectively.

Birth Control Methods

During 1994-95 (upto March 1995) 42.90 lakh sterilisations were performed in the country. The number of IUD insertions during the same period was 46.23 lakh. The total number of acceptors of different methods was 266.55 lakh. *Nirodh* besides being provided free is also sold under the social marketing programme which is being operated through a network of over three lakh retail outlets of eleven leading consumer goods, pharmaceutical and oil companies.

---

13. Burgess and Locke, *The Family*, (1950), p. 715.

With a view to make condoms available in rural and far-flung areas at reasonable prices, scheme of distribution of condoms through Public Distribution System has already been implemented in many states.

Oral pill programme under free distribution scheme was extended to all urban centres, including those run by local bodies and voluntary organisations. Besides this, social marketing of oral pill under the brand name '*Mala-D*', has been undertaken with the help of four pharmaceutical companies on zonal basis.

It is estimated that 43.5 per cent of 14.84 crore eligible couples whose wives are in the reproductive age-group of 15-44 years were protected by one or the other approved family planning methods as on 31 March 1994 averting 16.88 crore births since inception of the programme.

Medical Termination of Pregnancy (MTP)

It is estimated that about one fourth of the maternal morbidity and mortality are due to illegal abortions. In order to prevent these health hazards to women the Medical Termination of Pregnancy Act, 1971 was promulgated. Under this Act, medical termination of pregnancy can be done in pregnant women upto 20 weeks if, pregnancy is likely to result in birth of a congenitally malformed child or continuation of pregnancy is likely to harm the mother in the existing circumstances and in cases of contraceptive failure.

Research studies in India have shown that vacuum aspiration is a safe and effective methods for terminating first trimester (three months) pregnancy. During the last few years studies on first trimester MTP using antiprogestin compounds like RU 486, alone or along with prostaglandins are being carried out to see whether these could provide a safe, effective non-surgical method for termination of early pregnancy. It has been observed that about 10-15 per cent of abortion seekers come during second trimester of pregnancy. A wide variety of methods have been investigated for second trimester MTP. Whatever is the method used, second trimester of pregnancy termination is not as safe as first trimester pregnancy termination. All available data indicate that in order to minimise health hazards, women should come for termination soon after she misses her period.

To avoid the recurrence of an unwanted pregnancy women should be provided with concurrent contraception; IUDs, OCs, condoms, etc., or sterilization if she has completed her family. Since inception of the programme in April 1972, 97.5 lakh terminations upto December 1994, were conducted under MTP Act.

Maternal and Child Health Care Programmes

The National Health Policy (1983) in context of the global objective of 'Health for All by 2000 A.D.' has *inter alia*, set the following normative goals related to maternal and child health care: (a) reduction in infant mortality to less than 60 per thousand live births. In 1991 the infant mortality rate (IMR) stood at 80 per thousand live births, according to the results of the Sample Registration System (SRS) carried out by the office of Registrar General of India; (b) reduction in maternal mortality to below 200 per one lakh live births. According to estimates the current level of maternal mortality varied between 400-600 per 100,000 live births in various parts of the country; (c) reduction in child (1-4 year) mortality to less than 10 per thousand child population. The current level (1989) of child mortality is estimated at 29.9 per thousand child population.

As a part of the overall strategy to achieve these goals, the following specific programmes have been under implementation as cent per cent Centrally sponsored schemes: (i) universal immunization programme (under implementation since 1985-86), for reducing mortality and morbidity due to six vaccine preventable diseases namely diphtheria, pertussis, tetanus, poliomyelitis, measles and childhood tuberculosis. The primary target group for this programme is infants and pregnant women. When the immunization programme was launched in 1985 IMR for the country as a whole was 97 for every thousand live births. The intensification of immunisation programme has contributed to a significant decline in IMR in the last few years. The decline has been particularly pronounced in 1990 as compared to earlier years. During that year the IMR declined (by 11 points) to 80 per thousand live births from 91 in 1989; (ii) Oral Rehydration Therapy (ORT) Programme (under implementation since 1986-87) for reducing mortality and morbidity due to dehydration caused by diarrhoea. The primary target of this programme is children under five years of age. Diarrhoeal diseases are a major health problem in the country especially among children below five years of age. On an average, a child suffers three episodes of diarrhoea per year due to diarrhoea or diarrhoea related causes. The National Diarrhoeal Diseases Control Programme, initiated in the Sixth Plan, was therefore, intensified in the Seventh Plan with a conscious decision to promote Oral Rehydration Therapy; and (iii) Prophylaxis Schemes (under implementation since Fourth Plan period) against nutritional anaemia among pregnant and lactating women as well as children and against blindness due to vitamin 'A' deficiency among children under five years of age. Nutritional anaemia is one of the major public health problems especially affecting pregnant and lactating women and pre-school children. Anaemia affecting the mother also affects interuterine growth of the foetus. Similarly, nutritional anaemia among preschool children makes them susceptible to more diseases and death. Vitamin A deficiency is widely prevalent in the country among, the preschool children.

Child Survival and Safe Motherhood Programme

The package of services under Child Survival and Safe Motherhood Project are to be expanded under two major components: (a) child survival component under which the ARI control programme will be expanded along with provision of the kit based supply of drugs; and (b) safe motherhood component under which first referral units will be set up in the six states of Assam, Bihar, Himachal Pradesh, Orissa, Rajasthan and Uttar Pradesh.

SPECIAL SCHEMES

All India Hospitals Post Partum Programme

An all India hospital post partum programme (AIHPP) was introduced in 1969. It is a hospital-based, maternity centered approach to family planning. The primary objective of the post-partum programme is to improve the health of the mother and children through MCH and Family Welfare Programme which includes antenatal, neonatal, and postnatal services; immunization services to children and mothers; and prophylaxis against anaemia and blindness. The programme is based on the following rationale: (a) that women who have recently delivered are of proven fertility, and are at risk to become pregnant again rapidly; and (b) at the time of delivery and during the Lying-in-period, they are generally more receptive to adopt one or the other family planning method. The post-partum programme offers necessary facilities to such women. It has proved to be an efficient way of delivering family planning services. The programme now covers 550 medical institutions at national, state and district level inclusive of 104 medical colleges and two post-graduate institutions. With a view to provide MCH and family welfare services in rural and semi-urban areas, as well as to improve the health of mothers and children, the post partum programme has been extended to 1,001 sub-divisional and sub-district hospitals.

Post Partum Pap Smear Test Facility at Medical Colleges

In order to detect cervical cancer among women acceptors and non-acceptors of various family welfare methods, the PAP smear test facility programme has been introduced in all the medical colleges of the country. Under the scheme, a post of a cyto-technician as per state government's scale of pay and financial assistance or contingencies provided. The cyto-technician is required to work under the overall guidance and supervision of the professor of pathology of the medical college. The programme has been extended in a phased manner in 105 medical colleges all over the country. The state governments have sanctioned the programme in 80 medical colleges only.

Sterilisation Beds Scheme

Under the scheme, beds are provided to voluntary organisations/local bodies/ institutions on the basis of their performance of previous years and on the recommendations of the state government and regional director of Health and Family Welfare of the respective state. Maintenance grant under this scheme at the rate of Rs. 3,000 per bed per annum is provided to each institution subject to a minimum performance of 75/60 tubectomies per bed per annum for government institutions and local bodies/voluntary organisations respectively. A total of 3,610 sterilisation beds have been reserved under the scheme.

Urban Family Welfare Centres and Urban Revamping Scheme

Urban family welfare centres are on the ground since 1950 to provide Family Welfare services in the urban areas. These are of different categories depending upon the staff sanctioned and area covered by them. In all, 1,469 urban family welfare centres are functioning in the states/union territories, including 208 urban centres under Ministry of Railways and Ministry of Labour, etc.

On the recommendation of a Working Group it was decided to reorganise the existing urban family welfare centres to establish new health posts preferably in the urban slum areas. Accordingly, all the states/union territories were requested to send the proposals in respect of cities in their states. At present the scheme is functioning in 11 states through 870 health posts.

Training of Health Workers for Subscentres

Each sub-centre is manned by one female health worker and one male health worker Auxiliary Nurse Midwife. In order to train the required number of ANMs, there are 463 ANM training schools functioning all over the country with an annual admission capacity of 19,276. The requirement of Multi-purpose Worker (Male) (MPW (M)) for the sub-centres was initially met by the conversion of unipurpose workers to multi-purpose workers under the MPW scheme which has come to an end. Presently, basic training to MPW(M) is being given in MPW(M) schools, which is a cent per cent Centrally sponsored scheme. The training period is of one year duration and the basic qualification required for admission is 10th pass. There are at present 1,25,121 ANMs and 64,416 MPW(M) in position in the rural areas.

MOTIVATION AND EDUCATION

Family welfare programme in India depends on its voluntary acceptance by the people. To approach above 14.50 crore couples in the reproductive age group, living in urban and remote rural areas, a broad-based mass education and motivation programme has been launched. The multi-media campaign is being implemented by media units of the Ministry of Information and Broadcasting, state mass education media set-ups and other publicity agencies/ organisations. The Ministry of Health and Family Welfare lays down the communication strategy, develops plans and coordinates the media and extension activities of various participating media agencies. The mass mailing units of the Department of Family Welfare disseminates information in the form of printed material to various categories of opinion leaders through direct mail service. The Division brings out two monthly journals — "*Centre Calling*" in English and "*Hamara Ghar*" in Hindi.

AREA DEVELOPMENT PROJECTS

The area development projects have been taken up in different states with the financial assistance from external funding agencies like World Bank, United Nations Fund for Population Activities (UNFPA), Overseas Development Administration (ODA) and DANIDA with the aim of reducing maternal and child mortality and morbidity and birth rates. These objectives are sought to be achieved by improving the quality and availability of health and family welfare services through the strenthening of the service delivery infrastructure of the states and by making available facilities for upgrading skills of the concerned manpower through better training and programme management. Construction of institutional buildings for service delivery and training in addition to positioning of trained staff in the service centres received attention under the projects.

The Area Projects were initially taken up in 1973 in a few selected districts of Karnataka and Uttar Pradesh with the financial assistance of World Bank. During subsequent Plan periods, the scheme was continued and extended to cover more districts and states. Currently, 17 Area Projects are being implemented in 16 states with the assistance of donor agencies. All India Population Project VIII is also proposed to be taken up shortly for the urban slums of four major cities of Calcutta, Delhi, Bangalore and Hyderabad.

QUESTIONS FOR EXERCISE

1. What are the major functions of urban family?
2. Discuss the characteristics of urban family.
3. What are the basic functions of urban family? Have these functions changed during recent years? Would you call the modern family disorganised? Give reasons.
4. Is the institution of family disintegrating? Discuss.
5. Discuss the problems of modern family and suggest programmes for marriage and family.
6. Write short note on — Problems of modern family.
7. Discuss the factors responsible for the instability of urban family.

8

Urban Culture

Cultural Aspect of Urban Life

The important cultural institutions of a city are libraries, reading rooms, dance and music clubs, museums, art societies, writer's club, poetry clubs, associations and societies for the promotion of various cultural ideologies. In metropolises all these associations, institutions and clubs can be seen. In India there are scores of towns, Bombay, Calcutta, Bangalore, Cuttak, Delhi, Lucknow, Madras, Kanpur, Patna, Jaipur to mention some, in which all the above mentioned cultural institutions can be seen. Indeed, in Bombay, Calcutta and Delhi there must be scores of libraries, both Indian and foreign, government and private, besides museums, dance and music societies etc. Indeed in these cities cultural activity of every imaginable kind is to be found. In small cities we find libraries but no museums. The upkeep of a museum is an expensive affair and it is not possible in a poor country like India to have museum in every town. In majority of Indian cities we do find a multiplicity of libraries. In most of the cities there is a central municipal library which sometimes has its branches in different wards of the city. Any citizen is entitled to use these libraries on payment of small amount as subscription. In some towns there are mobile libraries which go from one place to the other on fixed days and take back previously issued books and issue fresh books to the members. There is considerable difference in the reading habits of people in different cities, there is also difference as regards the frequency of reading. Generally, in libraries we find books on fiction, biography, literature, politics, history and economics. There are also new books on psychology and sociology in these libraries. As a rule, these libraries do not stock books on philosophy, art, religion, science and commerce. This is so because an average reader is not interested in these subjects. Usually the books are in English and Hindi but now books in other languages are also stocked, particularly in non-Hindi areas.

In all big metropolises of India are art, music and dance clubs and societies. There are three central Academies in India whose function is to encourage art, literature and music. These academies have competent artists as their members. They select and award richly the best persons in every field of art, literature and music. These academies are : (1) Sahitya (Literature) Academy; (2) Lalitkala

(Fine Arts) Academy; and (3) Sangeet (Music) Academy. These academies are government sponsored bodies and have large funds at their disposal. Besides these official bodies there are also some non-official organizations devoted to the promotion of art and culture. The popular among these are Bharatiya Vidya Bhavan, Prayag Sangeet Sammelan etc. In all big and small Indian towns there are theatrical clubs which organize Ramlilas and other dramas and also give special performance on the occasion of some festival or independence or republic day. There are also some government sponsored agencies which give performance from one place to the other to propagate programmes and plans launched by the government. Now-a-days every important city has a film society which tries to promote art and other films which are not easily accessible. These societies arrange film festival from time to time. Besides these activities radio, television and cinema also play crucial role in the cultural life of the citizens, because their thinking and attitudes are shaped by these powerful media. Now-a-days, art and culture societies receive financial assistance from the central and state governments. The tenor of cultural life in a city is maintained by a few competent artists. Even if there is one outstanding artist in a city he can, by his dedication and devoted work, turn that city into a centre of art and culture. Besides cinema which attracts maximum attention from people, theater comes next in popularity.

COMMERCIAL RECREATION IN URBAN LIFE

What is Recreation ?

'Recreation' as the term suggests, aims at the recreation of the spent up energy of a human being. Recreation is a sort of relaxation. While relaxing the body, recreation tries to relieve the mind of its tensions by diverting its attention to other more pleasant aspects of life such as nature, culture, art, literature etc. Thus, recreation is as necessary to life as food and water.

Rural Recreation

In villages there is no need for a specific type of recreation as the work itself provides for necessary relaxation to a villager. Work within Nature satisfies most of his mental needs. The seasonal nature and variety of his occupations enables him to organize his recreation according to his needs.

Urban Recreation

But an urbantie's life is for the most part confined to the inside of a building and increased tension of work and increased unwanted leisure are both parts of urban society. Urban recreation consists of organizing communal feasts and festivals, creation of cultural organizations like ladies clubs, youth organizations etc. which provide an outlet for the talent in the community at the same time providing a moral base. Lounging in parks, sometimes with families is the most healthy form of urban recreation which relaxes both one's mind and body.

Mass Recreation

Urbanization has seen the development of a new form of recreation i.e., recreation for the masses. This aims at providing average recreation for the common masses. The media of this recreation include radio, television, newspaper etc. These are used for both recreating and educating people informally by organizations like city government, police etc., about the various aspects of city code and mass culture and mannerisms. These are financed by the city organizations in the interest of people.

Commercial Recreation

Lack of proper recreation leads a man to vice and crime. At the same time unhealthy recreation may also induce crime and vice in a person. Commercialization has entered into urban recreation. Professionals in the field have tried to seize the urban man's craze for recreation and to cash upon his instincts of cosy gains and adventure and thrill which are denied to him in the ordinary course of life. The main forms of commercial recreation include cinemas, gambling dense, night clubs, house of prostitutes, bars etc. Cinemas are to a greater extent, a healthy form of commercial recreation so far as they show movies which depict the healthier aspects of our social culture.

Injurious Recreation

The injurious effects of commercial recreation come into play in relation with the other contributing factors of life. The basic injury lies in the fact that they lead an urbanite into devious ways of earning money and recreation and thus destroys healthy social and personal life.

1. Gambling. Gambling is a universal phenomenon of contemporary urban society and it pricks the unsatiated urbanite's desire for some easy money. Thus it acts as a drain upon his personal income and leads to unnecessary mental tension and frustration.

2. Alcoholism. Excessive alcoholism to which an urbanite is led owing to the exigencies of urban life is promoted by the wide-spread network of clubs and bars. Excessive alcoholism, coupled with gambling, leads to personal and family disorganization and is a drain upon one's income. Alcoholism shortens a man's span of life and work while the effect of drink leads a man into unnecessary brawls and crime. It may lead him to mental frustration, isolation and ultimately to suicide.

3. Prostitution. The existence of cheap prostitution mars sexual morality and is a curse upon healthy family life. It encourages the innocent youth into the enjoyment of unhealthy and licentious sex without concern for consequences. Prostitution gives rise to sexual diseases like syphelis and gonorrea.

4. Vulgar Films. Vulgar films induce a bewildered adolescent into the first crime and to a life of crime, thrill and easy money.

The existence of commercial recreation acts upon common morality and decency and hinders the development of a healthy social life. Commercial recreation paves the away for development of deviant subcultures like hippi culture.

Commercial recreation promotes the development of professionals in recreation and the growth of deviency as a parallel culture in a city. It promotes crime and vice, creates confusion and chaos to the values of life and leads to personal, family and social disorganization. Commercial recreation hinders the effectiveness of normal social institutions like family, school, city, government etc.

URBAN RELIGION

Urbanism and religion at the outset appear as anomalies as urbanites mostly depend upon reason to find answers to most of their problems. But in fact, urban religion is also a part of the faith in reason of the urbanite. Urban religion is mostly secular. The importance of the religious institutions like temples, mosques and festivals in their traditional nature has been greatly reduced. The lack of strong religious feelings to guide man's life is sometimes attributed as the cause of many urban maladies. Magic plays no part in urban religion. However, the notions behind religious feelings still guide the urbanite's way of life. Urbanites use religion for social purposes such as Ganesh festival etc.

QUESTIONS FOR EXERCISE

1. Discuss the cultural aspect of urban life.
2. What do you understand by recreation ? Define the injurious effects of commercial recreation on urban life.
3. Write short note on Urban religion.

9

Urban Society

As the physical, psychological and cultural circumstances and conditions of urban society are quite different from those of rural society, the urban life is naturally quite different from the rural life. Now, we shall discuss the chief social aspects of urban life.

1. Impersonality of Social Relations. The most striking feature of the social aspects of urban social life is its impersonality. The chief reason for this state of affairs is that people in cities do not regard affectionately other persons and do not have any respect for them. They love and respect goods and things in preference to human beings. Every commodity and service in urban society is evaluated in terms of cash; therefore, everything in city is for sale and purchase. Nothing has intrinsic value in the urban context; all can be measured in terms of cash. Even human beings are buyable. Every service rendered by someone to someone has its price. Due to the overwhelming influence of materialism every kind of commodity and every kind of human relation has its price. The cash-nexus completely dominates the urban life. The most intimate of human relations, the man and woman relation has been made subject to money and cash by the profession of prostitution. In cities it is possible to buy sexual pleasure; something not possible in villages.

Thus, money and cash govern the behaviour of urban man. It is the cash and goods which matter; man plays a subsidiary role. A shopkeeper in city has no interest in the buyer as a human being : his only concern is to charge maximum price for his goods. Whosoever pays the price, irrespective of his character and background, is welcome to him; morals are irrelevant to him. In the bazaars, parks, cinemas, theatres and clubs of the city a human being is not a person having his distinctive character and appeal but is just a member of crowd, who has no distinction, no uniqueness about him. All these factors give impetus to impersonality of the character. In cities very little social control is exercised by institutions like family or caste, *Biradari* and society. The chief control exercised in urban society is secondary and not primary. The law courts, police and jail are the instruments of social control instead of family or caste. As long as man can escape these agencies he can be a respectable member of the society though in fact leading a corrupt life. In cities the needs of man multiply and in order to meet them he needs money. Living in urban environment one must have a furnished house, good clothes, membership of some societies and schooling of children in good schools etc. All these things require good amount of money. If a man in city has money and wealth he is respected, no matter how he has earned money. Indeed money can wash clean innumerable wrongs and sins of man in an urban society. Therefore, people in cities are mad after money. They are engaged in pursuit of money by hook or crook. In the pursuit of money, the city-dwellers do not shirk from adopting unscrupulous means; they even exploit their fellow human beings. Other persons for them are no ends but merely means. All these things add to impersonality and unattachment in human relations.

2. Mechanical Social Life. As a consequence of impersonality of relations, industrialization and the widespread use of modern sophisticated technical gadgetry the urban life has become mechanical. It has lost all creativity. What anyone has to do or not to do at any particular hour is determined by clock. The decisions about various things are not deliberate and free but guided by the hour of the clock. One dare not defy the dictates of clock. If the bus or train taking one to the place of duty leaves at 9-30 A.M. the labourer or the office clerk: must arrive at the bus stand or railway station, as the case may be, on or before 9.30 A.M., no matter what his mood or feeling is or whether he has eaten his food or not. He can defy this time table only at grave risk. Therefore, his life is guided by the clock and not by his will. He even goes to sleep, eat his food and play not when he is sleepy, hungry or playful but because time for all these activities is fixed and clock is the guardian of time. In cities no one lives as a human being, everyone wears a label. Someone is a doctor; someone is a professor; someone is rich; someone is poor, someone is industrialist; someone is a mill labourer and so on. Thus, in cities we see everyone under some category or class and a man in general is forgotten altogether. The reason for this state of affairs is that life in cities is so fast that no one has time to see anyone carefully, closely and with affection. No one has time or will to know anyone deeply or intimately. It is not love but self-interest which governs human relations in an urban society. Therefore, all relations are temporary and strictly guided by a particular purpose. It is this purpose that sustains the relationship and the moment the purpose is over, the relationship comes to an end. Outside of some self-interest nobody is prepared to recognize the other person. The professionalism so rampant in urban life comes in the way of development of deep and intimate relations, because no one is prepared to sacrifice his or her professional interest and the intimacy of personal relations militates against the professional interests. Therefore, love and sympathy are conspicuous by their absence in cities. The polite and civilized behaviour of city dwellers is a mere facade. It merely covers internal hollowness and mechanicalness. Inspite of meeting numerous persons daily, a city dweller rarely forms close relationship with anyone. Radio, television and newspapers encourage indirectness and formality of relationship because due to these one has not to depend on anyone for news and information. Due to temporary, casual and calculated relations among, individuals, few permanent, stable and deep relationships develop in cities. Even when the relationship is durable and long standing, it does not grow in depth and intimacy because of its utilitarian bias. Even where there is outward facade of intimacy of relationship there is no real love. One's own desires, needs and aspirations are so overwhelming and pressing that one has no spare time for thinking about the welfare of others. Even when people come together in closely-knit associations and become members of some club or society they are not averse to harming others, should it knit them and serve their interest.

3. Secondary Control. Due to impersonality of social relations and the mechanical nature of the social life, primary controls are not effective in urban context. There is little control of family, caste and *Biradari* upon the conduct and behaviour of the individual. An urban man is under the control of the law enforcing agencies of the government only. Therefore, in cities law and police assume great significance and play very crucial role. In the various clubs, associations and societies formed in the cities each is given its constitution which lays down the rules and regulations, violation of which attracts punishment. These constitutions are registered with government so that an infringement of them becomes a congnizable offence. Therefore, as long as an individual remains a member of the society, association or club he has to abide by its rules and regulation, and thus the constitution of the society or club regulates or controls his behaviour and conduct. Often the relations amongst the members of such societies become so intimate that the control exercised by them becomes the same as the primary control. Sometimes clubs and societies in cities performs the functions of family, church and neighbourhood. Like them they exercise primary social control. This is due to the fact that long associations among members of a club or society deepen and cement the ties between them. Thus, a member of club is very zealous about keeping the honour of club and tries to conform to norms and standards of the club or the society.

4. Ostentation and Show. In urban life there is too much emphasis on ostentation. Erich Fromm has elaborately depicted a forceful picture of the urban proclivity in his book, *The Sane Society*. The urban people are so addicted to ostentation that they value things more for their ostentation than for their use. It is not the utility of a thing which impresses them rather they are impressed if it is decorative, out of way, unusual or rare. They want to be popular, to be respected in recognition of the pomp and show of their possessions. There is indeed so much emphasis on the outward show, the brightness and glamour of dress, perfumes and such things that it is doubtful if the urban mass ever gets time to look into himself to reflect and ponder. The rich try to advertise their riches by building grand elaborate mansions, stuffing them with so called art pieces and by hosting gay and lavish party at which wine flows like water. The middle-class persons, inspite of their limited resources, only too anxious to ape; they try to follow rich and for this purpose overstrain themselves. But however, in as much as it is not possible to get any recognition and attract attention without pomp and show, the exhibitionism has become the style of life in cities. The middle class ladies put up an extremely crude show of themselves. Crazy as they are for praise and attention, they wear gaudy clothes of poor fabric, wear artificial silk and ornaments and decorate themselves with cheap cosmetics and strong perfume. Even poor in the cities try though not successfully to imitate the style and mannerism of rich. The office-going clerks and junior executives are out of money well before the end of the month. They are perpetually under debt. Besides daily extravaganza the money spent on marriage and other festive occasions is enormous. Every body spends beyond his means on marriages simply to attract attention. Exhibition of one's riches is the only means of getting attention, receiving praise and being treated with respect by others. The guard, bungalows, the fleet of cars, an army of attendants, scores of suits, dresses and regular trips by air etc. are undertaken not so much for their utility as for ostentation and face value. These are the means of acquiring status and respect in the urban society. Though the tendency of exhibitionism, is only too human and it is universal and there is also considerable show off, ostentation and extravagancy in village, there is an all important difference in rural and urban attitudes. In cities these things are approved and indeed one is expected to follow these, these are squarely condemned in the villages. The villagers frown upon those who indulge in show off and copy filmstars in fashion etc.

However, it must be borne in mind, in this context, that there is so much emphasis on ostentation in the cities not merely because people want to show off but also because there is an imperative need for show off in cities. As has been referred to earlier, the relations in the cities are temporary and in order to impress others and get business from them, one needs to show off. The shop keeper, the hotelier and an official have to be civil and well behaved toward every newcomer. This mannerism has to be there even if it is merely outwardly and hollow. This show off is very necessary for the successful operation of one's business.

5. Fashion. As a consequence of the tendency toward ostentation and show off, the fashion flourishes and is the order of the day in cities. The trends in fashion are determined by popular leaders, film actors and actresses. The ladies' fashion in hair dress, clothing, ornaments and mannerisms follow the trends set by the film personalities. Similarly, young men follow very closely the fashions of their film heroes in matters of dress, speech and even smoking. Whatever is an item of popular fashion naturally becomes a hot-sell. Once a thing is out of fashion its sale drops even if the thing is good and durable. Therefore, shopkeepers also stock only those commodities and items which happen to be in latest fashion. The fashions keep changing and only that businessman can succeed in cities who can sell fast and keep track of everything in latest fashion. The trends in fashion are usually set by leading metropolises. People of Bombay and Delhi lead in fashion and others follow their suit. In Europe, Paris and in U.S.A New York are trend-setters in fashion. As life is relatively non-competitive in the communist countries, fashions there do not change so rapidly as in the capitalist countries. Now-a-days, due to rapid means of communication, fashions also travel very fast. The leading fashion trends of New York and Paris spread to every corner of the world in no time. The popularity of fashions, however, does not mean that everyone in a city is affected by the fashions and that there are no persons who are orthodox and traditional in their wears and manners. Indeed fashions do not affect majority of persons. In every city there is a sizeable population which refuses to change dress and manner in tune with current fashions. They continue to wear traditional clothings. Whereas youth and women are fashion-prone and are easily carried away by changes of fashion, the religious-minded persons, old persons and nationalistic persons are, more or less, immune from changes of fashion. The political and social leaders of every country wear traditional dresses. As referred to earlier, the Western fashion is determined by the trends in New York and Paris. The modern fashion is sex and pomp oriented. Everywhere we find that current fashions are geared to heighten the sex feeling. The modern dresses are so cut as to bring out the bodily charm; displaying and not veiling the body is the aim of modern dress. The motivations behind fashions are complex. It is a mixture of an urge to conform and an urge to differ. In music and art fashion shows this tendency.

6. Dynamism. Another feature of the social life in the urban society is that it is far more dynamic and mobile than the life in the villages. The dynamicity and mobility of urban life is of many kinds. For example, we find frequent changes of residence in cities. This keeps people moving and shifting. The changes of residence in cities is due to the fact that the majority of people in cities live in tenanted houses. Therefore, they always so manage their affairs as to be able to shift easily and at a short notice. The change of residence can be due to a number of factors : such as transfer, quarrel between tenants and landlords; availability of better or cheaper accommodation etc. The government servants are transferred periodically, and they, therefore, have to change their residence from time to time. Besides, people live in suburbs and go to distant places for their work. They leave their residence in the morning and return in the evening of night. At times people have to travel ten to twenty miles to reach their places of work. In cities we find people moving on the streets practically whole of the day and most of the night. In cities people move about for a variety of purposes. Some are on the street because they are going to work; some move about plying trade and others are there just for the pleasure of moving about. The bus-stands, railway stations and airports in big cities are crowded day and night because people in city keep travelling in and out for business and other purposes. Daily there is considerable influx and exodus of population from cities. The movement of people is not uniform throughout the day. Indeed there are peak and slack periods. In the morning between 10 to 10.30 A.M. and in the evening between 4.30 to 5 P.M. are the peak periods. During these periods wave after wave of people surges onto the street and every means of transport is packed to capacity. In evenings clubs and restaurants are also packed to capacity. As the night falls and after midnight particularly the streets become relatively empty. In Bombay, Calcutta and Delhi, however, there is considerable traffic on the streets during night even. In mobility in towns, time factor plays an important role. This is so because everything in the town follows the clock. Every body works according to the hour of the clock. Not only are the city-dwellers guided by the clock in matters of business, they sleep, rise entertain themselves by the clock. Thus life in cities becomes mechanical. As life becomes mechanical, everything becomes routine and this leads to ennui and boredom. In order to escape this boredom, city-dwellers plan holidays and go to hill and health resorts in order to refresh themselves. On Sundays they arrange picnics and go out to nearby parks, river banks, lakes etc. Even businessmen and shopkeepers now-a-days take one day off in a week. This is done to escape the weight of routine and boredom.

The social mobility of urban life affects social relations. Generally an increase in the social mobility is accompanied by intensification of impersonality and unattachednesss of social relations. It also leads to personal and social disorganization. This lessens the social control. It obstructs the development of collective consciousness. All these factors result in breakdown of social relations. The breakdown of social relations and the lessening of social control give rise to corruption and moral laxity. However, the consequences of rise in social mobility are not only negative; on the positive side greater social mobility leads to greater awareness, heightened skill and efficiency and greater efficiency and tact in behaviour. A comparison in the behaviour of city youth with their rural counterparts clearly brings out this fact. For villagers it is a problem to cross a busy street in the city whereas even children of city do this very easily. Similarly, a man from village easily gets duped or cheated in the city whereas city people are quite shrewd and are able to avoid any cheating by others. A villager after a stay in the city becomes quite shrewd and clever. Thus, we can say that the urban atmosphere makes people shrewd, clever and efficient.

7. Lack of Neighbourly Feelings. In cities we find lack of feelings of neighbourliness. The social relations are motivated and calculated: they are totally devoid of love and sympathy. Generally speaking the feeling of neighbourliness is in inverse proportion to the size of the city and the density of its population. In cities the residential and industrial complexes are usually separated by great distances. Therefore people leave their homes early in the morning and return fairly late in the evening utterly exhausted. Sundays and other holidays are spent in doing house hold chores. Thus they get virtually no time to meet their neighbours and spend some time with them. Moreover most of their people live in insufficient accommodation and it is a problem for them to entertain their guests. This acts as an inhibitive factor in developing contacts. People in cities prefer to lead a life of anonymity. They do not want to be known thoroughly by any one. Therefore they are wary of developing contacts and friendship with others. It is natural to feel embarrassment if someone intimate learns one's secrets. Therefore, it is always advisable to avoid deep contacts. In big cities persons of all types live in one housing complex. It is quite possible that one's neighbours may be men of soady character. Thus so long as possible one avoids to be indulgent with his neighbours. This saves one from unnecessary complications. Generally one does not suffer any embarrassment in the presence of less known friends and neighbours and feels free to behave as one likes. Moreover, as the means of transportation and communication are rather fast in the cities one can easily maintain friendship with people in the other parts of the city and need not expose oneself to neighbours. The businessmen, shopkeepers and office goers prefer to contract friendship with their immediate neighbours. In cities people like to form friendship with their counterparts and avoid friendship with their immediate neighbours. In cities people like to form friendship with persons having similar interests and tastes; if their neighbours are of different tastes, they may not even know them in spite of long stay together. The clubs and associations offer far better and completer opportunities to fulfil their psychological needs of friendship. Therefore they do not need contract friendship with neighbours. In his '*The City and the Primary Groups*', Robert M. Wesley has made deep analysis of the causes of decline in the feeling of neighbourhood.

However, it may not be concluded from the above analysis that the feeling of neighbourliness has disappeared completely from the urban life. Whereas it is true that in some leading metropolises the feeling of neighbourliness is virtually absent, it is very much in evidence in the majority of the cities of India. Not only in small cities but in cities like Delhi and Bombay we find mohalla organizations which show great spirit of cooperation among neighbours. These organizations are formed for the defence of common interests. Even in big cities there are localities in which people from a particular region following a particular religion or belonging to a particular caste predominate and in these localities we find great deal of the feeling of neighbourliness. As a matter of fact decline of neighbourliness is a relative fact as far as Indian cities are concerned. There are many examples in which we find great feeling of neighbourliness in Indian cities. This fact is amply borne out by solidarity shown by city-dwellers during wars. Moreover, in India the role of women is still by and large confined to homes and professional women are an exception and not rule. Therefore women in mohalla or locality do get sufficient time to spend with neighbours. Therefore in this regard there is considerable amount of difference in Indian and Western conditions.

8. Heightening of Conflict and Competition. In urban life we find great deal of conflict and competition. With rise in the mechanical nature of urban life and its artificiality the mental conflicts are also on the rise. In the gaudy life of the cities a man is beset with so many desires some of which are at variance that it is small wonder that neuroses are so common in the cities. As a consequence of conflicting desires the life is full of discontent and sorrow. That is why we find abundance of psychiatrists and mental consultants in cities.

Besides social and mental conflicts there is also competition in the economic life. Everywhere we find cut-throat competition. As the needs of city-dwellers are enormous in comparison to those of the villagers, every city-dweller pursues money with a vengeance. This gives rise to no-holds-barred competition.

9. Rapidity in the Formation of Association. Another special feature of city life is the abundance of voluntary associations and the speed with which these spring up. In cities we find diversity of self interests, aptitudes, aspirations, aims and purposes. In order to meet this diversity a large variety of associations are covered by the following classification, this is fairly representative:

(1) Professional Associations. The examples of these are the associations of medicos, lawyers, teachers etc.

(2) Religious Associations. Such as Arya Samaj, Brahmo Samaj, Moral Re-armament Association, Radha Swami Sangh, Divine Life Society etc.

(3) Political Associations. The examples of these are B.J.P., Congress, Communist Party of Indias etc.

(4) Entertainment Societies. Such as Hotels, Cricket Clubs, Alexander Club, Indian Gymkhana Association etc.

(5) Spiritual Societies. Such as Ram Krishna Mission, Ruhani Satsang etc.

(6) Art Societies. Such as Kala Kendra, Lalitkala Academy etc.

(7) Welfare Societies. As Sewa Dal, Sarvodya etc.

(8) Brotherhood Societies. As Kayastha Sabha, Khukhran Biradari, Brahmin Mandali etc.

(9) Anti-Social Organizations. Gang of pick pockets etc.

As a consequence of participation in various groups and associations there is wholesome growth in the personality of city-dwellers. Sometimes people can be seen participating in groups having opposite characters. This reflects neurotic strain in their personalities. However, excepting anti-social groups all other groups are more or less, complementary to each other. All these things make the urban life diverse and colourful.

QUESTIONS FOR EXERCISE

1. Determine the influence of urban development and urbanization upon the social change in Indian Society.
2. Discuss social control in urban society.

10

Urban Politics

Some of the peculiarities of social life in an urban society are seen reflected in its political life. Like the social life in a city, the urban political life is also dynamic, conflict-ridden and full of intricacies. Broadly, the urban political life has two aspects: on the one hand, there is an administrator appointed by the state government and, on the other, there is municipal committee or corporation consisting of the elected representatives of the people. Every District headquarter has a District Magistrate who is the top most government official. This official, the D.M., is responsible for law and order in the district. Besides District Magistrate, Additional District Magistrate, City Magistrate, and a number of top police officials there are numerous police Sub-inspectors who are responsible for the law and order situation in their respective wards. There are many circles in a city and each circle has a Circle Inspector and some Sub-inspectors. Under a Sub-inspector there are numerous head constables and constables etc. Besides Station Officers who are chief police officials or Kotwals, there are Deputy Superintendents and Superintendents of police. A Commissionary is under a D.I.G. In most cities there is a Probation Officer who looks after delinquents and Juvenile Criminals. In big cities there are Criminal Investigation Departments. Besides all these officials there is a municipal board in each city. In municipal boards or corporations there are elected representatives who are elected on the basis of adult franchise. These elected representatives fight elections on behalf of their respective political parties. There are also some independent members who are not affiliated to any particular political party. These elected representatives known as city fathers look after hygiene, education, water, electricity, medical and cultural departments. For each department there is a committee of municipal members. Now-a days municipal boards are assisted by one Town Planning Officer.

From the above description it is clear that city administration is under the control of dual authority: on the one hand, there are government officials and, on the other hand, there are elected representatives of the people. Sometimes this dual authority comes into conflict. The municipal elections are fought on the basis of political parties and each political party wishes to control the municipal board. If the control of a Municipal Board goes into the hands of opposition party, the chances of conflict are high. Moreover, now-a-days elections have become very costly. Each candidate has to invest a lot of money for his election. It is natural that he should try to make good the money spent by him on elections. This means that as a member of municipality he must take recourse to corrupt practices.

The excessive expenditure during elections is an evil which keeps multiplying and producing uncontrollable corruption. Some city fathers are not the men inspired by the love of welfare of others. They are shrewd businessmen who calculate profit and loss and act accordingly. They manipulate and manoeuvre to get big contracts for their cronies and receive regular commission from them. An associated evil practice is the practice of casteism.

The urban politics has become a profession. It is no longer a service. Everyone wants to make profit by hook or crook. Politics of today is a business where operations work strictly according to the law of profit and loss. All evil practices have corrupted modern urban politics.

However, the picture is not altogether gloomy. As the functioning of municipal boards is under the authority of various official agencies there cannot be unfettered freedom of practice of corruption. Wherever matters deteriorate beyond a certain limit, the state government dissolves the municipal board. Therefore municipal boards try to maintain certain decorum and decency and also carry out faithfully the plans before them. Besides, the city fathers have first hand knowledge of the problems of their towns and are, therefore, able to do some genuine good and public service. For example, they may erect new water tanks, improve roads and make the living conditions of mohallas hygienic. Sometimes municipalities are lucky to have the service of some dedicated individuals and they are able to deliver genuine goods to the people.

In conclusion we can say that while it is quite true that urban politics now-a-days is beset with many evils and that influence of black money and casteism has extremely corrupting influence, there is a silver lining in the cloud. There are still some people who are inspired by the love of humanity and service to mankind and they do once in a while get elected to municipal boards. These persons do geniune good. Besides, the ultimate authority of the state government also functions as a check on whole-sale corruption.

City government is a minor form of national administration and it aims at bringing decency and order into the urban social life. It plans the structure of the city and favourable location of its functions. It looks after the executive administration of the city. It fixes land values and the norms governing zoning and construction of different varieties of buildings. It lays down and enforces the norms of city culture and traffic regulation. It is usually a body of elected representatives who represent different areas in a city proportionate to the city population. It derives its main income from federal grants and local taxes. It maintains its own police force and is supposed to keep control over the spread of vice and social disorganisation within the city. Today, city governments are playing a prominent part in slum clearance and urban renewal.

Although a common problem of all contemporary societies, rapid urbanization becomes more acute in a relatively less planned and unorganized country like India, it becomes a problem beyond a limit since the city at that stage becomes incapable of providing for the minimal products and services essential for a health and happy life of the urban dweller. Thus the problem of rapid urban growth is in reality a problem of improper planning and unbalanced development of the city. The problems created by rapid urban growth are immediate and are in the nature of affecting the day to-day life of the urban community. Hence they require immediate attention and handy solution. Some of them which are increasingly experienced by many of our cities especially the metropolises like Bombay, Madras, Bangalore, etc., include congestion, shortfall in the provision of essential services like water supply, housing, educational and medical facilities, public transportation etc., noise pollution and to some extent air and water pollution, growth of slums and consequent vices etc. It is a patent fact that services will not grow in population to proportion since they are products of man's creation.

The concept of a city government and city planning are novel to India. The city governments in contemporary India are modelled on the federal government structure and consist of a mayor and elected councillors representing, different areas of a city. A bureaucratic structure with technical experts looks after the day today administration. The city government has upon it the task of city planning as well as provision of essential services. City planning in relation to many of our cities refers to the amelioration of existing anomalies of urban growth.

Hence it becomes difficult to the city government to comprehend all the aspects of the existing, structure and possible future growth of a city and bring an order in the existing pell-mell of our cities. For example, one cannot forcibly remove a soap factory or a cotton mill like the Binny Mills of Bangalore from its existing location because of the inevitability of locating a housing suburb in the nearby area. Further, rapid urban growth causes constant law and order problems.

Thus, there is a paucity of technical experts and experienced city planners who can clearly assess and plan the future development of a city. Political factor also plays its own role in effective city planning.

PROBLEMS OF CITY GOVERNMENT

However, the immediate problems before our city government are provision of efficient and well balanced necessary services and intelligent location of various functions like business, housing etc., in proper areas and intelligent planning of future city growth. They may be called social.

1. Housing. The major problem that our city governments are confronted with today is housing. The basic requirement here is to provide well planned and compact independent houses with allowance for sufficient air and light, to all its dwellers according to their capacity. The city government can solve this problem by the construction of model houses of different sizes and shapes in various localities at all available vacant spots in the existing suburbs and by construction of new and well planned suburb at a not too distant place from the city centre with the provision of a retail shopping complex. Another novel ideal is to build multi-storeyed houses whereby houses in each storey are given to separate inhabitants. Many city governments are today asking, industrial establishments and commercial concerns like L.I.C. to build their own houses at reasonable cost for their employees. More than this the vital thing is the provision of poor and low income housing at selected spots at subsidized rates. Another problem connected with housing is congestion. The private owners build uninhabitable dwellings in a growing city with a commercial motive. The city government can put a check to this trend through its licencing system by which proper conditions for house building like distance from road, the area of a house, etc. may be laid down as prerequisites. Closely connected with this is the problem of water supply. This can be solved by laying down pipelines and tapping additional sources of water supply like digging of wells etc.

2. Transport. Another problem is the provision of efficient public transportation which forms the average man's means of commuting. This requires a proper calculation of the proportional requirement in relation to the existing population. This further requires the regular assessment of total population, the population of a suburb or its existing number of commuters and possible increases in this number etc.

3. Zoning. More than all this basic requirement of a city is proper zoning. This requires a careful calculation of the available space for particular activity, the existing number of units of that activity, the demand for them, the capacity of the area to support future expansion etc. On the basis of all these calculations the city planning must set limits for the future incursion of these functions on the available space. He has to find alternative location for existing surplus units without affecting healthy zoning pattern. Provision for different activities should be made in 2 calculated proportion, for example, there should be a school near 200-300 houses. Proper zoning also involves the transfer of existing units of a different activity, for example, factory near a subsurb should be transferred to its proper location at the outskirts as far as possible.

4. Provision of Commodities. Another crucial form of rapid urban growth is the provision of essential commodities to all citizens and maintaining a reasonable price level. This again involves a problem of calculation in relation to population and necessary imports and setting up of a proper distribution network through fair price shops throughout the length and breadth of the city.

5. Unemployment. A crucial problem of rapid urban growth is large scale urban unemployment. This results from a lack of proper manpower planning and haphazard influx of unskilled labour into our cities. Educated unemployment results from the lack of a functional educational system. The city government can tackle this problem by taking up massive city improvement works like road construction and repair, construction of new suburbs, etc. Educational unemployment can be solved by encouraging migration of the talented persons to the place of demand of their skills. This problem can also be solved by encouraging small scale ancillary industries for production of necessary products like soap and toilet articles in a planned manner after calculation of city's needs. Above all, this problem can be permanently solved only by future intelligent manpower planning.

6. Functional growth. A factor contributing to rapid urban growth is the haphazard flocking of various functions like commercial activities, industries, etc., to a common centre of attraction in excess of need with harmful consequences both to themselves and to the community. To solve this problem the city governments must look for areas in the nearby villages or towns or areas of relative scarcity of that product or service in the vicinity and force some units to shift to those areas by providing incentives and subsidies. In fact, the city government can follow this procedure in respect of excessive and ill-placed units of all functions if alternative space is available. The best thing is the development of satellite towns at an area of comprehensible distance from a city with provision of all essential services and shifting of the units there.

7. Diseases. Another problem of rapid urban growth is the increase in mental and physical diseases like nervous tensions and infectious diseases. The provision of sufficient preventive and curative medical services can solve this problem to some extent.

8 Traffic. The daily problem exposing the consequences of rapid urban growth is the constant traffic jam and traffic accidents in our cities. This can be minimised by the conversion of routes with heavy traffic into those of one way traffic and diversion of heavy traffic to alternative routes of less congestion and proper enforcement of traffic laws.

9. Expansion. A problem of rapid urban growth is the checking up of future urban expansion. This requires a careful appraisal of the city needs and capacity and allowing the migration of only the needed units and people. The city government can solve the law and order problems by maintenance of an efficient and well equipped police force.

Thus, the problems of rapid urban growth arise out of the haphazard influx of functions in excess of necessities and relative inability of essential services to expand in proportion. These may be solved by planning by the city government.

QUESTIONS FOR EXERCISE

1. Write short note on Dual Government.
2. Write short note on-City Government.
3. Explain the role of city government in solving the problems of rapid urban growth in India.

11

Industrialization and the City

To day as we hear the words "industry" or "industrial system" or just think of them, we automatically recall to our minds a picture of huge mill or factory fitted with giant machines, electrically and power operated, covering vast tract of land, having wide and huge expanse of buildings and employing hundreds of men. We also associate with it roar and rattling of machines, sky-high chimneys emitting thick clouds of smoke. However, even prior to the development of modern sophisticated industry, man was industrious. He was engaged in some industry, however, crude and underdeveloped that may have been in comparison to modern industry. We define man as a rational animal: but we may equally define him with full justification as an industrious animal. Thus, we find that the history of industry is as long as the history of man; they are co-eval. With the advancement of civilisation, man has advanced industrialization. For the sake of convenience, we can divide the history of industrial development into three periods: Ancient Industry, Medieval Industry and modern Industry. This division is done with a view to chronology and development.

HISTORICAL REVIEW

Ancient Period

In the ancient or primitive period of industry are included those works which were performed by man when he was neither literate nor civilised. In this period no systematic industry had developed. The main concern of man during these days was merely to provide for food and physical protection. The means which were adopted by him to meet these ends were symbolic of his industrial effort. For food the primitive man used to hunt animals and gather wild vegetables and fruits. For hunting he employed bow and arrow and certain instruments made by sharpening stone. These weapons were symbols of industrial development of that period. Besides, making fire by friction of stone or bamboos was industrial miracle of that time. For a pretty long time this state of affairs persisted.

Medieval Period

In medieval period there was sufficient development in industry. In this period the signs of industry became quite visible in the efforts of man. A number of manually operated machines were fabricated. Man also began using animal power to meet his ends. The signs of industrialisation, production of goods in excess of consumption and stocking of these, came in evidence at this time. The exchange of goods and division of labour also came into vogue. As a consequence of this, different industries started operating separately. For example, blacksmith, carpenter and weaver set up independent units. Thus began the specialization of jobs. The artistic spirit of the artisans was awakened.

The medieval industrial age in the West can be divided into three distinct industrial systems. The division is based on the nature of the industrial system. These three industrial systems are :

(1) Feudal system

(2) Guild system

(3) Domestic system

(1) Feudal System. Under this system, the primary industry was agriculture. Few persons controlled vast tract of land each and they engaged and employed hundreds of workers to do the farming. This system was in vogue in Europe between 9th and 12th century. Under this system the owner of the land was called feudal lord and persons engaged by him were called serfs. The serfs were virtual slaves of the feudal lord. Besides agriculture, other important professions were those of carpentry, black-smithy, pottery and weaving. Even these artisans were dependent upon feudal lords.

Under the feudal system, the serfs were required to give all kinds of services to their respective lords. In case required, they had to wage war against the enemies of their lord.

From 11th century onward, urban towns started coming up in Europe. With urbanization feudal system got a set-back. The labour or the working class now had an alternative to working as serfs. They could migrate to towns and find work there. As a result of urbanization, Guild system came into vogue.

(2) Guild System. The urbanization in Europe emancipated the serfs from their traditional slavery. Having emancipated themselves from serfdom under feudal lords, the worker started learning new trades and skills. As a result of specialization and proficiency in trades acquired by workers, centres of trade came up. Gradually, this process gave rise to Guild system.

In Guild system, trade associations representing various trades came into being. These trade associations worked for the promotion and development of their respective trades. These associations supervised the quality and quantity of goods being produced by the members of their association. They also fixed and regulated the prices of goods. Various kinds of relations are obtained among the members of a guild. They were related besides economic relations, by social, political and religious relations.

Under Guild system there used to be two kinds of guilds; the Merchant Guilds and Craft Guilds. The main task of the Merchant Guilds was to look after the interests of businessmen. They used to demand justice from government in a manner in which Chambers of Commerce of today function. The Craft Guilds were associations formed by craftsmen carrying on a particular craft. The craft guilds worked for the promotion of the crafts and protection of the interests of craftsmen. In craft guilds used to arrange weekly markets where craftsmen could sell their products. In craft guilds, master craftsmen played crucial role, though less skilful craftsmen were also given due share. They were helped to acquire proficiency in their skill. The master craftsmen used to belong to families of master craftsmen. The craftsmanship was supposed to be hereditary. In these days the craft guilds of blacksmiths, carpenters and weavers were particularly prominent.

The guild system occupies a place of pride in the history of Industrial development. This system was important in maintaining social harmony and unity. Remarking about the merits of this system Raj, K. Kohli says, "The builders of the great cathedrals of Europe (at that period) had achieved a unity of feeling and thought which the modern world has apparently lost."

Decline of Guilds

The guild system lasted for a pretty long time, but gradually it declined. From 16th Century there was a gradual decline and deterioration in this system. There were two chief causes for the decline of this system. The first cause was internal and the second was external.

The first internal cause of the decline of the guild system was that its functions and the rights of its officials were not well-defined. This gave rise to myriad conflicts. For example, the guild of goldsmiths was always warring with the guild of silversmiths. Moreover, there was gradual fragmentation of the guilds. Originally, there was only one guild of cloth merchants. But soon many sub-guilds like association of weavers, tailors, embroiderers etc. were formed.

The second cause of the decline of the guild system was external. Under this system there was one group of traders who were manufacturers and the other was that of middle men. This group of middle men later began exploitation of the manufacturers. It acted in the manner and style of modern capitalist. The middle men took over the control of all levels of production and arbitrarily used them for their own selfish ends. Generally, they took over the control of raw material. The arbitrary acts of these middle men gave severe set-back to the guild system.

Besides these two reasons, there were certain local and immediate causes of this decline. At this time America was discovered. The way to commerce was deeply affected. In the production and demand of goods there was sudden upward surge. During these days a religious factor also contributed its share in the decline of guilds. The protestant sect of Christianity had greater dominance at this juncture. The rise of protestant religion spelt the rise of individualism and this, too, proved inimical to guild system which was based on a sense of cooperation. In these days another factor which gave death blow to guild system was the invention and use of big machines and introduction of sophisticated techniques of production.

(3) Domestic System. After the decline of guild system, domestic system came into vogue. This system was a kind of capitalism. As far as the method of production was concerned, it was not much different from that of guild system. However, under domestic system there was no place and no role for various guilds and trade associations. Under domestic system a head of family who normally was a master craftsman controlled the entire production and everything was under his personal ownership. The head of the family used to provide for the raw material and also the manufactured goods. All processes of stages of production were under his individual control and supervision. Under this system the craftsman had not much freedom. The system is to be seen today in the form of cottage industries.

It was again the role of middle men and the money-lender which ruined the domestic system. The head of a trade in domestic system required from time to time extra funds for the purchase of the raw material. The extra amount came from the money-lender and he usually exploited the opportunity to the fullest. Besides, mechanization of industry rendered this system obsolete and revolution in industry and mechanizing it to the hilt, completely ruined the domestic system. Thus the domestic system came to an end and modern industry came into being.

Modern Period

A gradual rise in the population pushed up the demand for industrial goods. With the rise in demand for the goods, more and more machines were used and in place of cottage industries, factories employing hundreds of workers sprang up. With the establishment of factory system, industrial revolution became inevitable. Under the factory system there was considerable rise in the production and goods were sold at places far off from the place of manufacture.

For the introduction of factory system certain basic conditions had to be met. These were:

(1) An industry could be established only at a place where the raw material was easily available. Besides, workers should also be easily available and must be residing at nearby places.

(2) In a factory, man and animal power are to be replaced as far as possible by machines. This process was greatly accelerated by the invention of hydraulic machines. The successful application of mechanical power helped immensely to improve the quality and increase the production of goods.

(3) The factory system requires huge investment of capital in the form of

money. With the help of money power the capitalist is able to provide for raw materials, workers and machinery. In this manner the capitalist is able to raise production greatly. In factory system, besides production, the needs and requirements of consumers have also to be borne in mind.

Modern Industry and Individualism

As a result of industrialization the individualistic outlook on life became predominant. The capitalism grew fast in power and competence. The ideal of life became the maximization of the abilities, capacities and power of the individual. In contrast to individualism of industrial period, society and collective unit occupied the place of pride in the guild system as well as in the times of feudalism. As a result of the growth of individualism the entire trade and business came to be controlled by private individuals and foreign intervention in the form of social or government control was unthinkable. Now the individual had the right to buy and sell property. The credit system also came into vogue. Under these conditions wealth was concentrated in a few hands.

SOCIAL CONSEQUENCES OF INDUSTRIALIZATION

The industrialization had deep impact on society. The industrialization split the whole of the society into two fragments: the capitalists and the workers. As a result of industrialization the process of urbanization was greatly accelerated and the means of living were raised from economic as well as social points of view. More interest was shown in education, arts and science. There was political awakening and the society began to be democratized. Thus the process of industrialization had deep impact upon all aspects of society.

Impact on Relationships

The interweaving of human relations results in society. The human relations are determined by human attitudes. The pattern of human relations and the nature of civilization and culture mutually determine each other. The pattern of human relations in an agricultural society is quite different from that of the industrial society. The measure of social relation in the primitive society is widely different. In short, the structure of society is determined by the trade and profession of the society and the attitudes of the members towards these. The social relations found in modern industrial society are very complex and intricate compared to the simple and straightforward social relations found in ancient societies. The industrialization has affected the society in every respect. The customs and traditions, the fashions and manners, the ways and modes of living all have been deeply influenced by industrialization. The processes of industrialization are intimately related with scientific processes. Therefore, the attitude of the members of industrial society become scientific. In an Industrial society the superstitions and blind faith have no place. People expect and demand rational explanation of every phenomenon. The reason and not faith is the touchstone of every action and belief in the industrial society. The freedom of thought and individualism are the cornerstones of the industrial society. The methods and means of social control have changed. The ancient institutions of marriage and family have also changed. The old values and rules pertaining to religion and morals are undergoing radical changes. The new patterns of social stratification are being established. The caste system is being replaced by class system. Even the means of recreation and entertainment are undergoing change in industrial urban society. Thus, it is apparent that industrialization has influenced every aspect of society. It is not quite easy to judge if this impact is good or bad but it is possible to study the consequences flowing from industrialization. The following discussion is an attempt to make an in-depth study of the impact of industrialization upon various aspects of society.

Impact Upon Marriage

The institutions of marriage and family are to be found in every society. With the changes in the structure of society these institutions also undergo changes. Traditionally the Indian society has recognized marriage to be a sacred and religious institution but in the modern industrial society it has been reduced to a contract. In the past, marriage was considered to be permanent and inalienable bond which could not be terminated at will. But now, under the impact of industrialization, divorce and marriage go side-by-side. Now it is not considered an evil to terminate the contentious and miserable marriages. The following discussion will make explicit the impact of industrialization upon marriage —

(1) Marriage is a Social Contract. Prior to heavy industrialization in India, marriage in this country was considered to be a religious and sacred institution. It was commonly believed by Hindus that marriage was necessary for emancipation or salvation and that any one who did not marry could not find salvation in this life. Besides, marriage was regarded to be a permanent bond. Marriages were supposed to be settled in heaven and only God could severe a marital bond. But with the advance of industrialization these beliefs are considered superstitious and anyone holding them is frowned upon. Today marriage is regarded to be only a social contract between a man and a woman. The aim of marriage in modern times has ceased to be spiritual and now its aims are economic, social and biological only.

(2) Higher Age of Marriage. In Indian society only a few decades back parents used to marry their children at very early age. Child-marriages were quite common. But with industrialization the age of marriage is advancing; it is getting higher and higher. In metropolitan towns of India today boys and girls are generally marrying at the ages of 25 to 35.

(3) Practice of Non-marrying. As we have referred to above the aim of marriage in India is no longer spiritual: the marital bond is no longer looked upon as sacred or inviolable. As a consequence of rejection of the traditional beliefs and attitudes many young men and women in big towns prefer to live single. According to the thinking and beliefs of these young persons the major need filled by marriage is biological and this can be easily satisfied out of wedlock.

(4) Practice of Love Marriages. In Industrial Society men and women usually work together. In mills, factories, offices and other places men and women work together. Under these circumstances they get a chance of coming together, meeting and exchanging ideas and opinions. As a result of this human conourse individuals become intimate and this intimacy becomes love which untimately blossoms in marriage.

(5) Increase in Divorce. The industrial society is becoming more and more complex every day. The philosophy of individualism is flourishing in society. Even husband and wife have different outlook and attitude. Both of them as a rule work in separate social spheres. As a result of this, marital bonds are from time to time lent by discord. The mental conflict increases and the situation of divorce develops. In all industrial societies today there is legal sanction for divorce.

Impact Upon Family

The foregoing discussion makes plain the influence of industrialization upon marriage. Besides affecting the institution of marriage, industrialization produces effects upon the institution of family. Following are some of the important effects of industrialization upon family:

(1) Difference Regarding Functions of Family. As a result of industrialization the functions of family have changed considerably. Compared to today the family had much more functions in the past. Now a number of functions which used to be performed by families in the past have been taken over by other institutions. Traditionally an Indian family used to be a centre of birth, rearing and education of children. The children used to get training in the ancestral professions. The function of socialization of children too, used to be performed by the family. But in the industrialized society of today the family is not required to fulfil these roles. Today children are born in hospitals. Even for the nurture of the children there are today a number of official and nonofficial institutions. In big towns we find today a number of Infant-Care Centres and Children Homes. The education of children today is done in schools and not in homes. The professional training also is no longer the obligation of the family. What is even more, even feeding is no longer the exclusive obligation of the family. Many people in metropolises eat out of homes. In almost all big cities people rarely take lunch at home except on Sundays and holidays. In many families both husband and wife go out for work. In these circumstances the functions of a modern family are more formal than real.

(2) Breaking up of Joint Family. Traditionally most of the Indian families, were joint families. As a result of industrialization most of these joint families are breaking up and are being replaced by nuclear families. There are a number of reasons for this. Firstly, in industrial towns there is acute shortage of residential accommodation. Most of the people have to content themselves with a single or two room accommodation. In these circumstances it is physically exceedingly difficult if not impossible to retain the joint family system. Secondly. as a sequel to industrialization, family trades and professions have been eliminated. The sons of the same parents differ widely in respect of economic and social levels. This has given rise to individualism. As a result of all these conditions joint family is all but finished in industrial towns.

(3) Small Families. As a result of industrialization the cost of living has gone up. At the same time the standard of living has also gone up considerably. Every body wants good clothes, houses and other comforts of life. Obviously, it is not possible to maintain the standard with a big family. Therefore, people these days want to keep small families. The prevalence of contraceptives and abortions has made this goal easily attainable. Thus, we find that there is a strong trend towards small families in industrialized towns.

(4) Change in the Status of Women. In past the status enjoyed by women in Indian society was rather low. Women were shut up in the fourwalls of the home. From economic and social points of view woman was subject to man. The woman enjoyed no independence. Without husband the condition of a woman was miserable. As a result of industrialization there has been much improvement in the status of women. Along with men, women today work in all walks of life. They are, therefore, becoming independent economically. Their status and respect in society has, therefore, improved considerably. Now-a-days women consider themselves equal, even superior to men. As a result of this feeling, many women today do not like to marry. They wish to assert their independence by defying the laws of the society.

(5) Disintegration of Family. As a result of industrialization the outlook of intense individualism has grown. Everyone wants to have his own way; no one likes to be subject to any body. No body these days appreciates the need for adjustment and give and take. Thus, we find in modern society families cracking up under least strain. There is continuous tension and conflict in the minds of family members. As a consequence of this situation it is small wonder that families are breaking up fast in urban society.

(6) Difference in Family Goals. The goals and ideals which nourished the traditional Indian family were spiritual and religious. The housewives used to regard their husbands as gods or divine beings. They willingly subjected themselves to each and every whim of their husbands. Even children used to give unqualified respect to their parents. The father was regarded to be the head of the family and his command was rarely defiled. In Indian homes Ram and Sita were ideals of paternal devotion and wife's dedication to husband respectively. In industrial society there is no room for such ideals. For a modern wife the husband can be at best an honourable colleague and, under no circumstance, a god. The status of father in a family is being lowered as a result of industrialization. Compared to parents, children now have more say in the family affairs. In the past, functions which were regarded sacred duties and ideals are now considered acceptable only from utilitarian point of view. The father no longer holds sway over family members.

Impact on Social Stratification

From times immemorial human society has been riddled with inequalities and discriminations. From the very beginning of civilization we find some or other form of hierarchy in society. The society has always been divided into various classes having different rights and privileges and each enjoying a unique distinction and status in society. The classification and stratification in society have always been governed by some definite principles. As a matter of fact neither all persons in a society are equal nor are the various functions in society of equal value. Therefore, in order to maintain some system and order in society it is necessary to establish a hierarchy of functions in society. In different societies the principle behind the hierarchical arrangement of functions is different. In some societies the distinction between classes is based on the relationship of master and slave while in others it is based upon the idea of high, low and middle classes. Still in some other societies the governing principle of this distinction is caste system. In the modern industrial society the classification and stratification of society is based upon the concept of economic classes. The society today is divided into the classes of capitalists and labour.

As referred to above the basis of distinctions between classes in society is different in different countries and at different times. The basis is sometimes biologic, sometimes historic and sometimes religious. As a matter of fact in the stratification of any society are reflected its values and ideals. In a religious society the gurus and godmen enjoy a place of pride. In a martial society warriors and conquerors occupy top positions. On the other hand, in a capitalist society the wealthy persons are on top. In some industrialized societies like Japanese the technocrats occupy privileged positions. Thus, it is apparent that in different societies the basis of distinction among classes is different.

In industrial societies there is a unique kind of social stratification. In industrial society the different strata of society are known as social classes. The basis of stratification in an industrial society is different from that of other societies. Generally, social stratification in an industrial society occurs on the following four-fold bases:

(1) Occupation

(2) Education

(3) Income

(4) Birth.

Now we shall study these in a little detail

(1) Occupation. In industrial societies the main basis of social stratification is occupation. In these societies the status and prestige of an individual is determined by the position and rank he occupies, the nature of his profession and his rank and status in that profession. What is meant is that rank and status are of crucial importance in industrial society. Indeed in an industrial society rank and occupation are indicative of one's ability. The rank and status and occupation are not hereditary. In industrial society one has to strive and struggle for these. In a society where caste system is prevalent the occupations and professions are hereditary. The son of a Brahmin does the job of a Brahmin and enjoys the same status and respect in society as were being enjoyed by his father. The son of a Brahmin becomes automatically entitled to the respect and status of his father. On the contrary in an industrial society the son of a manager cannot claim the post of a manager after the retirement of his father. He must possess all the necessary qualifications for it, that is, he must earn the managership. In order to gain status in an industrial society one has to strive hard. In an industrial society there is no value for heredity but one has to strive for status.

(2) Education. In an industrial society education is an important determinant of the status of a person. The better educated are regarded more highly than the less educated. Of course in every society the poets, writers and learned have got top rank and status. However, in industrial society there is some difference in this regard from other societies. The industry has closer relation to science and technology than formal learning. This is why a person who is highly learned is not regarded so well as a person who is proficient in science and technology. In an industrial society it is not literary learning but the scientific learning that commands respect. As a consequence of industrialization the importance and value of subjects like philosophy and literature has gone down. The formal learning has been replaced by utilitarian subject. The predominant outlook in education today is pragmatic. Naturally, training in science and technology is conducive to industrial advance. It is applied science that is responsible for industrialization. On account of the utilitarian nature of science and technology, the scientists and technologists enjoy places of prestige in industrial society.

(3) Income. Now-a-days in industrial societies the measuring rod of one's social status is one's income; the higher one's income the higher one's social status. In materialistic societies one's material possessions are indeed the exclusive determiner of one's worth in the society. The rich are worshipped and poor are hated. According to the materialistic outlook, the possession of material comforts and luxuries is the paramount aim of life and the more one's material possessions the nearer is one to the *summum bonum* of life. For acquisition of material comforts money is needed. Therefore, a person's income or salary determines his status in the society.

There is another reason also for regarding money and wealth as criterion of social status. In the industrial societies the various types of qualifications are needed for earning money; without these qualifications it is not possible to earn wealth. A man must be laborious and hardworking in order to earn a lot of money. It is natural in this background that one's wealth should be regarded as a measure of one's abilities and qualifications. It is but natural to accord high status to a man of ability. Thus, from both points of view money and income are the determiner of one's social status.

(4) Birth. In the determination of social status one's birth and pedigree have always been kept in view. In different societies the family into which one is born has been regarded important in various ways. In the caste based societies the son of Brahmin was accorded the status of Brahmin without the slightest consideration of his actual merit. In feudal societies the family had great importance in determining one's social status. In industrial society, too, the family has unique importance in determining the social status of a person. However, the reasons for the importance of family in social stratification, in industrial society are not the same as in caste-based or feudal society. In an industrial society it is recognized that in order to develop or flower one's talent the family plays an important role. A successful manager technocrat need special opportunities of training etc. Only those families which can provide such facilities produce successful persons in industrial societies. A man born in a high class family naturally gets more opportunities of development than a person who is less fortunate in this respect. In socialization the family plays an important role. Thus, from the above discussion the role of family becomes apparent.

Impact on Caste System

In Indian society the caste system has had a unique role and importance. The social status of a person was determined by his caste The industrialisation has diminished the role of caste. Following are the salient features of the impact of industrialization upon Indian caste system:

(1) Disintegration of Caste-system. The industrialization has led to breakdown of caste-system. Under the impact of industrialisation the traditional caste-based structure of society is collapsing. Traditionally, the social status of a person in Indian society was determined by the caste into which he was born. As a result of industrialization the caste-based criterion of social classification has changed. In the industrial society it is the class and not the caste which fixes the social status of a person. Now the society is divided into classes. Man gets social status according to his class. Thus the caste system is now disintegrating.

(2) Reduction in Brahmin's Influence and Power. In the traditional social structure the Brahmin enjoyed the highest status in the society. But as a result of industrialization the influence of Brahmins is on wane, it is gradually losing its traditional hold on Indian society. Now there are other criteria of social stratification. It is no longer necessary that one should be a Brahmin in order to attain high social status. As a matter of fact the traditional role of Bramins in society is all but finished. Those who are unable to adapt themselves according to the changed circumstances have only a parasitic existence in modern industrialized society. That is why a Brahmin to day is looked down upon.

(3) Rise of Shudra. In the traditional Indian society a *Shudra* enjoyed the most inferior status in society. Indeed his plight was miserable and he was treated no better than a slave. The shudras were subjected to all kinds of calumny and obloquy. They enjoyed little respect in society. As a result of industrialization there is some improvement in the condition of shudras. In the industrial society the criterion of social status is work and not birth. Anyone proficient in industrial know-how is bound to get a place of pride in society irrespective of the fact that he is a Brahmin or a shudra. Today a number of persons born into shudra family are occupying high-ranking positions in society.

(4) Abolition of Caste-based functions. In the traditional caste-based society each caste had some functions. Generally, the entertainment was also caste based. The Brahmin had the role of teacher, the Kshatriya that of warrior. Now all this has changed. It is no longer obligatory upon a shudra to do menial jobs for upper castes. Due to these changes the traditional functions of the castes stand abolished.

(5) Division of Labour Now Proficiency-Oriented. Under the caste system the division of labour was based upon caste and upon the consideration of efficiency. A Brahmin was to perform the function of learned even if he was poor in learning. Under the influence of industrialization the criterion of division of labour has changed. The industrialization has encouraged specialization. Now-a-days a person is not given a task unless he is specially trained for it. In every department of society a specialized training is needed for the successful performance of a job. The Shudras are today doing the teaching jobs. On the other hand, Brahmins can be seen doing the manual jobs. A proficient Shudra can now easily attain the position of an industrial manager and a number of Brahmins may by working under him.

(6) End of Control of Castes. In traditional society the caste system was an effective instrument of social control. Each caste had its own code of conduct which was strictly adhered to and any violation thereof attracted strong social reprobation. The violation of caste-based code of conduct used to result in excommunication. In modern industrial society the control of caste has become loose and lax. The industrial society is highly intricate and complex. Now-a-days persons of all castes work together and it is, therefore, well-nigh impossible to observe the separate caste-based codes of conduct. In modern industrial societies the instruments of effective social control are provided by law and law enforcing agencies.

(7) Hold of Untouchability Loosening. Under the caste system there used to be no intercaste social mixing. The persons belonging to different castes did not get together and share a common board. As far as shudra was concerned he could not even sit, stand or walk near the person of upper castes. A shadow of a shudra was scrupulously avoided. On the other hand, there are cases where shudras themselves did not welcome the opportunity of being in the company of a Brahmin. They forbade Brahmin from entering their quarters. As a result of industrialization the spectre of untouchability is relaxing its grip upon the thought and imagination of people. Today members of all castes work together in mills and factories and eat food stuff from the same canteens and tusk-shops. Many a waiter in restaurants are *Shudras*. Even Brahmins willingly partake food prepared and served by these people. Besides, in parks and public places there are no restrictions on the entry of Shudra. Thus industrialization can be said to have come as a boon for the low castes.

(8) Prevalence of Inter-Caste Marriages. Under the caste system the inter caste marriages were a strict taboo. Hardly any one dared to defy this taboo and marry with a spouse of any other caste except one's own. The punishment for such marriages was nothing less then complete excommunication. In modern society these taboos are giving way. Though inter-caste marriages are not very common, people do marry into other caste without much disapproval. In mills and factories persons belonging to different castes come together, develop common interests and form friendships. Some of these contacts bloom and flower into mutual love and attraction. The mutual attraction breaks the caste barriers and such persons marry. There is another reason for the prevalence of inter-caste marriage. Due to frequent encounters with members of other communities one comes to realize the fundamental oneness of all human beings. One begins to appreciate that stereotyped thinking with regard to other castes is not valid. Thus the factors like caste pride and hatred for other castes which help accentuate caste barriers become inoperative. Thus there emerges a rational outlook. The factor of mutual regard and love comes to be considered the only relevant consideration in regard to marriage.

Impact on Religion

Industrialization has deeply influenced the course of religion. Following are some of the important features of this influence :

1. Decline of Orthodoxy and Superstitions. Under the garb of religion orthodoxy and superstitions flourish. As a matter of fact, the whole edifice of religion is built out of bricks of superstition and blind faith. Superstitions are due to ignorance. In practical life belief in superstitions and orthodoxy proves harmful. For material and Industrial progress it is very essential that men should be free from the clutches of superstitions. They must have rational and scientific outlook. The processes of industrialization help the spread and dissemination of science and practical knowledge. As a result of industrialization people learn the truth of physical reality. They begin to appreciate and value the practical results and are prepared to give up irrational beliefs. The knowledge disseminated and spread on account of industrialization subverts religious orthodoxy.

2. Development of Religious Tolerance. As a result of industrialization the outlook of general masses in respect of religion has become broad. Generally, orthodox religious persons are of narrow and parochial outlook. On account of their parochial outlook they regard their own religions as supreme and infallible. Their attitude towards other religions is that of contempt. As a consequence of industrialization the persons of different faiths come together and get an opportunity of knowing and understanding the truth about each other. This results in dispelling of wrong notions about other faiths and an appreciation of basic unity of all faiths. Therefore, as a result of industrialization there is development of religious tolerance.

3. Founding of Secular States. Previously, the states used to be theocratic each state subscribed to some or the other faith. Each nation had a national religion. The citizens professing faiths different from that of the state did not enjoy full rights and privileges : they were treated as second-rate citizens. But as a result of industrialization the concept of theocratic states has become obsolete. Due to industrialization every state now has a sizeable number of minorities whose claims cannot be ignored. Therefore, now-a-days it is a practice for almost all states not to consider any religion as special or state religion. The states today subscribe to the ideology of secularism, according to which state is neutral in matters of religion but accords equal status to all religions. This is secularism.

4. Social Aspect of Religion. Religion and religious functions have dual aspects. The first is its spiritual aspect and the second is its social aspect. In an industrial society the spiritual aspect of religion is not very important. Its social aspect, however, is quite important in industrial societies. Now-a-days, festivals are celebrated not so much as religious affairs but as social functions. Even going on pilgrimage today is more of a social necessity than a spiritual need. A visit to temple or mosque has come to assume social overtones.

Impact on Morals

Following are the ways in which industrialization has influenced morals:

1. Development of Rational Outlook. The Indian society has been traditionally based upon morality and religion. In India there has been little ciritical thinking in regard to moral principles and beliefs. The moral principles were accepted as universal truths beyond the sphere of doubt and reason. As a result of industrialization the outlook of common man has changed. Now people demand rational justification as to why a particular action is considered right or wrong. In industrial societies it is believed that moral principles are man-made and that morality is for the sake of human life and society and not vice versa. The tendency to examine and evaluate every moral principle before acquiescing to it is gaining ground in modern society.

2. Development of Materialistic Outlook. On account of industrialization the importance and value of physical progress and development has enhanced. An average citizen of today does not appear to be satisfied and contended. The maximum material acquisition seems to have become the aim of modern life. It is for this reason that a common man of today is averse to religion and spirituality. Today there is a strong competition for acquiring as much wealth as possible.

3. Individualism. The industrial societies are increasingly becoming complex and in all spheres of life there is a reign of specialisation. Due to industrialization large metropolises are coming up. In large communities there is a drop in fellow feeling. In such societies, therefore, the community feeling or the feeling of mutual belongingness is rather missing. The life becomes rapid and mechanical and people have little opportunity to look after the welfare of others. The life in industrial societies becomes self-centred. As a result of this there is growth and development of individualism in these societies.

4. Permissiveness in Sex Morals. As a result of industrialization the sexual mores have become lax. There are numerous reasons for this laxity. Firstly, the opportunities for the mixing-up of sexes have increased. Now-a-days boys and girls can meet without much difficulty and social opposition. In mills, factories and offices men and women work together. As a result of this frequent encounter of sexes there is laxity in sexual morals. Moreover, industrialization has given rise to materialistic thinking and according to the materialist outlook of life the traditional taboos on sex are harmful and free sex is consistent with healthy and sane life. This is why premarital sex is not considered to be criminal or immoral today. Indeed sex without marriage is coming to be considered quite normal, healthy and moral. In Western society all taboos on sex have broken down. A new highly permissive sex morality is the order of the day.

5. Increase in Crimes. As a result of industrialization there is an all round rise in the incidence of crimes. It is a common observation that the rate of crime is very high in industrial towns. In large metropolises family life is subject to many pressures. It is very difficult to have normal family life in those towns. On account of disintegration of family life the control of family over individuals is becoming lax. Due to absence of this control there is encouragement to crime. In every industrial town prostitution and liquor consumption are rampant. Besides, theft and dacoity also are commonplace things in industrial towns. The incidence of violence and murder is also high in industrial towns.

6. Loosening of Social Control. In industrial towns labourers and artisans from places far and wide come in search of jobs. Having found jobs, they settle in these towns. In industrial towns like Delhi, Kanpur, Bombay, Calcutta etc. workers from all over India are settled. As most of these workers are outsiders, they are not subject to usual social controls. Moreover, caste and clan considerations are almost non-existent in big metropolises. On account of all these factors the social control becomes loose and lax. In industrial towns it is neither the family nor caste and clan nor society in general that exercise social control. It is exercised by law and law enforcing agencies like police, courts etc.

Impact on Entertainment

The entertainment and relaxation are essential to life. Relaxation is indispensable for the health of every one. The means of relaxation and entertainment keep changing with time and circumstances. There is a big difference between the means of entertainment in pre-industrial and post-industrial societies. In India there has been significant change in means of entertainment as a result of industrialization. Following are the important influences upon entertainment due to industrialization:

1. Entertainment Outside Family. Traditionally, in India the family was the centre of entertainment. All entertainment was focussed upon family. Generally, all families used to be joint and therefore were very large. A single family used to have about a dozen adult members and a dozen children. On account of large families it was possible to find all kinds of entertainment within the family itself. The adult male members used to beguile themselves by playing cards or chess and females used to gossip, swing or sing. As there were very many children in every family the entertainment for children was easy. In the modern industrial societies the situation is just the opposite of the old state of affairs. The families today are not joint. The size of families has shrunk. A family today consists of husband and wife and their two or three children. Besides, in many families both husband and wife are employed. Under these circumstances there is no scope of entertainment within the family. Today almost everyone goes out for entertainment. The entertainment today has become institutionalized.

2. Professional Entertainment. In industrial societies the entertainment has become a business and a profession. Today there are a number of institutions of entertainment The cinemas clubs, dance and gambling dens are all centres of entertainment. We buy entertainment today. Throw money and have fun is the situation today.

3. Artificial Entertainment. Due to industrialization entertainment has become a business and profession. A professional entertainment, however, lacks the true spirit of entertainment. It is artificial and usually debases the man instead of relaxing him.

Besides, entertainment in industrial societies is not only artificial but is base and low also. Today classical music and dance are little appreciated. Moreover, these days entertainment by liquor and drugs is becoming common. In bigger towns prostitution is also a big source of entertainment. From all this it is apparent that the standard of entertainment has fallen steeply as a result of industrialization.

URBANIZATION AND RURAL LIFE

Urbanization concerns the movement of population from agricultural to industrial work and from rural to urban places of residence. People are attracted to the city by visions of a better life, or they feel compelled to leave rural places because they are disadvantaged there. For most urbanization migration, the attractions and compulsions are disadvantaged. For most such immigrants urbanization means a transition from one way of life to another. They become urbanised by going to where the urban way of life is.

Urbanisation through migration to urban centres is a global phenomenon. It is also centuries old and has always been more or less necessary to keep cities alive, since city populations are seldom able to reproduce themselves. They draw new inhabitants full-grown from their hinterlands. The modern city needs more than the migrant who is full grown and ready for work. Before he can be put to work he needs the kind of experience and training that can be used. Urbanization is not only cityward and toward industry migration, there is also the non-migration aspect of urbanisation. One can be urbanised by going to the city, but urbanisation can also come to him in a non-urban place. In this sense urbanism is outward reaching. People may be urbanised without migration to cities and without changing from agricultural to non-agricultural work.

The impact of urbanisation on rural life is not unimportant for sociological studies. The rural population is necessarily dependent on agriculture and allied occupations. But as a result of increased contact with urban centres, this means of livelihood is forsaken by many in the lure of better prospects in industry. There is general exodus from agriculture to industrial and semi-industrial centres. Also commercialisation of agriculture itself occurs. More and more cash crops are cultivated and the improved marketing facilities thrown open to the rural folk afford an opportunity to market agriculture products into the city. The increased demand for these products necessitates the introduction of specialization and sophisticated machinery, equipments etc. to face competing cultivators. Economically, there is increased production with a market in view. Due to the effects of urbanisation, "optimum" being the rule of the agriculturists.

The influx of urban commodities into the rural market is purely an exchange contract. The rural folk "aspect" the new products, be they food commodities or labour saving devices. The leisure time resulting in the use of such sophisticated gadgets helps diverse activities, commercialised in most cases.

Urbanisation necessarily involves the movement of a major population to urban centres. These migrants bring back with them new way of life, culture, way of thinking etc. These introduced influences or urbanism affect the majority of the rural population. The entire social structure of the rural community suffers a change. The old, traditional way of living based purely on kinship system, is shaken. Economic relations, neighbourhoods, universality of human actions, brotherhood doctrines are all thrown open to the gullible rural folk. As such new "classes" and "status" functions are derived in social life. Hereditary leadership gives way to "rational" leadership based on legality and authority as well as on voting choice. Efficiency gives the people a role of choice.

New forms of mass media like the radio, T.V., newspapers, magazines etc. are available to the rural folk who are influenced by these to a great extent. "Individualism" creeps in gradually replacing the age old collectivistic approach. Religion is less primitive, more rational. It is more a practical way of life than a threatening force.

The rural inhibitions no longer threaten the development of personality. The urban culture placing as it does adequate emphasis on individual's action, shatters the inhibited pattern of life and affords a broader perspective.

QUESTIONS FOR EXERCISE

1. Distinguish between urbanization and industrialization. Discuss the concept of over-urbanization.
2. "Industrialization is the last step in the process of urbanization". Do you agree with the statement ?
3. Discuss in detail the impact of industrialization on the (i) Marriage and Family; (ii) Religion and Morals; (iii) Caste and Class; and (iv) Recreation.
4. Throw light on the advantages and disadvantages of Industrialization.
5. What are the social problems of industrial urbanization ? Explain.
6. Discuss the impact of urbanization on rural life.

12

Urban Disorganization

In cities we find people professing a variety of faiths, belonging to various communities, castes, sub-castes and hailing from different regions of a country, even from many foreign lands. They speak different languages, dress and eat differently, following varying customs and traditions, practise different types of rituals at the time of marriage and death and belong to different political and intellectual strata. In metropolitan towns diplomats, business people and commercial representatives and agents from all over the world live and maintain their establishments.

EFFECTS OF HETEROGENEOUS POPULATION

The heterogeneous population leads to social disorganization in many ways. The chief effects are given below:

(1) Lack of the Spirit of Tolerance. Due to heterogeneous groups living in a city, there is little spirit of tolerance among them. In a village the population is homogeneous and people living there share many a common bond. They belong to same culture, practise uniform marriage and other rites. They share common memories of joy and sorrow and readily come forward to help each other. But in the city there are very few common bonds and the differences of religion and culture separating them are far more pronounced than the unifying elements. As a matter of fact people in cities are constantly at strife on one or the other account. The religious and communal antagonism erupts into violence from time to time. The different political parties have headquarters in cities and are busy in denigration and plotting against each other. Sometimes they incite trouble exploiting the linguistic grievance. Sometimes they fan religious hatred, sometimes they exploit economic grievances. In short, the political parties, for their personal gains, intensify and accentuate the heterogeneous elements in the cities. The people belonging to different cultures and religions consider their beliefs and customs superior and this naturally causes bitter reaction among people of other religion. For example, these days we find an influx of hippies in big Indian towns. They have caused many riots because of their extremely uninhibited ways of life. They peddle narcotics and live a life which other people consider very dirty and obscene. Most of all the, extreme difference in rich and poor in cities is a source of unrelieved bitterness and antagonism.

(2) Class-Struggle. As a consequence of vast disparity between rich and poor there is bitterness and frustration among the poor which is exploited by the vested interests. Therefore, trade-unionism, strikes, gheraos and noisy processions are permanent features of the city life.

(3) Multiplicity of Professions and Trades. A number of professional associations and trade guilds exist in cities. These associations and guilds are exclusive and have no connection with each other. Each professional association or trade guild is interested in protecting the rights and interests of its members. The union of Class IV employees and the union of officers class I each tries to push the interests of its members. This many a time leads to bitter controversy and rivalry among various unions. As the various professions are united among themselves, this at times entails working at the cross purposes. This heightens and accentuates the feeling of exclusiveness and the development of critical and unsympathetic attitudes towards others.

(4) Lack of Social Security. As in a heterogeneous group, people do not have common goals or interests and as their self interests clash with each other the incidence of crime is very high. Every city has a class of professional goondas who commit offences against payment. All these things are obviously detrimental to individual's security and accordingly, people in cities do not have adequate sense of social security. They feel insecure.

(5) Gross Disparities. Another consequence of heterogeneous population is that there are gross disparities, both economic and social, among city dwellers. On the one side we have multimillionnaire industrialists and capitalists and on the other hand there are extremely poor labourers, unable to get two square meals a day. The clerks in offices, labourers, shopkeepers and industrialists all form a separate society.

(6) Division of Labour. As a consequence of the heterogeneity of population, there is increase in the division of labour in the cities. In order to cater to the variety of needs and requirements of different groups, new industrial units are set up. Many types of shopping complexes, hotels and restaurants are opened. Due to too much division of labour many problems crop up and the balance of relations between different groups and individuals is disturbed.

(7) Family Disorganization. As people belonging to different cultures, religions and races reside in one city they come together. There are many points of contacts between them. As a consequence of the meeting of disparate culture outlooks the orthodoxy of any culture gets shaken and affected by new and different ideas and ideologies. This leads to gradual relaxation of rigidities of the culture. Particularly, there is liberalization of views with regard to sex and marriage. The young people begin to mistrust the old ways and question the reasonableness of traditions and customs of their ethnic groups. Due to meeting and exchange of ideas between different groups which hold permissive and non-permissive sex mores respectively, the family ties are loosened and people dare to flout the orthodoxy of their groups. The meeting of varying and opposite cultures also leads to impersonalness in social relations.

(8) Breakdown of Culture Barriers. The heterogeneity and diversity of people and cultures is not a cloud without a silver lining. While the heterogeneity of population has many bad effects, it also has good effects on the society. Due to contacts between persons of different cultures, religions, regions and lands people develop understanding of other viewpoints and sympathize with them. This widens and broadens the outlook of people and this promotes the spirit of tolerance. People of diverse faiths and cultures have to work intimately and unitely in educational institutions, government offices and factories. They have to tolerate each other and understand each other. As a consequence of this meeting between people, we find many young people of different religions falling in love and marrying each other. These things give rise to cosmopolitanism among people. Their thinking and outlook become international in vision and scope.

IMPACT OF IMPERSONALNESS

The Impersonalness of social relations has many consequences for the society. Due to industrialization of town and the rapid system of communication, people are busily engaged in their works and usually travel fairly long distances to come to their offices and factories. This leaves them tired and disinclined to mix up with their neighbours. The relationships between neighbours are usually confined to mere exchange of courtesies and sometimes even these are missing. They are hardly concerned with each other's woes and weals. In big cities it often happens that a dead body lies in the neighbourhood and nobody moves himself to lend a helping hand. Due to this impersonalness of social relations it is difficult to find an element of love and intimacy among social relations. What to speak of social relations, even in the family various members bear no love for each other and their relations are bare and formal. Each member of the family has his or her own friends and each may belong to separate clubs. Each pursues his or her individual goal and is not much bothered about its consequences for other members. The home sometimes is treated as a mere hotel where we take our food and spend our nights. As an indirect consequence of this impersonalness of relations, husband, wife, sons and daughters consider themselves as separate entities and wish to remain free and unsupervised in their activities. Sometimes this impersonalness becomes violent hatred and each member may thirst for the blood of the other. Instances of murders in family are not very rare. Directly, nobody bothers about the other but indirectly he is hateful and revengeful with regard to others.

Besides the above-mentioned adverse effects, the impersonalness of relation also has some beneficial and progressive effects. If the close neighboures do not care about each other, they do not equally plot against each other, do not wish unwell of others. This provides everyone maximum opportunity for personal development. The people belonging to different religions and cultures are tolerated if not indulged in. This promotes a healthy spirit of tolerance. In villages everyone knows almost everything about everyone. Anything slightly deviant of social norm meets with a chorus of disapproval. But in the towns one may live with wife, mistress prostitute or cousin, nobody bothers. Therefore, everyone has opportunity to live as best as he can think. One may even experiment without any detrimental social influences.

EFFECT OF IMPERSONAL RELATIONS

Thus we find that impersonality of social relations has both good and bad effect upon society. There is development and progress of the personality of the individual. There is also growth of the spirit of tolerance. Whereas due to impersonalness of the social relations there is increase in classism, self interest and hostility, the impersonalness of relations helps in breaking the cultural barriers. Following are the effects.

(1) Large Scale Trade and Commerce. The trade and commerce in the cities is not confined to any particular region but covers in its scope and ambit national and international markets. The trade and commerce in cities include importers and exporters, local and foreign traders and businessmen, industrialists, labourers, bankers, transporters and insurance companies. The businessmen engaged in different fields have their own associations to protect and promote their interests.

(2) Disparities of Intellectual proclivities ideas and ideals. In cities, people belonging to different religious and customs reside. There are differences in their intellectual capacities and ideals. They pursue different ideals. They form their own associations to pursue their end. There is wide difference in the outlook of villagers and town people. The city dwellers are individualists, intellectual, materialist and secular minded. They are liberal about personal morals and due to competitive life of city are mostly busy in their own works. Therefore, they are non-interfering.

(3) Family as an Association. In villages family is considered to be an institution and marriage is regarded a sacrament. But in cities family is more of an association than an institution. It is considered to be like a contract entered into for mutual profit gain. Usually each member of the family has his or her own aims and aspirations. Usually they subscribe to different associations and are members of different clubs. Thus we find much higher percentage of family association in the cities than in the villages.

(4) Dynamic Life. In comparison to rural life, the life in the cities is much more dynamic and busy. There is competition in fashions, educational attainments, money gathering, collection of luxury. Besides, there is intense competition of ideas and ideologies and economic interests. On the one hand, there are attempts at cooperation and collective efforts, on the other hand, there is severe competition and strife.

The following table would bring out with clarity the structure and problems of cities compared to villages.

City	*Villages*
1. Multiplicity of Industries	1. Lack of Industries
2. Huge Industries	2. Cottage Industries
3. Diversity of intellectual capacities, aims and outlook	3. Homogeneity of intellectual outlook
4. Family, an Association	4. Family, an Institution
5. Dynamic Life	5. Slow moving life
6. Rapid change	6. Gradual and slow change
7. Progressiveness and Rebellion.	7. Orthodoxy and contentment

DISORGANIZATION IN ART

In the modern urban culture we find a certain fall in the artistic standards. As a matter of fact, now-a-days we find a universal fall in the artistic standards and the degeneration of art in the urban industrialized society is a part of this universal phenomenon. Our attention towards this degeneration has been sharply drawn by the art historians and the aestheticians who have pointed out that whenever civilizations have declined and degenerated the first symptoms of this fall and degeneration have been found in the field of art. In the modern civilization all over the world the trend is towards gross and class materialism and naturalism. The fine and the elevated values of art are all but forgotten. The modern art does not address itself to the elevated emotions of the spirit and soul: instead the appeal is to low mass emotions. The art has become physicalistic and natural and realistic. The naked body of human beings is the most appealing subject of art today. However, the primary reason for the decline in art is its commercialization. Today, in dance and music as well as in paintings only those themes are touched upon which can be appreciated by the masses. Everywhere we find sex-oriented themes. This is so because sexual instinct has been repressed for long in society and now that it is being openly treated as it gives people a false sense of liberation. Of course, sex oriented art titilates and pleases. In cinema, in particular, an attempt is being made to introduce as much sex arousing material as possible. Thus we find cabarets in place of classical dances. In the western world currently a number of reputed film makers are treating themes like adultery, rape, group sex, voyeurism, exhibitionism, incest cunnilingus and fellatios most graphically. According to the famous historian, Toynbee this is a sure symptom of the rapid decline of the western civilization.

DISORGANIZATION IN REGION

As the man removes himself from the lap of nature and builds huge industrial towns where everything is artificial? the cultural pursuits of man are affected adversely. Man living in an artificial atmosphere and out of contact with the raw nature is so enslaved by the machine that his capacity for independent thinking and development is severely compromised. Commercialism and artifice invades all aspects of his existence. The commercialism is the bane of today's religious life and institutions. The piety, sincerity and innate respect for life, the religious virtues, have been replaced by commercial machinations. The religion has become subservient to selfishness and profit motive. Mostly, people, these days, build temples, mosques and endowments which are fruitful sources of tax evasion. Many religious institutions are run with a political motive. The work of Christian missionaries under British patronage was an example of this. The friends and foes of Anand Marg accuse each other of political motives. The priests and pujaris, maulvies and mendicants are busy inspiring fear psychosis among innocents and thus cheating them of their valuables. The various places of religious pilgrimage in India are busy centres of these religious crooks. They rob people of their possession by doling out promises of heaven and peace and in some cases do not shirk from sexual exploitation of women. Many a wives of impotent husbands fall prey to their trickestry. Many religious monastries have funds which are used to gain political leverage.

These days are marked for mass movements and commercial exploitation. These days there is little emphasis on personal piety and code of conduct in religion; the whole emphasis is on organized and institutionalized aspects of religion. People are more interested in religion for ostentation and display than in piety. For example, all places of worship are equipped with electronic trappings and prayers and hymn chanting are broadcast over amplifiers. The Devi Jagarans, so popular in North India these days, are performed by professional hymn chanters who sing thinly veiled popular sexy filmy songs to amuse themselves and the audience. They sing at topmost pitch supplemented by amplifier system all night. Hardly can anyone in the neighbourhood sleep peacefully on these nights. Besides, whenever the worship of body replaces spiritual worship, civilization declines. Today people have superficial interest in religion. They have made it an instrument of personal aggrandisement and gaudy display of their wealth.

DEGENERATION IN ENTERTAINMENT

Meaning of Entertainment

A man needs rest and entertainment after long hours of work and toil. Everyone gets fed up with routine and homogeneous life. Change sustains and recuperates life. However luxurious may be one's working conditions and however interesting one's engagement, the ennui is bound to overtake one sooner or later if life is unithematic and lacks variation. The change of routine is always rejuvenating and reinvigorating. It refreshes one mentally and physically. The entertainment is the best source of such change. In entertainment there is not only deviation from the routine but it also relaxes and removes mental tensions. During entertainment, even if one has to toil physically and do strenuous brain work, one is not exhausted, but, on the contrary, is refreshed and no strain is felt. As a matter of fact the entertainment dissipates strain. That is why people exhausted after day long work feel refreshed after a strenuous game of tennis, badminton or golf. Thus, entertainment is not equivalent to physical relaxation but means an activity undertaken for the sheer pleasure of it without any conscious end in which man becomes so engrossed that he forgets himself and his problems. In short, entertainment implies those activities which relieve ennui and boredom, and which besides providing mental, physical and emotional satisfaction help to develop the personality and promote in man the spirit of cooperation. While it is the aim of entertainment to provide personal satisfaction, it also satisfies the gregarious instinct of the man because most of the entertainments are collective and communal. A man confined to himself feels lonesome and is unable to relieve his mental tension, may these become more intense; but in the company of others he forgets his narrow self and is thus able to enjoy himself and dissipate the tensions. In communal atmosphere the man satisfies his gregarious feelings and gets a chance to come out of the narrow confines of his personal self. Thus the entertainment satisfies not only the biological needs but also the social needs of the man. The modes of entertainment which fulfil the social needs include various indoor and outdoor games and picnics, outings and collective tours. On the whole, entertainment fulfils the all round needs of man and develops an all round integrated personality. As one has written, "The entertainment which provides maximum mental and physical satisfaction is bad by engaging in certain specialized activities." Accordingly, young and old, men and women, rural and urban population, primitive and civilized people get entertainment out of different types of activities which vary according to time and circumstances. Generally, an entertainment likely to be most appropriate will depend upon the special tastes and interests of people, their sex and age. The cultural factors also influence the appropriateness of entertainment.

Importance of Entertainment

The above discussion clearly brings into relief the importance of entertainment. The following points should be borne in mind in this connection:-

(1) Removal of Mental Tension. The routine and humdrum of daily life exhausts the energy resources of man and he feels bored, listless and run-down. These conditions generate and aggravate mental tensions. These mental tensions in the long run produce gross physical disorders. The entertainment dissipates these tensions and keeps one physically and mentally healthy and fit.

(2) Improvement of Bodily Health. A man needs certain amount of physical exercise at all age levels. In the absence of physical exercise the body grows flabby and its general tone deteriorates. The physical exercise is a condition *sine qua non* of integral growth of man. The various indoor and outdoor games are great source of entertainment as well as physical exercise. For the old walking, badminton, table tennis are entertaining as well as reinvigorating. For the young strenuous games of Hockey, Football and Cricket are suitable. These utilize their excess energy constructively.

(3) The Development of Character and Personality. The various games and social reactions help in the healthy formation of character and personality. This is so because in the social entertainment the man has to mix up freely with others and learn to respect their legitimate claims and have his legitimate claims respected. This helps him to develop a mature outlook and his emotional life also matures. The emotional maturity, as we know, is the bedrock of healthy character and stable personality. For example, in games one learns that it is the spirit of the game which is important and not mere success in it. This is the secret of mature man.

(4) Development of Social Qualities. In as much as most of the entertainments involve social participation they help in the growth of social feelings and qualities. By participating in these we learn to sacrifice our interest for the legitimate genuine interests of others. In team games the team spirit and *esprite de corps* develops. In play there is no distinction of high and low, educated and illiterate, the prince and the pauper. Thus, games are most potent instruments of socialising and erasers of class and caste distinctions. It is proverbial that friendships developed during play are everlasting. Thus, it is abundantly clear that games and sports are sources of the development of social qualities.

(5) Development of Democratic Feelings. It is imperative for the success of democracy that a feeling of equality, freedom and fraternity should develop among people. Tho entertainment reduces tensions which give rise to violence and crime and impede the progress of democracy.

Rural v/s Urban Entertainment

The conditions and circumstances prevailing in the city and the village are very different. We can observe a distinct difference in the problems, frustrations, tensions and tendencies of villagers and city dwellers. Due to all these factors we find difference in the types of rural and urban entertainments. The rural entertainment is usually comprised of such games as Kabaddi and Kho Kho, and folk music, dance and drama. They also engage themselves in wrestling bouts, cock fights and hunting. The rural entertainment, as a matter of fact, is closer to life than the urban entertainment. The farming, cattle breeding, gardening and hunting are rural activities, performed in the lap of raw unspoiled nature, do not produce any adverse effect upon emotional and mental well-being. Therefore, the entertainment and useful work more or less overlap. The theory of entertainment postulates that greater the distance of man from nature the greater is his need for special entertainment. In the cities most of the population is totally cut off from nature therefore, the need for entertainment is more in the case of city-dwellers than in the case of villagers. As the life in the cities is more complex and variegated, the chances of emotional repression and frustrating experiences are great in cities. The types and varieties of tension and conflict are multiple in the cities, and for these specialized type of entertainment is needed to relieve these. Moreover, in the cities there are many commercial centres of entertainment in which varied types of amusement can be had against money. There are no such provisions in the villages. A reason for the availability of commercialized entertainment in the cities is that people here are rich and can afford to spend large sums of money on entertainment. Moreover, as people stay out of home for long hours in cities and are not obsessed with moral scruples, they spend a lot of their money and time on thrilling shows and highly entertaining fares.

The foregoing discussion makes explicit the differences between rural and urban entertainment. The main differences may be classified as follows:

(1) Whereas the urban entertainment takes place in artificial surroundings, the rural entertainment takes place in natural surroundings.

(2) Whereas the urban entertainment emphasizes diversion and relieving of tensions, the rural entertainment puts emphasis on body.

(3) Whereas entertainment in cities is available round the year, it is seasonal in the villages.

(4) Whereas entertainment in cities always involves certain amount of expenses, it is free of any cost in the villages.

Healthy Entertainment

Before discussing the various institutions providing entertainment in the cities, it is necessary to understand what is good and what is bad entertainment. There are certain types of entertainment, which, though thrilling, are morally depraved and desensitizing. Therefore, it is important to know the nature of healthy entertainment. Following are the main characteristics of good and healthy entertainment.

(1) Not Tiring. The real purpose of entertainment is to relax the physical and emotional tension of man. Too thrilling films, dancing under the influence of liquor and drugs and sexually exciting stage performance have the opposite effect. They highten tensions instead of relieving them. They can not, therefore, be considered healthy entertainment.

(2) Active Participation. The second feature of healthy entertainment is that there should be active participation. Though man does not attain relief by merely watching the entertainment programmes, it is only by an active participation that complete relaxation can be achieved. For example, the persons who actively participate in dancing get more pleasure and relief than those who are merely on lookers. This is the main reason why dance forms are getting more and more simplified. A dance form which does not require elaborate training can be enjoyed by a multitude of people.

(3) Must develop Character and Personality. A healthy entertainment not only amuses and beguiles but it must also lead to firming of the will and stabilization and maturation of the personality. If an entertainment demoralises and produces contrary and anti-social impulses in man, it can not be considered healthy. Therefore, sex-oriented entertainment is seldom salutary.

(4) Not Costly. A healthy entertainment must not be very costly, because if excessive cost is incurred it will produce adverse after-effects. For example, it may be very entertaining to visit posh hotels and mix up with beautiful persons. But if a person is poor he will repent for a long time the monetary thrills.

In a healthy entertainment following three types of activities may be included:

(1) Physical Exercise. The various types of games and dancing, horse riding, boating, mountaineering, skiling etc. help to relax the tension by diversion of attention and physical labour. They also develop man's physical capacities. Therefore, all entertainment involving physical exercise in a pleasant atmosphere is healthy.

(2) Social Functions. The social functions include dancing, singing and drama, picnic, competitive sports, community welfare, celebration of festivals and visiting fairs. All these help to develop and mature social aspect of man, and are, therefore, healthy entertainment.

(3) Cultural Activities. The cultural activities fulfil the intellectual function of entertainment. These lead to mental relaxation and development of the personality. These also enhance the social feelings in man and help to refine and advantageously use various instinctive tendencies in man. The cultural activities are comprised of music, dance, drama, satire, poetry symposia, Bhajans and Kirtan, debate, various sorts of competitions etc. These help creative development of the man.

For an all round development of the personality, the government and allied agencies should arrange cultural programmes, sports and games and social festivities in each and every village of the country. The educational institutions are by far the most important in this respect. They can play a vital role in providing healthy entertainment to young men and women. Besides dramatic and other clubs can be organized. The government should issue financial assistance to people engaged in providing healthy entertainment.

Decline in the Standard of Entertainment

These days there is commercialization in all walks of life. The world of entertainment has not escaped commercialization. In cities the entertainment has become a big business. The commercial entertainment has been defined as an activity which is of a limited scope and in which the audience is more or less passive. The commercial entertainment is controlled by the government. The aim of commercial entertainment is to thrill and emotionally arouse the audience and the aim of the commercial entertainer is to fleece the customers by bewitching them through exposing them to a highly emotional and sex-oriented fair. A commercial entertainment has an eye on profit and is totally indifferent to moral consideration. It is well known that man has passionate lower tendencies and these are richly exploited by the professional entertainer. This type of entertainment is provided by the cinema, the dancing halls, the night clubs, the gambling dens and bawdy houses. At these centres money flows like water. The entertainment provided at these centres is so bewitching that people who visit them become so addicted to them that nothing matters more to them in life than spending their time at these centres. They even borrow or steal money to satisfy their lust for thrilling entertainment. This leads to gradual deterioration of character and disorganization affects the marital relations and family life adversely and this leads to social disorganization. The biggest sources of such entertainment are cinema and clubs. The aim of film makers is to grab maximum profits and this can be done best by introducing maximum sex, violence and suspense in the films. In the West, film makers have produced films on every conceivable sexual theme. There are films not only on adultery but also on homosexuality, group-sex, necrophilia, voyeurism, sadism, masochism etc. No wonder there is no sanctity about sex in the modern western world. Many films glorify pre-marital sex and all this encourages sexual promiscuity in the youth. Many a film show crime minutely and these suggestions are picked up by gullible youth. It is not difficult to guess how persons who see Marlon Brando's *Last Tango in Paris* would feel encouraged to possess their beloveds roughly and sodomize them as the hero sodomizes the heroine in the film. The bawady houses and gambling dens are clearly demoralizing. All these things fire the imagination and take people downhill.

In the world of today we can not do away with the commercial entertainment, because in cities there are no natural sources of amusement and diversion, But the regrettable fact is the mode of exploitation of base human demands than an entertainment in the real sense. We come across in every big city numerous cinema houses, theaters, night-clubs, dancing schools, bawdy houses, massage parlours and gambling dens. A section of modern psychologists, sociologists and panel reformers are of the view that the uninhibited commercial entertainment helps to release mental tensions and relieve frustration. They plead for a greater freedom; even total removal of all restrictions on sex-oriented entertainment. They cite the example of Denmark where pornography is allowed. It has led to reduction in the incidence of crime. There is, however, great controversy over the real merit of such a move. Any way, the Indian conditions are not quite suited for such a thing though it has to be conceded, as Khosla Committee report has done, that certain amount of liberalization is called for. But an important fact to remember in this connection is that for satisfaction of the special needs of certain individuals we should not expose every member of society to highly sexy and suggestive entertainment. The pity of commercialization is that it precisely does that. In America and Europe many ignorant persons see literature which portrays graphically sex activity undreamed by them. Such a thing is highly objectionable. In the absence of healthy entertainment the prevalence of commercial entertainment is bound to demoralize the society.

MORAL DECLINE

Every society has certain moral principles which regulate and control the behaviour of its members. The moral principles are necessary concomitants of any culture. The existence of society without some moral principles is impossible. However, there are no uniform patterns of moral codes in different cultures. The moral principles also undergo change and modifications with change in the culture patterns of a society. The progress and decline of culture is by the order and hierarchy of values in a society. The lowest rung of values is bodily values; the mental and spiritual values are of a higher order. The cultures which emphasize the spiritual values and put the bodily values under their control are progressive. However, in modern cultures this hierarchy of values seems to have become topsyturvy. There is a strong tendency towards material values and the urge to satiate bodily functions is stronger than the passion for sacrifice of material values in service of higher spiritual and intellectual attainments. A man of modern culture is a hedonist for whom the heaven is the enjoyment of beautiful persons and dainty foods and drinks. The Bacchanalian existences celebrated in the quarters of Omar Khayyam seems to be the most popular goal of the cultural pursuits of our day. No disinction between means and ends is made. For example, wealth which is a means of enjoyment of wordly goods has become an end in itself and every body wants to accumulate wealth by any means, fair or foul.

Another measure for the quality of value is their extension or universality or comprehensiveness. The values which have wider acceptance and are respected by the majority of the human beings are of higher quality than the values with lesser extension and espoused by the minority only. However, in modern societies we find that each society has moulded the values to suit its parochial interests, nay, each individual modifies them to justify his selfish pursuits. For example, pre-marital and extra-marital sexual forays are described liberalism. Under the impact of science the biological values are getting upper hand over intellectual and spiritual values. The spirit of sacrifice is considered a psychological disease called masochism. According to this approach self-purification by fasting etc. is basically sexual gratification. Darwin has tried to prove that man is nothing but a highly complex animal and Freud has tried to prove that man does nothing altruistically. He is fundamentally selfish and sex pleasure is the goal of all his activities. Small wonder, then, that modern culture has become so blatantly sexualised. Besides, in modern days there is a welter of confusing opinions on every subject and there is crisis of values.

Due to this man knows not what he is expected today : therefore he adopts the path of minimum resistance and seeks his own satisfaction.

Some people think that a really free and creative life is one which is beyond the pale of morals beyond all considerations of good and bad. The evidence of this carefree a moral life is found in hippies of modern times. They refuse to earn a living by hard work. They eat, drink and sleep in the shabbiest possible manner. They do not mind to have homosexual or hetrosexual experience and even homohetrosexuality in one stroke, that is, indulge in group activities unmindful of the presence of others. They claim that a society which has brought them to earth must somehow feed them. All this is superficially attractive and use of LSD, DMT, psylocin and other halluciogenic drugs may bring many temporary ecstasy and extreme exhilaration but ultimately this is nothing but a fight from reality which can not be either worthwhile or successful.

Another cause for moral decline is the fact that modern man is offered life-goals which are low and have no redeeming values. This results in a crisis of faith and man becomes disgusted with morals and moralists. In Indian youth to-day there is an urge to experience what is different and taboo. They want to live a natural animal life and kick all social barriers. In newspapers sometime back it appeared that drug taking is becoming very popular among university students and that promiscuity is the order of the day.

The extent of moral degeneration in the modern world can be gauged from the following few examples :

(1) In Great Britain two women married formally and declared that lesbianism was the highest type of human relationship.

(2) In U.S.A., a mother married his own son formally.

(3) In most of the world's cosmopolitan cities exhibitions are held in which besides men and women, animals also participate.

(4) The political, economic and sexual corruption are extremely prevalent in Asian and Latin American countries.

(5) In the Soviet Union, writers and artists are persecuted for daring to express their free and frank opinions.

DEGENERATION IN MANNERS

The object and aim of etiquette and manners is to oil and smoothen the mutual relations between people of different sexes and various age groups so as to remove the possibilities of friction, bitterness and acrimony between them. For example, there are definite and well accepted standards of behaviour between young and old men and women etc. Among Indians the youngest person in a group is supposed to do the chores and obey the elders. In India there are reserved seats for ladies in buses but still if any lady is standing, males are expected to offer the seat.

In modern life there is degeneration in manners. There are many reasons for this. Many persons consider them bare formalities devoid of any real value or significance. For example, if a youngman vacates his seat to accommodate a pretty girl he is liable to be misunderstood and instead of receiving 'thank you', he is likely to be laughed at. A well-mannered person these days is liable to be considered high-brow and too formal. People wish to be informal.

The fall in moral standards is very much responsible for deterioration of morals. It is no longer considered sacred to pay respects to elders; on the contrary elders are considered to be old fashioned and over critical. The world of today is a world of youth. The old are parasites. In America people send their old parents to veteran homes. The deterioration of morals is so steep that it is considered an enlightened attitude to discuss sex matters openly and crudely.

The third reason for the fall in morals and manners is that there is commercialization of culture. The sweet manners and sweet tongue is suspect these days.

The fourth reason for deterioration in morals is economic. These days the shopkeepers show no curtesy to customers because demand far exceeds the supply. Therefore they can afford to insult the customer with impunity. The labourers and clerks have unionized. They disrespect, ridicule and abuse their superiors because no action can be taken against them due to their militant unity.

The fifth reason for deterioration of morals is excessive sexualization of culture and the glorification of crime in cinema and art. These days a crook, a dacoit, a scoundrel is made hero of the film stories. Too much display of female body in the cinema has degraded womanhood. She is considered only a sweet candy or luscious flesh.

SOCIAL MALADJUSTMENTS

If we are to combat deterioration in manners we shall have to attack the problem on all the above mentioned fronts and remove anomalies of our economic, sexual and cultural lives.

In modern India we find various types of maladjustments. As a matter of fact, the whole Indian society is seriously maladjusted. This state of affairs is due to the fact that we have successfully adopted western science and technology to transform our material civilization. We have industrialized our society; built big towns with modern sophisticated amenties. But in our thinking, beliefs and attitudes, there is little or no forward movement. Inspite of receiving very high education and learning the philosophy of liberalism, non-explotation etc., the educated youth of India is unable to kick the dowry system. As a matter of fact, they desire it just as much as their parents. We find that modern Indian women are not backward than their western counter parts in seeking employment and economic freedom; but, unlike the western girl an Indian girl still prizes virginity highly. In the political sphere, an attempt is being made to encourage nationalism and determined efforts made at national integration: but on the other hand regional tendencies are gaining ground. Inspite of a century of effort to integrate Hindus and Muslims and to avert communal violence, the Hindu-

Muslim rioting keeps erupting from time to time. Inspite of constitutional abolition of untouchability, the discrimination against Harijans by higher castes persists. In the economic sphere, we find proliferation of big industrial units, the unemployment is also growing. With the production of new goods the prices, instead of coming down, are rising. Our education, instead of reducing maladjustments, tends to make the situation worse. Our education does not equip our young men and women to adjust better with the complexities of life. We do not find that young girls after finishing education become better housewives than non-educated. The educated men are not more skilled in handling the complex issues or life than uneducated persons. The educational institutions are full of indiscipline and unrest. The relations between teachers and students are strained: the element of respect and regard is totally lacking. The spectre of unemployment ever haunts the students and initiates their motivation and own urge for knowledge. The political parties try to grind their own axes and mislead the students. Thus we find maladjustment and unrest in each and every field of life. The family, community, school, college are badly disturbed due to maladjustment.

Nature of Mal-Adjustment

Following points are notworthy with regard to the nature of maladjustment in India:

(1) Communal Tensions. The communal tensions are at the back of various types of maladjustment. The political affiliations and rivalries, allotment of residential areas, admission to educational institutions and economic favours are guided and governed by communal considerations. The multifarious divisions of society into small fragments on the basis of caste, religion, sex, age, politics, economics and profession is playing havoc with the health of the Indian Society. The reason for this is not far to seek. In a country like India where the economic resources lag much behind the needs, the groups assembled on various criteria assume violent postures.

(2) Tensions due to Poverty. As remarked above the economic factor plays a very vital role in accentuating social tensions. Many a psychological tension is due to poverty which is the most potent breeder of frustrations. When a man is ill-fed and ill-clothed he tends to vent his fire on other persons or opposite groups. Thus conflicts between labour and capitalists, government servants and government show their ugly head from time to time.

(3) Change in Values. Fundamental changes are occurring in the family, educational and religious institutions due to change in the beliefs, customs, traditions and usages: in one word, due to transvaluation. As we know, nothing stays put in this world; change affects all. Even our values change with time. An uneven change in values is a great source of conflicts and tensions. In the institutions of marriage and family due to change in values, love marriage, intercaste marriage, divorce, breakdown of joint family etc. are in vogue, today. The modern educated persons are practising family planning, whereas the old generation still considers children to be the gifts of God. The moral values have undergone sea-change. What to speak of men folk, even women do not consider drinking, gambling, smoking etc. as immoral. The practice of non-vegetarianism is increasing and many Hindus feel liberated in taking beef and liquor. The fashions are changing frequently and many ludicrous dresses are coming into vogue. The modern dress is so fashioned as to reveal than to conceal the bodily charms. Incurring large expenditure on partying and entertainment is becoming fashionable. In the political field, money, wine and woman are freely used to gain power. In education the educational institutions are likened to shop which must guarantee satisfaction of customers, namely, students. In family, father has ceased to hold authority. Democracy and secularism have helped relaxing the hold of casteism and religion a bit, but the practice of free adult franchise in political elections has revived the importance of casteism and communalism.

The wide-spread maladjustments in the Indian society are fundamentally due to psychological causes. The personal frustrations and tensions of individuals give rise to social tensions. The psychological tensions are wide-spread in our society due mainly to economic and sexual frustrations coupled with the ascendance of competition over the spirit of co-operation. A dominant need to excel others often than not causes severe disappointments and mental shocks. In urban areas the psychological tension is much more rampant than in the villages. This state of affairs is due mainly to two things: (1) the spirit of competition is more strident in the cities than in the villages and (2) the marriage age is far more advanced in cities than in villages. A proper study of maladjustment requires psychological approach.

Causes of Maladjustment

Following are some of the important causes of maladjustment in India:

(1) Social Change. Due to the application of science and technology to society, rapid industrialization or political or social or natural upheavals, radical changes in social structure occur. Due to this the relations undergo change and call for fresh adjustments. Many people are not mentally equipped to change themselves quick enough to cope with the changed atmosphere. This inability or incapacity for adjustment gives rise to maladjustment.

(2) Industrialization. As a consequence of rapid industrialization in this country the labour force now runs into many millions. So many people work for so few men who have come to control the economy of this country. Thus, whereas the coffers of these few capitalists are loaded with gold, diamonds and currency notes, the workers do not get even subsistance wage. Any increase in their wage is more than offset by the rising price spiral. Therefore, it is a patent fact that rich are getting richer and poor are becoming poorer. As a result of this widening gap between the labour and the capitalists, the relations between the two are strained and uneasy. The workers do not put their hearts in work and the capitalists try to reduce their bargaining power by sowing the seeds of dissension among them. All this has resulted in maladjustment of workers as well as capitalists. Another effect of industrialization is the alienation of the individual. In industrial production no one manufactures more than a part of a thing. Accordingly, no one feels the sense of ownership or belonging to the goods he help to produce. All this results in estrangement and alienation of the individual from his own products and the socicty. Because of this, man feels empty and the process of dehumanization starts. The labourer takes to drinking, gambling, prostitution and thieving. He comes to consider himself and others as mere goods which have some definite price. Due to this subversion of the moral individual in man, every type of illicit practice is condoned. Paddling contraband goods, prostituting one's kith and kin for profit is grimly accepted as a fact of life. Thus, industrialization has encouraged crimes of every variety. Thirdly, industrialization has uprooted the cottage industries and created vast amount of unemployment. The political parties thrive and flourish by exploiting people's unrest and inject virulence of class hatred among people. The groups are turned against each other. Fourthly, as a consequence of big, huge and sprawling industrial units employing labour force in lakhs there is virtually no contact between the employer and the employed. A class of intermediaries has sprung up who act as go between the employer and the labourers. Only by placating the intermediaries can the labourer get employment. These intermediaries have to be bribed or given other satisfactions. Thus the poor and labourers are further improverished and often feel compelled to augment their incomes by conniving at prostitution by their wives and nubile daughters. Thus, we find that the industrial man is corrupted to the core and is callous and indifferent to the pain and misery of others. The industrial disputes have become the order of the day. An unrelieved tension between the labourer and the capitalist persists. Even government agencies are quite helpless. While their orientation is labour based, the power of money subverts the cause of justice.

(3) Urbanization. We find more maladjustments in cities than in villages. The main reason for this is that life in the city becomes impersonal and the sense of community and fellowship is superseded by the sense of gain, profit or status. Therefore, people in cities do not care or bother about others. The sex-oriented entertainment provided by the cinema, the club and television keeps people in. a state of perpetual excitement. This gives rise to personal disorganization. The old restraints of religion and morality are giving way to a sense of independence and emancipation. Everyone thinks himself quite competent and is afraid to lean on others for help. In cities in many families husband and wife both work out of home. This leads to forced neglect of children. Moreover, woman comes to feel and think herself equal of man and wants her husband to share household work. The rate of crime is very high in the cities because it is easy to buy anonymity in the cities and escape police detection. Finally, the gap between rich and poor is very wide in cities. The palatial mansions and hutments exist side by side The spectacle of many people eating the left over of rich people and sleeping on the pavement cannot but deepen the bitterness and conflict between rich and poor.

(4) Political Causes. In India politics has also contributed its share to production of maladjustments. The political groups want to wrest power by means, fair and foul, by hook or crook. The political parties raise their funds by indulging in and encouraging others to indulge in corrupt practices. The party in power makes use of the official machinery to collect funds to fight fresh election. It does not desist from issuing of threats and favours to achieve its selfish ends. The open handed corruption by government encourages the capitalist to buy the officials and the M.Ps. and thus by the backdoor keeps control over the government. Some frustrated politicians stoop so low as to encourage communal violence to gain their political ends. Some political parties receive large funds from outside powers and work on their biddings. For them personal gain is more vital than the national honour and strength. As an eminent political scientist has observed, it is in the nature of political parties to suppress the truth and spread falsehood. The government officials detected of having sympathies with anti-government elements are harassed. The government wants its servants to help it in elections. Political parties encourage strikes foment all sorts of troubles and use every means to harass the party in power. All this results in maladjustments. Politicians are true to none and always exploit others. The government officials cannot behave naturally and are forced to act against their conscience.

(5) Casteism and Untouchability. The evil of casteism and untouchability is a potent cause of maladjustment. The system of election by open free adult franchise has greatly revived the casteism. The castes have come to realize that the source of political strength lies in keeping the caste feeling alive and to exploit their real and imaginary grievances in order to cement the bonds of caste and encourage caste exclusiveness. The M.Ps. and M.L.As. elected on the strength of caste affiliations perpetuate casteism by using their power in favour of caste. The national interests are thus ignored. Accordingly there is conflict of national and parochial interests. A successful politician professes nationalism but works really for his caste interests. Not only in the political sphere but in the economic field also the selections for appointments are made on the basis of caste. In the educational institutions the influence of casteism is most glaring. Barring emergency, appointments in the educational institutions are as a rule made on the basis of caste consideration. The government officials too staff their department with their own men irrespective of the consideration of merit. The eminent sociologists have correctly observed that without the eradication of the evils of casteism and untouchability no stable progress towards sound social organization can be made.

(6) Regionalism. At present there is widespread and powerful influence working to promote regional interests at the expense of national good. The main factor at the back of this regionalism in politics is the motive of personal gain aggrandisement. The leadership exploits people in order to gain higher status in the government because rationally the progress of one region at the expense of other is self defeating and the ascendancy of regionalism is bound to slow down the wheels of progress of one region at the expense of other is self defeating and the ascendancy of regionalism is bound to slow down the wheels of progress rather than quicken them. And the slowing down of economic progress is bound to add to maladjustments. An important offshoot of regionalism is a sense of insecurity among the minority groups.

(7) Linguistic Fanaticism. India is a multilingual nation. There are more than 15 highly evolved languages spoken in India. These languages are spoken by millions of people and possess rich heritage. The people are proud of their own language and do not want supremacy of any language other than their own. So far English served as link-language. But with imminent replacement of English by Hindi the people of southern states became panicky as the immediate effect of such a step would have been deprivation of all India services to southern people. There was violent hue and cry and in violent agitation the property worth hundreds of crores of rupees was destroyed. This resulted in assurance to southerners that it shall be seen that displacement of English does not harm them. Three language formula was evolved. But to-day we find further intensification of linguistic fanaticism the solution of which does not appear to be in sight. The minorities living in any region are worst hit by this fanaticism and feel insecure and maladjusted.

(8) Communalism. The British Government adopted a policy of divide and rule to strengthen their clutches on India. In the historical animosity of Hindus and Muslims the British statesmen found a fertile field to push their policy. They encouraged Muslims and directly and indirectly helped them to divide India into two nations. Unfortunately even after the departure of the British the virus of communalism erupts in epidemic from time to time. The minorities whether Hindu or Muslim feel constantly disturbed by a sense of insecurity. This leads to maladjustment.

(9) Regionalism. In the recent past a strong regional sentiment has affected politics and economic planning in India. In all fiscal and economic matters each state presses its claim for lion's share. There are bitter disputes between states and center over setting up of new Industrial units. Recently a bitter and violent agitation was launched for pressurizing the centre to set up a steel plant n a particular province. The disputes over river water sharing are frequent and of extremely bitter nature. Even courts are moved to have the matters sorted out. Such interprovincial rivalry at time takes an ugly form and the lives of persons of other provinces are jeopardized and this starts a chain reaction. This type of attitude is both psychologically and economically harmful and promotes naladjustments.

(10) Law and Law Courts. Normally the rule of law and the existence of mpartial judiciary should promote stability and organization in the society, but uriously in India law and law courts have also been instrumental in promoting naladjustment. It is truly said that the justice delayed is justice denied. But in ndia we find even minor suits taking very long to be settled, and by the time udgement is pronounced both litigants may have become paupers. Most of the villagers find going to courts pastime though it may cost them dearly both in money and time wasted. The lawyers directly or indirectly encourage illiterate people, to file suits and caution against out of court settlement. Rich people, the goondas and politicians have corrupted the judiciary by their illicit ways of getting things done. Therefore inspite of laws and police and judiciary the poor and common man feels insecure and persecuted. Such a psychology most obviously leads to personal disorganization and maladjustment.

(11) Abuse of Science. Today science is in service of business and commerce. Instead of being an emancipating force it has become enslavening and destroyer of liberty. The science has put at the disposal of man instruments and gadgets which can destroy all privacy. Evesdropping, clandestine photography and bugging have made everyone feel unsafe. No one can express himself freely lest the opposite group expose him by unusual means.

(12) Means of Communication. The fast system of transportation, spread of news media like newspaper, radio and television can help greatly the cause of national unity and integration, but their abuses like spreading rumours, writings, speeches inciting communalism, regionalism etc. can have just the opposite effect, that is promotion of maladjustments. Many political groups publish their own newspapers and other literature by means of which they incite dissension, communalism, linguistic fanaticism etc. This pollutes the body politic. Though Radio and Television are under government control and are supposed to be impartial in the dissemination of news and views, however it has been strongly and persistently alleged by the opposition that Govt. has used radio to promote the political interest of party in power. It will be good if radio and television are controlled by a corporation and newspapers let the leaders of different political groups speak for themselves through their columns This will eliminate the disadvantages of partial and prejudicial reporting.

(13) Defective Education. In India the education is not integral and wholesome. The government does not make adequate investment in education Therefore, most of the schools and colleges are ill equipped. The teaching staf is low paid generally but what is more, the teachers in government and private schools are given different salaries. Such discrimination affects the morale o the staff.

(14) War. The wars cause widespread destruction of life and property Many homes lose their bread earners. Many newly married women becom widows. The country's economy is upset and economic progress is retarded There is increase in crimes after war, particularly sexual offences becom common. The wars fan hatred and bitterness. In Bangladesh, the retreating Pa army destroyed everything, raped every woman whatever her age they cam across. The women raped in wars by the enemy and those who become pregnar have to live a life of shame. They are unacceptable to their own people. A such things produce personal disorganization on a vast scale.

(15) Partition. India received its independence only after the country wa partitioned. As the basis of partition was religion, communal violence erupte at massive scale and there was mass influx of Hindus into India. This gave rise to spread of epidemics, destruction of property, loss of honour of many women. The influx of about one crore refugees from former East Pakistan has upset Indian economy. Anything which increases people's poverty produces maladjustment.

(16) Influx from Abroad. There are many lakhs Indians settled in various countries. Due to changes in the policies of different governments, Indians are ordered out. When they come to India they find Indian society too orthodox and narrow for their tastes. They bring with them a style of free living which may upset people here. All these things cause maladjustments.

(17) Conspiracy by Foreign Powers. The Pakistani and Chinese agents are ever busy spreading communal hatred and violence in India. They try to indulge in subversive activity and give financial and arms assistance to organizations working against India's national interests. The border of Punjab, Rajasthan and Assam and Nagaland are hot beds of anti-Indian activities. The Chinese agents encourage labour unrest and try to subvert everything Indian.

(18) Cultural Lag. Finally the fundamental cause responsible for social maladjustment is the cultural lag. Due to English Education India came in contact with western civilization, science and technology. But whereas the application of technology has resulted in numerous benefits there has been little change in the attitudes, beliefs, customs and traditions of India. In short, the rapid economic advance has not been matched by the cultural change. Due to cultural lag there has occurred wide chasm of generations. The difference between the attitudes of older and younger generations is unbridgeable. Western civilization has broken up the joint family and caste-barriers. There is a crisis of old and new cultures and the two are unreconciled.

By understanding the above causes of social maladjustments we can chalk out programme to remedy them and restore normalcy.

QUESTIONS FOR EXERCISE

1. What is the impact of social disorganization of religious life and institutions? Explain with the help of examples.
2. Discuss the available sources of entertainment in urban India of today. Give your suggestions to make them more appropriate and useful.
3. Discuss the nature and modes of urban recreation.
4. Discuss the degeneration in morals and art in modern times.
5. Write a short note on Degeneration of Manners.
6. Explain the causes and nature of maladjustments presently found in India.
7. Write short notes on :

   (a) Over Urbanization, (b) Push back factors in migration

   (c) Urban unemployment, (d) Slum improvement programme.

13
Corruption in Public Life

In cities corruption in public life can be seen in all the spheres of individual and social life. For a detailed study these fields can be divided as follows:

1. Political field,
2. Administrative field,
3. Economic field,
4. Social field,
5. Religious field,
6. Individual sphere of life.

1. Corruption in Political Field. In this we may take the activities regarding the formation of the government. India has a democratic form of government in which leaders elected by the people form the government. Hence in order to get success in the election, political parties use even the lowest type of evil means in defeating the rival candidate. Money is distributed among the voters, votes are purchased, drink is supplied, grand feasts are arranged, boarding and lodging is supplied free of cost to the voters processions pass through the markets with a great pomp and show raising slogans. All these performances are merely wastage of money, resulting in corruption. In democracy, there is no difference between a literate and an illiterate, male and female etc. All are equally treated before the law. Every one has equal rights. The people have right to cast their votes in favour of any person they like. They can't be forced to cast their votes to a particular person. Therefore, it becomes very difficult to check the voters from employing corrupt means at the time of election. Again, the political parties allow only those persons to fight election who have a high social status, two or three big factories, some powerful gangs with them, and can spend money lavishly without the least consideration of their ideas, morality and character. The parties have nothing to do with the evil means the candidate has employed in earning and collecting money. It is a usual practice among the leaders of the country that they earn a lot through various corrupt ways and then come on the stage to fight election, because they know that they would be able to compensate their loss if they win. The political parties hold power and pelf in higher esteem than the character of a candidate. There are many political leaders who have been defamed for corruption since long but who are enjoying the privilege of being all India political leaders for more than twenty years because through party politics and other evil means, they have acquired a unique prestige and power without which the parties can't pull on their work. Not even a single person has the courage to utter a word against them. These leaders degrade the new generation morally, resulting in new corruption in the society. Political pressures increase corruption even in the field of administration and justice. Undue pressure of political leaders increases corruption in almost all the departments of the government.

2. Corruption in the field of Administration. All the various offices of the government, whether they are concerned with the police, railway, justice, municipality, military, transport, or with any branch of administration, are all counted in the field of administration.

(i) *Corruption in the government offices.* In every office of the government there is a large scale corruption. One can get any work done by the employees of these offices only by paying some money. There is bribery everywhere. If one thinks it a corruption and does not give any extra money the employee shall not do his work at all. If any employee wants to avoid the evil means, or possesses a moral character, other employees discard him, befool him and even force him to do the same as they themselves are doing. Even the officials turn against him, harass him and if possible he is dismissed for his good character. In such a critical position, either he resigns from his post or adopts the same evil way of corruption. In many offices of the government a fixed and regular sum of money is taken from the businessmen, contractors, inspectors and officials, clerks of the educational institutions and so on. In railway departments the businessmen have to pay a definite amount to the booking clerk for his pocket in order to send their parcels in time. Many a time even for the reservation of a seat or a berth one has to bribe at the booking window. The free medical aid given by the government to its employees has created a lot of corruption among them. Some employees prepare the annual medical bills demanding money more than the annual total salary they get. For it they have to give bribes to the doctors as well to the officials concerned. Forged certificates are produced in order to get long leaves. In the public works department without bribing the Overseers and Engineers, no construction work can be passed and no contractor can get his tenders accepted. It is a plain fact that some persons by taking undue advantage of their powers and posts openly indulge in corruption and whenever they are caught red handed they by employing the same means easily get out of the trap. Such persons, often use to say, "Every man can be purchased by giving him some money." Having this belief they continuously throw money at the corrupt officials and clerks. The sanitary inspectors, lawyers, income-tax officials, parcel booking clerks, ticket checkers, educational officers, marketing inspectors, doctors, etc., all are busy in making money through evil means. Due to this corruption the planning of the government remains unsuccessful, and the state of the country remains as before. Even after spending a huge amount of money over planning, the standard of living of the citizens, and the problems of the country are left untouched.

(ii) *Corruption in police department.* In India, whenever the government has appointed commissions, they have pointed out towards the corruption in police department, but all in vain. Only recently, at Lucknow, a retired judge of Allahabad High Court expressed his views regarding corruption in this department. He was of the opinion that it was the police of the state which encouraged dacoities by its support. The prostitutes, thieves, cheats, dacoits and the persons indulging in many crimes, get themselves free by giving bribes to the police and freely do their jobs. The police officials take a definite amount regularly from the centres of corruption. After handing over due shares to the police officials, gambling dens, drinking bars and brothels become free to operate. They are not afraid even of violating a law. Corruption in this department sometimes crosses the limits by entangling the innocent persons in their traps. They force these persons to give them undue money. They thrust upon them many crimes only to harass them. The police men realise money by showing them fear of law and imprisonment, disgrace and humiliation. The businessmen mostly fill their pockets now and then. The rich men try to please these police men in order to avoid imprisonment because every one of them earns his money through evil, illegal and corrupt means. Many police men are habitual of drinking. They attend brothels and drinking bars regularly. The centres of corruption work freely under their patronage and shelter.

(iii) *Corruption in the law courts.* A country where there is corruption even in the courts of justice cannot be called a truly democratic society. On the contrary it is a disgrace to democracy. Today in India corruption is not only increasing in the political field, but also in the field of justice. Corruption in the courts of justice is a curse to humanity. Postponement of dates of a case is very easy only by giving bribes to the clerks of the judges. Allurement of money changes the decisions taken by some judges in these courts. Some advocates also try to full up the pockets of the judges. They are well aware of the fact that after a heavy bribe the decision would be done in their favour and that the advocate of the opposite party will have to look back even after a successful pleading. The professional witnesses are trusted and regarded as true witnesses by the law courts, whether they have been present on the spot or not. In addition to criminal courts there is bribery even in the civil courts. The industrialists and owners of big mills give bribes to the judges and the magistrates and as a result do not care for the labour laws while running their factories and mills. Presentation of gifts to the judges on all occasions or festivals, has become, somewhat customary. Alongwith it a large sum of money is sent to them regularly, on account of which they fulfil their endless desires through corrupt means. In the field of justice there is such a large scale corruption that the profession of a lawyer has become morally degraded. It is now rightly called the profession of a liar.

(iv) *Corruption in the local self-government.* In India Village Panchayats, Municipalities, Corporations and District Boards etc. are centres of corruption. Many of the Chairmen, Presidents, Secretaries, Mayors, accept bribes and cheat the government by producing forged documents and other certificates before the officials. They suck the poor people of the country, make money and lead a luxurious life. "Eat, drink and be merry" is their motto. The main cause of corruption lies in the fact that they have to spend money lavishly during the election period. They have to purchase votes. And after getting success they compensate their loss done, by taking and giving bribes. They make every possible effort, fair or fowl mean and discarding in order to fulfil their target. After the election is over, they arrange dinners, feasts, drinks, dances etc., to please their supporters and other high officials. These leaders will naturally accept bribery. For the election of chairman lakhs of rupees are wasted. When the chairman holds his office he will try to compensate his loss from the pocket of the public. In such a condition it is quite natural that these bodies turn into centres of corruption. The members, employees and the peons too begin to take bribes and committing thefts. Every body knows that with the help of money nothing is impossible. Without getting the plans passed in advance, houses and buildings are built and if afterwards an inquiry committee is appointed, again there is bribery and the committee gives its report in favour. For obtaining licences, permits, contracts, the men employ the same evil means and are successful. Even for having connection for electricity and water one has to give bribe.

3. Corruption in Economic Field. In the economic field also, there is corruption at large. For example, dishonesty in the Stock Exchanges, bribery in the commercial field, forgery and cheating in advertisements etc. are usual practices in this field. The contractors take contracts through corrupt means and then try to fill their pockets by adulteration in the cement etc. The industrialists and the businessmen deposit money of the public but when the people want to withdraw their money, these men declare themselves bankrupt. The shopkeepers cheat the public and the innocent customers by weighing less. Millionaires avoid taxes by giving bribes to the officials concerned. Sutherland, in his research found out that there was a large scale corruption among the businessmen of U.S.A. Forged and false advertisements were very common. Alongwith false publicity violation of laws of copy right and patent trade marks was also a usual practice.

If we cast a glance over the history of big capitalists in India, we may find that some of them have been employing every possible corrupt means in order to achieve success in the economic field. The shopkeepers make adulterations in the eatables and medicines also for the smallest gain. They keep forged weights and scales to loot the customers. Again, there are black-markets everywhere in the country. The capitalists loot the public in these markets by selling the articles which are not available any where except in their godowns. They take full advantage of the economic law of demand and supply. By following this rule the capitalists are becoming wealthier day by day. The practice of imitating well-known articles is becoming more popular. The imitators prepare an article so cleverly that it looks like the original. In Calcutta there are a number of markets in which only imitations are sold. The government is making no provision of any law so as to check these markets. Besides, in big cities like Calcutta, Bombay and Delhi it is very difficult to rent a house or shop in a well located area. For it one has to pay a big unreturnable amount called 'Pagri' to the owner. Many of the businessmen make all possible efforts to avoid taxes. They hide their income and other facts of their business, prepare bogus accounts to produce before the officials concerned and by giving a heavy bribe easily get clear of. In economic field the main cause of corruption is the throat cutting competition among the businessmen. It is only due to this competition that they involve themselves in corruption. In the words of Bernard, "A...problem posed by competition is its effects on character and personality... profit rather than production of goods is sought and throat cutting, unfair practices and shoddy workmanship are constant temptations. Businessmen often complain that they have to do things they are forced to do under pressure of competition. They sworn themselves for doing what they feel they have to do. They suffer self-hatred and a sense of guilt". The businessmen, in spite of suffering from self-hatred and a sense of guilt, have to indulge in corruption knowingly, enforced by evil circumstances.

4. Corruption in Religious Field. In this field corruption is found in religious places in the form of immoral deeds in the name of religion. People generally build 'Dharamshalas', 'Temples' and 'Gaushalas' inspired by religious spirit but the priests and 'Purohits' who look after these holy places, spread corruption. They corrupt these places by involving into many immoral activities. They drink in these places, gamble and indulge in many impious acts. The women who come here with a holy heart are insulted and humiliated by these men. They entangle them in and loot their money and honour. 'Prasad' is sold in the markets and money given by religious persons is wasted in drinking, gambling and merry making.

5. Corruption in Social Field. The organisation of human relationship is weakened by some evil practices prevailing in the society. For example, illegitimate sexual relations corrupt a family and then the society. If such type of relationship is brought to an end social ties would be strengthened. Such illegitimate relations were found in the society very often when there was no provision of widow remarriage. But even now when it has been allowed by law, illegitimate relations are increasing. The public still discards the widow remarriage act and remarriage of a widow is regarded as an immoral act, and a sin. As a result thousands of young widows are not allowed to marry again. As they find it very difficult to control their desires, they indulge in corruption. The availability of mechanical and chemical means of family planning are also responsible for increasing corruption in sexual relations. The virgins as well as the married women both can use these contraceptive means, and as there remains no danger of pregnancy, it increases illicit relations among males and females. One more cause of corruption is illmatched marriages. For example, a girl of sixteen years is married to a middle aged man only for a monetary gain. Selling away of girls like this is social evil. It leads them towards prostitution and illicit relations. In marriage dowry system plays a very important role in increasing corruption. Parents of a girl are forced to give dowry in the marriage of their daughter. If it is not given according to the demand of the other party, either the marriage party goes back or the bride is severely dealt with. The women of the opposite party humiliate and discard the new bride. Sometimes parents of the boy compel the girl to leave their house for ever. Under these intolerable circumstances the girls revolt against the society and flee away to lead an independent life. Mostly they become prostitutes and call girls. Most of the institutions like Orphanages, Rescue shelters, Mahila Ashrams Salvation Homes, are the centres of corruption. Though these institutions may serve the society successfully but the persons who are to look after these increase corruption by indulging in many sex-vices. They always try to make money through corrupt means.

The same corruption may be found even in educational institutions. Members of executive committee force the staff to do immoral things. The poor teacheresses, by their circumstances act as these members desire. Managers or managing bodies of these institutions compel them to put their signatures on a particular salary which is not actually given to them. The employees accept whatever they are given because they have neither money nor courage to revolt against injustice. In schools and colleges undue money is taken from the students in the form of building fund, poor boys fund etc. The students have to give bribes to the principals and clerks in order to get admission in a particular institution. There is corruption in the field of art also. Girls are invited to learn music, dance, drawing and painting, sewing and knitting etc. by the institution concerned. Instead of giving them a good knowledge the instructors mislead them to adopt corrupt ways. They fail to stand against the allurements and sooner or later, indulge in corruption. In educational field a number of institutions receive grants-in-aid by the government showing forged figures regarding the staff, students and other employees of the institution. These very institutions are recognised by the government. In private institutions there is an absolute monopoly of the management. The members of the managing committees employ their own relatives, friends and persons belonging to their own caste. In cases of admissions also they follow the same corrupt rules and regulations. To sum up, there is corruption in most of the educational institutions upon which depends the future of the country.

6. Individual Corruption. Individual corruption means a corruption due to some individual deformities. Though the individual having deformities causes harm to himself also but social relations are affected greatly as the society is merely an association of individuals. Morally or physically degraded individuals can't be fruitful to the society. It needs good citizens. Drinking, gambling, sex-vices and prostitution etc. are some examples of individual corruption. Such corruption degrades the individual from every point of view. He needs money in order to fulfil his endless desires. If he does not get enough money through fair means, he tries to get it by fowl means. Thus individual corruption increases corruption in the society.

SUGGESTIONS TO PREVENT CORRUPTION IN PUBLIC LIFE

Prevention of corruption from public life has become so important that without it no further reform in the society is possible. After a critical study of different aspects of human life reformers have reached the conclusion that raising the moral standard of each individual is a very urgent need of the country today, so that they may fulfil their responsibility and duty towards the country. Good citizens can perform their duties more efficiently. Hence each individual must avoid corruption. Some suggestions to eradicate corruption in the public life are as follows:

1. Proper Education. The most important suggestion to remove corruption from public life is to impart fruitful and proper education to the individual of the country. In this direction proper guidance is very necessary. The education code should also be amended so that the educational institutions may not employ evil means and harass the teachers and the students. The best remedy to prevent corruption in the society is to introduce the best type of moral education. It is only a proper type of education which may divert the attention of the individuals towards goodness. An educated man know the consequences of an act more vividly in comparison to an illiterate man; he can to some extent avoid corruption and follow some ideals and values of life, like honesty, truth, nonviolence, fulfilment of duty, the roots of a country's progress. He only shall be able to differentiate between good and evil, social values and personal gain, morality and religion. In brief, an educated person knows what he is doing and what would be the consequences. The circumstances may force him to do an evil act, but at heart he may be suffering from a sense of guilt. In the near future he may avoid corruption and be an ideal citizen. To impart moral education in every educational institution will raise the moral standard of each individual. In giving employments, emphasis should be laid on the ability of a person, instead of his caste, religion, sex, status and the family to which he belongs. If this suggestion may be brought into practice, corruption from the government offices, law courts, police departments, educational institutions, reformatories, etc. may be eradicated. In education institutions only ideal teachers should be appointed without any consideration of caste, sex, family, religion or nationality. Such teachers alone would be able to draw the attention of the students towards morality, duty, goodness, obedience and faithfulness. They must be given a higher start so as to meet their necessary requirements, a better residence, sufficient medical aid, chances for further studies, leaves with pay and benefit of provident fund etc. The undue interference of the managers in the school or college affairs should be strictly prohibited. The appointments should be made on a permanent basis so that teachers might feel safe and secure from that side.

2. A change in the standard of political parties. The political parties in India have increased corruption in the democracy of today. They are killing the real sense of democracy. They think themselves above law quite free to do any thing. A change in the standard of political parties is very necessary if we want to bring a change in the structure of the government. In a democracy only elected leaders by the people rule over the country. That is why every leader with his party makes every possible effort to purchase votes at any cost. Crores of rupees are spent for them, motor cars are sent to bring the voters, money is distributed among the poor. The money wasted now shall be compensated tomorrow. It is also a form of corruption. Voters can bring a change in the political structure of today. It is their responsibility to send good leaders to form the government. They should evaluate the candidates. A candidate, if morally degraded, must be discarded even if he has huge money, a high social status, high powers and is well known in the public. The party in power must enforce laws to eradicate corruption from political parties. It can amend the constitution also. It can suppress the party in opposition, which helps in spreading rumours about the present government. The government should give a heavy punishment and rigorous imprisonment to the persons responsible for spreading corruption during the election period. They should be severely dealt with. Besides taking these steps, it ought to put high ideals before the public by raising its standard of living, making some social reforms, introducing morality in the educational and other institutions, following the path of truth, nonviolence and brotherhood shown by Gandhiji and other great men. If the party in power is itself corrupt, it will be quite impossible to prevent corruption in this country. It is only the government which can remove corruption by employing every possible means. One more suggestion may be given that only educated citizens should be given a right to vote. The white collar criminals then shall not be able to cheat and befool the illiterate voters by giving them some money, or by making false promises. The government can check the white collar criminals. In the words of E.H.. Sutherland "white collar crime is crime committed by a person of respectability and high social status in the course of his occupation". The government should check the capitalists also who directly or indirectly support the white collar criminals. They spend crores of rupees over them at the time of election. If such persons are caught red handed their fundamental rights should be taken away by the government.

3. Information of law in the areas of trade, industry and commerce. There is a large scale corruption in the field of commerce. In industrial areas, people generally violate laws by giving bribes to the officials and ministers concerned. If these persons are caught red handed at the time of adulteration or black marketing they are left without any penalty. The businessmen, when found avoiding taxes, the officials overlook them, and indirectly encourage them to adopt the same means because their pockets are filled with money. For these people there is no provision of heavy punishment or rigorous imprisonment. They are often left free. Capital punishment should be given to the persons, engaged in adulterating edibles, medicines and other articles, necessary in life. In the industrial areas, the owners of big factories and the industrialists, often violate the laws and save themselves from being punished. In this direction, to remove this corruption the government should make laws and enforce them strictly in such areas. The violaters should be severly dealt with. Heavy punishments such as life imprisonment, rigorous imprisonment, corporal punishment and heavy penalties etc. are fit for such corruption so that other persons may also learn a lesson.

4. Reforms in government offices. Mostly, corruption is found in the government offices. There should be separate body to keep an eye over the conduct of the employees. Every activity should be watched carefully. If they are found engaged in corruption, they should be dismissed then and there so that other employees may have an example. The laws must be obeyed by them. The rules and regulations must be amended. The public should not encourage the employees by giving bribes for the work they do. If any official demands undue money he must be reported to the anti-corruption department of the government. The leaders, ministers and other higher authorities should go deep into the matter and make proper inquiries personally. A quick decision is very necessary so that the employees may not get a change to give bribes to the authorities concerned. During the middle ages some kings used to move in disguise to know the welfare of the subjects and tried to remove the grievances. The same practice may be adopted even to-day by our leaders and reformers. In this way they can prevent corruption from the government offices. Some ideal leaders have adopted this method of enquiring and have been successful in catching the corrupt employees.

5. Reforms in police department. A number of enquiry committees have been appointed by the governments to find out corruption in the department of police. In the reports they have indicated towards the large scale corruption prevailing in this department. A few years back, justice Mulla called the police of Uttar Pradesh a gang of looters. Undoubtedly, everywhere, the police support the criminals such as the gamblers, prostitutes, and persons selling drinks, etc. The support of the police has increased corruption in the society. Reforms in this department are very necessary. This will lead to two advantages. If corruption from this department is removed the officials and other employees of the department will cooperate in removing corruption in the public life. If the police of a country is watchful, corruption can't take root. It can no longer exist in the society. For preventing corruption from this department it is also very necessary to pay proper attention towards the complaints made by a publicman against the police. After a proper inquiry, a quick action against the corrupt person should be taken by the authorities. Some heavy punishments should be given to such corrupt persons. Getting a man merely transferred for corruption will not suffice. It will be a very light punishment to bring him on right lines.

Undue interference of the political leaders in the cases of corruption discourages the police to do its duty. It should be strictly prohibited. The leaders have no authority to force the police to do a particular action. As the executive body has no connection with judiciary, in the same way the political leaders should make no interference in the duty of police.

6. Reforms in the law courts. The law courts are the places where a man goes with pockets full of money, but returns empty handed. There are persons who have lost everything after these law courts. Justice, here is sold and purchased. Advocates attend the courts to loot the innocent villagers, to shop and search for some customers. From a peon of the court to the highest officers all accept bribes and sell themselves for a monetary gain. They all run after money. A suggestion in this direction is that our trusted leaders, in disguise, should try to catch these corrupt persons red handed and they ought to be awarded rigorous imprisonment.

7. Reforms in Industrial area. There is a large scale corruption in these areas. Man has become only a tool of a machine. In the words of Bertrand Russel, "In the development of science the power of impulse has increasingly prevailed over the love impulse." Again, Erich From writes, "Our gods are the machines and the ideal of efficiency the meaning of our life is to move, to forge ahead, to arrive as near to the top as possible." Thus we can say that the machines have increased corruption in the industrial areas. People have lost their moral values. They are busy in corruption, for all the corruptions such as adulteration in edibles, imitation, forgery, cheating, black marketing, avoiding taxes, preparing false accounts, taking signatures of the employees on a blank sheet and paying a little amount to the labourers etc., the government should enforce laws, alongwith it there must be a provision of severe punishment. Violation of the law should not be tolerated at all. A few days ago the police arrested a gang of gamblers. All of them were taken to the law court in a procession. A slogan, "we are gamblers" was written in bold letters on the cardboard sheets. The procession was passing the open markets. All of them were highly ashamed for what they had done. Inspectors, advocates, capitalists and some other officials were also arrested by the police as they were also gambling. An example of such a punishment was given recently in Pakistan. The persons involved in black marketing were seated on the donkies, with the faces painted black, and were taken to the law court in a procession passing through open markets. Such type of punishment aims to prevent corruption by causing a fear of insult and humiliation in those who might otherwise indulge in evil practices.

8. Reforms through social welfare institutions. In order to prevent corruption in the public life social welfare institutions should be established, almost in each city of the country. Our trusted leaders and persons having high moral ideals should participate as the active members of these institutions. Though such types of institutions are serving even today but the managing body is very corrupt. The persons who are to look after these institutions are corrupt persons. They mislead the widows, orphans and the poor exploited virgins, who take shelter for the betterment of their lives. Young enthusiastic persons of new generation should cooperate with them in social welfare work and try to remove evil elements working in such institutions. There should be a revolution which can be successful only if the young men having high moral character and reformative spirit, take an active part vigorously.

9. Reforms in Penal System. The penal system of today is very defective. It is very expensive, rigid and puzzling. Ordinary illiterate people can't follow its procedure. They have to give bribes from top to bottom and only then they can hope of getting justice. The procedure of approaching law is very long. It takes a long time. The criminals do not feel any kind of terror. They go on doing their own job violating every law, because the punishments which are given by law courts are very light. There must be some reforms in the penal system. The punishment and penalties should be to some extent desirable and reasonable. Getting a man merely transferred, if he is found guilty is not a desirable punishment. Such types of punishment encourage more corruption. The punishments should provoke terror in the hearts of criminals and mischief mongers. Even the hardest punishment may be given. In its Justification Cicely M. Craven writes, "Capital punishment aims to prevent crime by causing the fear of death in those who might otherwise be criminal." He again writes, "The procedure of approaching law courts should be simple and less expensive." Sometimes the persons who make a complaint, or give some clues of corruption in a particular area are caught and imprisoned. Hence everybody feels fear in making any complaint against somebody. The law courts should take a quick action on the complaints that any criminal may not get time to give bribes. Pleaders should be available to the poor people also without any payment. The executive should not interfere in judiciary. Both should be quite separate from one another so that the judiciary may not feel any undue pressure while deciding a case. It will remove bribery to some extent. The poor and it literate people would also be able to get advantage. They may bring their complaints in these law courts.

SMUGGLING

India is surrounded by Bangala Desh in the East, Nepal in North, Pakistan in West and Ceylone in South. While Ceylone is separated from the country through ocean the boundaries of the country in East, North and West are marked on the land. These boundaries can be easily transgrassed by miscreants. Smuggling means illegal import or export of some goods through illegal means. This involves great financial loss to the excise department besides involving so many criminal activities. It is a big activity in the villages, towns and cities situated on the boarders. Its cause is high excise duties in different countries, rigid checks upon export and import and big difference in the prices of different commodities in the two countries. Smuggling from India is not only to the boarder countries but also to the far off countries of middle east and far east. Smuggling of gold from Arab countries and silver from India to Arab countries had been a great headache to Indian police of Bombay and other ports situated on the western coast.

Smuggling activity is maximum through land routs since land border can be easily crossed. In Punjab the border between India and Pakistan is very easily crossed by the villagers on the two sides. This is due to the fact that the border is so long that it cannot be easily checked by the police of both the countries. Similar is the case with the border between India and Bangla Desh. In North, the border between Nepal and India is long and passes through difficult terrain. This makes guarding of the border all the more difficult and increases smuggling activities on both the sides. The second important route for smuggling is through water since it can be operated through power driven boats and small steamers. The Indian coast is very vast and it is physically impossible to guard the entire sea coast, against smuggling. Therefore, it is a big time activity on the coasts in India. The third route for smuggling is through air. This involves minimum amount of smuggling due to rigid checks at airport and due to the difficulty of obtaining private planes for smuggling purposes. Vehicles on roads and boats and steamers can be easily procured by the smugglers but procuring of an aeroplane or a helicopter for smuggling purposes is almost an exception.

The above description of the three routes of smuggling makes it clear that in order to stop it or minimise it more checks are needed on the land and sea borders. Sociologically speaking, the reasons for smuggling are: economic ambitions, lure of earning big money quickly, criminal tendencies, lack of sufficient guarding of the borders and last but not the least the prestige of money in society even though earned by dubious means. The famous novel *Godfather* revealed that the government in U.S.A. and the industrialists are in league with Mafia gangs to run their operations. Similarly in India smugglers had been giving big donations to the different political parties. During the time of emergency smugglers were nabbed on a large scale for the first time. They were put in jails, their premises were thoroughly searched and they were prosecuted. This gave a setback to smuggling activities for sometime but as soon as the period of emergency was over, smuggling activities started again on a large scale. In the present time it can be definitely said that the big international smugglers are phenomenally rich and enjoy political patronage. Recently in Bombay a very famous smuggler was openly guarlanded and praised by a cabinet minister of the state government. In Bombay and other big cities of the country so many smugglers wield financial, political and physical influence. Therefore, it is not easy to root out smuggling from the country.

The above analysis of the causes of smuggling in the country leads us to the following suggestions which may be adopted to root out this biggest cause of black money in the country.

1. The borders of the country should be everywhere more strictly guarded against smuggling activities.

2. More strict punishments should be provided for the convicts of smuggling activities.

3. The policy of import and export should be revised and reoriented with a view to reducing smuggling activities to the minimum.

4. Public opinion against smuggling should be made strong so that smugglers may be socially ostracized.

5. Spending by political parties in elections should be checked and if found too much exaggarated its sources should be scrutinised. This will remove political patronage of the smugglers.

6. The lure for foreign goods should be curbed through propaganda and increase of the quality level of the indigenous goods.

7. Police officials involved in checking smuggling activities should be given financial and non-financial incentives for their special abilities in checking this evil.

8. The net of income tax raides upon smugglers should be more tightened and steps should be taken to recover income tax penalties and arrears from them.

BLACK MONEY

Besides corruption, nepotism and smuggling an important current social evil is black money. Black money is primarily known as an economic evil. It leads to inflation and all round increase of the prices accompanied with fall in the value of currency. Black money is associated with luxury, white collar crime and so many other social evils. In Bombay it plays a very important role in the film world. In political sphere again it plays an important role with the result that it gets political patronage. In India the amount of black money is equal if not more than the white money. This results into parallel economy of black and white money which upsets so many business, industries and the prices structure. It leads to considerable loss of different types of taxes to the government exchequer. Therefore, one often hears about the worry of the state and central government over the curbing of black money in the country.

Some of the causes of the increase of black money in India are as follows:

1. The income-tax structure in the country is such that no one can become rich without evading income-tax. It is hence that most of the moneyed persons are motivated to gather money in the black form.

2. In several industries as in the film world transactions in white money are not appreciated and more transactions are required in terms of black money. This again increases the amount of black money circulating in the market.

3. Black money is the biggest cause of so many illegal and criminal activities, economic and otherwise.

The following are the consequences of the rise of the amount of black money in the country:

1. As has been already pointed out, it increases inflation resulting in rise of prices and fall in the valuc of currency.

2. It is the economic backbone of different criminal activities such as smuggling, hoarding, black marketing, grafts, criminal activities and white callar crimes.

3. Increase of black money not only ruins the economic world but also leads to social disorganisation.

4. Black money encourages prostitution, murders, crimes, callgirl rackets, political intrigues and almost all the social evils. It is because the owner of black money is required to spend it as much as possible otherwise it increases fast and becomes difficult to hold. Therefore, those who have black money spend it more and more in women and wine and other social evils.

The following suggestions can be made to curb the social evil of black money in the country.

1. The income tax structure should be so revised that it may discourage black money and encourage earning in white money.

2. More incentives should be given for the betterment of economic conditions in the country.

3. Public opinion against black money should be created.

4. The government should take all such steps as are suggested by the specialists from time to time to curb this social evil.

QUESTIONS FOR EXERCISE

1. Explain corruption in public life found in urban centres and megapolitan cities in India.
2. Write short note on smuggling and Black money in Indian cities.

14

Urban Problems : Over-Crowding

In major cities in India like Greater Bombay, Calcutta, Pune, Kanpur and Ahmedabad the population between 85 and 90 per cent of households lives in one or two rooms. This shows an acute shortage of housing in urban areas. This will be further clear by the report of over-crowding in Greater Bombay. In 1971 the sequence of the first 10 largest cities in India was as follows : Calcutta, Greater Bombay, Delhi, Madras, Hyderabad, Ahmedabad, Bangalore, Kanpur, Pune, Nagpur. According to Registrar General of India the urban population is likely to increase to 278.3 million by 2001.

OVER CROWDING IN INDIAN METROPOLITAN CITIES

Life in Indian metropolitan cities like Calcutta, Bombay, Delhi and Madras is becoming a nightmare for a majority of the people and if the present trends continue, there will be a total failure of the urban system by the end of the century, according to environmentalist Rashmi Mayur. Dr. Mayur points out that while there is an appreciable decline or stabilisation of large cities in industrialised countries, the pace of urbanisation is increasing significantly in the less developed nations, Mexico, India and Egypt being prime examples. Dr. Mayur lists the present urban growth rate at four per cent yearly, approximately twice the rate of population growth, half the growth being natural and the rest due to migration from rural areas. The present rate of urbanisation he says, will be accelerated after 1985 and by the end of the century, the approximate number in various urban centres all over India will reach 335 to 350 million people.

Bombay : A profile of Present Over-crowding

1. Area and Population etc. Area 43.771 sq. km. Population 8.2 million (1981 Census), Density of population per sq. km. 18,73,386 Sex ratio 775 females per 1,000 males, Percentage of literacy 68.2, Slum-dwellers 35 lakhs, Birth rate per 1000, 81.6, Death rate per 1000, 26.9.

2. Education and Health. Pre-primary and primary schools 1,859, Secondary schools 115, Number of higher and special education institutions

437, Pre-primary and primary students 7.55 lakhs. Secondary schools students 4.25 lakhs. Higher secondary school students 1.52 lakhs, Number of hospital beds 25,000.

3. Entertainment, Hotel and Restaurants. Cinema houses 142, Total number of seats, 95,000, Residential hotels, 635, Number of rooms 25,000, Eating houses and restaurants 11,520.

4. Transport. Total railway length 167 km. No. of commuters carried per day 5.5 million. Total road length 1,41,060 km. Buses 2,052 (93% operational efficiency), No. of passengers carried per day (BEST) 4.5 million, Contract carriers 250, Lorries 65,000, Taxis 50,000, Private cars 30,000, Slow moving vehicles (including handcarts and bullock-carts) 15,000. Petrol Stations 257, Motor spirit used 18,374 kiloliters, High Speed diesel used 14,710 kilo-liters, Daily vehicle coverage of Cars 5,10,000 km, Daily coverage of diesel vehicles 2,45,000 km.

5. Communication. Total number of assorted mail pieces daily 2.5 million (10% of the country's total), Number of postmen 4,500, Marriage invitation cards 20,000, Parties cards 28,000. Functions cards 3,200, Greeting cards 12,140, Airmail sent to 140 countries, Telephone connections 2,80,366, Telephone revenue Rs. 95.69 crores. Telephone waiting list 1,23,156, Telex waiting list 1,800. Street side hoardings 6,000, Pole Ads 15000, Kiosks Ads 6,000, Bus fleet Ads 2000.

6. Immigration. In 1980 : 2,00,000, influx per day 3,000 families, rate of growth due to immigration 50% (Mexico, Cairo and Jakarta 5%), Initial area 26 sq. miles, Megalopolis area 169 sq. miles.

7. Housing. Dharavi, the biggest slum in Asia, population .5 million, footpath dwellers .5 million, persons living in buildings likely to collapse 15%, number of buildings likely to collapse 11,000, Cost of apartment Rupees 2,000 per sq. foot, Shortfall of public housing 5,000 units per year, private housing construction 20,000 units per year, backlog of housing units 8,00,000. Yearly shortage of housing units 55,000.

8. Social Problems. Average income of 75% families Rs. 630 per month, income of 10% persons Rs. 250 per month, Beggars 2,00,000, Unemployed 5,00,000, Partially employed 1 million, water to slum dwellers 10 gallons per person, Daily garbage generation 3,200 tons, road accidents (in 1980) 23,000, accidental deaths 706, daily pollutants discharged in the air, 1,500 tons, incidence of lungs diseases 9 to 20%, noise pollution 72 decibels in busy areas, rate 9 million, sick and hungry dogs 2 million, amount of pollution in slum areas equal to smoking of 30 cigarettes per day.

9. Industrial Units. Large and medium units 798, small scale units 14,531, per capita income Rs. 1800, textile mills 54, industrial daily employment, 164,187, wholesale merchants 8,000, paid up capital Rs. 67 crore, City mills consumption 111 million cotton bales, chemical industries 45% of the national production, dyestuff units 70% of national output, Film industry biggest in

Asia. Total industrial investment Rs. 10,000 crores, major trade unions : CITU, AITUC, INTUC, HMS, BMS, etc.

10. Banking. Banking offices 940, Banking offices (cooperative) 210, Registered money-lenders 2,140.

11. Revenue and Finance (Rs. crores 1980-81). Income Tax 900.00, Corporation Tax 376.59, Non-Corporation Tax 458.37, Wealth Tax 20.32, Gift Tax 1.36, Estate Duty 4.32, Interest Tax 23.09, Sales Tax 600.00.

12. Miscellaneous. Cement consumed per quarter 2 lakh tons, rice sold per day 100 kg. bags), 45,000, Wheat sold per day (100 kg bags) 42,000, Meat sold per day 45,000 kg., Vegetables arriving daily 2,700 tonnes, annual rain-fall 19.2 mm, registered shops 1,21,430, commercial establishments 17,626, daily average water supply 430 million gallons, share of Bombay port in India's total foreign trade 21.1% Total volume of foreign trade carried by foreign trade 5,637 crore, Private markets 19, Milk consumed daily 1.9 million litres, Newspapers dailies 42, Magazines 764, Municipal markets 74, Income of Municipal Corporation in 1981-81 Rs. 263.86 crores (More than the income of H.P. state Rs. 218 crore).

13. Future Predictions for 2001 A.D. Slums population 75%, shortage of housing units 2.4 million, growth of suburbs 50%, sex ratio 1,000 to 900 females, number of people aged 60 and above 1 million, increase of railway travel 300 per cent, demand for bus services 150%, total demand of bus trips per year 1.5 billion, number of vehicles 6,50,000, water shortage 350 million gallon per day, garbage collected per day 6,500 tonnes. It will be difficult to quantify the institutional breakdown, crime, corruption, alienation, etc. arising out of the giganticism of the city.

Alternative to doom. 1. Available resources must be judiciously and selectively used. Efforts should be made to create new and indigenous resources. 2. The benefits of resources must be distributed equitably and for the total development of society. 3. A fair system of sharing and contribution of resources as between the Centre and the State Government must be created.

The over-urbanisation is evident in various ways. One is underdevelopment by which certain types of urban technology necessary for modernisation is scarce, unavailable or not used. Secondly, urban forms, city governments and economic planning are archaic, with little relevance to the Indian setting.

Dr. Mayur argues that the urban social structure reflects institutions, attitudes, values and rituals of rural India, determining policies and influencing development which conflict with the building of healthy and progressive urban society.

Finally, the continuous accentuation of the urban-rural dichotomy has led to the parasitic relationship between the city and the hinterland, by which, because of the disadvantageous relationship of the latter, much of its vitality is drained away and is concentrated in the urban areas for the benefit of a limited number of people.

At the outset it seems that if the trends continue as projected, the future of urbanisation in India will be disastrous if not catastrophic. Broadly speaking, there will be 20 cities with a population of about one million each and at least 600 cities with a population between 50,000 and 5,00,000, small towns will decline in number.

The spectacular population growth, specially in urban ares, will strain all resources and social institutions beyond any Malthusian calculation. Even if the food production is doubled by the end of the century to 220 million tonnes per year (which is likely), there will be a deficit of at least 30 million tonnes per year.

He says that if the economic growth picks up again and the per capita NGP increases at the rate of two per cent yearly on an average over the Rs. 950 GNP per capita today, by the end of the year 2,000, it will hardly be Rs. 1800 GNP per capita, which will not take the masses above the poverty line. On the contrary, since much of the surplus will be absorbed by the increasing population, at least 65 per cent of the urban population will be living below the desired minimum.

Dr. Mayur says that for the projected population 70 million dwellings will be required. Water needs will touch 8.75 billion gallons daily. Transportation will shockingly halt due to enormous disruption and dislocations generated by continuously inadequate facilities.

Probably the most gruesome problem will be that of energy shortage. The problem of environmental pollution will plague Indian cities and towns even more seriously.

The literacy rate, which is 32 per cent today in the urban areas, will reach 60 per cent in the next 22 years. The relevance of the present education system to the future development will be increasingly questioned but the present entrenched system will hardly go through any major changes. The manufacturing sector will remain the main employer.

The cost of health will grow in geometrical progression, yet for a large number of people ill-health will be the way of life. The joint family system, the backbone of Indian society for centuries, will experience the strain of modernisation.

Urban development, Dr. Mayur says, should be made part of the regional planning based on the resources requirements, economic viability, optimum productivity, cultural growth and integrated development, halting any further growth in major metropolitan areas.

Every region, city and town should have a data bank, supplying scientific, up-to-date information for planning, integrated long-range development and proper resources allocation. Dr. Mayur says it is not necessary for urban society to suffer from various social ills such as loneliness, crime, breakdown of social relations or alcoholism as many aspects of family relations can be restructured to accomplish the goal of building a new and happy society.

However, the more pervasive picture he paints of urban life in India today is pockets of glistening modern skyscrapers, surrounded by squalid slums, stretching far into the suburbs with all the concomitant problems of poverty, unemployment, pollution, traffic congestion, crime, filth and misery.

NATIONAL CAPITAL REGION PLANNING BOARD

The National Capital Region Planning Board (NCRPB) has been set up with statutory powers under the National Capital Region Planning Board Act, 1985, to plan and promote a balanced and harmonised development of National Capital Region (NCR). This is a unique concept of regional development providing partnership approach with the Centre taking lead and three participating states Haryana, Rajasthan and Uttar Pradesh and Union Terriotry of Delhi and evolving an integrated development framework for the region. NCR development is expected to cost nearly Rs. 3,000 crore.

NCR being one of the most urbanised regions of the country has been facing serious problems of unplanned and haphazard development particularly in Delhi and its adjoining areas which are growing at an alarming rate. Delhi itself is besieged by a host of serious problems due to shortages in water supply, power, public transport and sanitation. This is further aggravated by constant migration mainly because of its high employment generation capacity and better quality of living. Besides Delhi, metropolitan area towns are growing very rapidly because of their close proximity to the national capital resulting in rapid growth around Delhi.

NCRPB has prepared a Statutory Regional Plan-2001 for NCR which came into force from 23 January 1989. Two important goals are (i) a balanced and harmonised developed region leading to dispersal of economic activities and (ii) population. The plan is an integrated policy framework relating to population distribution, settlement, system, transport and telecommunications, physical and social infrastructure, regional land use, environment and eco-development, management structure of plan implementation and counter-magnet areas for development outside NCR.

NCRPB has identified priority towns/complexes in the region for induced rapid growth through creation of economic activities with a view to attracting potential Delhi-bound migrants. It will help reduce pressure on Delhi. In addition, the Plan envisages development of sub-regional centres, service centres and basic villages in various sub-regions of the National Capital Region.

QUESTIONS FOR EXERCISE

1. Write an essay on over-crowding in Indian metropolitan cities with special reference to Bombay.
2. Write short note on NCRPB.

15

Problems of Housing

The problem of housing in India is a complex one requiring finances on a huge scale and is dependent for its solution on the concerned efforts of individuals, cooperatives and central and state governments to be planned and executed over a number of years. There is acute shortage of housing in urban and rural areas and much of the available accommodation is qualitatively of sub-standard variety. The shortage in urban areas has been largely on account of considerable increase in population since 1921, the steady shift of population from the rural to the urban areas, the haphazard growth of towns owning to lack of proper town planning and the comparative inability of private enterprises to keep pace with the growing demand.

Size of the Problem

With a growing population and the steady shift of population from the rural to urban areas, the problem has become more difficult both in qualitative and quantitative terms. Housing inadequacies in India have both qualitative and quantitative aspects. The problem of housing has tended to worsen over the years due to (i) rapid increase in population, (ii) fast rate of urbanisation, and (iii) proportionately inadequate addition to the housing stock. There is a qualitative difference in the problems for urban and rural housing. Whereas the problem of urban areas is, by and large, that of congestion, slums and squatter settlements, the rural areas are characterised by the absence of essential services and poor environmental conditions. Any comprehensive solution of India's housing problem cannot afford to ignore either.

Since Independence, India has changed a great deal. Post Independence policies of providing greater employment opportunities and better health care have led to many more people having higher disposable incomes, and to a growing population which is living longer than the earlier generations. These changes are being reflected in the growing number of new households needing housing and the rising standards of expectation where housing standards are concerned. Housing policy in India thus concentrates on increasing the number of houses built and encourages people to own their own houses. Although living standards have improved for many people, it has also become abundantly clear that the fundamental inequalities have remained unaltered.

Housing Finance

Housing finance is the most crucial element in house construction and building activities. In the field of housing, the public sector has a marginal though promotional role to play. The bulk of the investment in housing is, however, expected to come from the private sector.

A number of specialised agencies have come up in recent times in the country yet the bulk of the finance for housing originates from a selected group of Central financial institutions comprising the Life Insurance Corporation of India (LIC), the General Insurance Corporation of India (GIC), Housing and Urban Development Corporation (HUDCO), the Employees Provident Fund Organisation, etc. Funds are also provided and channelised through the state apex co-operative housing societies, state housing boards and housing and urban development authorities, nationalised commercial banks, etc.

Urban Development

The Sixth Plan emphasised the development of small, medium and intermediate towns. Urban development is seen as complementary to rural development so that policies affecting the process of urbanisation would strengthen the links between the cities and their hinterland. The objective of the Sixth Plan is to strengthen the small and medium towns for increased investments in housing, water supply communication, education; medical care, recreation, etc. It is envisaged that positive incentives would be given for setting up new industries and other activities in these towns accompanied by improvement in power and telecommunication facilities. With this objective in view, a centrally sponsored scheme for the development of small and medium towns with a population less than one lakh has been in operation since December 1979.

The Sixth Plan has made a provision of Rs. 96 crore in the Central sector in order to support the integrated development of 231 small and medium towns during the plan period. The Central Government would finance schemes for shelter, transportation and economic activities to the extent of 50 per cent of the project cost or Rs. 40 lakh, whichever is lesser subject to matching funds from the sate agencies. The state governments would further undertake investment in water supply, sanitation, slum improvement and social facilities as a part of the integrated project. Low cost sanitation has also been introduced as an item for Central assistance under the scheme. State Governments will be entitled to Rs. 15 lakh over and above Rs. 40 lakh available under the scheme for low cost sanitation provided they propose to spend at least Rs. 12 lakh on low cost sanitation schemes out of their own funds. The projects are appraised by the Town and Country Planning Organisation.

Socialisation of Urban Land

The Urban Land (Ceiling and Regulation) Act, 1976 came into force on the 17 February 1976. It provides for: (i) imposition of a ceiling on both ownership and possession of vacant land in urban agglomerations, the ceiling being on a graded basis according to the classification of the urban agglomeration; (ii) acquisition of the excess vacant land by the state governments with powers to dispose of the vacant land to sub-serve the common good; (iii) payment of an amount for the acquisition of the excess vacant land in cash and in bonds; (iv) exemptions in respect of certain specific categories of vacant lands; and (v) restricting the plinth area for the construction of future residential buildings. The Act provides for granting permission to hold land in excess of the ceiling limits for utilising them for the construction of dwelling units for the weaker sections of the society.

The Act applies to all the states and union territories except Jammu and Kashmir, Kerala, Nagaland and Sikkim, which have not adopted the Act so far; and excludes Tamil Nadu which had enacted its own law in 1978.

Environmental Improvement of Urban Slums

The Sixth Plan period envisaged of one crore slum dwellers at an estimated cost of Rs.151.45 crore in the various schemes of environmental improvement of urban slums (EIUS). The scheme forms part of the minimum needs programme. This is in continuation of the scheme introduced in 1972 under which amenities like water supply, sewerage, sanitation, paved pathways, community latrines and street lighting were provided to slum dwellers in selected urban areas. During 1983-84 and 1984-85, an amount of Rs. 10.97 crore and Rs. 80 crore respectively was released to the states under the Central incentive grant scheme introduced in 1983-84. During the Sixth Plan period as on 31 December 1984,84.6 lakh slum dwellers have been covered in the various slates and union territories as per the progress report received from them.

URBAN WATER SUPPLY AND SANITATION

Urban Water Supply and Sanitation is a State subject. Schemes are formulated, implemented, operated and maintained by the state governments/ union territory administrations. Funds are provided for the purpose under the state plans. As per the information available, the coverage of urban water supply and sanitation till December 1991 was 85 per cent and 46 per cent respectively. The working group for the formulation of the Eighth Plan recommended to provide drinking water facilities to cent per cent population and with sewerage and sanitation facilities to 75 per cent of the urban population by the end of the Eighth Plan (1992-97). In order to achieve the objective, the Working Group envisaged amount of Rs. 23,634.56 crore for the Eighth Plan. However, only an outlay of Rs. 5,757.28 crore has been provided by the Planning Commission for the Eighth Plan period, of which an outlay of Rs. 1,114.54 crore has been provided for the Annual Plan 199394 under the state sector. During 1994-95, an amount of Rs. 16.99 crore was distributed amongst those states which were considered earlier for the first instalment. Various training programmes have been initiated for human resource development in planning, design, operation and maintenance and management of urban water supply and sanitation schemes. The Government has introduced use of micro-computer for planning and designing of water supply distribution and sewerage systems besides imparting training to public health engineers. Financial assistance was provided to several state agencies dealing in urban water supply and sanitation sector for procuring micro-computers. The agencies have procured the computers and accessories and installed them in their organisations.

The Ministry sponsors research and development projects to various institutions in the country in order to develop appropriate technologies in the field of water supply and sanitation which can be applied not only in implementation of the project but also in their operation and maintenance and to achieve an overall improvement in the sector. The Urban Development Ministry has developed a Management Information System (MIS) which has been disseminated to state public health engineering departments and water supply and sewerage boards for implementation. The Ministry provides technical advice and accords technical approval for urban water supply and sanitation schemes in order to get loan assistance from LIC, World Bank and other bilateral agencies.

URBAN BASIC SERVICES FOR THE POOR

The Scheme of Urban Basic Services for the Poor (UBSP) was launched in 1990-91. The scheme is based on the convergent provision of social and physical inputs in low income, urban neighbourhoods through the programmes of various specialist departments with the active participation of community groups. The cardinal objective of the scheme is to improve the overall quality of life of slum dwellers. The Cabinet has approved the scheme for the Eighth Plan period. From the inception of the Eighth Five Year Plan, the programme is being implemented on a 60:40 sharing basis between the Central and state governments. Further, the per capita expenditure will be Rs. 75 in the first year and Rs. 50 from the second year onwards after the basic infrastructure has been established. A total outlay of Rs. 100 crore has been provided for the scheme for the Eighth Plan period. The scheme is to be implemented in collaboration with the state sector scheme of Environmental Improvement of Urban Slums and the Centrally-sponsored scheme of Nehru Rozgar Yojana. By the end of the Eighth Plan period, it is expected that the benefit of the scheme will extend to urban areas having a total slum population of about 70 lakh and, on a national basis, targets 500 cities and towns. The National Plan of Action (NPA) on Children which is a follow-up of the promises made by the global fraternity at the World Summit for Children in 1990, reiterates and re-affirms India's commitment to the cause of women and child development. NPA goals became operational from early 1992. One of the major objectives of the UBSP scheme is to achieve the goals of the NPA on Children in the urban poor localities by planning and organising various programmes being implemented by different ministries/departments.

Upto March 1995, over 3,622 neighbourhood development committees comprising primarily of urban poor women have been set up in around 283 towns taken up for provision of basic services all over the country. This represents community based structures covering around 48.26 lakh low income women and children. It is expected that approximately 70 lakh beneficiaries will be covered under UBSP programme by the end of Eighth Five Year Plan. On a national basis, the Eighth Five Year Plan targets 500 cities and towns. Around 2,997 mini plans have already been prepared and 460 community organisers are in the field working as catalysts for enriching community participation. In order to monitor the scheme a National Level Monitoring Committee has been set up under the Chairmanship of Secretary, Ministry of Urban Affairs and Employment.

INTEGRATED DEVELOPMENT OF SMALL AND MEDIUM TOWNS

The Scheme of Integrated Development of Small and Medium Towns (IDSMT) was launched in the year 1979-80 with the following objectives: (a) achieve more balanced urban development in the country; (b) provide infrastructural facilities to support employment generating activities; (c) evolve resource generating schemes for local bodies for the purpose of proper operation and maintenance of the infrastructural facilities so created; (d) develop growth poles for the betterment of rural hinterlands adopting a regional approach; and (e) arrest migration from rural areas to large/metropolitan cities.

The budget allocation for IDSMT Scheme has been raised from Rs. 80 crore in the Seventh Plan to Rs. 155 crore in the Eighth Plan. It is expected that 300 towns will be covered under the scheme during the Eighth Plan period. Upto 31 March 1995, 232 towns have been covered under the revised scheme of IDSMT and Central assistance of Rs. 57.5 crore released. This amount includes Rs. 45.84 crore for 232 new towns and Rs. 8.15 crore for on-going schemes in 57 towns. It also includes Rs. 3.52 crore approximately on account of grant-in-aid released to 20 state governments and one union territory administration for defraying the expenses incurred on preparation of project reports of 190 towns covered under the revised scheme of IDSMT.

Mega City Scheme

Large metropolitan cities like Calcutta, Bombay, Madras, Hyderabad and Bangalore make significant contributions to the national economy. Therefore, their prosperity and efficient functioning are of national concern. Many problems in these cities are due to massive migration from rural areas and smaller towns all over the country on which the city authorities have little or no control. The state governments are not in a position to make adequate investments in infrastructure in such cities on account of their limited resources and their priority to sectors like agriculture, irrigation, education, health, etc. Keeping in view of the persistent demands from the state governments and based on the recommedations of the National Commission on Urbanisation, a Centrally-sponsored scheme for infrastructure development in mega cities having population of four million and above as per 1991 Census has been introduced from the year 1993-94. The scheme is called the Mega City Scheme. The main features of the scheme are: (i) the scheme would be applicable to Bombay, Calcutta, Madras, Bangalore and Hyderabad; (ii) the scheme would be administered through the Ministry of Urban Development and funds would be channelised through a special institution at the state level; (iii) the funds from Central Government are to be used as equity support/seed capital for the institution. The sharing between Central Government and state government would be 25:25 per cent and the balance 50 per cent is to be met from institutional finance, through public financing institutions or capital market; (iv) the institution would provide project related finance for urban infrastructure including water supply, sewerage, solid waste management, etc; and (v) finance will not be provided for health, education, electricity, MRTS/LTRS, etc., under this scheme. The projects to be included under the scheme would be under three categories: (a) Projects for basic services where minimum returns are not expected — for these loans could be at 8.5 per cent; (b) Projects in which user charges could be levied — for these loans could be at 12 per cent and (c) Projects which are remunerative and for which loans would be given on - market rate of interest.

To ensure viability of the institution described at (iii), the above three categories of projects would be financed in the ratio of 30:30:40 as a rough indication. The intention is that the overall package (rather than each project) should be viable in the sense of creating a sizeable corpus for future investment.

The scheme would be implemented during the Eighth and Ninth Five Year Plans. The following Plans allocations from the Central Government are proposed for the five cities.

(Rs. crore)

		Outlay	Central funds allocated during	
Name of the City	Project Cost	Eighth Plan	1993-94	1994-95
Bombay	800	200	20.1	16.1
Calcutta	1,600	200	20.1	16.1
Madras	914	100	15.1	11.1
Hyderabad	913	100	15.1	11.1
Bangalore	805	100	0.1	20.1

The project for each mega city should consist of a judicious mix of remunerative and non-remunerative schemes so that the total basket is economically viable. The project outline envisages a mix of projects with different gestation periods; as far as possible, projects with long gestation periods are to be avoided. Projects of regional significance are to be given priority. The priorities would be decided by the state governments. However, the criteria for prioritisation of projects could be: (a) compatibility with the perspective structure plan for the metropolitan region; (b) selectivity in terms of significant impact in particular and desirable sectors or complementarity to an existing or completed large project for speedy accrual of benefits; and (c) shorter gestation period so as to ensure completion of a significant proportion of the project during the Eighth Plan period.

The state governments are required to designate one institution as the coordinating and monitoring agency for the entire range of mega city project activities. The following agencies are since chosen to be the designated agencies: Bombay Metropolitan Region Development Authority (BMRDA); Calcutta Metropolitan Development Authority (CMDA); Madras Metropolitan Development Authority (MMDA); Hyderabad Urban Development Authority (HUDA); and Karnataka Urban Infrastructure Development and Finance Corporation (KUIDFC). The designated agencies will monitor the implementation of various schemes as well as resource mobilisation for the revolving fund. A state level project sanctioning committee will approve the projects during 1995-96. A budget allocation of Rs. 84 crore has been made as Central assistance for the scheme.

CENTRAL PUBLIC WORKS DEPARTMENT

The genesis of Central Public Works Department (CPWD) can be traced to 19th century when Ajmer Provincial Division was created in 1863. The department acquired a size and stature from the year 1911 when it had to play a key role in creation of infrastructure for shifting of National Capital from Calcutta to Delhi. During this period, the Department constructed the Rashtrapati Bhawan, North Block, South Block, Parliament House, etc. The Department was formally constituted as CPWD in 1930. Presently, the CPWD with its headquarters located at New Delhi, headed by Director General (Works), is having its offices all over the country. It has zonal chief engineers at Delhi, Bombay, Calcutta, Madras, Siliguri, and Shillong. The CPWD provides integrated construction management services from project concept to completion stage. The scope of its activities extends to construction of residential, non-residential, institutional and educational buildings, sports complexes, hospitals, runways, airports, computer centres, embassies, *samadhis* and landscaping works. The CPWD has even gone to the borders of the country at the remote and difficult areas and has executed fencing roads and flood lighting.

The *Vigyan Bhawan* at Delhi which was extensively damaged by fire in April 1990 has been renovated and refurnished to the international standards recently by CPWD. It has constructed a highly challenging and time bound project at Hall of Special Displays at Pragati Maidan, Delhi costing nearly Rs. 20 crore within six months time to meet the deadline for India International Trade Fair 1994. The Hall was inaugurated and dedicated to the nation by Hon'ble Prime Minister of India on 19 November 1994. The CPWD constructed fencing in Punjab, Rajasthan sectors in over 780 km length. Another about 700 km of road in Indo-Bangladesh border in West Bengal sector has also been completed and fencing in 185 km has been completed. The Indo-Pak borders have been provided with flood lighting in over 800 km length. The works of re-development of *Vijay Ghat* and *Kisan Ghat Samadhis* are nearing completion and *Vir Bhumi*, the *Samadhi* of former Prime Minister late Shri Rajiv Gandhi, is in progress. The other important buildings in progress in Delhi are Parliament Library Building, Intelligence Bureau building and Indira Gandhi National Open University and extension of Supreme Court, National Security Guard Project at Gurgaon and *Bhasha Bhawan* (Ministry of Culture) at Calcutta. Infrastructural support for National Festivals such as 15 August at Red Fort and 26 January at *Rajpath* in Delhi are being managed by CPWD.

The CPWD has taken a lead in environment friendly construction. The landmark decision has been taken to ban the use of solid wood in its construction starting from April 1993. It has introduced various possible wood substitutes available such as medium density fibre boards, waste wood particle boards, pressed steel, cement based particle boards and PVC. Further, some more wood substitutes like red mud, polymer glass, reinforced gypsum board and rice husk are being developed with the assistance of research laboratories. Usage of plantation timber like rubber wood, eucalyptus and bamboo is also being promoted. This will help protect the environment both by stoppage of cutting of forests and usage of waste which otherwise litter up the usable land. The flyash bricks, which are eco-friendly, are being used on some works as a substitute for traditional bricks. The energy efficient housing project consisting of 135 quarters adopting solar passive architecture at Delhi has been completed. The efforts are also in progress for developing appropriate housing cluster and design of individual dwelling units with thermal comfort and day lighting.

The CPWD also provides consultancy services for various public sector organisations and autonomous bodies for their planning and designs of major buildings, projects, complex structures, air conditioning and electrical installations, etc. It has all in-house facilities for planning, designing construction management and human resource development and undertakes deposit works of various nature from different autonomous agencies. CPWD has a mind set for quality assurance and has taken a quantum jump in this field by establishing the first ready mix concrete plant facility for all consumers in the city of Delhi. It has also risen to the need of the present day project management system, considering the modem client-contractor relationship, and has modified its contract forms which are used by almost all Government/semi-government bodies in India.

NATIONAL CAPITAL REGION PLANNING BOARD

The National Capital Region Planning Board (NCRPB) has been set up with statutory powers under the NCR Planning Board Act, 1985, to plan and promote a balanced and harmonised development of the region which covers an area of 30,242 sq km comprising the whole of Delhi (1,483 sq km) and parts of the three adjoining states of Haryana (13,413 sq km), Rajasthan (4,493 sq km) and Uttar Pradesh (10,833 sq km). The NCR is envisaged to be developed in accordance with the policies and programmes enunciated under the Regional Plan-2001 for NCR which is in force since January 1989. The development steategy evolved by the NCR Planning Board include, *inter-alia*, the integrated development of new townships alongside the existing priority towns selected for accelerated development, by providing commensurate infrastructure support both at regional and local levels to create economic momentum in their growth and expansion, which, in turn will generate abundant employment opportunities and higher income for its people. In accordance with this strategy, the Regional Plan envisages to deflect about two million people by the year 2001 of the following priority towns: (i) Meerut; (ii) Bulandshahr; (iii) Khurja; (iv) Hapur; (v) Panipat; (vi) Rohtak; (vii) Palwal; (viii) Rewari; (ix) Dharuhera; (x) Bhiwadi; and (xi) Alwar.

Besides the above, the Regional Plan also envisages to develop 34 subregional centres within the NCR and five counter-magnet areas outside the NCR located in Punjab, Madhya Pradesh, Rajasthan, Haryana and Uttar Pradesh. This development can be made practically functional only if it is backed and supported by regional physical infrastructure and economic linkages. With this in view, the Regional Plan also emphasises the development of proper transport (expressways and highways and railways), telecommunications, power and other regional infrastructure along with providing for a package of fiscal measures to help decongest the Capital.

For the overall development of the Region in accordance with the Regional Plan-2001, the Board has estimated an overall investment of Rs. 45,000 crore by 2001, out of which, about Rs. 17,000 crore is required for infrastructure development by the public sector (Centre, NCRPB, states and their implementing agencies), and Rs. 28,000 crore by the private sector for creating economic infrastructure as well as housing and other facilities. For the Regional development projects both by Central ministries and the NCRPB jointly with state governments, the Board has approved an investment programme of Rs. 3,813 crore for the Eighth Plan (1992-97) of which Rs. 1,868 crore is for state sector projects, and Rs. 1,967 for Central sector projects.

The Central sector schemes relate to the augmentation of rail network, construction of expressways, laying of telecommunication network, etc., while those under the state sector involve the development of new townships, construction and maintenance of regional roads and providing transmission and distribution network for power supply.

QUESTION FOR EXERCISE

1. Write a short note on problem of housing in India.

16

Urban Crime

Crime is anti-social behaviour which a group rejects and to which it attaches penalties. In this way all those activities for which the state lays down punishments are crimes. Those activities to which no punishments are attached may be sinful but they would not be criminal. But some thinkers have deemed it comprehensively. In the words of C. Darrow, "Crime is an act forbidden by the law of land and for which penalty is prescribed."[1] This constitutes a definition of crime from the social viewpoint. From the legal viewpoint, violation of law constitutes crime. In the words of Barnes and Teeters, "The term 'Crime' technically means a form of anti-social behaviour that has violated public sentiment to such an extent as to be forbidden by statute."[2] This definition does not include those anti-social activities which are not prohibited by law. Actually criminality should attach both to anti-social activities and to activities forbidden by law. Though no punishment is prescribed for anti-social activities, the public opinion always condemns them.[3] According to Garofalo even the actions contradictory of the prevalent conceptions of pity and truth should be considered criminal.[4] To quote Elliott and Merrill, "A crime *ipso facto* implies a disturbance in a social relationship and a social definition as to what such a disturbance is."[5]

THEORIES OF CRIME

Several theories are current as to why an individual commits a crime. Some of the major ones are the following:

1. Theological School. According to this school, crimes increase when the religious tendency diminishes. But it is not inevitable that a religious person will do no criminal act while an atheist will do it. Sometimes even religious people are seen committing the most heinous crimes.

---

1. Darrow, C., *Crime — Its Causes and Punishment*, (1934), p. 1.
2. Barnes and Teeters, *New Horizons in Criminology*, Prentice Hall, (1959), p. 70.
3. Sutherland, E.H., *Principles of Criminology*, J.B., Lippioncott Co., New York (1955), p. 14.
4. Garofalo, R., *Criminology*, Little Brown (Boston), p. 59.
5. Elliott and Merrill, *Social Disorganisation*, Harper & Bros., New York (1950), p. 91.

2. Hedonistic school. According to this school, an individual indulges in criminal activity when he thereby stands to gain more pleasure than pain. Cesare Beccaria, the protagonist of this school, maintained that crimes can be checked only when the pleasure attained by them is lesser than the pain consequent of punishment.[6] The followers of this school were against the punishment of children and insane because they cannot compare the pleasure and pain resulting from a crime. Jeremy Bentham also supported this view. According to this view the punishment for a crime should be proportionate to the pleasure attained by it, so that the motive of crime may be defeated. The hedonistic interpretation of crime has attained much support everywhere but modern criminologists do not consider pleasure to be the sole motive of crime. It goes without saying that many people commit crime by causes other than the search for pleasure.

3. Geographical school. According to Montesquie, the author of *Spirit of Laws,* the rates of crime increase near the equator while they decrease as one proceeds towards polar region. Adolf Quetlet has pointed out that generally in the hot countries one finds violent crimes and crimes against persons while in cold countries there are more crimes concerning property. Thus according to geographical school the causes of crime are the geographical factors like climate, weather, etc. In fact, none can deny that indirectly the geographical conditions exert an important influence over the rates and kinds of crime. But neither the geographical situations explain all types of crime nor do they explain all causes of a particular type of crime. Hence Cohen has rightly pointed out that the conception of Geographical school is more imaginative than factual.

4. Ecological school. According to this view ecological elements play the most important role in the determination of crime. The followers of this view have compared crimes in Urban and Rural ecological situations and found close relation between ecological situations and the kinds and rates of crime. This type of study was first conducted by Park & Burgess in 1926. Clifford Shaw maintained that while one finds large number of juvenile delinquents in the centre of an urban area, their number goes on decreasing in the suburbs. Though it is not possible to accept the view that ecological situations alone determine crime, modern criminologists accept the fact that the ecological situations determine the environment which in its turn determines crimes.

5. Typological school. According to this view a criminal is a particular type of person. This type has been determined both on anthropological and psychological basis. Lombroso has maintained an intimate relation between physical structure and mental tendencies. The criminal, according to him, is a prototype of the primitive man. He is morally insane. Right from the very birth he is of a particular type having peculiar facial characteristics. This particular type of person must commit crime whatever may be his conditions. Thus, according to this view, the criminal is a particular type of person. According

6. Beccaria, C., *Essay on Crime and Punishment*, Stephen Gould, New York, pp. 5-32.

to Lombroso different types of criminals have distinct physical characteristics. This theory has been proved to be baseless by means of several large scale studies. In his work *The English Convict*, Doctor Charles Goring has proved that it is not possible to establish any marked-distinction between the physical characteristics of the criminals and those of the normal persons.[7] According to modern criminologists, criminal tendencies are not innate but acquired. Hence the anthropological or typological school has only historical significance.

6. The view of mental testers. According to Goddard nearly 25% criminals are feeble-minded persons.[8] Thus some mental-testers consider feeble-mindedness to be an important determinant of crime. On the other hand, it has been found that not all criminals are feeble-minded nor do all feeble-minded persons turn into criminals.

7. Psychiatric view. According to the psycho analysts, the criminal is a psychopathic person and the causes of crime are in the repressed desire, emotional imbalance and different types of mental diseases. For example, persons suffering from Kleptomania have a tendency to steal whatever thing they may find within their reach. Though this view may explain crimes committed by some mentally abnormal persons, it is not applicable to every criminal. It goes without saying that this view gives no importance to social and economic causes of crime.

8. Socialistic view. According to socialists, the main causes of crime are economic conditions and class struggle. This view also has a grain of truth and yet being one-sided, it is not applicable to a large number of crimes.

9. Sociological view. According to this view the main determinant of crime is the social endowment which determines the responses of the criminal. The form of social organisation has an important relation with the type and rate of crime. Crimes are determined by social factors such as social mobility cultural conflict, economic competition, social stratification, political, religious and economic aims and ideals, the density and quality of population, the distribution of wealth, etc. Social psychologists like Dewey, Mead and Thomas have pointed out that the processes leading to crime are not qualitatively different from the normal processes. According to Sutherland, the author of Principles of Criminology, the criminal behaviour is very much influenced by bad company. The sociological explanation of crime is one of the most important theories in this connection, though like all other theories it too has its obvious onesidedness.

Modern Criminologists believe that the causes of crime are multiple and no single theory is sufficient to explain all the causes. Thus, while all the theories of crime, hitherto discussed, involve some grain of truth, they do not explain all types of crimes. While several crimes may have their origin in some one cause, some one crime may be the result of several causes. In fact, the

---

7. Charles Goring, *The English Convict*, London., pp. 99-100.

8. Goddard., H.H., *Feeble-mindedness*, The Macmillan Co., New York (1914).

causes of crime are of many kinds such as social, economic, geographical, ecological, etc., and the reasons for a person's having committed a crime can be discovered only after investigating his personality and environment. A catholic, comprehensive and synthetic approach will be most useful here. To conclude in the words of Elliott and Merrill, "The factors in relation to the whole, rather than the sum of the single isolated factors, must be considered in any satisfactory analysis... The behaviour is a resultant of all the forces impinging upon the individual plus the characteristics of his personality."[9]

CAUSES OF CRIME

The main causes of crime are- (1) Social, (2) Economic, (3) Physical and developmental, (4) Geographical and (5) Political.

Social Causes of Crime

The main social causes of crime are as follows:

1. Broken family. The broken family is the most dominant factor in the social causes of crime. Now-a-days family disorganisation may be seen in India. The control previously exercised by the family over the individuals is now lacking. In urban areas, all the members of a family are to be seen pursuing their individual paths. With the lifting of family control there are no restrictions on the criminal tendencies of children. Now that the natural relations between parents and children are devoid of love, both young boys and girls are prone to criminal activities. Even in the villages adolescents and young men and women do not respect their elders, and they want to lead a carefree: unrestricted individual life. Due to all these causes, sex crimes are increasing. One main cause of adultery, abortions, miscarriage, prostitution and juvenile delinquency is the undesirable domestic conditions.

2. Absence of Social Control. A second social cause of crime in India is absence of social control. Previously, the caste panchayats in the villages kept control over the behaviour and conduct of the members of the caste. It was extremely difficult to conceal crime in the village and when any crime was revealed, the caste panchayats meted out very stern punishment, going to the limit of exterminating the guilty persons from the caste. This tended to control and check crime effectively. Today, these social organisations no longer exist. They have been deprived of all their authority. Secondly, with better facilities of transport being available the criminal can commit the crime and abscond from the village to the town or to the village from the town. In urban areas no one is bothered about caste organisations. Now-a-days in big cities, even doing favour to neighbourers is a defunct practice because few have intimacy with their neighbourers and social relationships have become impersonal. Any individual can commit a crime and conceal his identity in the city mob. In this way, the disappearance of the control of caste organisation is another cause of crime in India.

---

9. Elliott and Merill, *Social Disorganisation*, Harper & Bros,., New York (1960)., p. 110.

3. Defective education. Modern education in India is very defective. It does not develop the character of students in right direction. Instead it has led to an increase in selfishness, disorderliness and impertinence. Ethical and religious education have no place in the modern education system. Besides this, even after completing his education an individual does not become capable of earning his livelihood and many well educated people remain unemployed for many years. Late employment leads to late marriage. All these causes tend to aggravate criminal activity.

4. Cinema. Cinema has helped in the increase of crime in India. According to Blumen and Hansen, cinemas indirectly influence the male criminals. The cinema arouses criminal tendencies in men by teaching crime techniques by exhibiting many kinds of crime, by stimulating the desire for wealth and comforts, by showing ways and means of appropriating them illegally, by arousing the feelings of bravado, toughness and adventure, by arousing profound sexual urges, by stimulating day dreams of criminal jobs. In much the same way it directs or urges many young and inexperienced women to illegitimate relations and crimes by setting alight the sexual desire, the desire for exhibition, love making, independence and variety.

5. Newspapers. Besides cinemas, newspapers also have a hand in increasing criminal activity. Newspapers increase criminal activity by publishing methods of crime through news items by printing many news items relating to crime, by making crime a general subject, by printing news of major crimes and showing their advantages circulating the names of criminals, by highlighting causes which tend to increase in the name of studies of crimes and by warning and alerting criminals by publishing police methods. The recent wave of dacoities in India was to some extent indirectly assisted by newspapers.

6. Use of Alcohol. The consumption of alcohol also is one of the major causes of crime in India. Drinking is more prevalent among those who have a low standard of life and it is also from among them that the greatest number of criminals are coming. There are large number of crimes committed under the influence of alcoholic stimulants. Drinking affects not only the drinker and makes him a criminal but it also has a deleterious influence on his entire family and inclines men, women and children towards crime. In this way drinking increases crime both apparently as well as indirectly.

7. Prohibition of Widow Remarriage. In India widow remarriage is now legally accepted as valid but it is still looked down upon in society. Consequently, many young widows do not remarry for the rest of their lives but such a decision does not annihilate their sexual passion and these rather lie dormant in a corner of the mind and wait for a suitable opportunity. Even if the widow is religious and saintly, she is pursued by men and is lured to the path of evil and sin by many threats and coaxes. In this way, there is an increase in adultery, miscarriage, abortion, infanticide etc. When their sinful practices are made public many women commit suicide.

8. Defects of the marriage and dowry system. In India the dowry system also is among the social causes of crime. On the one hand the dowry system urges the fathers of girls to earn money through illegitimate means for their daughters' marriage, it on the other hand, leads to suicide by many young girls who can not bear to see the degraded condition of their parents, the dowry system has further encouraged late marriages, both in girls and in boys. In extreme cases, the lack of wealth compels a girl to remain unmarried throughout her life or at most she is married to an old man or to an unsuitable partner. All these also tend to increase sex crimes in society. Very often the parents do not care to ask the girl or boy for opinion and sometimes even proceed against it. This also results in suicides and other crimes.

9. Religion. Religion has also been one of the causes of crime in India. This does not mean that religion itself encourages crimes but the encouragement has come from the different sects which originated in the differences of opinion between people on matters of religion and in the hatred for other religions. In a general way, of course, communal riots and crimes, such as looting, murder and so on, perpetrated in order to increase the followers of one's own religion and to injure another religion, have always been happening in India, but the crimes committed during communal riots in the name of religion, when the country was partitioned in 1947 are unequalled in the history of the world. Helpless women were denuded and taken in procession through the main roads all the time being whipped. Their breasts were cut off they were violated and mutilated, their children's hearts were cut out in front of their eyes. The most heinous crimes that can be discovered in the history of criminal activity have been perpetrated in India.

10. Changes in Social values. There has been a tremendous change in social values in recent times in India. Now-a-days, new notions such as materialism, individualism, rationalism, the respect for wealth, absence of sex restrictions, etc., are becoming very popular in the country. This has led to a disregard of ancient social values and new values have been reinstated in their stead. There is no one common opinion of any kind in them. This disordered state of values also inspires crime because any individual can manage to produce an agreement to justify even that which is improper.

The preceding exposition on the social cause of crime in India will have brought to light the extent to which the defects of such social organizations as family, caste, religion, marriage, etc. have on geographical, economic, political and other causes, but it is intended merely to show the important part played by social organisation in crime.

Economic Causes

1. Poverty. In India one sees extreme poverty. Poverty is a major cause of crime, since a hungry man can do literally anything in order to appease his hunger. One comes across instances where a criminal commits a crime immediately on his release from prison in order that he may be imprisoned again where he is assured of a square meal. Outside the prison he has no such assurance. Dr. Haikerwal has investigated that during the period 1917—1927 thefts increased in number when the prices of wheat went up, and decreased when wheat prices fell. In this way, a close relation is found to exist between the number of crimes and the prices of foodgrains in India. It was found in the course of a study conducted upon the prostitutes of Kanpur that one major cause of prostitution is poverty. Poor girls are easily entranced by men who violate them, take away their virginity and put them on the market. One even comes across news of suicides and murders of families due to poverty.

2. Unemployment. Unemployment, much like poverty, is major cause of crime in India. Many young men commit suicide when they are frustrated by extreme poverty and continued unemployment. Many others turn to thieving, picking pockets, robbery, etc. Among the people who are seen creating disturbances, causing, violence, etc., the majority are the unemployed. Most gangsters do not work. Gangsterism is their only occupation.

3. Industrialisation. Industrialisation is also an important cause of crime in India. It has destroyed the family life of millions of labourers. They work very hard for eight to ten hours in the day during which they have to suffer many indecencies and for this they have to live in towns far away from their families. Continued existence of this life leads them to indulge in drinking alcohol and in prostitution and this encourages other crimes. In India, the most prospering centres of prostitution are important industrial towns which, at the same time, foster crimes such as murder, assault, disturbance, robbery, etc. Industrialisation has encouraged crime also due to another reason. Housing becomes a problem in an industrial town when the population increases beyond limits. In some towns thousands of families live in houses having no more than one room each. In such conditions the married women have no privacy and children and unmarried members witness happenings which they should not see. This has a bad influence upon them and sex crimes increase among them. Sex crimes increase tendencies to other crimes which then take place. In industrial towns many thousands of labourers and men otherwise are compelled to live alone and this tends to split the ratio of men to women, which consequently encourages sex crimes. Many girls from rural areas are deceived with promises of employment and brought to towns where they are forced to adopt prostitution

4. Urbanization. Urbanization is the result of industrialization and other causes. Hence all those crimes caused by industrialization are also caused by urbanization. In cities the society fails to exercise control over the individual who loses his identity in the mob after having committed a crime. There is no such facility however redoubted in the village. In towns there are better opportunities for picking pockets and practising deception in a crowd. There is absence of healthy recreation in the town and hence the cinemas are crowded. Gambling dens, indecent theatres and wine shops provide means of superior recreation. This encourages crime.

It is evident from the foregoing account of the socio-economic causes of crime in India that there the main causes of crime are social and economic. Absence of reliable statistics makes it difficult to say definitely that the causes of crime here are hardly psychological. But what can be said is that since life in India still lacks some of the velocity and crowdedness of western life, the psychological causes of crime in India do not compare favourably with their counterparts in America and other Western countries.

MEANS TO PREVENT CRIME

Roughly speaking the way to prevent crime is to counteract the various causes that have been mentioned above. Even suggestions are being made in this connection. Some important means are–

1. Probation. Probation is the postponement, on certain conditions laid down by the prosecuting authority, of the punishment due to a criminal by law. These individuals are kept in the guardianship of some one instead of being imprisoned. According to the Probation Act 1938 of U. P., first offenders below the age of 24 who have committed crimes not punishable by death or life imprisonment may be placed on probation. The decision to place criminal on probation is taken after due consideration of such factors as his age, his way of life, his conduct, physical and mental condition and others. All criminals placed on probation live under the probation officer's care. Mostly, it is the minor offender or the juvenile delinquent who is released on probation.

The probation officer performs the following activities for curing the criminal—

1. To keep criminals in his own care.

2. To try to improve and reform criminals.

3. To compile the life histories of criminals and to try to trace their tendencies through them.

4. To send relevant information to courts regarding the criminals.

5. To render assistance to criminals in getting employment.

6. Solution of family problems of criminals such as solving domestic strife and contracting marriage of their daughters, etc.

7. To make efforts to make them good citizens by every conceivable method.

8. To send the criminals to prison once again if they show no signs of improvement.

In this way, the probation officer is both the helper as well as the saviour of the criminals and tries to put them on the right track by convincing and cautioning them.

2. Parole. Parole is also a means of reforming criminals. Under probation the criminal is given over to the protection of the probation officer without being punished but a criminal is placed on parole after he has served a short prison sentence. He is also placed under the parole officer. The parole officer maintains contact with the criminal, keeps an eye on him and tries to reform him. Probation is more popular than parole.

3. Reformatory. In 1876 the Elmira Reformatory was established in New York, U.S.A. Since then this method of reforming criminals has been gaining favour in all civilized countries. Reformatories are of two kinds–

(i) *Juvenile Reformatories.* The oldest of this kind of reformatory is in India. In this efforts are made to reform criminals, to educate them and to make them successful citizens. Previously, only those who had been given a life sentence were confined in them but now criminals serving shorter prison sentences are also allowed.

(ii) *Adult Reformatories.* Only adults who commit some specific kinds of common crimes are confined to the reformatories. They receive education in military discipline, physical exercise, religions, the principles of citizenship etc. There are very few reformatories of this kind in India at present. Their success depends mainly on those who run them.

4. Borstal schools. Another means of reforming juvenile offenders is the Borstal school. Only criminals between the ages of 16 and 21 are kept in these schools. There are many institutions of this kind in different states of India. Here the juvenile delinquents are educated and efforts are made to turn them into good citizens by providing adequate care.

5. Prison. Prison is a universally accepted means of preventing crime but now-a-days efforts are made to reform rather than to punish criminals in jail. A model prison has been constructed at Lucknow, U.P. where the inmates are provided with all the opportunities to develop their personalities and provision is made to make them able citizens. An important experiment has been made in this direction in U.P. The name of this experiment is Sampoornanand Camp. In 1954, 200 criminals were employed to build a dam across the river Chandraprabha in Benaras district. There was no police to look after them. The warden of the prison was their guide. The criminals lived in tents on open ground like ordinary labourers. All arrangements and facilities such as canteen, hospital, reading room, radio, library, cinema, etc., were provided for them. Teachers and welfare officers educated them. They were paid wages, a part of which was retained to be given to them on release in order to enable them to start some business. This experiment was a complete success and it shed new light on the problem of preventing crimes.

Actually, these means are to reform criminals and to prevent them from subsequent criminal activity. These cannot prevent all those factors which must be eliminated from the social, economic and political life of the community in which crimes originate.

QUESTIONS FOR EXERCISE

1. Evaluate the role of social organisation as a contributing factor in crime in India.
2. How far do social conditions determine crime?
3. Briefly describe the relation between urban conditions and crime.
4. What are the causative factors of crime? Discuss briefly the programmes for crime prevention.

17

Urban Juvenile Delinquency

In modern civilised countries a criminal is not looked upon as a sinner or a bad person, but rather as a mentally diseased individual or one who has been victimised by circumstances. There was a time when even small children were severely punished if they committed some crime. But as psychologists proceeded to draw the attention of the civilized world to the causes of juvenile delinquency, the tradition of punishing children lost favour, to be replaced by efforts at improving and rehabilitating them. Now-a-days, in every nation efforts are made to correct the juvenile delinquent rather than to punish him. To make the deviant once again a healthy and responsible citizen of society, efforts are made through reformatory schools, probation and other measures.

What is Juvenile delinquency ?

From the legal point of view a juvenile delinquent is a person between the ages of 15 and 17 who indulges in anti-social activity. In the U.S.A., the Ohio Code defines juvenile delinquency in some such manner as this: A juvenile delinquent is one who breaks the law, is a vagrant, persists in disobeying orders, whose behaviour endangers his own moral life as well as the moral life of others or one who tries to marry without the consent of his parents. It may as well be pointed out that the ages of the so-called juvenile delinquents have not been similarly determined in all countries. It varies from country to country but is within the usual limits of 16 and 20. Normally, it is the 17 year old adolescent who qualifies for this term, but in India, according to the prevalent laws, the maximum age of a juvenile delinquent is fixed at 16. Laws pertaining to this subject have been passed in U.P., M.P., Bombay, Madras, Mysore, Delhi, West Bengal, Orissa, and East Punjab. In those States in which the juvenile acts have not been passed, the reformatory act of 1897 prevails. In these the maximum age of a juvenile delinquent has been determined at 15. In Bombay and Madhya Pradesh it is 16. According to the reformatory act, the term Youthful Offender will be appended to any individual below 15 who has been sentenced to life imprisonment or has been convicted of some crime.

Differing from the legal definition of the controversial term, psychologists lay much emphasis upon the causes of juvenile delinquency in defining it. From the legal viewpoint all those who are not apprehended are not criminals but from the psychological viewpoint all such offenders also are criminals. Consequently the psychological definition of juvenile delinquency is more comprehensive than its legal definition. Psychologically, any and every child, of either sex, between the ages of 15 and 18, who commits a crime, irrespective of the fact that he is apprehended or not, is a juvenile delinquent. In this manner, juvenile delinquent is one who forcibly takes away the property of another, or causes it damage, indulges in anti-social activity, creates danger to another's life or hinders the activities of others. Hence, a child who throws stones at a car and runs away, one who sets things to or creates dangers for the life of others just for the fun of it, are all juvenile delinquents, from the psychological viewpoint.

Defining juvenile delinquency, Dr. Sethna has written, "Juvenile delinquency involves wrong doing by a child or a young person who is under an age specified by the law (for the time being in force) of the place concerned." Newmeyer puts the same idea in these words, "A delinquent is a person under age who is guilty of antisocial act and whose misconduct is an infraction of law."

CRIME AND DELINQUENCY

The following are the main distinctions between crime and delinquency:

1. Age. The main difference between a juvenile delinquent and a criminal is one of age, while both indulge in anti-social and subversive activities. In this way, if a criminal is below a certain specified age, he will be designated a juvenile delinquent.

2. Criminal activities. But sometimes criminals and juvenile delinquents differ not only in ages but also in the type of crimes they commit. A classification as wide as juvenile delinquent can include the vagrant, cruel, obstinate, or young boys who keep the company of thieves, dacoits, other vagrants and prostitutes, those who keep away from the house for long periods of time without the permission of their parents, those who roam the lonely streets late at night. It should be remembered here that such activities are, strictly speaking, not illegal or infringing any legal statute. Hence, the juvenile delinquent who chooses to act in these ways cannot be included in the same class as ordinary criminals. Another thing that sometimes happens is that the unemployed, unhoused and wandering child may be included in the category of juvenile delinquents along with the beggar, the farce being carried so far as to present the young person before a court and to try to mend his ways.

3. Other characteristics. Kohen has distinguished criminals from juvenile delinquents on the basis of the following distinguishing characteristics:

(a) A juvenile's mischiefs are lacking in utility as he performs actions that do not benefit him in the least, such as roaming about the streets without cause. On the other hand, the criminal acts with the intent to gain something. A juvenile is sometimes even unaware of the objective of his own actions.

(b) Sometimes a juvenile commits a crime with only an intention to enjoy himself and indulge his sense of humour. It finds expression in practical joking like breaking car glasses, putting boulders on railway tracks or pushing people into a pond of water just for the fun of it. A criminal does not find this a suitable mode of manifesting his sense of humour.

(c) The juvenile delinquent does not commit a crime on a preplanned and well organised basis, being more apt to things on the spur of the moment. A hardened criminal is more inclined to plan his moves and organise crime with a certain show of skill.

Briefly, criminals and juvenile delinquents are to be distinguished by their differences of age, kinds of criminal activities, objective of activities, mode of working etc. Yet, normally it is the difference in age alone that is considered the sole basis of making distinction between the two classes.

CAUSES OF JUVENILE DELINQUENCY

According to modem criminology, the causes of delinquency may be divided into two classes — personal and social, internal and external. Internal factors include physical and psychological factors while the external factors consist of of social elements. In the present chapter, the causes of juvenile delinquency will be divided into three classes for convenient study — (A) social causes, (B) psychological causes, (C) economic causes.

A. Social Causes

Of the various causes of juvenile delinquency, the most comprehensive are the social causes. Among them, the main ones are - (1) defects of the family, (2) defects of the school, (3) criminal area, (4) bad company, (5) paucity and inadequacy of recreation, (6) war, (7) social disorganisation, (8) displacement.

(1) Defects of the family. Of the causes of juvenile delinquency, Elliott and Merrill accept distorted family influence to be the most potent. Of 4000 juvenile delinquents in Boston, Healy and Bronner found that about 50 per cent of them came from divided or broken families. The major situations in the family that cause it are— (a) broken families, (b) attitude of parents, (c) character and conduct of parents, and (d) effect of criminal relatives. In order to understand the importance of family as a cause of juvenile delinquency, it is necessary to comprehend these factors :

(a) *Broken families* : A study of juvenile delinquency has revealed that the maximum number of delinquents come from broken families. A broken family, as the term indicates, is one in which family ties have been destroyed. A family is not constituted by a number of people living together but by their mutual intimate relationships. Absence of this intimacy results in the breaking up of a family, and it is in broken families that juvenile delinquents come to live. In any such family, a child is not looked after properly. In the opinion of some specialists broken families are more apt to arouse criminal tendencies in females than in male juveniles. The Child Care Society of Bombay had 386 boys and 169 girls under its care in 1947. Of these children, the parents of two boys and two girls were serving prison sentences, two boys and five girls were guilty of extreme indiscipline, six boys and nine girls were the victims of moral insecurity. In a broken family, the relationships of husband and wife, parents and children, brothers and sisters lose their healthy nature. Hence, it is only natural if the children choose the wrong path that ruin their lives.

(b) *Parent child relationship* : According to the preface writer of *Women of the Street* a probing and searching analysis of the prostitutes of London, the problem of the prostitute has its origin in the relationship between the child and parents. Often when the child is deprived of love and is scolded constantly on every occasion, he develops feelings of revolt and hatred so that he runs away from the house at the earliest opportunity and falls into a life of crime. Disregard on the part of parents induces feelings of insecurity in the children with the result that they develop mental complexes. If the parents try to conceal their own life from children, the tendency towards crime is aggravated. One of the most common query that children are apt to put before their parents is where did they come from, or where their younger brothers and sisters have come from. When they are told all sorts of lies by their parents, while they learn the truth from their servants or other people outside the family, a sense of insecurity is induced in them, because they feel that their parents do many things which they fear to tell their children and this injures their feelings. This sense of insecurity leads many children to sex crimes..

(c) *Character and conduct of parents* : The child's personality is considerably influenced by the character and conduct of its parents. One rarely comes across a child who has been able to mould his behaviour according to socially accepted values and conceptions in the face of his parents telling lies, hypocritical behaviour, sexual immorality and thieving . In a study conducted by Miss Elliot, 67 per cent parents in broken families and 44 per cent parents of united families were engaged in immoral behaviour. If the mother is already involved in prostitution, the child will have little hesitation in following suit, and with the worst conceivable consequences.

(d) *Influence of brothers and sisters* : A child's personality is susceptible to the influence of his brother's and sister's personality apart from the personality and mutual relationship of the parents. This influence is more potent in the case of girls as they are not exposed to external influences as much as boys who remain in the home for a considerable less period of time. If the senior children in the family manifest criminal tendencies, the youngsters are invariably influenced by it. If the elder sister is engaged in immoral behaviour, the younger sister is more apt to follow her example.

It is evident from the foregoing description that the situation within the family has a major part to play in turning children into criminals. But this need not lead one to the conclusion that all children in a broken family will turn out to be criminals. Healy and Bronner[1] studied 372 broken families and in only 20 per cent of them one of every two children was a delinquent. In 336 families in which each had 6 children, only 12 children were engaged in criminal activity. Such a study seems to indicate that the family being broken is not the sole cause of juvenile delinquency, but no criminologist will refuse to accept the fact that such a condition is undoubtedly a most potent cause.

2. Defects of the school. After the family, a child's personality is next influenced by the school. But one major form of juvenile delinquency is absconding from school. In 1947. Willamson found in his study that playing truant from school, theft and sex crimes were the major forms of juvenile delinquency, and even among these running away from school or roaming outside the school claimed the greatest attention and interest among children. Analysing the causes of such behaviour, Willamson came to the conclusion that it was caused by criticism at the hands of parents, gaining membership of a gang of criminals, punishment by the teacher, weakness in some subject and a level of education that is above the child's ability and capacity. Children who run away from the school usually spend their time in the worst sort of company and commit all kinds of crimes. This is one major problem confronting the teacher. It is for this reason that in most big cities, students are not allowed to view matinee shows in film exhibitions, but preventions of this nature do not help to solve the problem. One of the major causes of increasing indiscipline in the present time is that education is neither recreating nor interesting, in addition to which it lays emphasis upon stuffing the brain with information rather than building up character. It need hardly be expressed that it is these factors that make the child lose interest in study, try to avoid school with the result that he falls into a life of crime.

3. Crime dominated areas. According to the result of a study by Clifford, Shaw and Mckay, some areas are not appropriate for the development of children. It is a matter of common knowledge that the neighbourhood casts important influences upon the child. Using the statistical method. Maler came to the conclusion that in New York, juvenile delinquency was maximum in those quarters where the level of life was very low, child mortality was very high, means of recreation were almost absent and the residences were not

1. Healy and Bronner, *Delinquents and Criminals : Their making and unmaking.* The Macmillan Co., New York, pp. 121-125.

permanent. In a community that is unstable there are no social taboos or laws. Pickpockets are found in great abundance in and around hotels and other places where travellers stay, since there is always some traveller or the other there. Clifford, Shaw and Mckay studied juvenile delinquency in nearly 15 towns to discover that the rate of juvenile crime was highest in the centre of the town and lowest at its furthest reaches. From this they concluded that the social traditions of backward and low economic status areas distinguish the pattern of crime from the average groups. And these patterns are maintained in juvenile delinquent group. In this way, big towns have certain red light areas where there is an abundance of criminals. It should be remembered here that Shaw and his assistant Henry Mckay have not accepted the place of residence as a cause of crime. They have tried to show that crimes are found to be the highest where conditions of poverty, mental aberrations, family disorganisation, diseases, infant mortality and other forms of disorganisation are constantly maintained or existing. Tendency to displacement is also found to prevail in criminal areas. Having studied crime in Chicago and other cities Shaw and Mckay came to the following conclusion:

(a) Rate of crime differs from one settlement to another. In some areas boys are not arrested, while in other areas a fifth of the criminals were captured every year.

(b) In winter, the rate of crime increases around the factory area and decreases in the suburbs. Rate of crime decreases in proportion to the distance from the town's centre.

(c) The rate of crime is also high in the areas where there is a greater tendency to abscond from school.

(d) Rate of crime was high in 1930 in the areas where it was high in 1900, despite the fact that the constitution and size of population underwent considerable change during these years.

4. Bad company. According to the famous criminologist Edwin H. Sutherland,[2] criminal behaviour is acquired through interaction with others. An individual becomes a criminal when there is excess of conditions that promote the infringement of law over conditions that prevent such infringement. And among children, some get good company while others don't. The child who gets bad company turns towards crime while the child who gets into good company progresses to become an able and useful member of society. An individual's behaviour is influenced to a considerable extent by the conduct of his companions. In order to induce the children to accept and respect the value and assumptions of adult society around them it is necessary to create such an atmosphere in which inspiration to criminal behaviour is reduced to the absolute minimum.

5. Absence of recreation. Means of recreation have an important place in the child's development. It is only a good and healthy atmosphere that can

---

2. Sutherland, E.H., *Principles of Criminology*, New York, 1955.

provide the right sort of inspiration to the children for sensible and healthy behaviour in their spare time after school. Inability to make proper use of one's spare time is an added instigation to criminal behaviour. Play and games are essential elements in the socialization and ethical training of children. Inadequate, uncontrolled and improper recreation in a town is an important cause of juvenile delinquency. In Thurston's study of 2507 juvenile delinquents it was found that their spare time had hung heavy on their hands.

(b) *Defective recreation*. In modern times, the one means of recreation available to everyone is the cinema, which is responsible for juvenile delinquency and antisocial activity to quite an extent. New pattern of crime are presented to an individual through scenes of adventure and romance. Some films have such potent influence upon the adolescents that after their screening in some towns, certain kinds of crime increased manyfold. But the reactions of children to films are determined and guided by patterns within the house or around the neighbourhood. And different children react differently to it. Scientific studies have determined that the direct influence of cinema upon the behaviour of children is very little. In fact what is even more important than the cinema is the child's reaction to it which keeps on functioning on the basis of his previous experience and reaction to social and cultural circumstances.

6. War and post-war conditions. Increases in the rate of juvenile delinquency have been found during war and post-war periods. In countries that actually participate in the war, the children's education is considerably hindered and affected. It often happens that in wartime the father is on the front fighting the war, while the mother goes to the factory to earn. Hence, children are not properly looked after. Lack of any control leads to much promiscuous mixing between girls and boys with the result that sexual crimes increase. In wartime, wherever there was bombing, the adolescents took the greatest part in looting and smashing houses. Hence, the situation of war definitely encourages criminal tendencies.

7. Social disorganization. Social disorganization leads to disorganization of individuals. And disorganization of society leads to increase in criminal activity, hence, it too is one of the causes of juvenile delinquency. In modern industrial society there is lack of synthesis and equality which creates tension. This tension inspires young men and women to crime.

8. Displacement. Displacement also influences juvenile delinquency. In studying the town Berkeley Stuart discovered that juvenile delinquents lived in an area where there was considerable displacement, but as compared to their own respective families, they themselves are much less active and dynamic.

B. Psychological Causes

Till now we have been discussing the social causes of juvenile delinquency, the data for which have been collected by the statistical method. The application of the case history method, and psychoanalysis on the other hand, has thrown light on the psychological causes of delinquency, of which the important are the following

(1) Intellectual weakness, (2) mental disease, (3) characteristics of personality, (4) emotional instability.

1. Intellectual weakness. Dr. Goring advanced the theory that intellectual weakness is a cause of crime. Goddard[3] was the main exponent of the idea that mental weakness is the cause of crime. He has written that the greatest single factor or cause of crime is mental weakness. After examining 4000 children, Healy and Bronner came to the conclusion that 13 per cent of them had an intelligence quotient below 70.[4] This conclusion was supported by S.S. Glueck and E.T. Glueck who studied 1000 criminal children in 1934 and came to the conclusion that 13 per cent children have an intelligence quotient of below 70.[5]

This contention has been objected to on the ground that it is based on the study only of those juvenile delinquents who have been produced before the courts. Naturally, the intelligent and shrewd juvenile delinquents will be apprehended far less than the backward ones. In one of their studies, C. W. Mann and N. P. Mann have confirmed this view and shown that children with an intelligence quotient of less than 90 stand a far greater chance of being apprehended than brilliant children.[6] They calculated the median of the intelligence quotient of 1061 criminals in which the boys were discovered to have an I. Q. of 94.88 and girls of 83.77. In 1947, Merrill calculated the average of the intelligence quotients of 500 criminal children measured on the modified Binet scale; and found it to be 92.5. Examining 2904 healthy children for their intelligence level it was found that their average intelligence quotient was 101.8. From both these enquiries Merrill concluded that a low level of intelligence cannot be accepted as a cause of crime since the level of intelligence in juvenile delinquents is not distinctly different from that of healthy children. There may be no denying the fact that it is comparatively easier to mislead backward children, but intelligent and shrewd children are also liable to get involved in crime.

2. Mental diseases. Some criminologists have tried to establish a definite relationship between mental disease and crime. In the several studies carried out upon criminals,, some mentally diseased individuals were also found. According to this view, a criminal is a kind of mentally diseased individual who is in as much need of treatment as of punishment. Some, psychiatrists and

---

3. Goddard, H. H., *Mental Efficiency and levels of Intelligence*, Princeton University Press, 1936.
4. Healy, W., and A. F. Bronner, *Newlight on Delinquency and its Treatment*, Yale University Press, 1963.
5. Glueck, S.S., and E. T. Glueck, *Unravelling Juvenile Delinquency*, Harward University Press 1940, p. 356.
6. Mann, C.W., and H.P. Mann, Age and Intelligence of a group of Juvenile Delinquents, Jr. *of Abnorm. Psychol*, 1930, Vol. 34, pp. 351-360.

neurologists believe that the psychopathic personality is a cause of crime. Psychopathic children are born in families where there is almost total absence of love, affection and control. Concerning psychopathic children, Tappan has written that he is very unsocialised, irritable, cruel, obstinate, suspicious, self-centred, lonely, full of feelings of revenge, backward and hypersexual or uncontrolled in his sexual behaviour. In an extremely advanced stage, he lacks the ability to sympathize, and is completely devoid of repentance over his own cruel doings and the pain or suffering of others. A psychopathic child of this nature has the existence of an uninvited guest in his own house. He is never loved by any one, but is instead the butt of every criticism and abuse in the house. It is only natural that the child should react to such behaviour with feelings of unhindered obstinacy and homicidal tendencies. To illustrate, Tappan has described the case of a psychopathic child, Isaac.

Isaac was a very intelligent child of 14, accused of theft, truancy from school, unnatural sexual practices and general indiscipline. He was a beautiful child who almost invariably impressed the strangers. He was the only child in the family and his mother died while he was an infant. His father deserted him at the age of 2, following which he was disgustedly and disinterestedly cared for by one relative after another for short periods. Finally, he was sent to an orphanage. All these causes led to the manifestation of many complexes and aberrations in his childhood.

Isaac never paid attention to daily routine and showed no respect for authority, always giving evidence of obstinacy and bitterness in his conduct. He put forward all kinds of impossible and unrelated demands. His behaviour towards the two individuals whom he loved very much did not differ from his general attitude. They did their best to cure the child. Gradually, he was made aware of the folly of his ways and the nature of his behaviour. His interest in agriculture was encouraged. As a result of sympathetic behaviour over a considerable period, these two individuals came very close to Isaac, consequently becoming his ideals that went so far as to assume the form of his inner self. He came to seek their advice in whatever he did. A sense of disgust with his previous ways was aroused in him. When Isaac manifested this tendency towards better adjustment, ideals of better behaviour were gradually put before him. Due to the self-confidence and persistence of the two individuals, Isaac succeeded in reorganising his future, to be selected in the United States Air Force in 1941 at the age of 21.

Some psychologists and criminologists have criticised the conclusions reached by the study of psychopathic criminals. Sutherland writes that a neurologist studied the prisoners in Illinois prison. And studying the symptoms he found that 98 per cent prisoners were psychopathic. When some other psychologists studied the prisoners in the same prison they found only 5 per cent of them to be psychopathic. In fact, this term has been used in so many varied senses and on the basis of so many varied symptoms by different psychologists and psychiatrists that it has been left with no specific meaning that can be used to elucidate scientific facts.

3. Characteristics of personality. The tendency to crime was also found to have close relationship with characteristics of the personality. Personality is the method of an individual's adaptation to environment. Criminal children resort to illegal modes of such adaptation. Hence juvenile delinquents have been found to possess some characteristic features of the personality that shed light on the causes of their delinquency. Glueck has pointed out that the degree of freedom, irresponsibility, revolt, homicidal tendency, suspicion, lack of control, some forms of sadism, emotional and social maladjustment, extrovert behaviour, etc., in juvenile delinquents is much higher than in normal children. Immaturity in sentiment and lack of emotional balance were found to be some eight times more than in the normal child. A normal child is comparatively well-behaved, less explosive, peaceful, obedient and social. The juvenile delinquent, on the contrary, is found to be naughty, explosive, anything but peaceful, disobedient and unsocial. Glueck also discovered considerable difference between the general interests and forms of recreation of normal and delinquent children. Delinquent children were found to take much interest in works of an adventurous and dangerous nature. They were found to take considerable interest in seeing pictures and films. Among his interests and modes of recreation were found such practices as cigarette smoking, travelling without ticket, etc. He is often the member of one or the other gang. On the contrary, normal healthy children were found engaging in games. In some study it has been proved that female juvenile delinquents exhibited considerable emotional instability and immaturity.

4. Emotional instability. Thus emotional instability is one of the most important causes of crime. A child's personality is rendered unbalanced through lack of love and affection, emotional insecurity, very strict discipline, feeling of insufficiency and inferiority and reaction of revolt. Such a state of mind inspires the child to criminal behaviour. In their studies, Healy and Bronner found that 23 per cent of all juvenile delinquents manifest symptoms of emotional imbalance. A detailed analysis of these juvenile delinquents presented the following emotional patterns and influences:

(a) 46 criminals showed feelings of insecurity, lack of acceptability, extreme discrimination of an unfavourable nature, inferiority and not being properly understood.

(b) In 28 criminals, lack of affection had led to suppression of their normal desires.

(c) 54 criminals showed that they felt inferior or inadequate in school life, family life, in the friends circle or in play.

(d) 34 criminals showed signs of emotional imbalance as a result of bad behaviour of the parents, conditions of family life, mistakes of parents and lack of proportion in the family.

(e) In 31 criminals, feelings of extreme hatred and jealousy towards fellow mates were very strong.

(f) In 17 criminals, illusions of an unhappy life, based possibly on past experience, were found to be existing.

(g) 9 criminals clearly evinced the presence of self-condemnation and awareness of having committed crime due to some past criminal behaviour. These feelings were both conscious and unconscious.

C. Economic Causes

Crime and poverty are intimately related. Study conducted by Shaw, Mckay and Elliott revealed that among juvenile delinquents a majority belonged to families of unskilled workers. This discovery has the support of Bonger and Fornasiri, as they maintain that poverty acts as an incentive to crime. Concerning these juvenile delinquents, Merrill has written that a low family income compels the children also to share the burden and to neglect their education. Atmosphere in the factories and mills leads the male and female children to crime. Sometimes children are entrusted with carrying messages to the homes of persons where they often see all kinds of sexual practices. This has the worst effect on them, and they become tendencious towards crime. Statistics show that among juvenile delinquents, employed youngsters involved in crime number ten times than the unemployed ones. Girls working in hotels or restaurants are easily lured into sex crimes since their wages are low, their residences are dirty, hours of work are long, and there is no shortage of individuals who want to lure them to a life of crime. In fact children in poor families have many desires that remain unfulfilled, and it is to satisfy them that they turn to crime. Poverty also induces sense of dissatisfaction and inferiority, another spur to criminal tendencies.

Yet, this is no reason to conclude that crime and poverty are invariably related. In fact, poverty is not the cause of crime: rather, the cause of crime is the psychological factor that arises in poverty and impels boys and girls to crime. In the treatise *Juvenile Delinquency* Tappan has written that poverty is related to crime, but mainly because along with the subnormal economic situation other elements of the child's training and experience are also active, and these elements are more important in determining the reaction to character, values and laws. Family quarrels and dissensions, delinquent gangs and inadequate education are factors that are more active; than the preferred attraction of non-conformity to law and order. With the help of his study, Cyril Burt has demonstrated that one cause of there being such a large number of poor people among all criminals that are apprehended is that being poor, they cannot escape the clutches of law and police whereas the richer elements find it comparatively easier to avoid embarrassment. In the study conducted by Cyril Burt, only about 19 per cent Juvenile delinquents were to come from extremely poor families, while another 37 per cent of them came from the average poor families. But, according to Burt, the main reason for this large proportion was not poverty but instead the ability of the children of richer families to avoid being apprehended. Whatever the cause to which the high rate of juvenile delinquency among poor families may be attributed, no criminologist can contradict the fact that poverty and juvenile delinquency are closely related. When children of poor families see individuals of rich families using many different kinds of things, but are prevented from doing so by the lack of wealth, they develop feelings of hatred, avarice and jealousy that ultimately lead them to crime.

The foregoing exhaustive treatment of the social, psychological and economic causes of juvenile delinquency makes it clear that the principle of specific causation does not properly apply to this phenomenon. In fact, no modern criminologist and psychologist can refute the fact that the causes of delinquency are many and varied. A person's activities are his modes of adjusting to his environment. And in this adjustment individuals who apply socially acceptable means are called healthy while those who use unsocial and abnormal means for it are called criminals. Thus, a child becomes a criminal through the cooperation of many causes, social and individual, familial, psychological and economic. Hence, in order to rehabilitate the juvenile delinquent as a healthy member of society, it is necessary to understand all these causes and to remove them.

Modern welfare states aim at reforming the juvenile delinquents so that they may become responsible citizens when they grow old. The following are the most important methods to realize this objective :

1. Probation. In this method the juvenile delinquent is kept under the supervision of a probation officer whose job is to look after the delinquent, to help him in getting established in normal life and to see that the delinquent observes the rules of bail-bond. Thus the delinquent not only gets a chance to reform himself but also gets advice and concrete help for this purpose.

2. Reformatory institutions. Institutions such as reformatory schools, certified schools, auxiliary homes and borstal schools are devised to reform inmate delinquents. These institutions provide an allround progress of the delinquent.

Whereas the above measures are adopted by the state, the psychologist adopts psychological techniques for the reform of juvenile delinquents. Of these the important ones are the following :

(i) *Play therapy*. In this technique the delinquent children are given opportunities to participate in such plays as give expression to their repressed motives and help in the development of creative energy. In play therapy individual as well as group play are utilised.

(ii) *Finger painting*. In this method the child is given plain papers and some colours. He is allowed to paint in his own way by means of his fingers. The purpose is not painting but expression of repressed motives in the child, which leaves him sensible and healthy.

(iii) *Psycho-drama*. In this technique the child is allowed to participate in different roles in group drama and thereby manifest his repressed motives.

STREET CHILDREN

Surveys of street children (sponsored by the Ministry of Welfare-UNICEF

1992-93) in eight major cities have indicated that a large number of street children suffer destitution, neglect, abuse and exploitation due to the circumstances beyond their control. The surveys have also shown that, due to a variety of reasons, basic urban services do not reach them in an effective and integrated manner.

Under the Scheme for the Welfare of Street Children, grant-in-aid is given to voluntary organisations to provide integrated community-based non-institutional basic services for the care, protection and development of street children. The focus under the scheme is on reduction of exploitation and abuse and withdrawal of children engaged in hazardous work. Priority is given to girls, children without family ties and those amongst them who are victims of abuse and exploitation. For younger children, priority interventions focus on reinstating them in their families and facilitating their participation in the formal primary education. For older children, efforts are directed at enhancing their education and providing vocational training for equipping them with productive skills for adult life.

The Scheme has been started in 1993-94 with a view to supporting and strengthening voluntary organisations engaged in the welfare and development of street children to enable them to reach out in larger number in the cities of India and providing linkages with existing programmes, schemes and infrastructural services of the Central/state governments and municipal corporations. Under this Scheme, each voluntary organisation is expected to implement one project for 300 children. Ninety per cent of the cost of the project is provided by the Government of India and the remaining 10 per cent by the non-government organisation (NGO) concerned. Each project is supported by a core staff with professional qualification and facilities for maintenance, rehabilitation, training and learning material.

All the 23 million-plus cities and state capitals (total 37 cities) are covered under the Scheme and the implementation of the projects is closely monitoried by a city-level Task Force Committee comprising officials from the welfare, municipal and police administration and representative of each NGO implementing the Scheme. The budget provision for the scheme for the year 1994-95 was Rs. 500 lakh.

PREVENTION AND CONTROL OF JUVENILE SOCIAL MALADJUSTMENT

It is a Centrally-sponsored scheme which has been implemented by the Ministry of Welfare through the states/union territories since 1986-87 for the neglected and delinquent children for effective implementation of the Juvenile Justice Act, 1986. The main objectives of the scheme are:(i) to provide for full coverage of services contemplated under the Juvenile Justice Act, 1986 in all districts so as to ensure that no child under any circumstances is lodged in prison; (ii) to evolve system for separate handling of non-delinquent children; and (iii) to develop infrastructure for an optimum use of community-based welfare agencies in the care, protection and rehabilitation of maladjusted Children. Under the scheme grants of Rs. 18.06 lakh and Rs. 25 lakh are provided for construction of observation homes and juvenile homes/special homes respectively. Grants are also provided for upgradation of existing institutions. It also envisages grants for maintenance of inmates at the rate of Rs. 300 per child per month, contingency of Rs. 10 per child per annum. The above expenditure is shared on 50:50 basis between state and Central Government and when incurred through NGOs, it is on 45:45:10 basis. As per the information available, there are 280 observation homes, 251 juvenile homes, 36 special homes and 46 aftercare institutions in the country and a total number of 32,162 inmates presently being maintained in these institutions. The budget allocation for 1994-95 was Rs. 300 lakh.

CRITICAL EVALUATION

Children Acts are in force in the states of Andhra Pradesh, Gujarat, Kerala, Madhya Pradesh, Madras, Maharashtra, Mysore, Punjab, Uttar Pradesh and West Bengal and all the Union Territories. The Borstal Schools Acts, which are slightly different in scope, are in operation in the states of Andhra Pradesh, Gujarat, Kerala, Madras, Maharashtra, Mysore, Punjab, Uttar Pradesh and West Bengal. The Reformatory Schools Act of 1897 has also been enforced in all the bigger states and some Union Territories.

The problem of Juvenile delinquency is mainly the concern of State Governments. The Central Government, however, have sponsored a Care Programme under which the states are given assistance. Under this programme, 40 remand homes, 17 certified schools, 5 borstal schools, 15 boys clubs and 5 probation hostels have been established.

Beside formal education, vocational training in a number of trades is imparted to the inmates of the certified reformatory and borstal schools. Some of these institutions also provide juvenile delinquests on their release with implements and money to enable them to settle down in trades learnt by them in schools. Other institutions provide follow up services. The inmates of the certified schools are given training in citizenship and democratic living and are encouraged to take part in extra curricular activities, such as sports, debates, dramas, music and scouting.

Recently, seventy-two children also escaped from the home at Majnu-ka-Tila, Delhi, making it the third escape this year. Sources confirm escapes are common. Recently some inmates also fled from another custodial home. As a matter of fact, most children do not want to remain in these homes.

The state-managed homes, set up under the Juvenile Justice Act, were created for the care, protection and rehabilitation of neglected and deviant children who are "destitute or have unfit parents found begging, or living in near brothers and are likely to be abused or exploited for immoral and illegal purposes." Reportedly, the number of such children (mostly from Bihar, Assam, Bengal, UP, Andhra Pradesh and also Nepal) are increasing daily. In Delhi about 500 children are picked up annually. The city has about 100 custodial institutions. According to one estimate children's homes across the country have a capacity to house some 3,50,000 inmates, while 80 million children remain outside schools.

Although the Juvenile Justice Act, which replaced the Children's Act 1960, is in line with the UN Standard Minimum Rules for the Administration of Juvenile Justice, the Indian juvenile justice system has totally failed to imbibe the spirit of the Act. The world of custodial institutions is murky, full of horror and neglect that is most shocking. Some members of the committee, now set up to look into the functions of the homes say on condition of anonymity : "The food is extremely bad. The kitchens stink unbearably. The toilets and the drains have been found to choke with sewage. Many homes do not provide cots to the children who sleep on the floor with poor cushioning even in the cold winter months. In some homes the walls are stained with urine and betel juice. The sick are seldom attended to properly. The use of soaps and phenols are not quite evident though there are funds for these items."

Observes Sandhya Sharma, social worker and member of the Juvenile Justice Board. "I think even two hours of sincere work would bring some improvement. As adult-child communication is zero, in the absence of any emotional anchor, the children run away. If children fail to go to school, no one is bothered. At one home there is only one bat in the name of sports. The officers-in-charge keep attending meetings, the ladies keep kintting or basking in the sun. Even as a Board member, I am not aware where all the money is spent."

The Juvenile Justice Act, however, states the homes are to provide services for the physical, mental, moral and spiritual welfare of children and facilities for self improvement. "Rather than providing custodial care like parents provide, juvenile homes have degenerated into jail-like custodial centres. The JJ Board, despite its authority, has remained a mute spectator to the pitiable conditions of the Homes," comments Amod K Kanth, ACP, Delhi Police and secretary, Prayas Juvenile Centre for Neglected Children, Kanth adds, "The Juvenile Justice Act strongly advocates that children should not be kept in lock-ups as juvenile justice is distinguished from criminal justice. Most children arrested are non-offenders but the two categories — neglected children and juvenile delinquents are wrongly clubbed together."

Admits Balbir Singh, secretary, social welfare, "We'll not dispute it — there are bound to be certain deficiencies as the homes were established a long time ago. But there are also deficiencies in our own homes. A committee will soon make proposals for making these homes meaningful and livable."

QUESTIONS FOR EXERCISE

1. Distinguish between crime and delinquency.
2. What do you understand by delinquency? Can it be prevented or cured?

3. What are the chief causes of delinquency? How would you prevent a boy from stealing?
4. Describe some of the factors that have been found to be related to criminal behaviour and juvenile delinquency.
5. Write short note on Reform of juvenile delinquents.

18

Urban White Collar Crime

In the modern capitalist system the white collar crime assumes social importance. Normally by the term white collar crime we mean the crimes committed by educated and cultured persons who are well-clad and would not be normally reckoned as criminals. These persons utilise their economic and social status as a cover for the nefarious activities. In this category are also included those persons who exploit their religious status and position to commit various types of crimes. A poor and obscure individual committing crime is easily apprehended, but the white collar criminals so cover their criminal activities that they are not easily caught. The white collar criminal by the use of money, political influence or religious status keeps the long hand of law at abeyance. Thus, in the capitalist society the white collar criminal has become a serious problem. This phenomenon may be regarded as the symbol of capitalist exploitation.

Definition of White Collar Crime

The eminent criminologist E.H. Sutherland has defined white collar crime thus, "White collar crime is committed by a person of respectability and high social status in the course of occupation." Further elaborating the same point Sutherland writes, "The white collar crime is committed in the course of one's economic and fiscal activities." It is evident that in the gamut of white collar crime are included only those crimes which are connected with and are committed in the course of professional and business activity. Normally, in the capitalist societies the white collar criminal is not punished. Therefore, the modern criminologists have emphasized this point. In this respect the contribution of Sutherland is significant.

CHARACTERISTIC OF WHITE COLLAR CRIME

From the foregoing discussion of the white collar crime the following points emerge :

(1) The general traits of white collar crime are similar to those of other crimes. A crime is an act or a complex of activities which are against society and which violate the provisions of law. Similarly, the white collar crime is against society and law. It is obvious that like all crimes the white collar crime is punishable.

(2) The white collar crime is punishable. E.H. Sutherland has written this about the concept of white collar crime, "It does not only emphasize punishment but includes punishability." Thus, it is plain that from the view-point of penology the white collar crime has the same place and status as any other crime. Mr. Sutherland is very critical of the fact that the laws enforcing authorities in capitalistic societies tend to ignore or minimize the evil of white collar crime.

(3) The white collar crime is based on violation of trust. According to Sutherland, "White collar crime is based on violation of trust". For example, many a management of educational and other institutions pay much less salary than stipulated by law but compel their employees to put their signatures on false documents: and, thus, draw more money from government than actually disbursed. Many financial institutions cheat their subscribers. The Chit Fund and like schemes are instances of such bungling. Many manufactures boost their sales by offering cheap gifts at nominal cost or free but more than make good their investment by quality deterioration or by reduction of quantity. The government is daily cheated of huge sums of money by unscrupulous contractors who grease the palms of concerned officials. Even smuggling is masterminded by high placed persons who escape detection due to huge pay-offs to police.

(4) White collar crime is related with differential implementation of law. This is the observation of eminent criminologist Sutherland that white collar crime flourishes and is rarely punished whereas the other criminals are shown no such mercy. This preferential treatment to white collar criminals is due to two facts: (1) White collar crime apparently relates to abuse of money and does not pose threat to life, that is, it is an offence against property and not a physical violation of any one. (2) Since the government and police themselves are susceptible to corruption, they are reluctant to move against persons well-placed and politically and economically powerful. The white collar criminal usually makes it a point to involve government agencies in his nefarious activities and, therefore, is protected even upon detection lest the government people themselves were exposed.

CURATIVE MEASURES

The urban discussion brings into relief the fact that white collar crime has assumed serious dimensions in the capitalist society. In order to combat these tendencies it is essential that political corruption be firstly eradicated and that government should refuse to yield to political and economic vested interests. In democracy every government wants to retain power and for this it is very necessary that it may not alienate any powerful political lobby. But if the problem is to be tackled, the government should be prepared to take risks. The judiciary should be very well paid and selection should be strictly on merit. The judges must be persons of high intellectual and moral calibre. They should be persons of proven integrity and must be incorruptible. Only by these bold steps can the white collar crime be combated and contained. But it seems that in a capitalist society where the golden key opens all locks, the eradication of such crimes seems virtually impossible. For effective control and eradication of white collar crime it is very essential that there should be some curb on vast accumulation of money in the hands of individuals, and also monopolization of any trade by private persons should not be permitted: otherwise the abuse and corruption of money cannot be contained. In socialist countries the white collar crime is not of serious nature and proportion because no men have so much money as to be able to influence or buy the government machinery. As a matter of fact the basic cause of these crimes is the vast accumulation of wealth in few hands so that even the government has to depend upon them for survival. As long as this state of affairs persists, there is no hope of any reduction in white collar crime. It is possible to control or at least contain such crimes if liberal labour laws are enforced very strictly and if the government servants are so well paid that they have little temptation to accept bribes.

QUESTION FOR EXERCISE

1. Define white collar crime. Is white collar crime on increase in India?

19

Urban Prostitution

G.R. Scott writes in *A History of Prostitution:* "An individual (male or female) who, for some kind of reward (monetary or otherwise) or for some other personal satisfaction and as a part or full time profession, engages, in normal or abnormal sexual intercourse with various persons who may be of the same sex, or the opposite sex is the prostitute." This is a very comprehensive and adequate definition of the prostitute. A prostitute, contrary to ordinary beliefs, may not always be a female: may not indulge in heterosexual intercourse; may not be a full time professional, may not accept monetary rewards. Positively, a prostitute has normal and abnormal sexual relations with more than one person: experiences some novelty in his or her activities and receives more personal satisfaction. Of course the most distinguishing feature of prostitution is sexual intercourse with various individuals.

When any female allows use of her body for sexual relations against payment of some money to many persons, this is an immoral activity which poses a threat to the society. The man availing the services of such women is called prostitute monger. The prostitution is considered immoral and unsocial because it commercializes and degenerates love and asserts the supremacy of bodily values over social and moral. Some people consider prostitution a safety valve through which excess of social concupiscence releases and thus the sanctity of family is preserved. However, while there may be some truth in this opinion, it is an undeniable fact that prostitution poses a great threat to family peace and that the cases of marital dissolution multiply due to prostitute mongery. Prostitution demoralizes and debases man. Accordingly, all civilized societies are trying these days to eradicate or at least minimize prostitution. In India also prostitution has been made a legal offence and a person is liable to be punished for being a prostitute or visiting one.

Causes of Prostitution

The social research made so far into the causes of prostitution reveals that females are drawn into it for a variety of reasons. A study of Kanpur prostitutes has revealed that though a majority of prostitutes have taken to their profession due to extreme poverty and hunger, there are many who have willingly adopted it after a series of love exploits Though, the economic factor is quite important, it is liable to be over emphasized. The citing of hunger and poverty as reasons for prostitution seems to absolve the prostitutes of all blame and they feel that in this way they can win over the sympathy of society. Like the causes of prostitution the cause of prostitute mongery is lust for novelty in the field of sex. Too much familiarity breeds contempt. This is nowhere more true than in the case of sexual instinct. Repetitive sex is extremely boring and depressing. Through his monumental researches into sexual behaviour of American men, Dr. Kinsey has reported that people go to prostitutes because this is the most economical means of having variety of sexual experiences. Compared to the marriage, concubinage, adultery and illegitimate liaisons going to prostitute is safest, least risky and least complicating.

The chief causes of prostitution can be classified into the following categories:

(1) Economic causes,

(2) Social causes,

(3) Psychological causes,

(4) Biological causes,

(5) Religious and cultural causes.

(1) Economic causes. Though, the economic compulsions constitute the major factor in the causation of prostitution it is, by no means, the only and exclusive cause of the phenomenon. It is not the case that every prostitute accepts money for her services or that all prostitutes hail from indigent homes. There are many prostitutes who hail from well to do families. In India, of course, there are many prostitutes who are compelled to adopt prostitution to feed themselves and their dependents. However, poverty is not the only economic factor, there are many other factors which are not economic. The economic factors are comprised of: (i) Poverty. (ii) Under-age employment, (iii) Unhealthy working conditions, (iv) The pollution and corruption in industrial centres and (v) Immoral traffic in women and children.

(i) *Poverty*. As referred to earlier, poverty is the main economic factor responsible for prostitution. A woman who is unable to get any gainful employment and who has no supporter must either starve to death or earn livelihood through prostitution. The illiterate and semiliterate women cannot easily get employment. More often than not they have to sexually gratify their prospective employers. Many parents feel so utterly helpless that they prostitute their own children. The maid servants are often object of the lust of their employers. The concept of poverty however is relative. A woman may prostitute herself in order to live well and give first class education to her children.

(ii) *Under-age employment*. Many females have to work in hotels, offices, industry and shops at immature age. At this impressionable age they are easily misled by lust-seekers.

(iii) *Bad working conditions.* In India many women are able to get employment through intermediaries. These intermediaries and agents recruit women and keep them under their mercy. Whenever opportunity offers itself they exploit it fully and often succeed in receiving sexual bribe. Once a woman falls prey to their lust they, in no time, make a professional out of her.

(iv) *Pollution and Corruption in Industrial Centres.* The living conditions in most of the industrial centres are barbarous in India. Living accommodation is scarce and whatever is available is in slums. Due to paucity of accommodation most of the workers are compelled to leave their families and live alone. The absence of family and cinema going, gambling etc. make prostitute mongers of these persons. The industrial towns have busy brothels and innumerable prostitutes. In India women are paid less wages than men. Therefore, contractors make it a point to recruit maximum number of women in the labour force. These women are easy prey to the lusts of contractors and their friends. Due to poverty their bodies are exposed to full view of these lust seekers. In slums the unmarried girls have to witness sexual activities of their relatives and are often seduced prematurely. The precocious development of sex often drives women to prostitution.

(v) *Immoral Traffic in Children and Women.* Many tender girls are kidnapped from their homes by unscrupulous gangsters. They properly train them in the art of prostitution and when these girls mature, they are sold.

(2) The Social Causes. The social causes are extremely important factors in encouraging and promoting prostitution. The social factors are comprised of (i) Family causes, (ii) Marital factors, (iii) Bad neighbourhood, and (iv) Illegitimate motherhood

(i) *Family Factors.* A study of London prostitutes published as Women of the Street reveals that most of the prostitutes are connected with family troubles. Their parents were either living separately or their family relations were so strained that children were left to their own machinations and received no love. An unloved child when she grows up offers all of herself to any one showing any degree of love and affection. The children of criminals show a marked tendency to become prostitutes. If the character of the mother is bad and she has to carry her clandestine liaisons, she rarely escapes the eager eyes of her daughter. Often it happens that a man sleeping with mother succeeds easily in seducing the daughter.

(ii) *Marital Factors.* Many a superstitions prevalent in India force women into prostitution. For example, widow-remarriage is still frowned upon. But as a recent Hindu film ''Phir Bhi'' depicted even a middle aged woman is unable to eliminate and repress her physical needs and that the more you fight against them, the more passionate and demanding these become. Therefore, the widows, unable to remarry due to social stigma, may fulfil their physical needs by self abuse, seducing of young etc. But as these are poor substitutes for the real sex, they may choose to become prostitutes. Secondly, in India it is still common to marry persons very young. If these girls become widows they often do so when they are very young. In Indian homes, particularly among villagers and poor, the illicit connections are common. Even brothers-in-law stoop so low as to have sex connections with their sisters-in-law. As a matter of fact, there is no relationship so sacred that it does not get sometimes consumed by the fire of passions. Evidently, these illicit connections are temporary and do not meet the sex needs of young women fully. Therefore, they seduce their servants or expose themselves to out-siders. Due to the irregular sexuality, unable to satiate their desires, they take to prostitution as a last resort.

(iii) *Bad Neighbourhood.* The children living near brothels or in the company of immoral persons become so used to seeing sex trade that they come to accept it as normal. The brothel keepers usually haunt these areas for their prey. The children who get exposed to sex business want to have these exhilerating experiences at the first available opportunity. The young boys are lured to serve as sex slaves of wealthy sex crazy women. A recent survey of an American slum revealed that a lady of more than fifty would lure a couple of boys to her apartment, and offer them food and drink. Thus in a subtle manner she would develop intimacy and engage in weird sex circus with them.

(iv) *Illegitimate Motherhood.* The women who become pregnant as a result of their liaisons and who cannot get abortion are exposed in society. No body wants to marry them but everybody wants to enjoy them sexually. Desperately such women prefer to become regular prostitutes.

(3) Psychological Causes. There are some psychological facts which tend the person towards prostitution. A woman who is frigid becomes desparate. She tries one man after another. Because of frigidity she is unable to experience pleasure and becomes a prostitute by trial and error. Some women are incapable of submission. In order to assert their independence they can flirt with other men. There is a psychological abnormality known as troilism. A husband who suffers troilism wishes to watch his wife submitting to the embrace of another men, sometimes he wants another woman to embrace his wife sexually and at the same time he sodomies her. It is not possible to go into the full range of psychological factors.

(4) Biological Factors. The persons born with defective sex organs or overactive glands may feel compelled to sex gratification in a bizarre manner.

(5) Religious and Cultural Factors. In India there has been religious sanction to prostitution. In South, every family was supposed to offer one daughter to the temple where apparently she was supposed to serve gods with total dedication. They were known as Devadasis — god slaves. But in actual practice they lived a life of prostitution. In ancient and medieval India prostitutes enjoyed the status of courtesans, that is, a pleasure girl of courtiers and kings. These courtesans enjoyed high status in society. There are certain religious sects in India as well as abroad in which the priest has the right to deflower every newly married girl. The polyandry and polygamy sanctioned by many societies are sophistications of prostitution. A man with numerous wives has to countenance lesbianism and illicit liaisons with servants in his family. Even eunuchs are used by such women to obtain relief. It is natural that if a person lives in highly lascivious and erotic atmosphere his or her desire is multiplied and seeks release in normal as well as abnormal channels. In many cultures a guest is honoured by the offer of wife or daughter by the host.

All causes enlisted above contribute more or less to prostitution has a very long and varied history. As a matter of fact it is considered to be the oldest profession in the world. In modern times it is becoming fashionable to consider prostitution a necessary part of the society. Many favour development of the art of prostitution on the pattern of geisha girls of Japan. That prostitution is and may be a preferred profession and avocation with some people is clearly shown by the following remarks of George Ryle Scott; "In many cases the mother is a prostitute herself, the father is a pimp and they send their daughters in the streets with slightest compunction often themselves initiating her in sexual intercourse."

PROSTITUTION IN INDIA

In India prostitution is a grave problem. Though exact data is not available, the number of registered prostitutes must be well over one million. In Bombay there are 70000 to 10,00,00 prostitutes. In West Bengal there are 5,695 brothels 45,000 prostitutes. In Bihar, in Mirzapur and Patna there are 100 brothels. In Motihari and Champaran there are 14 and 12 brothels respectively. In Orissa, in city alone there are 200 brothels. In U.P. there is a sizeable number of prostitutes in Allahabad, Banaras, Kanpur, Meerut cities. As a matter of fact there are sizeable number of prostitutes in every big town in India.

Prostitution or legal sex gratification on a mercenary basis has existed from the beginning of human society and is considered as a vice. Prostitution which existed in a limited way in earlier societies has thrived much and expanded in the contemporary industrial societies with its insistence on late marriages. Prostitution or pre-marital and extra marital sex has become an inbred feature of our urban societies with its comparative freedom in sex relations, availability of contraceptives faulty sex education existence of pornography, a loosened moral code etc.

Prostitution in Indian Cities

As everywhere else prostitution has become a prominent occupation and vice in our cities and metropolises and has assumed various novel forms in relation to an economy of scarcity. Bombay is the nerve center of urban prostitution. There we find the existence of specific houses of prostitution. The owners of such houses call their houses as centres of artistic entertainment like music and dance. These houses procure their girls through pimps who lure these girls from distant villages in India with promises of a lucrative jobs. These houses provide the services on payment ranged in a gradation. Besides this, prostitutes are attached to night clubs, cabarets, etc. They pose themselves as dancers or pop singers and carry on prostitution as a part of their trade. Hotel waitresses, receptionists etc., also do this. Besides these regular and recognized types of prostitution in India we find a type of prostitution of high society women, middle class girls, married women, etc. Even in a city like Bangalore this type of prostitution is found to be increasing in its alteration. High society girls and women carry on prostitution to escape from boredom and also to test their charm and attractiveness.

Middle class and low class girls carry on prostitution sometimes to get extra money to satisfy urgent need or to satisfy their craze for cosmetics. Married women carry on prostitution either to get some extra money or due to lack of marital satisfaction. In our economy of scarcity and constant need it may not be surprising if we hear of college girls acting as prostitutes at times to cater to an urgent economic need. The areas of low class housing and slums in our cities are more or less areas of prostitution. The existence and expansion of call girl activities of receptionists, typists, female clerks, telephone operators, has added a new dimension to the prostitution picture of our cities.

Diffusion of Prostitution

Prostitution becomes all the more of a social problem because of its diffused nature in relation to high society prostitution and the profession of call girls. Prostitution of high society women affects the morals of their children and their family life. The development of middle class prostitution in recent years has been affecting the morals of middle class women and young girls. Thus, widespread prostitution questions the efficacy and value of order and a moral code in the society and places the young mind in a state of confusion about the choice of alternative values of conduct. Call girls act as initiators and promoters of prostitution among young girls. They tap on young middle class girl's unsatisfied need for jewels and sarees through constant persuasion and may lead the susceptible into occasional prostitution which may afterwards affect the mental health and morals of that girl and affect her future. These call girls many a time solicit in public place like city bus stops in a city like Bangalore. They are a constant public menace and affect the attitudes of the school going children. They exhibit various flirtatious ways of soliciting which may indirectly induce the watchful child or girl to imitate with harmful consequences. The existence of prostitution also encourages kidnaping of young girls by a man with an eye on money by the sale of the beautiful girl to a prostitute. The constant exhibition of prostitution may lead a mentally confused and disturbed youth to prostitution against his will. Further, prostitutes and their procurers pose constant law and order problems. It may be accepted that prostitution in a healthy and controlled manner is necessary for certain classes of a society. However, the increased diffusion of prostitution over the whole social net work in a healthy community becomes a social problem in many ways.

In Indian cities prostitution has acquired its own forms in an economy of scarcity. It is increasingly becoming a constant social menace which is affecting the maintenance of healthy social life. This problem becomes more insoluble as it receives much support from the law enforcing agencies for its existence.

Evils of prostitution

Prostitution as such is considered as a vice social problem since it affects healthy sex life, loosens the value of family norm, promotes the spreading of universal diseases and affects the morals of youngsters. It is a constant social problem in our cities. This fact can be substantiated by the regular news items appearing in our newspapers of raids on illegal houses and imposition of fines on girls for soliciting. The statistics on venereal diseases for Bombay published from time to time show an increasing trend and this is an indirect indicator to the amount of prostitution practised in that city. Prostitution is encouraged by the conditions of city life such as constant tension, mental worries, the practice of free sex, late marriages, absence of responsibilities and provision of sex gratification at a low cost etc. In its turn the existence of prostitution affects the morals of the city-bred youth, students, adolescents and high society boys and unemployed youths. Prostitution or extra-marital sex is the cause of many of divorces in our cities and broken homes or homes with insufficient care and bringing up of children. In many cities a group of prostitutes rent a house in the midst of a residential suburb and the existence of such a house becomes a constant menace and nuisance to the inhabitants of that subrub. Moreover, seasonal prostitutes who pose as respected employees of firms or a government concern make casual acquaintances with innocent young girls and girls in their teens and lure them to a job in prostitution.

Some even take girls with them with an inducement of a chance to act in a "movie" and by manoeuvering make them take on a job of prostitution inevitably. The difficulty in getting married in our society with its dowry system and the relative poverty of parents also leads some girls into prostitution out of desperation. The existence of prostitution has affected the morals of our low class society and has led to the breakdown of healthy social and personal life among them.

India being a welfare state, all-out effort is under way to control and eradicate the curse of prostitution. Several laws have been enacted for this purpose. In 1956, Suppression of Immoral Traffic in Women and Girls Act was enacted, under which it was declared a legal offence to keep brothels, to entice girls and women and use them for prostitution.

All the provisions of the Act have been enforced throughout India from May 1, 1958. The Act prescribes punishment for brothel-keeping, for living on the earnings of prostitutes, for detaining a woman or girl in premises where prostitution is carried on, for prostitution in or in the vicinity of the public places and for seducing or soliciting for the purpose of prostitution. The setting up of an adequate number of protective homes for the rehabilitation and the education and vocational training of women and girls recovered and detained under the Act is also envisaged.

Rescue Homes and Reception Centres established under the After-care Programme can also be utilised as Protective Homes. About 294 Protective Homes (Government as well as private), are reported to be functioning in the country.

Besides, there are 80 Rescue Homes and 32 Rescue shelters to enable stray women and prostitutes to find a place where they can receive preliminary training for rehabilitation in society. In the 3rd Five Year Plan five Protection Centres were opened in U.P. Besides above-mentioned agencies, following other agencies are active to help and reform prostitutes and find them useful work. The Women Home, Madras; Shradhanand Ananth Ashram, Bombay, The Good Shepherd Home, Madras, Christians Home, Poona; The Salvation Army Home, Bengal; The Feudal Home, Bengal; All Bengal's Women's Union Home, Bengal; Khushal Bagh Mission Orphange, Gorakhpur; Mahila Anathalaya, Varanasi are some of the important centres for rehabilitation of fallen women. But the measures being adopted to check prostitution are inadequate. It will need a concerted effort on the part of both public and government if the problem of prostitution is to be controlled.

QUESTIONS FOR EXERCISE

1. Define Prostitution. What is being done by the state to eradicate Prostitution?
2. What is Prostitution?
3. Explain prostitution as a social problem in Indian cities.

20

Urban Alcoholism and Drug Addiction

Though alcoholism does not invariably lead to personal disorganization, it is undoubtedly an important cause of personal disorganization. In particular, the drinking habit among the poor and labour class has generated serious problems all over the world, and alcoholism among poor is dangerous morally, socially and economically. The poor drink usually to escape from their besetting worries which are largely due to indigency, but as is obvious, drinking can help only to perpetuate poverty and insolvency and by no stretch of imagination can be regarded as a solution of this problem. The excessive drinking robs man of his sense of discrimination; he is unable to distinguish between good and bad, right and wrong. This leads to loss of control and behaviour becomes involuntary and capricious. Thus, alcoholism produces personality disintegration and is a chief cause of family disorganization. The poor in India remain permanently poor on account of alcoholism; their will to improve collapses and they accept their despicable existence as ordained and irretrievable. Thus alcoholism causes poverty and leads to huge waste of national wealth. The broken homes are invariably concomitants of alcoholic habit. In particular, alcoholism affects the life of children and women very badly.

FORMS OF ALCOHOLISM

Some people take to liquor because of mental afflictions and emotional complexes; others drink though they suffer from no mental or other disease. Following are the main types of alcoholism :

1. Daily Liquor Consumption. With the exception of certain specific diseases this is invariably harmful. The liquor reduces tension, dialates arteries and produces euphoria. In some exceptional cases its moderate daily consumption relieves nervous tension and induces good sleep. However, medical advice is necessary in all these cases and it must not be self-prescribed.

2. Escapist Drinking. Some persons take liquor because under its euphoric spell a sense of well being supervenes and thus they become oblivious of their magging problems and worries. Though liquor does not provide temporary relief, it makes the problems worse because forgetting a problem does not mean that it has been solved. As a matter of fact, man's capacity to cope with life situations, becomes less and less due to the use of liquor. Thus poor remain poor or even become worse — moral degenerates and financial bankruptcy results.

3. Addictive Drinking. One may begin consumption of liquor for any reason but gradually it enslaves the man, he cannot kick it inspite of his best efforts. It is like a dangerous animal which as an infant, looks so harmless, even charming; but as it grows it eats up the man.

The consumption of liquor is widespread in India. On Holi and other festivals a sizeable majority of villagers and labourers drink. Even otherwise the habit is very widespread. Not only is liquor consumption common in India; but other intoxicants like Ganja, Charas, Bhang, Dhatura and Opium and its derivatives are widely used.

Though the rate of liquor consumption is very high in India, but undoubtedly there is some reduction in it due to prohibition policy of the government. But of late there are determined attempts to scrap prohibition and there is growth of liberalism and collapse of traditionalism. These factors are fast pushing up the sales of liquor in all states in India.

HARMFUL EFFECTS OF LIQUOR

The use of liquor and other intoxicants is harmful for every progressive and growing individual and society. It is harmful in as much as it impoverishes intellectually and morally softens and spiritually deteriorates the person addicted to liquor. Without weaning the poor from liquor no great economic or social progress in any country is possible. The following is the list of its harmful effects :

1. The Wastage of National Wealth. It has been estimated that a successful enforcement of Prohibition Policy would increase the purchasing capacity of people by rupees 44 crores; of this rupees 40 crores will be invested for productive purposes. It is obvious, therefore, that prohibition would save the country from huge wastage of national wealth.

2. Low Standards of Health. The consumption of liquor leads to deterioration of health. This may happen due to any of the following two reasons :-

(1) Liquor is narcotic and leads to nervous degeneration, liver cirrhosis, high blood pressure and a host of other diseases and (2) money spent upon liquor reduces one's resources and may not leave one with sufficient funds to buy nutritious food. The money which can buy gallons of milk is wasted on litres of liquor. The country made liquor is often a great health hazard. Only in last two years more than 500 people have died after consuming poisonous liquor in various parts of India.

3. Lowering of Efficiency. With fall in the standards of bodily health and mental agility, the fall in efficiency is but a corollary. The alcoholic is whimsical and incapable of sustained attention, concentration and putting in long hours of work.

4. Mental Imbalance. A man under the influence of liquor has no control over his will and is fickle-minded. He is unable to think and work constructively. His vision and thinking get blurred if intoxication is strong.

5. Increase in Poverty. In India the villagers and labourers drink inspite of their poverty. This obviously increases their poverty though it may provide them temporary well-being and euphoria.

6. Individual Disorganisation. The consumption of liquor makes a man wayward in habits and whimsical in moods. He also loses all control over his desire to grow and progress becomes feeble. He grows careless and indifferent and finds little difference between morality and immorality. All this produces personality disintegration.

7. Family Disorganisation. More homes are broken due to drinking than due to any other single cause. This is easy to understand. As the moral sense of man is destroyed and his inhibitions removed, prostitution mongery and adultery are normal consequences of alcoholism. An alcoholic shows little respect to his wife or children. This leads to divorce and constant family tension.

8. Increase in Crime. Under the influence of liquor people act in unsocial way as their inhibitions are removed. This includes murder, rape and other crimes. Moreover, in order to meet the expenses of drink a man may take to gambling or even theft.

DRUG ADDICTION

Delineation of Drug Addiction

According to Sri K. Mitra the term 'drug addiction' refers to a condition of uncontrollable, habitual craving wherein a person seeks the sleep, torpor, or stupor resulting from the consumption of a drug. Such torpor producing drugs are described as being narcotic. There are three main groups of such drugs: (a) Opium, cocaine and their compounds including their derivatives, and related synthetics such as morphine, pethedine, methadon etc.; (b) sedative (soothing) or hypnotic (sleep-inducting) drugs such as vernal, bromides, aspirin, barbiturates and (c) *ganja, bhang* and other preparations of the hemp plant, botanically included under the genus "cannabis."

Effect of Drug Addiction

The body acquires a tolerance to it and gradually increasing doses become imperative to produce the desired degree of intoxication or satisfaction. Once accustomed to any of the drugs enumerated specially those listed under the first group. The desire to continue the drug is so over powering that the addicts very frequently resort to any means, at times even to crime, in utter disregard of the adverse effect on their physical fitness and mental condition. Such drugs interfere with metabolism of the tissues of the body specially of the nervous system. The result to that the withdrawal of the drug may cause nausea, vomiting and mental discomfort. The addict develops a psychological and even physical dependence on the drug. He loses his healthy, intellectual and moral stamina. Thus he becomes a liability to his own family and the society of which he is a member. The drugs listed in group (b) may be said to be less harmful than those in group (a). Drugs included in the group (c) do not have such adverse physiological effects on the addict as those under the first two groups.

History of Drug Addiction

Herbal concoctions, exhilarating in character, were prevalent in use in India from ancient times. This was the condition even earlier than drug addiction in China. References to "*somarasa*" abound in old Indian literature. However what was "*somarasa*" cannot be established with any certainly. *Bhang* has been mentioned in the *Atharva Veda* and even in other old Sanskrit literature. The consumption of alcoholic drinks and hemp drugs like *ganja* and *bhang* seems to have been in vogue prior to the advent of Muslims in India. These drugs produce a sedative effect and also induce pleasing dreams during the period of intoxication,. Probably opium was introduced in India by Muslim traders during the 9th century A. D. The beverage "*Chanabargha*" (four leaved) compressing alcohol, opium, Indian hemp, and poppy capsule was popular drink among the richer classes during the Mughal regime. After it opium cultivation was undertaken in India on large scale. As early as 1857 and 1878 the object of the Opium promulgations by the Government of India was chiefly to reinforce the fiscal monopoly. In 1893 Royal Commission was appointed to enquire into the prevalence of the opium habit. In 1895 the Government of India appointed another Commission to study the problems arising out of the consumption of hemp drugs. The attention of medical men and social workers was attracted in the reports of both the Commissions. In 1912, the British Government of India subscribed to the first International Convention restricting the external trade of opium to the genuine manufactures of medicinal preparations. However, it reserved the right to sell opium within its domain for "legitimate purposes." In actual operation, opium was available to the public through licensed excise vendors. Thus, there was no control on consumption and on the illicit traffic of the commodity.

The excise laws, differed widely from State to State. Gradually, popular feeling against drug addiction was voiced in the legislatures. In 1920 the Indian National Congress pledged itself to a policy of total prohibition of liquors and intoxicating drugs.

Study of Drug Addiction

Father of the school of pharmacology in India, Colonel Ram Nath Chopra of the Indian Medical Service, made an elaborate study of the drug addiction problem in India. During the third decade of the present century he published his findings in a series of articles in the reputed though now defunct, periodical, 'Indian Medical Gazette.' Some of the salient points of his observations were the following:

1. Opium ganja and bhang. These were the drugs commonly indulged in by the Indians.

2. Cocaine. Cocaine was imported from Java in India since the nineties of the last century. It was consumed by sizeable group of the population in some of the big cities in India. At one time it posed a problem but, fortunately, rigid preventive measures gradually eliminated it.

3. Hypnotic drugs. These, mainly barbiturates hardly constituted a problem in India. The number of regular consumers was few and scattered all over the vast country.

4. Synthetic Drugs. A big problem in certain parts of the world, viz addiction to drugs of synthetic origin, was almost absent in India.

PROBLEM OF DRUG ADDICTION

Due to the development of quicker modes of travel and the growth of a peculiar psychological atmosphere in rapidly multiplying industrial communities many were tempted to look to drugs as a means of relief from the stresses and strains of modern life. The vastly-improved chemical methods, for the extraction of alkaloids from opium and coca leaves and also synthesising similar narcotic drugs, combined to extend the drug-addiction habit to almost all the world. Thus a localised threat to the health and well-being of people in certain countries gradually extended to all the parts of the globe. Illicit traffic in these commodities thrived. Consequently, the crime rate increased by leaps and bounds. International opinion gradually hardened. Preventive laws and rules and regulations were framed to tackle the drug addiction evil in an organised manner during last fifty years. Among the international bodies concerned with narcotic drugs, the most important ones were the Commission on Narcotic Drugs of the Economic and Social Council and the Permanent Central Opium Board. The World Health Organisation appointed an "Expert Committee on Drugs Liable to Produce Addiction" during the latter half of the forties. The latest meeting of the Expert Committee was held in 1963 at Geneva. The problem of addiction to synthetic drugs featured largely in its proceedings.

The reports of the United Nations have made it clear that the habit of smoking of opium has been prevalent mostly in the countries of the Middle East and of the Far East. Addiction to "cannabis" preparations is not only found confined in Asia and Africa, it also extends to Europe and the America. "Marijuana" (cannabis cigarettes) is popular with addicts in the U.S.A. However, the western countries, are concerned more with the steadily growing menace of addiction to synthetic drugs like diacetylmorphin (heroin), pethedine and the like. It has been found that every addict is capable of infecting four others with this pernicious habit. Illicit trade in narcotics has assumed alarming proportions in most of the parts of the world.

Legislation for Control

A notable measure was the Dangerous Drugs Act of 1930 (which covered opium) enacted by the Government of India soon after the conclusion of the International Convention of 1925. With it for the first time in the country, greater emphasis was laid on the social aspect of drug addiction than on the revenue aspect.

(iii) The last date for the nonmedicinal use of *ganja* be extended to 31st

March, 1961 for the few States that find it difficult. In view of the recommendations made by the Yodh Committee, set up by the Government of Bombay, and as a result of representations made by the proponents of *Unani* and *Ayurvedic* schools of medicine, not to ban the use of hemp drugs in medicinal preparations. The UN Commission on Narcotic Drugs had impressed on the Government of India the viewpoint of the WHO that use of "cannabis" (hemp) drugs for medicinal purposes was unnecessary.

(iv) The final decision of the Conference was kept pending till a scientific investigation on the subject was made.

The efforts made by the Central and state Governments in India have been widely recognised outside this country particularly by the UN Commission on Narcotic Drugs. The incorporation of the Indian system of control over the production of opium in the United Nations Protocol of 1953, was one of the many tributes paid to Indian efforts.

Treatment of Addicts

An important part of the programme for the control of drug addiction is the treatment of addicts who should be regarded as psychiatric patients rather than as criminals. On the recommendations of the 1956 Conference the Government of Assam initiated a drug addiction rehabilitation programme. Some of the other States were reported to be interested in the measure. *Medical Tribune*, a reputed medical periodical in the U.S.A., reported that the National Institute of Mental Health, U.S.A., has pointed out in a monograph that the number of know narcotic addicts has declined from 60,000 to 40,000 in the decade 1950 - 1960. 90 per cent of the 1,900 addicts returned to their addiction within a six months of their treatment 70 per cent of the addicts were men; Addicts often resort to minor crimes to support their habit.

Soon after their assumption of office in 1937 the implementation of the policy of prohibition initiated by the Congress ministries in at least five Indian States. In some of the other States, prohibition was introduced on an experimental basis. One of the earliest measures was closure of excise shops. These efforts received a set-back when the Congress ministers vacated their office in 1939. These were revived soon after the popular ministries returned to power.

In March 1948, the Government of India, made a solemn declaration in the Constituent Assembly indicating their determination to root out the evils of intoxicating drinks and drugs. Thus was later incorporated in Article 47 of the Directive Principles of State Policy of the Indian Constitution.

All India Conferences on Narcotics

Besides legislation, all India conferences sought to check drug addiction . Since 1947 three All India Conferences on Narcotics have been held.

1. All India Opium Conference was convened at New Delhi in August 1949. All the State Governments participated in it. A unanimous decision was taken to launch a ten-year prohibition programme. All the State Governments agree to reduce their demand by 10 per cent every year, the aim was that by

1959 complete prohibition except for medicinal and scientific use should be achieved. Under the Narcotics Commissioner to the Government of India Central Narcotics Department, was created in November 1950. Its aim was to rationalise and unify the production and distribution of opium. The Commissioner was also appointed the Opium Agent under the Opium Act, 1857. His job was to superintend the cultivation and manufacture of opium. The Narcotics Department ensures the production of opium to meet the internal and external requirements for therapeutic purposes. It keeps a preventive watch over possible leakages from the sources of production and supply. The first Conference also agreed that non-medical use of *ganja* and *bhang* should be banned after 1949.

Earlier, under Article 19 of the Opium Protocol, 1963 the Government of India declared that "consumption of opium for non-medical and nonscientific purposes would be totally eliminated by 1959."

2. The Second All India Narcotics Conference was held in 1956 in Shimla. It reviewed the position regarding the ban on narcotic drugs. Some of its important recommendations were the following:

(i) After the date of 31st March, 1959 the opium supply should be restricted to addicts only on the strength of valid medical permits.

(ii) Closure of all excise-licensed opium shops by 31st march, 1959.

(iii) Provision for treatment of opium addicts in hospitals.

(iv) Introduction of a phased programme for stoppage of the use of *ganja* for non-medical and non-scientific purposes by 31st March, 1959 and *bhang* by March 1961. A later date was set for *bhang* because of its use in certain parts of the country for social and religious functions and because of the wild growth of the herb.

(v) Control over the import, sales and manufacture and possession of pharmaceutical preparation of narcotics and a preventive watch on illicit trade of all narcotics.

3. The Third All-India-India Narcotics Conference was held in Hyderabad in 1959. It reiterated its determination to adhere to the earlier recommendations. It discussed some of the problems arising out of those recommendations. Following were some of the highlights of the Conference.

(i) Medical opium should be issued under strict control through government-managed depots. All leaks to illicit channels should be stopped.

(ii) Inter-State export of poppy capsules should not be allowed except on requisition for medical purposes.

PROHIBITION IN INDIA

Indian constitution enjoins on the State of endeavour to bring about prohibition of the consumption of intoxicating drinks and drugs. In December 1954, the Prohibition Enquiry Committee appointed to suggest a programme and a machinery for the implementation of the directive in the light of the experience of the States in implementing their prohibition policies in the past.

The committee's main recommendation that schemes of prohibition be intergrated with the country's development plans was affirmed by resolution of the Lok Sabha on March 31, 1956. The resolution recommended the formulation of a programme to bring about nation-wide prohibition speedily and effectively.

The Third Five Year Plan had laid emphasis on prohibition being a voluntary social welfare movement, whose success depends upon (i) its acceptance as public policy accompanied by concrete administrative steps to make the policy a reality, (ii) support of large section of public opinion and active participation of social workers and voluntary organisations, (iii) finding practical solutions to problems arising out of it, such as employment, and (iv) enabling State Governments to meet possible loss of revenue on account of progress of prohibition.

A Central Prohibition Committee has been set up to review the progress of prohibition programmes, co-ordinate the activities in different States and keep in touch with their practical difficulties. The Committee also suggests ways and means to intensify propaganda in favour of prohibition, promote research on the economic and social implications of prohibition and recommends measures to encourage and assist official and non-official agencies devoted to prohibition and temperance propaganda, care and rehabilitation of alcoholics and drink addicts and scientific research in respect of problems associated with prohibition.

The progress in the enforcement of the prohibition policy in the different States and Union Territories of the Indian Union is briefly dealt with in the following paragraphs.

1. Andhra Pradesh. Complete prohibition is operative in the districts of Anantapur, Chittoor, Cuddapah, East Godavari, Guntur, Krishna, Kurnool, Nellore, Srikakulam, Visakhapatnam and West Godavari. In the other districts toddy and liquor shops have been shifted from populous areas.

2. Assam. The dry law is in force in the districts of Kamrup and Nowgong, covering 19.2% of the area and 15% of the population of the State. In the other districts, measures to discourage the sale and consumption of liquor have been set in motion, the more important of which relate to increase of rates of duty on both foreign and country liquor, stoppage of issuing new liquor licences, removing of liquor shops from industrial areas and the gardens, the prohibition of serving liquor in public places and closure of liquor shops on national days.

Total prohibition of opium has been in force throughout the State since 1947. Seven opium addicts treatment centres have been opened. With effect from July 1959, consumption of *ganja* and *bhang* has been totally prohibited.

3. Bihar. A prohibition board to consider details of policy and to review the programmes of its implementation has been established. The work of preparing a phased programme bas been entrusted to a technical committee. Among other steps taken to introduce gradual prohibition and to prepare the ground for total prohibition, mention may be made of the enhancement of duty and retail prices of counter spirit, introduction of the sliding scale system of settlements in respect of distillary liquor and drug shops, stoppage of sale on national days and closure of liquor shops for a period of 8 days in a month in certain areas of the State and a reduction in the sale hours of country liquor shops.

The supply of opium for oral consumption, except on certificates granted in limited number by approved medical authorities, has been completely withdrawn since April 1, 1959.

4. Gujarat. There is complete prohibition in the whole of the Gujarat State. Taluk prohibition drive committees and sub-committees of the block advisory committees have been set up. Similar committees at the village level are being formed with the help of the Panchayats.

5. Kerala. Complete prohibition has been in force in the whole of the Kozhikode, Palghat, Cannanore and Trivandrum districts as also five taluks in the Quilon and Trichur districts and for Cochin area of Ernakulam district covering 58% of the area and 56% of the population of the State. Advertisement and public inducements relating to drink have been prohibited. No fresh licences for liquor shops are granted. A State Advisory Board has been set up. Six District Advisory Committees have also been established to enlist public co-operation for prohibition in the dry areas of the State.

All opium and ganja shops in the State have been closed with effect from April 1, 1959.

6. Madhya Pradesh. Prohibition is in force in the districts of Sagar, Damoh, Narsimpur, Hoshangabad, Khandwa and Vidisha districts and portion of Bilaspur, Raipur and Durg districts covering 16.4% of the area and 12.8% of the population of the State. A system of permits has been introduced in one tehsil of the Jabalpur district and one of the Betul district. Among other steps taken are progressive reduction in the number of liquor shops, ban on advertisements relating to drink, prohibition of liquor drinking in public, progressive increase in the number of days on which liquor shops remain compulsorily closed, shifting of liquor shops from industrial and populous areas, enhancement of the price of intoxicants and encouragement of the consumption of healthy and refreshing drinks

The oral use of opium, except on permits issued by competent medical authorities, has been totally banned since April 1, 1959.

7. Madras. Total prohibition has been in force throughout the State since October 2, 1958. The enforcement of the prohibition law has been strengthened by providing enhancement of sentence, summary trials and control over sale and transport of molasses.

8. Maharashtra. Total prohibition has been in force since April 1, 1961. Besides a State Prohibition Board, Taluk prohibition sub-committees have been set up in district development boards. Taluk prohibition drive committees and social committees of the block advisory committees have also been established. Efforts are now being made to establish similar committees at the village level. Subsidies are paid to welfare institutions, co-operative societies, village panchayats and municipalities for conducting Sahkar Kendras (Recreation Centres) for prohibition propaganda.

9. Mysore. Prohibition is in force in the entire state except in the districts of Bangalore, Gulberga and Raichur. The dry area account for 81.1% of the area of the state and covers 79% of the production. To facilitate the successful implementation of the prohibition policy of Government of Maharashtra, a ten mile dry belt zone on the Mahatashtra-Mysore border in the Gulbarga district was created in July 1959. Prohibition Board has also been set up for advising the State Government in the matter of effective implementation of the prohibition policy. The sale of ganja, except for medicinal and scientific purposes is totally banned in certain districts of the State. Consumption of opium, except for medicinal purposes and by addicts on medical certificates, has been completely banned from April 1, 1959.

10. Orissa. The dry law operates in the districts of Ganjam, Koraput, Cuttack, Balasore and Puri. Sale of foreign liquor to addicts in these districts is limited through licensed shops and on production of permits. In non-prohibition areas, steps have been taken to reduce progressively the number of liquor shops and to increase the number of days when liquor shops remain closed.

Oral consumption of opium has been prohibited since April 1, 1959, and all opium shops in the State have been closed.

11. Punjab. Total prohibition exists only in the districts of Rohtak and steps have been taken in other districts to reduce sale and consumption of liquor through restriction of the grant of licences and sale of liquor etc. Other steps taken by the State Government include imposing restrictions on advertisements relating to drinking and closure of liquor shops once in a week with effect from April 1, 1962.

Complete prohibition of the oral consumption of opium, except on medicinal grounds, has come into force since April 1, 1959.

12. Rajasthan. Prohibition is in force only in Abu taluk in the district of Sirohi. A phased programme has been put into effect since April 1, 1956. Among the more important aspects of this programme are the ban on serving drinks in public places, closure of liquor shops on pay days and other important national days, reduction in the number of country liquor shops, removal of liquor shops from populous areas and enhancement of duty on liquor and licence fees. A Prohibition Advisory Committee was established to introduce prohibition by stages.

13. Uttar Pradesh. There is total prohibition in the three pilgrimage centres of Brindaban, Hardwar and Rishikesh and the districts of Badaun, Etah, Farrukhabad, Fatehpur, Jaunpur, Kanpur, Mainpuri, Pratapgarh, Rae-Bareli, Sultanpur and Unnao. This covers 17.05% area and 21.4% population of the state.

The sale of ganja has been prohibited throughout the State and oral consumption of opium has also been banned with effect from July 1, 1959.

14. West Bengal. Prohibition has not been introduced in any area of the State. Among steps taken to discourage the drinking habit are the declaration of dry days in industrial areas, reduction in the hours of transaction in excise shops and in the grant of licences for retail sale, enhancing rates of taxation on liquors, etc.

15. Union Territories. A policy of gradual prohibition is in progress in Union Territories. Toddy shops have been closed, liquor shops are closed for five days in a week and import of foreign liquor is banned in Andaman and Nicobar Islands.

In Delhi, restrictions on the saleable strength of country liquor and the number of country liquor shops have been imposed. Advertisements relating to liquor consumption have been banned and various steps have been taken to stop public drinking. Sale of liquor in clubs is restricted to members only. The number of dry days have been increased and duty on all various kinds of country liquor has been enhanced. From April 1, 1959, supply of opium is available only to addicts on production of medical certificate.

There is total prohibition in the Bilaspur district and subdivisions of Mahasu, Mandi and Chamba districts covering nearly one fourth of the population in Himachal Pradesh. Elsewhere the quota of country liquor has been reduced, as also the number of liquor shops. Drinking in public places has also been banned. An Advisory Board has been set up to advise the administration and prohibition committees are being constituted in all the districts.

In Manipur, the issue of licences for local distillation of country liquor has been discontinued since 1958 and special permits are issued to individual tribals for local distillation of liquor on festive and religious occasions. Public drinking, advertisements relating to drinking have been banned and a district prohibition committee has been set up to ensure the successful implementation of the prohibition policy and to seek public co-operation. The oral consumption of *ganja*, *bhang* and opium has been prohibited.

In Tripura, excise shops are closed for one day in the week and selling hours have been reduced. Advertisements relating to drinking have been banned. Steps are being taken to remove excise shops away from populous areas. The sale of *ganja* through government agencies has been completely withdrawn with effect from April 1, 1959.

QUESTIONS FOR EXERCISE

1. What is alcoholism? How far can this problem be resolved by the enforcement of prohibition?
2. Write short note on — Prohibition in India.
3. Write short note on — Drug Addiction.

21

Urban Suicide

Every six minutes a person commits suicide in India and the total number of such deaths was 89,195 during 1994, an increase of 5.9 per cent over the previous year.

There were nearly 5,000 more suicides in the country in 1994 compared to 1993 and the suicide deaths increased at a compound growth rate of 6.2 per cent per annum against the population growth of 2.1 per cent, the National Crime Records Bureau (NCRB) said in a report.

West Bengal, which ranks fourth in the country's population, accounted for the highest number of incident of suicidal deaths consecutively for seven years, recording 12,389 suicides during 1994.

Followed by West Bengal; the other top risk states which reported high rate of suicides were Maharashtra (10,782), Tamil Nadu (9,248), Karnataka (9,050) and Kerala (8,533). Uttar Pradesh, India's most populous state, accounted for 7.8 per cent (6,938) of suicides in the country.

Among the Union Territories, Delhi and Pondicherry had maintained the status of reporting the highest and the second highest number of suicidal deaths during 1994. While Delhi reported a total of 803 suicides, Pondicherry accounted for 589 suicides during 1994, the report showed. Lakshadweep reported one case of suicide during 1994, the NCRB said.

A study on suicidal tendencies revealed that undesirable conditions at home like use of intoxicants, immorality, lack of parental love, poor parent-child relationship, too much of disciplining induce persons to take extreme step, the NCRB said. Too harsh treatments, authoritarian attitude, parental discrimination in favour of a child and personality clashes affect the emotional balance adversely and may force persons to resort to taking the extreme step, the NCRB added.

Among the 14 specified causes, "dreadful disease" is the most important cause having 13.5 per cent share in total suicides, quarrel with parents-in-law or with spouse together account for 10.7 per cent of the suicides, implying that the three causes were responsible for nearly one-fourth of all the suicides in the country.

Poison remained, as in the past, the prevalent means for committing suicides. It accounted for 34.8 per cent of suicidal deaths followed by hanging (23.4 per cent), fire/self-immolation (11.5 per cent), and drowning (9.4 per cent). The four means accounted for 82.8 per cent of the total suicides leaving 17.2 per cent share to other means, the NCRB side.

The study showed that 18 per cent more males committed suicides than females during 1994 and in the state of Jammu and Kashmir females outnumbered males. The cause profile of minors (under 18 years of age) showed a different scenario with highest suicides due to "love affairs" (13.2 per cent) followed by 'failure in examination' (9.4 per cent) and 'dreadful disease' (8.8 per cent), it said.

The highest incidence of suicides for both the sexes occurred in the age group of 18 to 30 years (43.8 per cent) followed by 30 to 50 years with 32.2 per cent.

In rural areas, girls work on an average of nine hours a day, 315 days a year and shoulder manifold responsibilities notably sibling care as early as at the age of six or seven. Early marriage, also thrusts a girl into the role of a wife and mother at a time when she is still a child herself, the NCRB said, adding that unable to cope up with the tension and vagaries of the life she is sometimes forced to take the drastic step of suicide.

Stating that it was a serious concern that very large number (11.2 per cent) of children were driven to commit suicides, the study said that perhaps children feel more neglected and emotionally vulnerable than before due to changed scenario of social order.

"There is an immediate need to take up extensive studies in this sphere so that remedial measures could be taken to curb this high rate of suicides amongst children", the NCRB noted.

DEFINITION OF SUICIDE

1. Encyclopaedia Britannica. "The act of voluntary and intentional self destruction." This emphasizes two salient features of the act of suicide: (1) that suicide involves the "will" of the person, which consents and acquiesces in willing self destruction; and (2) "Knowledge" that death is being preferred to life and that reason in person concerned is aware of and has acknowledged this as a fact and accepted it as inevitable and nonavoidable. Another important fact brought out by this definition is that there is some sort of purpose behind the act of suicide and that can be no intention; and desire presupposes some object or goal, that is, some purpose which has to be attained.

2. Ruth S. Caven. "The intentional taking of one's life or the failure when possible to save one's self when death threatens."

3. Social Definition. If someone indulges in self destruction or commits suicide, not only the members of his family but society as a whole is affected. This is true more or less in every case of suicide; but this is particularly so if the suicide is committed by an eminent scientist, scholar, artist, writer, social reformer etc.; because this death deprives the society of their valuable services and may mean an irreparable loss to the society. This fact is illustrated by suicides in recent years by eminent personalities Marilyn Monroe and Dr. Shah etc. by consuming an over does of sleeping pills. Recently a Japanese writer of world renown and a recipient of Nobel prize killed himself by cutting his throat. The loss of such persons is deeply regretted by society because society is poorer on account of their deaths.

4. Symptomatic of Personal Disorganization. Only if there is total disintegration of the personality of man and he has lost his equilibrium, a person commits suicide. There can not be an urge to put an end to one's life so overwhelming as to suppress or counter the deep-rooted instinct of self-preservation unless there is some fundamental spiritual unrest and to the soul, so to say, undergoes searching and is topsy-turvy. The suicide implies complete loss of sense of value in the person and the consequent feeling of emptiness and unwholeness of everything, every aim or aim--or object of living. There is so much mental and physical disintegration that the ultimate escape through death appears to be the only way out.

5. Symptomatic of Social Disorganization. Besides, being a case of personal disorganization, suicide also indicates or is symptomatic of social disorganization. The personal disorganization, as a matter of fact, is disorganization of a social unit; and in as much as a change or deterioration in the unit spells change or deterioration in the whole, individual disorganization is a product of and as well as produces social disorganization. Therefore, the fact of suicide entails some defiant disorganization in the society. In the least, it clearly foreshadows following facts: the norms and values which underlie and govern the society are being seriously questioned and challenged in some quarters and that society lacks the flexibility to cater to or accommodate the serious distent.

CAUSES OF SUICIDE

A person who commits suicide must be doing so under extreme pressure and in a very complicated and involved set of circumstances. When, due to some reasons, the condition of a person becomes utterly miserable and all hopes die before him, he feels driven to a precipice of life where a plug into abysmal sea of nothingness seems to be the only possibility and hope. It is certain that there is no single factor responsible for suicide; but there is a concentration of such factors. Of course, in some cases, a particular factor may prove crucial and decisive and in others, a different factor may fill the bill. It is not easy to enumerate and study all the factors involved in suicide. Some of the important factors are the following:

1. Psychological Causes of Suicide. The psychological factors play vital role in causing suicide. In majority of the cases of suicide, the persons committing suicide, are mentally disturbed or mentally imbalanced. The chief psychological factors leading to suicide can be classified as follows:

(i) *Abnormal Feelings.* There are certain feelings and emotions, which are universally present but in acute and abnormal form these produce unsetting and upsetting effect upon man. Fore example, fear anxiety, frustration, hatred, violence, vindictiveness, guilt and inferiority feelings can assume such dimensions that man loses his sanity. Overwhelmed by anyone or a combination of theses he loses his capacity for discrimination and rational thought. Consequently, he becomes abnormal and over-reacts to various stimuli. In the result, what will not even move an average man produces deep tremor and earthquake in over-reactive person.

(ii) *High level of Intelligence.* Compared to the individuals of average abilities and intelligence, far more suicides are committed by persons of bright intelligence and highly talented. It is a commonplace fact that highly talented doctors, scientists, writers, and artists are usually the persons who commit suicide. The suicides committed by practical-minded persons of average talents are relatively fewer in number. The main reason for this is of course higher level of intelligence; but, besides, the life-problems of such individuals are far more complex, intricate and involved. It is precisely on account of life that these persons commit suicide.

(iii) *Peculiarity of Personalities.* The various surveys conducted regarding the personality structure of the individuals committing suicide reveal that those individuals who commit suicide arc introverts and serious. Extroverts and social mixers are rarely found to commit suicide. Whereas the extrovert persons are social and have many friends they share their joys and sorrows and rarely take anything to heart, the introvert persons are in the habit of feeling deeply and internalizing various emotions to which they are subject. Thus introverts are many more times suicide-prone than extroverts.

(iv) *Mental Illnesses.* There are Mental Illnesses which become important factors in suicide. The mental Illnesses and abnormalities are resultants of the loss of emotional equilibrium and frustrating life situations which imbue deep anxiety, dismay, despair and forlornness. The chief mental Illnesses are Schizophrenia, Melancholia, Depressive mania, acute Paranoia etc.

2. Geographical Causes. Certain climatic and topographical factors are considered contributory to the phenomenon of suicide. The incidence of suicides is much higher in colder climates and mountains than in thc warmer and tropical climates and plains. Many reasons are given for this phenomenon.

3. Economic Causes. The economic factors, too, play very important part in inciting suicide. Many other factors too are attached with the economic factors and act like adjutant causes or subsidiary factors. For example, the rise and fall of economic status lead to corresponding rise and fall in the prestige of a man. It is, therefore, not unusual to find that loss of fortune leads to suicide by a businessman. But actually the economic factor does not operate directly, because loss of fortune may not, and usually does not mean that the man is going to starve. Then why commit suicide? The real reason is that the prestige and social status enjoyed by a multimillionaire is different from a millionaire.

Therefore even when a multimillionaire finds himself reduced to the status of a millionaire he suffers a loss of face and feels so depressed that he commits suicide. Below we shall discuss some of the categories of persons who commit suicide because of economic factors:

(i) *Suicide in Businessmen*. The pursuit of business is directly governed and influenced by economic factors like supply and demand, market trends, public tastes, governmental, policies, war and peace etc. Due to any of these factors, change in government, outbreak of war or cessation of war, there can be havoc and great upheaval in the economic fortunes of businessmen. Suppose there is revolution and the new government divests businessmen of their economic possessions, to-day's multimillionaire becomes a commoner. Unable to cope with the economic catastrophe, many a businessman commit suicide. Again, outbreak of war with a neighbouring country may spell ruin of a businessman who has all his business contacts with that country. The loss of fortune means loss of face, too; and loss of face so upsets certain individuals that they prefer death to dishonourable life. In business many evil practices flourish. The defection of funds, blackmail, giving and taking bribe, sea-laden entertainment of high business executives and officials etc. are some instances of them. Anyone who is found and caught may find his image darkened overnight and then life looks meaningless. In such circumstances, too, many people commit suicide.

(ii) *Special Occupations and Suicide*. Persons involved in certain special occupations are suicide-prone. Generally highly mobile persons commit suicides. An English survey reveals that the incidence of suicide in England is very high among hoteliers. In Germany and France call-girls and pornographers often commit suicide. Some of them commit suicide on such trivial matters like death of a pet animal. Middle aged prostitutes are very much suicide-prone. The bankers, the playboys, the cinema theatre personalities and artists are also very much suicide-prone. Another category of professionals who are predisposed to suicide are military top brass; they always prefer death to professional disgrace. The harakiri of Japanese army generals is proverbial.

(iii) *Suicides among Unemployed*. Another category of persons who are forced to commit suicide on account of economic factors are persons who are unemployed and feel therefore wretched and failures. A talented artist, engineer, scholar or scientist, if unable to secure employment, feels deeply let down and this produces in them symptoms of manic-depression and the person feels he has no alternative except death. In India the incidence of suicides in this category is progressively rising on account of growing unemployment among highly educated.

(iv) *Family and Marriage*. By family factors in suicide is meant divorce, marital incompatibility, death etc. Below we shall discuss the various factors one by one:

(i) *Suicides due to love*. Since times immemorial there has been a strange attraction, a feeling and an urge to commune, between sexes. This has taken numerous forms such as courtship among young boys and girls, a strange desire to be near, to possess each other. Marriage is an institution invented by society to control this impulse and regulate it into socially acceptable channels; but there have always been some people who have defined the bonds imposed by the society and pursued their instincts unwaveringly. These people have to put up with the guiles and deceptions of lovers or beloved. There are cases in which a lover is jilted by the beloved or she cheats him to settle the score. In these cases, some persons of highly emotional type are unable to suffer separations or the shock of deception and they put end to their lives. In certain cases, a young girl allows full rein to her natural instincts and in the process gets pregnant. She is shocked, asks the lover for marriage; but the lover quietly gives her a slip. Under these circumstances, many girls are known to have committed suicide. Still there is another category of cases in which the social and financial status come in the way of successful romance. Young couples are driven to suicide. Many Bombay films are based upon this theme.

(ii) *Marital Problems and Suicide*. In India, marital problems at times assume vicious proportions and produce a lot of mental ills. According to religious sanctions and social conventions and traditions, the parents of bride are required to pay handsome amount of cash, ornaments, clothes, furniture and many other things by way of dowry. In some communities this involves exorbitant expenditure and the parents of many a young women are unable to marry their daughters on account of fabulous sums involved in dowry which they simply cannot afford. Many such girls are condemned to prostitution and many of them put an end to their lives on account of the miseries they undergo. When some of these girls happen to remain unwed for a long time, they feel highly depressed. This is because an unmarried woman is looked down upon by the society. Unable to cope with social contumely, calumny and disgrace, many of these unfortunate women put an end to their existence.

(iii) *Suicide in Marriage*. There are occasions in the marriage span when suicide appears to be inevitable. In accordance with the Indian traditions marriage in an overwhelming majority of cases are arranged and the boy and the girl have had no chance of any premarital acquaintance. They are utterly ignorant about the habits, likes and dislikes of each other. There are some cases where these habits are so divergent, that quarrel between husband and wife becomes inevitable. There are cases where the mates are sexually incompatible. This incompatibility leads to an ever-increasing psychological tension and dislike. This mutual recrimination gradually becomes more and more vicious and in certain cases are a source of so much unrest that the person concerned commits suicide. Sometimes sexual habits, performances and failures can be a great source of shock, disturbance and disequillibrium, all of which leads man to commit suicide. If a person is weak in sexual performance or incompetent or impotent the contumely of his spouse many become unbearable and he may end his life. Similarly a barren wife is subject to great deal of ridicule and a sensitive wife may commit suicide unable to cope with social criticism.

(iv) *Suicides among women due to Family Causes*. In many Indian homes the condition of women is not satisfactory. In many homes women are maltreated. They are severely ridiculed for insufficiency of dowry, for failure to conceive, for bringing ruin to the family. The bitter and persistent quarrels of mother-in-law v/s bride, sister-in-law v/s bride are proverbial in Indian homes. These become so vicious that the bride may feel so utterly humiliated as to commit suicide. A widow in Indian Society has very hard time. She is not supposed to marry; she is not to dress properly, but must remain shabby. If the widow is young, she is prey to evil impulses of many. Being human, she craves love and thus is easily seduced. All these factors in certain cases lead the widow to commit suicide. A barren woman is queer phenomenon in Indian Society. She has no relief, no escape from constant social calumny, contumely and ridicule. She seeks help from quacks, fakirs and god-men but all this increases the burden of her heart and she ultimately embraces death as the only honourable course open to her.

5. Physical causes. Many individuals commit suicide under the impact of certain physical affections. As regards the suicides induced by physical conditions one thing must be borne in mind, that is that in India more women than men make attempts to commit suicide even if they are not always successful. A survey regarding suicides reveals that maximum number of attempts at suicide are made by women between the age of 15 to 25. This is the age when a woman discovers her sexuality and is greatly perturbed by the complicatedness of her sex-mechanism. A regular monthly discomfort and feeling of ill-at-ease mark the life of the women. This biological phenomenon upsets quite a few and they attempt to finish their lives. Besides this there are many chronic diseases which are incurable and a source of unrelenting mental and physical pain. The sufferings of cancer, paralysis, diabetes, impotence, and certain mystery disease prove so uncomfortable that life becomes a continuous drama of pain having no episodes of pleasures. Under these conditions many persons finish their existence by committing suicide.

6. Religious Causes. There are some religious cases of suicides too. The true religion always dissipated the urge to suicide. All great religions of the world condemn suicide. Only in Greek religion, which is really prehistorical, was suicide considered admissible. No true religion, however, sanctions suicide; it considers it a heinous sin. The line of argument is that since man has no power to make life; he has equally no right to take life whether his own or of somebody else's. Therefore killing whether homicide or suicidal is a sin. But with the decline in the sanctity of religion in modern times, the people do not have such implicit faith in religious beliefs as they used to have in past. Consequently, religion no longer acts as a powerful prohibition against suicide.

7. Social Causes. The social structure and cultural system under which an individual happens to live greatly affect and influence his beliefs, ideas and behaviour. A well organised and balanced social system help a man a great deal in leading normal and useful life . On the contrary, a disorganised society and divided or contradiction-ridden culture have the opposite effect that is, due to cultural and social conflicts the individual also suffers from contradictory hopes and fears and in the process he becomes like a house divided against itself. If there is any cultural lag in a society it has adverse and injurious effects upon the individual. This adverse effect is at times so cataclysmic that it leads to suicide. Below we discuss some of these factors category-wise in order to appreciate the cultural impact fully:

(i) *Social Disorganization*. Consequent upon social disorganization, every social norm and value becomes a casualty. Along with disintegration in the social fabric, there is chaos in values. This chaotic situation of social norms and moral sanctions leads to relaxation of social control over human behaviour. In the result, there is rising spiral of crimes in society. Drug-addiction, religious and moral experimentalism, prostitution, violence, theft and dacoity become the order day-to-day. In such a vicious and polluted social atmosphere, the day-to-day life becomes chaotic, a senseless movement. In the extreme cases of individual disorganization, suicide results.

(ii) *Urbanization*. The ancient India was a country of villages. Now there is rapid urban development and big towns and cities are springing up fast. With the rapid industrialization and urbanization the basic rural structure of society with its norms and values has undergone sea-change and all around there are crises, in particular the crisis of values. The intimacy and communal character of living so characteristic of the rural society has undergone overnight change and given way to informality and aloofness characteristic of urban life. Thus life and behaviour has become artificial. This outward artificiality seeps into the soul of man and renders his life rapid and meaningless. A gradual change from rural to urban society would not produce so much social and personal disorganization as is the case if this change is rapid and sudden. The rapid and sudden change produces varying degree of imbalance in individuals. Some are able to absorb the change and make adjustments with it, while others fail. The extreme cases of those who are unable to make adjustments are potentially suicide-prone.

(iii) *War and Suicide*. The wars also have direct impact upon suicides. The period of war is a period of great excitement and thrills, particularly if the war is not directly involving the populace. The cessation of war suddenly leads to depression because all of a sudden quiet and slow movement replace excitement and thrills of war. Certain individuals are so deeply affected by this change that they commit suicide. Besides, in vanquished the sense of defeat depression and failure is pervasive and may induce an urge to end the sorry state of affairs by plunging into the abysmal sea of nothingness.

(iv) *Unbalanced Socialization*. The incidence of suicide is also directly affected by the processes of socialization, their proper and improper ways and means. If the socialization of the child is not proper and according to social standards and expectations, his mental and emotional development is retarded. Under these circumstances the child grows into an unbalanced, illadjusted person who feels himself a misfit everywhere. Driven by desperation of construct humiliation and failure such a man commits suicide.

The above discussion makes explicit some of the major factors of suicide. As a matter of fact, suicide is a complex phenomenon; their is a variety of factors and numerous causes responsible for it. In a particular instance of suicide, psychological factors may be dominant, but in other instances social or cultural factors may be dominant and still in another case the cause of suicide may be stoppage of war or fall in the share value. Therefore, it is not possible to assign primacy as a causal force to anyone of these factors. Therefore we may conclude by saying, that it is not possible to assert that this or that is the most crucial factor in suicide. We need to analyze the cases individually before we can say what are the factors of suicide in a particular case.

REMEDIES TO SUICIDE

The problem of suicide poses serious danger both of the individual and the society. As the social organization becomes increasingly complex, the rate of incidence of suicide also rises. In India, consequent upon industrialization and urbanization the social organization is rapidly changing and this leaves many individuals maladjusted. On account of the increasing maladjustment, the incidence of suicide is showing an upward trend. The suicides have adverse effect upon the society and the nation, because, due to suicides, the nation loses the invaluable services of many persons. In critical social situations, as a rule, the suicides are committed by persons of high sensitivity, intelligence and talent. Naturally, it is a matter of grave concern to any nation if it starts losing its elite in suicides. However, suicide also has a chain reaction impact. If some notable personality commits suicide many persons who are some how holding themselves together, are deeply affected and their impulse to suicide is further strengthened. The suicides by famous scientists, writers, artists and politicians produce chain reaction. On account of these incontrovertible facts it is the duty and obligation of the society and the nation to find correctives to the problem of suicide. But the important question is, what are these correctives? What steps can a society take to prevent occurrence of suicide? Towards this end we have to eliminate those causes which lead to psychological and social tensions, cultural contradictions and produce personal and social disintegration. Following are the suggestions calculated to reduce or eliminate those irritants which induce suicide:

1. Elimination of Factors Inducing Social Disintegration. In a disorganized and disintegrating society the incidence of suicide rises; therefore it is the duty of every nation and society to stem disintegration of the society and evolve ways and means which would produce social harmony and promote social peace and tranquillity. The society should try to check and control crimes like violence, drug-addiction, sex offences and marital infidelity etc. as these lead to rapid personal disorganisation.

2. Economic Reform. The economic factors play an extremely important part in causing suicides. The wide economic disparities and consequent class distinctions play havoc with the life of individuals. Due to widespread disparities society is divided into rich and poor. In such a society the money-power comes to play so vital a role that the social class, prestige and reputation rise and fall with economic possessions and dispossessions. Such a society cannot be harmonized; it will always breed conflicts and contradictions, till the society eliminates aggressive economic competition and reduces the overwhelming role of money and peace.

3. Religious Preaching. Indeed religion is always opposed to suicide and considers it to be a sin, a violation of the will of God. However in the modern society the spirit of religion is becoming weak and the restraint which was exercised by religious injunctions upon human behaviour no longer holds. Therefore it is of fundamental importance for every society that the spirit of religion should be revived and it is made to play the role of preaching love and harmony, forbidding violence and hatred. For this it is essential that various religious institutions should use their influence to propagate the sanctity of life and the value of love and harmony.

4. Reform in the Institution of Marriage. A number of suicides in India are due to defective and retrograde traditions and conventions of a marriage. For example, due to the institution of dowry, many deserving females are condemned to live the life of spinsterhood. This is obviously an abnormal condition of a nubile young damsel; but what is worse, such persons are socially stigmatized. Consequently, many such girls unable to cope with the insistent natural urge become unwed mothers. Therefore, they are left with no alternative to suicide. Obviously, it is the duty of every society to remove from its social fabric irritants like these and also all other orthodoxies and harmful conventions which plague the society and undermine the moral and natural health of its members.

5. Social Acceptance of Unmarried Persons. Our society is highly orthodox and conservative and in this society marriage for every young man and girl is considered an inevitability and anyone stepping out of this social barrier is subject to ridicule, calumny and contumely. However, it is now recognized by every enlightened person and society that the belief that marriage is an inescapable destiny of every man and woman is false and ill conceived. There are in every society some persons whose fundamental nature and habits are incompatible with the institution of marriage. If such persons are forced to marry because of social pressure they find themselves in hell and to avoid and escape from the disgust and shame of life they commit suicide. No society has any right to interfere with the natural development of man and force upon him some artificial pattern. On the contrary society must recognize the peculiar needs and urges of its members and suitably cater for these.

6. Reform in Retrograde Social Traditions and Conventions. Generally the social traditions and conventions facilitate smooth movement of social life; but with passage of time they grow into orthodoxies and their observance becomes an end in itself instead of being a means of smooth social intercourse. These orthodoxes become hindrances in the way of social and personal developments. In Indian society evil customs like dowry, taboo on widow remarriage, casteism and untouchability destroy the real purpose and value of education and help increase psychological and social tension. The customs and traditions are indeed blots on the society and must be eradicated if there is to be peace and progress in the society and if the society is not to crumble under the wight of modernization, urbanization and industrialization. These orthodoxies are the chief causes of cultural lag and backwardness.

7. Promotion of Healthy Entertainment. Entertainment is as necessary for the healthy and happy life as good food, home and other things. Entertainment is a great source of dissipation of tensions. Bad or sex-laden entertainment may thrill and produce temporary euphorias but in the long run it tells upon the mental health of the man. Therefore, it is the duty of the society to check wild pornographic display of dance, drama and cinema and to provide good natural and refreshing entertainment.

From the above discussion, it becomes plain what steps are necessary for the prevention of suicide. Indeed, the main cause of suicide is personal disintegration and the consequent imbalance of personality. Therefore, all our efforts should be directed towards checking the factors which produce imbalanced and disintegrated personality.

QUESTIONS FOR EXERCISE

1. What is suicide? Discuss its cause.
2. Write short note on Suicide in India.

22

Urban Beggary

The beggary is a curse for any society under any conditions and circumstances; but for a poor country like India it is not only curse but a great financial burden, too. At present there are more than half a million beggars in India and if we include among these those persons who occasionally beg, the number will swell into a few millions. The beggars perform no useful social function: their existence is parasitical. They contribute to the impoverishment of the country. But the problem of beggary is not only economic, it has social and moral aspects also. As a rule, the beggars are chronically diseased, physically weak and they are morally corrupt. It is a very common sight to see swarms of ill-clad but apparently healthy young women carrying young babies in their arms and continuously nursing them. The beggars are a fruitful source of disease spreading and also spread reprehensible moral ills. The beggars represent a section of society which was rotted and is putrifying. This requires drastic and immediate tackling: otherwise the beggars would contaminate the whole of society. The foreign press and television have put India to shame by graphically showing pictures of beggars fighting like dogs for a few coins, swarming like bees for good left over in hotels and restaurants, naked women sleeping on floor and children sucking. Such scenes show India in very lurid colours. When, in past, India was a land of plenty and no economic problems existed, there were, no doubt, beggars in India. There is a great difference between contemporary beggars and the beggars of past days. The beggars of today are either too ill to do any useful work or too idle for that, they, therefore, prefer to beg to fill their bellies to doing work. But the mendicants of ancient times were dedicated souls who renounced all material goods and performed the vital function of maintaining and sustaining the moral standards of the society. They were spiritual seekers who were supposed not to earn livelihood and were permitted to beg for day-to-day needs of food. The Hindu scriptures and moral code provided for living by alms for celibates and those who had renounced the world. But the beggars of today have adopted beggary as a profession. They do nothing except begging and leading a life of hortible moral corruption. Moreover due to less productivity and all-round backwardness even a labourer in India is unable to earn enough to have two square meals a day in spite of daylong toil and moil. It is a patent fact which can not be overemphasized that our society cannot afford to have social parasites. Only those who do some productive labour should be fed; none has a right to food without putting inadequate work. Though many superstitious and orthodox Indians consider it a moral duty to give charity, but any intelligent man can easily appreciate the fact that giving of charity amounts to perpetuation of social and moral cancer in the body of society. If we seriously consider the social and moral aspects of beggary, we cannot help concluding that beggary must be uprooted from a society which wants to progress.

DEFINITION OF BEGGARY

Before attemping a detailed study of the problem of beggary in India it is necessary to define the terms Beggar and Beggary. Two important and illuminating definitions of these terms are given hereunder:

(1) The Bombay Beggary Act, XXXIII of 1948 defines begging thus: "A person without means of subsistence and wandering about or found in public places or allowing himself to be used as exhibit for the purpose of begging is covered by the definition." According to this definition three features are to be observed in a beggar: No apparent means of livelihood; (2) to beg at public places and (3) exhibition of one's suffering, bodily defects etc. in order to elicit public sympathy.

(2) The Mysore Prohibition of Beggary Act, XXXIII of 1954 defines beggary in the following words: "Begging includes wandering from door to door, soliciting alms, exhibiting or exposing sores, wounds, bodily ailments or deformities, or making false pretence of them for exciting pity for securing alms." This definition has the same elements as the earlier one though it lays special emphasis that beggars exploit their physical miseries and gross and repelling bodily defects for the purpose of eliciting pity in others and that such exhibition may not be genuine. Usually elaborate make-up and artificial devices are employed to put on an appearance of blindness, mutilated limbs, bleeding open sores and such other bodily affliction.

Beggary in India

As per the Census Report of 1951, there were 4,80,904 beggars and loafers in India. Of these 3,44,215 were males and 4,43.641 were women. To-day this number must have gone up by 100% or more. In thickly populated areas the number of beggars is much more than in sparsely populated areas. Usually, temples, mosques, Railways, roads and Bus stations, fairs, shrines, bathing ghats are the popular haunts of beggars. There are, of course, many roving beggars who move from door to door. Many beggars beg collectively and in an organized manner. They come in large numbers and by sheer shouting and aggressive postures compel people to give them some coins. The places where many people come and go daily are the favourite haunts and like specially located shops carry pugree or overhead price. The beggars also distribute between them mohallas or localities. They live on pavements or in the open under improvised huts. The beggars are found both in villages and towns. In India the places of pilgrimage are the most prized haunts of beggars.

SURVEY OF BEGGARS

Now-a-days many non-governmental social research institutions have carried out survey of beggars in order to assess the real dimensions of this problem. In this connexion a reference has already been made to Madras School of Social Works. The J. K. Institute of Social Work, Lucknow made a survey of 300 beggars. The following facts were revealed by this survey:

(1) Age. The sample had beggars between ages of 5 and 73. The maximum portion was beggars in 35-45 age group.

(2) Sex. The male-female ratio was 6 to 1, that is, there was one female to every six males. Among children, male outnumbered the female. Most children were in 10--15 years age group. The majority of women beggars were in 35-40 age group.

(3) Religion and Caste. Little over 66% of beggars were Hindu and little over 30% were Moslems. Among Hindus, only 1/10 belonged to highers castes; rest were low-caste.

(4) Education. 6% beggars were literate.

(5) Family Status. 60% of beggars had anomalous family status, the unmarried, widower, widow, married, separated, that is, the beggars belonged to all categories.

(6) Earning. 59% beggars earned Rupee one per day 30% earned Rupees two per day and the rest between 3 to 5 Rupees per day. At present, this earning must have grown at least ten times.

MODE OF BEGGARY

There are many ways to beg. All beggars try to arouse pity in others so that they may be moved to relieve the miseries of beggars and try to make an appeal to the religious sentiment of the people. Giving of alms is considered a laudable act by the religious traditions and it is claimed that by giving alms one earns merit and secures a place for himself in the heaven. The beggars learn to exploit all these techniques. Some women beggars manage to take bogus certificate in which the mention is made of the tragedies that have befallen the holder of the certificate and a fervant appeal for-all out help is made. There are, of course, many blind and deaf among beggars. There are lepers who extract money by the chorus of their pitiful and heart-rendering cries. Some beggars kidnap children and mutilate their limbs in order to use them for beggary. A survey conducted by Madras School of Social Work revealed that out of 5000 beggars in Madras city, as many as 3500 were able-bodied. Some beggars are in league with thiefs and dacoits and provide them useful clues to enable them to rob and burgle successfully. Some beggars beg by claiming that they have been ruined by drought, flood or earthquake. Some beggars beg by singing songs and claiming payment for their services.

CLASSIFICATION OF BEGGARS

As referred to earlier. a number of surveys have been conducted into the problems of beggary. These surveys have revealed the variety of beggars. Broadly, the beggars may be divided into following categories :

1. Religious Beggars. In this category are included those who have renounced the world and are carrying on the orthodox tradition of spiritual seeking and enlightenment of the householders. They are Yogis, Sanyasis Sadhus, Dervish, Fakir, Vairagi, Udasi etc.

2. Pseudo-Religious Beggars. The pseudo-religious beggars are those who have no spiritual quest and belong to no order of sadhus. They merely put on the saffron garb as a convenient way of receiving alms.

3. Tribal Beggars. These are professional beggars who beg by singing folk songs and giving dance performance on the roadside.

4. Able-Bodied Beggars. These are healthy persons who prefer beggary to work as it suits their queer temperament. They are usually in league with bad characters and act as agents of thiefs and dacoits.

5. Invalid Beggars. These are the persons who cannot earn their livelihood because they are too ill to work. They include lepers, old-aged and chronically ill.

6. Psychically handicapped Beggars. These are the beggars who are blind, deaf or dumb or one-legged or legless. They are easily able to arouse public sympathy and pity and are considered deserving cf public help. However, in this category are also beggars who have been subject to most inhuman and cruel treatment by other beggars. As mentioned before, many beggars kidnap children and mutilate them in order to use them as their pawns in beggary.

7. Mentally Unsound Beggars. These include psychotics, schizophrenics, idiots, morons etc.

8. Child Beggars. The children in misery arouse great pity. They cry, whine, wail so pathetically that they are given alms simply in order to be free from their painful presence. Many clever beggars pretend blindness, hunch-backness or old-age and use children for beggary.

9. Professional Beggars. Those who are either physically unable or mentally disinclined to any work and will only beg are called professional beggars.

10. Part-time Beggars. These beggars are those who are engaged in some petty work and beg in spare time.

CAUSES OF BEGGARY

1. The Economic Factor. Poverty and unemployment are the most crucial causes of beggary. The persons who cannot get any job of any kind and are left with little option but to beg, borrow or steal. The later two are rather difficult. Borrowing requires credit which is unthinkable in the case of indigent person and stealing is unlawful and risky. It needs a mental attitude which is not easy or common. Accordingly, begging appears to be the safest course left for indigent and impecunious.

2. Religious Factors. The widespread and evergrowing incidence of beggary in India is very largely due to the religious superstition of the common masses that by giving alms one earns special merit and attains righteousness. The attitude of people renders the task of beggars not only easy but least painful. Thus, many persons who have to toil and moil hard and sweat from each force to earn livelihood feel tempted to join the ranks of beggars. In particular, at the places of pilgrimage huge army of beggars bee-line the routes and people going there consider it a sacred duty to offer them alms.

3. Physical Causes. In India there is no adequate provision for the treatment and social rehabilitation of blind, deaf, dumb or handicapped. In the absence of any reasonable alternative such persons feel compelled to beg.

4. Social Causes. There are a number of social factors responsible for generating beggary. As is common knowledge, Indian society is highly orthodox and traditionalist. The widows are not allowed to remarry and are often maltreated by their in-laws, hence in order to escape mental torture they move out of family. If, unlukily, they possess no skill or education they are left with little choice except prostitution or beggary. The old have not even the first option. The women who get raped or themselves commit some offence are unacceptable to both parents and husbands.

5. Mental Causes. The idiots, morons and psychotics, unless cared for by society or relatives, have no option but to beg.

6. Natural Calamities. The earthquake, flood and drought compel people to leave their homes. Many such persons are unable to find any work and feel compelled to beg to control the hunger pangs.

SUGGESTIONS FOR PREVENTION

Following suggestions can be made for the prevention and eradication of beggary:

1. Eradication of Unemployment and Poverty. In order to eradicate beggary, its root cause must be removed, that is, we must provide everyone a right to work and also raise the minimum wages. In the absence of these essential steps, no other measure can be effective. You cannot ask a person to die of starvation but not to beg. You can ask him not to beg provided you can arrange for his food and shelter.

2. Legal Sanctions. Every state must pass law to declare beggary a legal offence.

3. Centres for Cure of Chronic Diseases. There should be special hospitals to take care of those who are unable to pay their own expenses.

4. Care of Orphans and Handicapped. The orphans and handicapped should all be taken care of by opening rehabilitation centres.

5. Treatment of Mentally Ill. The poor persons suffering from mental ailments should be given free treatment in psychiatric centres.

6. Rehabilitation Homes for Fallen Women. The women who become unacceptable to their relatives should not be left to the mercy of rouges and scoundrels; but should be given shelter in rehabilitation centres.

7. Public Opinion against Beggary. In as much as Indian people suffer from the religious superstitions that by feeling poor one can buy ticket to haven, the people should be educated about the realities of beggary and harmful effect of their current practices.

It is a great pleasure to find that the Indian government is alive to this problem and taking every possible step to eradicate beggary.

REMEDIAL MEASURES

The Criminal Procedure Code treats vagrants and vagabonds alike and provides penalties under sections 55 (i) (b) and 109 (b). Beggars may be proceeded against under Section 133 as those committing public nuisance. Beggary within railway premises was prohibited by law on February 15, 1941. Special Acts have been passed by most of the States to prohibit begging in public places. In others, municipal and police acts provide measures against begging. To deal effectively with persons who kidnap children for the purpose of exploiting them for begging, the Indian Penal Code (Amendment) Act, 1959, was enacted.

At present most of the states in India have passed laws declaring Beggary a legal offence. In the year 1959, the Government of India amended the Indian Penal Code so as to make beggary and abuse of children culpable crimes. Prior to this amendment in the Indian Penal Code by the Government of India, various states had passed laws making beggary a legal offence. Some of the important acts are quoted below :

(1) The Hyderabad Prevention of Beggary Act, 1941.

(2) The Bengal Vagrancy Act, 1945.

(3) The Mysore Prevention of Beggary Act, 1945.

(4) The Bombay Prevention of Beggary Act, 1945.

(5) The Madras Prevention of Beggary Act, 1945.

(6) The Cochin Vagrancy Act, 1945.

(7) The Travancore Prohibition of Beggary Act, 1947.

(8) The Bhopal Prevention of Beggary Act, 1947.

(9) The Bihar Prevention of Beggary Act, 1962.

All the above-mentioned Acts declare beggary an offence and provide for punishment of going to jail or payment of fine. They have also classified the beggars into various categories. The provision of punishment, its nature and severity is made in accordance with the categories of beggars. Besides the above Acts, the municipal acts of Punjab, Madhya Pradesh, Uttar Pradesh also prohibit beggary and declare it a legal offence. In the big Indian towns like Calcutta, Bombay, Madras, Delhi and Bangalore where foreigners come in large number there are strict laws against begging and begging at these places is not tolerated. In order the check the problem, there are poor homes in these towns where beggars are kept. They are given food and shelter and are encouraged to do some useful work or learn some skill.

QUESTION FOR EXERCISE

1. Define Beggary. Suggest remedies for its eradication.

23

Urban Poverty

According to Gillin and Gillin, "Poverty is that condition in which a person either because of inadequate income or unwise expenditures, does not maintain a scale of living high enough to provide for his physical and mental efficiency and to enable him and his natural dependents to function usually according to the standards of society of which he is member."[1] Thus, poverty is a condition of extremely lower standard of living. In it even the necessary wants are not fulfilled. As Goddard puts it, "Poverty is insufficient supply of those things which are requisite for an individual to maintain himself and those dependent upon him in health and vigour."[2] Therefore, a man is called poor when he is unable to gather the means to keep himself and his family in health. But poverty is a relative concept. It can be more or less. Its increase or decrease can be ascertained by the more or less proportion of the necessary things of life for the individual and his family. In the words of Adam Smith, "Man is rich or poor according to the degree in which he can afford to enjoy the necessaries, the conveniences and the amusements of life."[3] Hence in different countries the criterion of poverty also differs. In U.S.A. a person earning Rs.400 a month will be called poor, while in India a person earning Rs. 50 a month will be called poor. But in fact a condition of the absence of the fulfillment of the minimum necessities of life should be called poverty everywhere. The form of these minimum necessities, however, changes according to place and time.

CAUSES OF POVERTY

Different thinkers have pointed out to different causes of poverty. According to Henery George, the main cause of poverty is the personal ownership and monopoly of the individual on the land . He writes, "In the great cities, where land is so valuable that it is measured by the foot, you will find the extremes of poverty and of luxury. And this disparity in condition between the two extremes of the social scale may always be measured by the price of the land."[4]

---

1. Gillin and Gillin, *Cultural Sociology*, The Macmillan Co., New York, (1950), p. 758.
2. Goddard, J. G., *Poverty, Its Genesis and Exodus*, p. 5.
3. Adam Smith, *Wealth of Nations*, Book 1.
4. Henery George, *Progress and Poverty*, Condensed edition, (1936), The Hogarth Press Ltd. London, p. 5.

According to Marx the main cause of poverty is the exploitation of the labourers by the capitalists. To quote him, "He creates surplus value which for the capitalist has all the charms of a creation out of nothing."[5] According to Malthus, poverty increases because while the food production increases in arithmetical progression, population increases in geometrical progression.

All the above-mentioned views lay emphasis on certain one particular cause of poverty. But modern thinkers consider poverty the result of multiple causes. In the present complex economic organisation fate or the efforts of an individual are not the sole causes of poverty. As Landis and Landis have correctly said, "In a world where economic hazards are so numerous, the individual cannot always be blamed for poverty. " Hence besides the personal causes there are geographical, economic and social causes of poverty.

Personal Causes

Though one may not believe in fate in the modern time but no one can deny the importance of personal capacity, efforts and characteristics, in the economic status of the person. The important personal causes of poverty are as follows:

(i) *Sickness.* Hunter has written, "Poverty and sickness form a vicious partnership each helping the other to add to the miseries of the most unfortunate of mankind."[6] Due to sickness while a man is unable to work and his income decreases, a major portion of his income is also spent on the cure of the disease. Thus sickness increases poverty and poverty also increases sickness since hard labour in the absence of sufficient nutrition increases many diseases among the labourers.

(ii) *Mental Diseases.* Due to mental diseases also a person becomes incapable of doing anything. This decreases his income and increases poverty. On the other hand, poverty also increases mental disease since it is difficult to maintain the balance of the mind in a stale of uttar poverty. As Pashley rightly points out, "Poverty alone directly produces a very large proportion of the whole number of cases of insanity among the indigent poor."[7]

(iii) *Accidents.* Accidents either make a person entirely incapable of work or considerably reduces his capacity for it. If the earning member of a family is involved in some serious accident the whole family becomes poor."

(iv) *Illiteracy.* Poverty and illiteracy are mutually related. Illiteracy increases poverty since the capacity to earn of an illiterate person is very low. On the other hand, many persons are compelled to remain

---

5. Karl Marx, *Capital*, Vol. I Foreign Language Publishing House, Moscow (1954), p. 217.
6. Hunter, R., *Poverty*, p. 144.
7. Pashley, R., *Pauperism and Poor Laws*, p. 124.

illiterate because of poverty. Thus poverty and illiteracy together form a vicious circle to increase the troubles of the poor people.

(v) *Idleness*. Idleness is also a cause of poverty. Many persons, in spite of sufficient opportunity to work, do not work because of idleness and hence remain poor. In hot countries idleness is an important cause of poverty and backwardness.

(vi) *Extravagance*. It is well known that an extravagant person can waste any amount of money in no time. In fact the cause of poverty is not a lower income but excess of expenditure over income. Some persons are so much extravagant that they always remain poor in spite of whatever they earn. In India extravagance on the festivals and marriages can be easily observed everywhere, with the result that sufficient money is not available for education, sanitation, light, medicine and other necessities of life.

(vii) *Demoralization*. Demoralization or the lowering of character and morale leads to personal disorganisation and finally to poverty. Drinking, prostitution, gambling and other evil habits reduce to poverty even the persons of sufficiently high economic states. They reduce the capacity and cause escapism thus leading to poverty.

(viii) *Other personal causes*. Besides the above-mentioned personal causes of poverty there are some other important personal causes. If a man has too many children to bring up, his standard of living is definitely lowered, and he becomes relatively poor. This is the main cause of poverty in India. Old age, death of earning member, natural calamities, also lead to poverty. In rural India constant fragmentation of land leading to uneconomic holdings is a serious cause of poverty among the agricultural class. Abnormalities of personality also cause poverty by creating maladjustment. Such a person cannot stay in one job at a particular place. In fact, every defect of personality reduces man's capacity to work and thus leads to poverty.

Geographical Causes

Besides the above-mentioned personal causes, the following geographical factors are also responsible for increasing poverty:

(i) *Unfavourable climate and weather*. Favourable climate and weather is very much necessary for work as well as for production both agricultural and industrial. Hence in the extremely cold climates and weathers the amount of work and production is considerably lowered. This increases poverty.

(ii) *Absence of natural resources*. No country can become rich in the absence of sufficient natural resources, e.g., fertile land, sufficient water, minerals and other natural products. In the absence of natural resources the inhabitants of the deserts, high mountains and extremely hot and extremely cold countries generally remain poor.

(iii) *Natural calamities*. Besides unfavourable climate and weather, natural calamities such as the eruptions of volcanoes, typhoons, floods, earthquakes and lightning cause serious damage to property and agriculture. In Japan earthquakes cause serious damage to property. In China floods are a major cause of damage to agriculture. In India the absence of timely rains, excessive or deficient rains cause serious damage to agriculture. This increases poverty everywhere.

(iv) *Pests*. Pests are a major cause of damage to agriculture and movable property such as books, furniture, etc.

Economic Causes

Besides the geographical causes the main causes of poverty are economic. Of these the important ones are as follows :

(i) *Agricultural causes*. Absence of sufficient manure, improved tools, implements and machines, means of irrigation and cattle of high breed; diseases, absence of sufficient means to protect the fields from pests and animals; superstitions; exploitation of farmers by the landlords and constant fragmentation of land are some important agricultural causes which increase the poverty among people of the agricultural class.

(ii) *Unequal distribution*. Even if production is sufficient, millions of farmers and labourers remain poor in the country where distribution of wealth is unequal. In the capitalist system, the rich go on becoming richer and the poor poorer.

(iii) *Economic depression*. Economic depression causes decrease in trade and commerce, lockout of mills and factories and unemployment of millions of labourers and small traders. Thus it is a serious cause of poverty.

(iv) *Unemployment*. Unemployment is the most serious economic cause of poverty. In India it is a major cause of the lower standard of living of the people both in urban and rural areas.

(v) *Unproductive hoarding*. If a major portion of the wealth of the country is hoarded in unproductive forms such as jewellery, etc., the economic development of the country is seriously handicapped. This is a serious cause of poverty in India.

(vi) *Unwise economic policy*. Sometimes in spite of the presence of sufficient resources and manpower in a country, the people remain poor because of the unwise economic policy of the government. This was an important cause of economic backwardness of India under British rule.

Social Causes

Besides the above-mentioned economic causes the following social causes also increase poverty:

(i) *Faulty educational system*. An important social cause of poverty is faulty educational system. It is because of this that in India thousands of educated persons are unemployed and leading a life of poverty. A grave defect in Indian system of education is lack of sufficient opportunities for technical education. Another defect is the high cost of education and absence of sufficient scholarships.

(ii) *Faulty and insufficient housing*. In India due to family and insufficient housing, millions of people are forced to live in dirty and unhealthy slums. This reduces their capacity to work by increasing diseases and frustrations. Hence it leads to poverty.

(iii) *Absence of training in home science*. Mismanagement of household is a serious cause of poverty everywhere. This is because of lack of sufficient training to women in home science. Without such a training many middle class families remain poor.

(iv) *Evil customs and traditions*. Evil customs and traditions in society are an important social cause of poverty. In India, for example, the system of dowry compells many families to remain poor in spite of all the efforts of their menfolk to earn.

(v) *Insufficient provision of medical aid*. Insufficient provision of medical aid causes delayed cures, prolonged diseases, permanent displacements and untimely deaths. All these increase poverty.

(vi) *War*. War devastates prospering lands and rich countries. It leads to heavy loss of property and manpower. It upsets the balance of society by disrupting the moral standard and socio-economic system. It gives a serious blow to trade and commerce both national and international. Epidemics spread after war thus adding to the misery of the people. All these lead to poverty.

The above mentioned personal, geographical, economic and social causes do not exhaust all the causes of poverty. In fact, they differ from man to man and society to society. But the above mentioned are the important causes of poverty everywhere. Eradication of poverty requires removal of all these causes. This requires efforts from the government as well as from the people.

QUESTION FOR EXERCISE

1. What is poverty ? Explain causes of poverty in cities.

24

Urban Unemployment

Defining unemployment, Karl Pribram has written, "Unemployment is a condition of the labour market in which the supply of labour is greater than the number of available opening."[1] According to Fairchild, "Unemployment is forced and involuntary separation from remunerative work on the part of the normal working force during normal working time, normal wages and under normal conditions." Generally speaking, unemployment means the nonavailability of work even though there is a desire to do it.

FORMS OF UNEMPLOYMENT

The forms of unemployment have been given different names by different scholars. Some main forms in this connection are the following:

1. Cyclical unemployment. It is that unemployment which results from trade cycles, profit and loss and fluctuations in the price level. For example, when there is a depression in trade, thousands of people are thrown out of work.

2. Sudden unemployment. That form of unemployment which is in evidence in those business which engage workers periodically, for example, workers are turned out from time to time when the work in the factories decrcases.

3. Unemployment arising from failure in industry or business. Many factories close down after a short period of existence and their workers are left without work.

4. Unemployment resulting from deterioration in industries. When industries deteriorate due to lack of success in competition or one of the variety of causes, many people become unemployed.

5. Unemployment arising from seasonal business. Seasonal business stops when season comes to an end. As a result, the people engaged in it are thrown out of work.

1. Pribram, K., *Encyclopaedia of Social Sciences,* Vol, XV, p. 147.

From the standpoint of factors affecting unemployment, it may be divided into the following two types:

(i) Subjective unemployment. This is caused by physical or mental shortcomings of the individual.

(ii) Objective unemployment. This is caused by factors beyond the control of the individual and is related to objective circumstances.

Distinctions of Objective Unemployment

Objective unemployment may be divided into the following four forms:

1. Seasonal unemployment. This is the unemployment caused by the shutting down of seasonal industries.

2. Cyclical Unemployment. This is due to the cyclical economic inflation and depression.

3. Structural unemployment. This is due to the defects in the economic structure, for example, while thousands of people are unemployed in Kanpur there may be a heavy demand for labour in Delhi. In this situation the unemployment is not due to the excess of supply over demand but rather due to the defect of the economic structure.

4. Normal unemployment. This form of unemployment prevails in almost all countries. In a complex economic organisation it is difficult to provide full time employment for everybody.

UNEMPLOYMENT IN DIFFERENT FIELDS

Besides the above mentioned types the following three forms are accepted according to the fields of unemployment:

1. Agricultural unemployment. This form includes the unemployment of the people engaged in the agricultural sphere.

2. Technological unemployment. This includes the unemployment resulting from advances in technological techniques. For example, as the machines in any industry or factory increase they continually displace beings.

3. Educational unemployment. It includes the unemployment of all those people who are educated in some respect or other.

Of the above mentioned type of unemployment the first is the most important in India. This will be now discussed in sequence.

Categories of Workers

For 1991 census, population was divided into main workers (classified into nine broad industrial categories), marginal workers and non-workers. Data released so far gives total workers sub-divided into main workers and marginal workers and the distribution of main workers into four broad categories of workers viz. cultivators, agricultural labourers, household industry workers and other workers in rural and urban areas, as on 1 March 1991.

UNEMPLOYMENT IN INDIA

Number of persons on the live registers of the employment exchanges gives an idea of the trend of unemployment subject to certain limitations. Employment exchanges cover mainly urban areas. Not all the unemployed register their names in exchanges. Further some already employed, get registered for better employment. Number of job-seekers on the live registers of employment exchanges increased from 178.38 lakh as on 31 December 1981 to 367 lakh on 31 December 1994. Table 24.1 gives registrations, vacancies, placements and job-seekers on the 'live register' for the period 1981-90.

National Sample Survey Organisation

National Sample Survey (NSS) was set up in 1950 with a programme of conducting large-scale surveys to provide data for estimation of national income and related aggregates especially relating to unorganised sector of the economy and for planning and policy formulation. Today, it is a major fact-finding body and occupies a unique position in the nation's statistical system. It carries out annually socio-economic surveys covering various facets of population. It also undertakes field work of Annual Survey of Industries and carries out sample checks of area and yield of crops to improve quality of estimation of agricultural production prepared by the states, besides updating the urban frame work for selection of samples in urban area. Its personnel strength is now about 6,000 in 170 offices is spread over throughout the country.

It was reorganised in 1970 by bringing together all aspects of survey work into a single unified agency known as National Sample Survey Organisation (NSSO) under the Department of Statistics. The activities of NSSO are guided by a Governing Council with requisite independence and autonomy in the matter of collection, processing and publication of data. Besides the Chairman, the Council comprises five academicians, six data users in the Central ministries and state governments and six functionaries of the Department of Statistics. It is headed by the Chief Executive Officer, who is also the member-secretary of the Council. NSSO has four functional divisions, namely; (i) Survey Design and Research Division (ii) Field Operations Division (iii) Data Processing Division and (iv) Coordination and Publication Division. Each division is under the charge of a Director.

The subject coverage of the socio-economic surveys conforms to a well-defined cycle of the surveys extending over a period of ten years. Survey on consumer expenditure, employment and unemployment, manufacturing establishments and enterprises and trading establishments and enterprises in the unorganised sector are to be repeated once in five years, while subjects like land-holdings, livestock holdings, debt and investment are to be covered once in ten years. Thus, out of a cycle of ten years, pre-assigned subjects are allotted for seven years while three years are kept as 'open rounds' (two full-year rounds and two half-year rounds) to cover special topics of current interest to meet the demand of data users. Integrated with the main topics of a round, annual survey on consumer expenditure was reintroduced from 42nd round (July 1986 - June 1987) with a relatively smaller size of one-fifth of the usual quinquennial round during the intervening period between two quinquennial rounds on the subject. From 45th round (July 1989 -June 1990) it was decided to extend the scope of annual survey to cover employment - unemployment as well.

TABLE 24.1

Population by Category of Workers

(In crore)

	Rural	Urban	Total
1991 Census			
Total Population	63.13	21.53	83.66
Total workers[1]	24.93	6.56	31.49
Marginal workers[2]	2.77	0.17	2.95
Main workers	22.16	6.38	28.54
(i) Cultivators	10.74	0.32	11.06
(ii) Agricultural labourers	7.04	0.42	7.46
(iii) Household industry workers	0.68	0.36	1.04
(iv) Other workers	3.70	5.28	8.98

P. Provisional

Notes : 1. The figures exclude Jammu and Kashmir where the 1991 census has not been held.

2. Figures may not tally due to rounding off.

SELF EMPLOYMENT PROGRAMME FOR URBAN POOR

The programme was launched by Government of India on 1 September 1986 with the objective of encouraging families living below subsistence level in metropolitan, urban and semi-urban areas to undertake self-employment ventures with the help of subsidy and bank credit. The programme covers cities and towns having population exceeding 10,000 as per 1981 census and all urban areas administered by municipal committees/town area committees/notified area councils which are covered under IRDP, irrespective of their population.

Under the scheme, assistance upto Rs. 5,000 depending on unit cost is admissible to an eligible beneficiary for undertaking any of the eligible vocations. The borrowers are eligible for a capital subsidy of 25 per cent of the total amount of assistance. Applicant should have lived at least for three years in the city/town area. The family income of the beneficiaries should not have exceeded Rs. 600 per month.

TABLE 24.2

Registrations Vacancies, Placements and Job-Seekers on the Live Register

(lakh)

Year	Number of Employment exchanges[1]	Registrations	Vacancies notified	Placements	Applicants on Live Register	Percentage increase in Live Register over previous year
1981	663	62.77	8.97	5.04	178.38	10.1
1982	692	58.63	8.20	4.73	197.53	10.7
1983	726	67.56	8.26	4.86	219.53	11.1
1984	745	62.20	7.08	4.07	235.47	7.3
1985	800	58.21	6.75	3.88	262.70	11.6
1986	821	55.35	6.23	3.51	301.31	14.7
1987	835	60.12	6.01	3.34	302.47	0.4
1988	840	59.63	5.43	3.28	300.50	—07
1989	849	65.76	6.00	2.89	327.76	9.1
1990	851	65.41	4.91	2.64	346.32	5.7
1991	854	62.36	4.59	2.53	363.00	4.8
1992	860	53.00	4.20	2.39	357.58	—
1993	887	55.32	3.85	2.32	362.75	—
1994	891	69.28	3.97	2.05	366.92	—

Note : Total may not tally due to rounding off.

1. Including University Employment Information and Guidance Bureaux.

During 1991-92, an amount of Rs. 48.86 crore (provisional) was sanctioned to 1.11 lakh beneficiaries. The Self Employment Programme for Urban Poor (SEPUP) was merged with the Scheme for Urban Microenterprises (SUME) under the ***Nehru Rozgar Yojna*** (NRY) with effect from I April 1992.

SCHEME OF URBAN MICRO ENTERPRISES

The Scheme of Urban Micro Enterprises (SUME) was introduced on 15 June 1990 with the objective of providing employment to the unemployed and under-employed poor in urban areas. It covers unemployed urban poor living below the poverty line with an annual family income of Rs. 7,200 (which has since been revised to Rs. 11,850) and below for the Eighth Five Year Plan with effect from 1 April 1992 in metropolitan areas, cities and towns not covered by IRDP. The urban local bodies are primarily responsible for identifying beneficiaries. Maximum loan amount presently permitted is Rs. 15,000 in the case of SCs/STs and women beneficiaries and Rs. 12,000 in the case of others with a subsidy at the rate of 25 per cent of the project cost, subject to ceiling of Rs. 5,000 for SCs/STs and women beneficiaries and Rs. 4,000 for others. The subsidy is routed through the urban local bodies.

Self-Employment Scheme for the Educated Unemployed Youth

The scheme for providing self employment to the educated unemployed youth (SEEUY) which was introduced during 1983-84 was continued during the financial year 1990-91 also. Under the scheme, educated unemployed youth who are matriculates and above and are within the age group of 18 to 25.

QUESTION FOR EXERCISE

1. Discuss the problem of unemployment in Indian cities and suggest remedies.

25

Urban Labour Problems

It is regrettable fact that there have not been sufficient reform and improvement in the conditions of Indian Labour. The Indian labour is not properly organized and does not have its own leadership but depends upon outside guidance. The labour leaders are politically motivated and not really interested in the labour welfare. As a matter of fact they more often than not use the labour unrest as a means to grind their own axes instead of helping the labour genuinely. The government has not paid enough attention to the real problems and needs of labour and though there is much labour legislation intended to help the labour but in actual practice there is little improvement in the condition of labour. Following are the chief problems of Indian labour:

1. The Problem of Migration. One of the main problems of India labour is the problem of migration. The increasing pressure on land due to population explosion, the ever growing army of landless tillers, the social stigma on Harijans, increased indebtedness, breakdown of joint families, fast means of communication, ravaging of cottage industries and city oriented education are some of the causes responsible for the exodus of villagers and their influx into industrial towns. While by joining the army of industrial labour, there is some improvement in the economic conditions and relenting of pressure on land the family and social life of these new recruits gets upset. This creates problems of social adjustment, decreases efficiency and comes in the way of development of healthy employer-employee relationship.

2. The Problem of Recruitment. The second main problem of the Indian labour is that of recruitment. As yet there is little direct recruitment. Most of it is done through intermediaries. The services of Employment Exchanges are available to very few. As most of the workers are dependent upon intermediaries and as intermediaries have special type of relationship with the Employees they can afford to behave arbitarily with the workers. They receive cutbacks and have also to be propitiated by other gifts.

3. The Problem of Absenteeism. The labour force hailing from villages is usually unable to cope with the alien environment of the city. The fresh food, air and light is unavailable in cities. Besides, slums in which the workers live are extremely unhygienic and great breeders of disease. Accordingly, the workers are usually unwell. They consume liquor and visit prostitutes. All these factors combined result in large absenteeism from factories.

The chief causes of absenteeism in India are illness, nightshifts, alcoholism; migrating instinct, industrial accidents; prostitution; laziness; frequency of festivals and litigation. The absenteeism produces adverse economic effects on industrial production and the earnings of labour. Besides, it causes rift and tension between employer and employee. The various measures presently taken to meet this problem are grossly inadequate. A Committee set up by the Bombay Textile Mills to investigate the causes of absenteeism and make suitable recommendations for remedying the problem came to the following conclusion: "Proper condition for work in the factory, adequate wage protection from accidents and sickness and facilities for obtaining leave, rest and recuperation constitute the most effective means of reducing absenteeism."

4. Problem of Trade Unions. In India the trade union movement is not as yet well organised and developed. The lack of education, susceptibility to religious influence, generally fatalistic outlook, deep indebtedness and opposition by employers and intermediaries are some of the factors responsible for slow and uneven growth of trade union movement. The labour does not have its own leadership and has to depend upon politicians who have furtherance of their own interest rather than labour welfare at heart.

5. The Problems of Industrial Disputes. The capitalist economic and social structure, the policies of creating dissension among workers by intermediaries, retrenchment of workers to circumvent labour legislation and paying compensation are the problems which lead to frequent strikes, lock-outs, gheraoes and sit-in by workers. At times these disputes turn violent and labourers suffer heavily.

6. Problems of Wages. The chief problem of workers is that they are poorly paid. In some cases these are below subsistence level.

The statistics show very clearly that the chief problem of workers is poorpayments. In some cases these are below subsistence level. The statistics show very clearly the pathetic condition of the workers. Due to lack of adequate wages, the labourer is unable to give proper education to his children. He cannot maintain his health. This leads to decline in his efficiency and in the ultimate analysis the productivity falls.

7. The Problem of Indebtedness. On account of low wages, bribes to intermediaries, drinking and prostitution, most of the workers are permanently and deeply under debt. It has been estimated that more than 2/3 workers of big industrial towns are under debt and the average amount of debt exceed their 3 months salary. Due to heavy indebtedness the worker cannot think progressively and considers whole of his life an unrelieved drudgery. The causes of indebtedness are many. Usually the worker is born in debt and due to drudgery becomes demonetized; therefore he takes to drastic and powerful means like liquor and woman. This further complicates his problem and drives him to die a pauper in debt.

8. The Problem of Living Standard. Due to low wages and rising spiral of prices, the living standard of Indian workers has been dropping constantly. A comparison of wages in India with other countries will bring into relief the pathetic plight of the Indian labour. There are may causes of low living standard. The main among them are: (1) Low wages; (2) Illiteracy; (3) Population explosion; (4) Intoxications; (5) Lack of skill; and (6) Fatalism.

9. The Problem of Health. Due to lows wages and low standards the workers are unable to eat wholesome balanced diet. What is worse, most of them are addicted to smoking, tobacco chewing, drinking and visiting cinemas and bawdy houses. All these reasons coupled with unhygienic living conditions, inadequate clothing in inclement weather heavily dispose workers to disease and infection. According to Professor B.P. Adardar a worker loses 14.6 days in a year to ill health.

10. The Problem of Inefficiency. According to the report of Tariff Board a worker in India can handle 180 spinals whereas his counterparts in Japan, England and America can handle 240, 450 to 600, 1200 spindles respectively. As a rule the efficiency of Indian workers is 1/2 or even 1/3 of the worker in progressive countries. Ill-health, lack of education, lack of will to learn and progress, addiction to bad habits are some of the factors responsible for the low efficiency of the Indian worker.

11. The Problem of working condition. The conditions of work of the majority of labourers are extremely bad and deplorable and leave much to be desired. Most of the factories are ill ventilated and the illumination is improper. The living and working conditions are making workers prone to accident. At many places even facilities for drinking water, toilet etc., do not exist. In extreme weather there is no provision to minimize its effects. Due to lack of amenities and hazardous working conditions the efficiency of workers drops and they are exposed to accidents and infection.

12. The Problem of child labour. Though it is illegal to employ workers under certain age, these provisions are frequently flouted and circumvented. The problems of child labour in India are the following:

(i) More work and less wages.

(ii) Loss of education of children.

(iii) Lack of proper rest and play essential for proper growth.

(iv) The unhygienic and rigours working conditions.

(v) Low and below standard productivity.

13. Problem of women workers. Following are the main problems faced by women workers:

(i) Unsatisfactory working conditions.

(ii) Lack of amenities and facilities for maternity leave, child welfare etc.

(iii) Rigours labour unsuited to delicate constitution of women.

(iv) Maltreatment and enforced immoral life.

It is a matter of gratification that the Government of India, Trade Unions, Progressive and enlightened capitalists and industrialists, state governments and many non-government organizations are alive to the above mentioned problems and are doing everything under their power to remedy them and relieve the conditions of workers.

TABLE 25.1

Consumer Price Index Number for Industrial Workers

Year	Bombay	Ahmedabad	Calcutta	Madras	Kanpur	Delhi	All India	
							All Items	Food
Linking Factor	5.12	4.78	4.74	5.05	4.69	4.97	4.93	4.98
1970-71	182	176	182	170	190	199	186	201
1971-72	190	181	187	182	196	211	192	205
1972-73	203	198	197	203	212	222	207	223
1973-74	233	245	228	229	251	265	250	279
1974-75	289	305	288	301	323	337	317	358
1975-76	300	293	287	314	299	333	313	342
1976-77	298	281	297	288	294	332	301	317
1977-78	318	310	320	311	330	358	329	345
1978-79	325	323	331	318	337	368	331	347
1979-80	359	348	351	350	357	389	360	373
1980-81	400	376	382	388	396	426	401	419
1981-82	460	441	414	446	439	472	451	476
1982-83	502	487	447	475	473	508	486	508
1983-84	564	544	511	550	528	551	547	581
1984-85	609	570	576	576	554	597	582	607
1985-86	654	599	610	630	614	648	620	630
1986-87	717	657	671	681	672	707	674	700
1987-88	791	724	714	756	725	788	736	767
1988-89	856[1]	763[1]	783[1]	802[1]	763[1]	852[1]	786[1]	820[1]
	172[2]	163[2]	172[2]	167[2]	172[2]	177[2]	166[2]	172[2]
1989-90	179	171	178	172	178	182	173	177
1990-91	201	196	203	189	202	201	193	199
1991-92	234	225	223	216	228	225	219	230

1. Average based on six months indices only – April September 1988 on 1960 base.

2. Average based on six months indices only – October 1988 March 1989 on 1982 base.

Note : Old Series (1960-100) has been replaced by the New Series (1982-100) from October 1988

Linking factors between 1960 series and 1982 series are operative from October 1988.

Source : Labour Bureau, Shimla.

All-India index is compiled as weighted arithmetic average of centre indices with weights proportionate to aggregate estimate expenditure of each centre.

TABLE 25.2

Consumer Price Index Number for Urban Non Manual Exployees (Base 1960-100)

Year	Bombay	Calcutta	Madras	Delhi/ New Delhi	All-India
1970-71	168	170	175	174	174
1971-72	172	174	188	180	180
1972-73	183	180	203	190	192
1973-74	204	204	231	217	221
1974-75	241	238	291	262	270
1975-76	246	243	306	273	277
1976-77	255	251	294	274	277
1977-78	269	265	311	288	296
1978-79	285	279	321	303	306
1979-80	315	297	350	321	330
1980-81	347	331	390	352	369
1981-82	393	367	439	395	413
1982-83	440	384	470	428	446
1983-84	493	418	531	468	492
1984-85	538	451	577	508	532
1985-86	568	481	611	551	568
1986-87	612	530	671	597	613
1987-88[1]	666	562	736	645	656
1988-89[2]	130	135	141	135	136
1989-90[2]	139	146	152	143	145
1990-91[2]	154	164	168	156	161
1991-92[2]	180	181	189	177	183
1992-93	204	198	212	196	202

1. Average is based on seven indices (April 1987 October 1987)
2. A new series of index Numbers on Base 1984-85 — 100 has been introduced from November 1987. All-India Index on New Base may be converted to Old Base by multiplying the conversion factor 5.32. Conversion factors in respect of Bombay, Calcutta, Madras, Delhi/New Delhi are 5.38, 4.51, 5.77 and 5.08 respectively.

THE PROBLEM OF HEALTH

Two Perspectives

The problem of health of industrial workers may be viewed from two perspectives First, the health hazards, which are common to all citizens and secondly, the occupational health risks, to which industrial workers are exposed in certain industries.

1. Health History. Industrial worker shares the common health history with all other members of the community and his needs are met by the general health services.

2. Occupational risks. These should be met by properly constituted health services which can deal with the science and art of preserving and improving the comport of workers through the recognition, evaluation and control of the environment factors which adversely affect the health of industrial workers.

Present State of Health in India

The Royal Commission on Labour in India recognised the fact that ill health and sickness are the most widespread causes of absenteeism, lower morale and bad time-keeping leading to decreased production, spoiled work and bad labour management relations. The poor state of health can be gauged from the low expectation of life, which is much lower than that of other countries. Though data regarding general health conditions in India may be found in a number of publications, but data regarding the health of the industrial workers in this country are scanty. There is no machinery for providing health information about the industrial workers. However, statistics relating to absenteeism due to sickness show that the percentage is fairly high.

Causes of Bad Health

1. Prevalence of insanitary conditions in industries. This is the main cause of bad industrial health. Basic facilities such as facilities of drinking water, latrines and urinals etc. are not provided by most of the employers in India. This adversely affects the health of the workers.

2. Low nutrition. The industrial workers does not get the required calories of food to maintain his health because he is low-paid and cannot arrange for better nutritive values from the available means.

3. Inadequate facilities. Existing medical and preventive health organisations are inadequate. The employer are indifferent to the problem.

4. Illiteracy and Poverty. Workers in India are uneducated and poor and therefore they do not care much for their health.

5. Industrial causes. There are several industrial causes of bad health. They are:

(i) Long hours of work and low wages;

(ii) Migratory character of workers. They daily commute from and to their villages.

(iii) Bad climatic conditions under which work is performed.

Measures to Improve Health Conditions

1. Legislative measures. The Government of India enacted several labour legislation protecting the health of the industrial workers. These include: The Factories Act 1948, The Mines Act 1952, The Plantation Labour Act 1961, The Indian Dock Labourers Act 1934, The Motor Transport Workers Act 1961, The Coal Mines (Conservation and Safety Act) 1952, The Employees State Insurance Act 1948. Under these Acts several provisions have been made to protect the health of industrial workers from the occupational disease. These pertain to both the curative and the preventive aspects of the industries health. The employees are held responsible for carrying out the provision of the concerned Acts.

2. Special Advisory Committee. A Special Advisory Committee on Industrial Health has been set up under the Indian Research Fund Association to conduct Research on health problems peculiar to Indian industries. Some of the problems investigated by the committee are the following:

(i) Effect of excess noise on workers. The research show that industrial noise adversely affect the efficiency of workers and their auditory acuity in the long run.

(ii) Sickness and absenteeism due to accidents,

(iii) Incidence of bad intoxication in printing presses, and

(iv) Assessment of toxicality of industrial dusts.

3. Education in Industrial Health. An Industrial Health and Safety Bulletin is being published regularly to educate the workers. A special course in Industrial Hygiene has been introduced at the All India Institute of Hygiene and Public Health, Calcutta for training medical personnel and medical practitioners connected directly with the industries. In Bombay, a Council of Health, Hygiene and Safety has been constituted to promote safety-mindedness among the workers and employers. The U.P. Government has also established an Industrial Health Organisation with a view to investigation and improving conditions and the general health of the workers in the factories.

4. Inspection. State Inspectors of factories are given training by the Chief Adviser, Factories. Medical Inspectors are appointed in the states of Maharashtra, Assam, Bihar, Orrisa, Mysore and West Bengal.

5. Training. A number of training organisations have been set up by the controllers of the state Governments in the country and the services of several foreign organisations are made available to undertake surveys in industrial health, safety and welfare programmes.

Evaluation and Suggestions

The various efforts made by the Government of India and the Governments of various states to improve the hygienic conditions of industrial workers are not sufficient. Prevention of disease and health depend to a large extent upon the environment in which people are born, grow, go to school, eat, drink, travel, work and relax. Therefore, the health of industrial workers cannot be improved unless their standard of living is improved and better working conditions are provided. Following suggestions may be forwarded in this regard:

1. Nutrition and Housing. Malnutritions and the insanitary conditions of living are the main causes of bad health and thereof, efforts should be made towards improving the diet and housing conditions first, rather than concentrating mainly on the improvement of medical facilities.

2. Medical Check up. As suggested by National Commission on Labour, there should be a regular medical check-up of all new employees and regular periodical check-up of all employees from time to time. This will help to:

(i) Eliminate those whose health is not fit for job and those who suffer from communicable diseases.

(ii) Detect and provide for remediable disease, and

(iii) Maintain the health of those who are healthy.

3. Study and the Prevention. It should be the duty of every employer to study the effects of environment factors on the health of the workers and devise the preventive measures.

QUESTIONS FOR EXERCISE

1. Discuss problems of Indian Labour.
2. What is absenteeism? What are the various causes of absenteeism and how are they removed?
3. Write short note on problem of Health in Indian Industries.
4. Write short note on Industrial Sickness in India.

26

Urban Outlook and Social Change

No man is born with either Urban or Rural outlook; he acquires it through his life experiences. Though, heredity does play a significant role in determining and fashioning one's outlook and attitudes towards various things, it is the environment and social circumstances of man which primarily determine his outlook — whether it will be rural or urban. As a matter of fact, it is the physical and social environments of man which fashion and determine his attitudes, aptitudes and interests in life. As we have just mentioned, the environment to which man is subject is of two kinds; Physical and Social. Both physical and social environments affect man and help to determine his outlook. However, in certain contexts it is the physical environment which dominates while in other context social environment is predominant. Depending upon the physico-social context man is influenced more or less by each type of environment. In villages, for example, it is obvious that it is the physical environment which is dominant whereas in cities the physical environment is subsidiary and the social environment is dominant. In cities due to the widespread use of modern electrical gadgetry and congestion of localities the physical environment is progressively receding into background and man is getting virtually alienated from nature. Thus, an urban is subject to social environment more than the physical. Therefore, in fashioning the urban outlook of a city dweller his being a resident of a city and subject primarily to social environment play crucial role. The urban environment is productive of such social conditions that, in turn, help produce and fashion an urban outlook. The urban outlook is a particular way of looking at things. A man having an urban outlook looks in a special way at life, society, wealth, nature, religion, art, politics and morality.

NATURE OF URBAN OUTLOOK

Before we may explain the nature of urban outlook we must bear in mind the limits within which such an explanation can be made. As we have referred to earlier the heredity also plays some role, though subsidiary, in fashioning human outlook, attitudes, aptitudes and interests. Second, the family background, the educational orientation, the social and professional environment of each city-dweller differs from the other in some small respect; it is by no means the case that each individual has the same family, educational, social and professional background. Therefore, there is no identity in the urban outlook of various citizens. Besides, as we had occasion to refer to earlier, the difference between a village and a city is relative. Accordingly, it is not possible to define the urban outlook in absolute terms. The distinction between rural and urban outlook is relative.

CHIEF CHARACTERISTICS OF URBAN OUTLOOK

Now we shall describe and discuss the chief characteristics of urban outlook. As noted earlier, these characteristics are to be found more or less in every citizen though no two persons have identical characteristics. The main characteristics are as follows :

1. Dynamism. The first and foremost characteristic of the urban outlook is its dynamism. Evidently, the urban man is far more dynamic in his thinking and outlook than his rural counterpart. The urban man is more open to change and is far more liable to adopt new trends, fashions and manners than a villager. The speed of formation of voluntary associations is more rapid in cities than in villages. Besides, city people are receptive to new fashions, thoughts and ideologies. They are far more easily aroused against exploitation and injustice than villagers; they are more sensitive to wrong doing and easily incensed by unjust actions. There is greater variety and diversity in the life experiences of urban people and they come across people of diverse outlooks, manners, faiths etc. As a consequence of this concourse, their outlook becomes dynamic and liberal. However, it should not be inferred that there are no orthodox persons in cities. Indeed conservatism and liberalism coexist in cities. But on the whole the liberal trend has an upper hand in the cities, whereas the conservative tendency is the order of the day in villages and has definite priority over liberal tendencies.

2. Liberalism and Tolerance. In comparison to rural people urban people are much more tolerant and liberal. One reason for this phenomenon is the fact that whereas rural people subscribe to and steadfastly hold to absolute moral values and norms, the city-dwellers, on the other hand, have flexible attitude in this regard and subscribe to and gracefully accept a relativism in moral values and norms. For example, the city-dweller accepts without challenge and ruefulness a variety and diversity in regard to fashions, manners and ways of life, and is, therefore, not very critical of variations and deviations from customs and traditions in behaviour whereas a villager considers these deviations to be indicative of degradation and a fall in moral standards. Thus, a city-dweller is not very particular to foist his will upon others. Though he may hold to certain norms and moral values and may consider certain things to be good and desirable, yet he is not disturbed if he finds other people not falling in with his opinions and beliefs. Indeed he is prepared to make compromise in this regard. The spirit of give and take is developed much more in city-dwellers than in villagers.

However, it is not possible to verify and prove experimentally that a city-dweller is more liberal than a villager. Murphy and Newcomb have referred to a study regarding the comparative attitudes of rural and urban Americans towards negroes. It was discovered that in the Southern states there was no perceptible difference in this regard among urban and rural people. In the Northern States, however, urban boys were found to be more prejudiced than the boys in villages. Though there has been no systematic study in India to evaluate the comparative attitudes among city-dwellers and, villagers in regard to Hindu-Muslim misunderstandings and tensions, it is nonetheless a fact that more communal frenzy is to be witnessed in cities than in villages and that the majority of communal riots have been confined to urban areas. It is well known that the outbreak of communal frenzy is rare in villages. Moreover, whatever communal tension is to be found in the villages is a direct result of urban machinations and propaganda. Thus, in-so-far as the problem of communal tension and frenzy is concerned, we find that in India at least the villagers show greater liberalism and tolerance in this regard. As a matter of fact, while it is true that city-dweller is exposed to multiplicity of cultures as a result of which he develops flexibility and tolerance in his outlook, it is also a fact that the city-dwellers are usually preoccupied with their own concerns and problems. Their preoccupation is so extreme that even if they want to take interest in the welfare of others they have neither time nor the opportunity to do so. The villagers are very particular about the uprightness of the conduct and keep a vigilant eye on the behaviour of every other villager. Therefore, the scope of falsehood, deceit and double-thinking and double-talk is much less in the villages. It is due to this factor that we do not find much communal tension among villagers. Moreover, there is rigid control over individual behaviour in villages by caste and community. As a result, there is little freedom of action and movement in villages. This atmosphere at times proves too stifling to be bearable and people want to migrate to cities. It is possible that city-dwellers do not interfere with the conduct of others because they are selfish and irresponsible. They wish to enjoy life as much as possible and they realize that interference in the behaviour of others would invite counter-interference. It is to be usually seen that the parents do not check the behaviour of their children because they themselves want to enjoy life and would feel embarrassment in asking their children not to do things which they themselves are doing.

Taking everything into account it must be realized that though there may be certain instances and things in which we may find a villager to be more tolerant and liberal, it is the city dweller, who, on the whole, is relatively more liberal and tolerant.

(3) Individualism. The third characteristic of Urban outlook is individualism in personal conduct and impersonalism in social conduct. The society and social institutions do not excercise the kind of control over individual's behaviour in cities as these do in villages. In villages a man usually functions as a member of a family, caste or group and there is little personal choice and thinking in behaviour. The rural behaviour is strictly governed and controlled by the expectations, norms and standards of the group. In villages the community feeling is very strong whereas it is very weak in the urban societies. In cities the social group is secondary and not primary. However, it will not be true to say that rural behaviour is rigidly controlled by society. As a matter of fact we do find that the factor of personal choice operates in rural society as well. There is family and personal disorganization in the villages and, on the other hand, there are quite a few instances of social co-operation in cities. But relatively speaking, it is true that individualism is an important characteristic of the urban outlook.

The Urban Outlook and Social Change

Broadly speaking any change occurring in society is social change. The society is a hierarchy of social relations. Therefore a social change affects the relations within a family, that is, among the family members and also the relations between various families. In cities the social change is quicker than in villages. In cities we can see constant changes in man-woman relations, in relations between father and son, brother and sister, teacher and taught and among neighbours. In comparison to the rural world the urban world is much dynamic and changeable. The rural world is relatively stable and secure. On account of conflicting moral values and standards, cultural traditions and customs, the urban man is much more liable to encounter social conflicts and strifes than his rural counterpart. This constant scene of conflicts and tensions produces, on the one hand, tolerance towards opposite moral standards and social norms, but on the other hand, it also undermines one's faith in one's own system of beliefs and hierarchy of moral and social values. This results in one's faith becoming pliable. Therefore under some pressure or on account of some great benefit and advantage, the urban man is prepared to give up his faith and adopt a new faith.

However, this does not mean that the orthodoxy and conservative outlook is altogether absent in the urban society. While it is a fact that rural society is highly orthodox and conservative, the opposite is not wholly true of an urban society. While undoubtedly the urban society is liberal in comparison to rural society, none the less, we find pockets of orthodoxy and conservatism in cities. We can easily find societies and associations in cities which are avowedly formed to protect and preserve orthodoxy. Thus, along with associations preaching radical social changes, we find others which wish to preserve the tradition. It should come as a surprise to no one that even highly literate persons are subject to superstitions.

A reason for the quicker pace of social change in the urban society is the fact that the percentage of highly educated persons is much higher in cities than in villages. An urban man is much better informed about social changes taking place all over the world. Therefore, every social change has a greater impact on the mind of a city-dweller than on the mind of a villager.

QUESTION FOR EXERCISE

1. What is Urban outlook? Discuss its relation with social change.

27

Urban Planning and Slums

Along with the industrial progress there is increase in the urban population in India. With the increase in the urban population the pressure on urban space is also growing. With the coming up of new industries, offices, shops and markets there is crowding and congestion. As the space becomes less and less and the demand for it keeps growing, the prices of land shoot up. In Delhi the land prices vary between 1,000 and 20,000 Rupees per square meter. In Bombay and Calcutta the prices of land are still more fabulous. With the appreciation of land prices the house rents are also shooting up. In Delhi, Calcutta and Bombay a two-room flat costs anything between Rupees 200 to Rupees 4,000 per month. Due to fabulous rise in rents the poor cannot afford a roof over their heads. The labourers live in slums, dingy dark houses. In Bombay, Calcutta and Delhi the problem is so acute that lakhs of people sleep on footpath or in open. The railway platforms, Bus stands, even sewer pipes are used for sleeping. The crowding, the congestion, the slums and such things are a grave threat to moral and physical health of people. Due to crowding in cities traffic jams are becoming regular features. Besides, the air of industrial cities is so highly polluted that there is a constant threat to the health of the people. Due to congestion and fast traffic the number of daily accidents in big cities is alarming.

IMPORTANCE OF THE URBAN PLANNING

It is an ungainsayable fact that there is crowding and congestion in cities as a sequel to industrialization. Indeed, the relation between industrialization and population rise is direct: the population rise is in direct proportion to the extent of industrialization. Therefore, there is no remedy to check the population growth if there is to be industrialization anywhere. The population is an inevitable and ineluctable result of our mechanical civilisation. Nowhere has it been possible to achieve industrialisation without increasing the population. As the proverb has it, you cannot eat your cake and have it too. You can not industrialise without allowing population increase. Then, is there no way out of the above mentioned problems? Indeed, town planning is the answer to all urban problems, because the above mentioned problems are not just the results of population rise but are due to unplanned and disorganized growth of towns.

FUNDAMENTALS OF URBAN PLANNING

By town planning proper care is taken of public places, parks and playgrounds. As regards houses, rules and regulations are made to see that lanes and by-lanes have been left and are adequate. Besides, these rules ascertain that the house will be airy, sunny and unspoilt by future expansions. The town-planning authority supervises removal of slums and illegal construction. It also makes arrangement to prevent recurrence of slum. The town planners are also responsible for providing fresh water and the disposal of used water and garbage. Broadly speaking, the following are the fundamentals of urban planning:

(1) Transport and Traffic Control. In town planning provisions are made for transport by water, air and land. Therefore, the width of street is so determined as to enable easy control of traffic. New roads are constructed at important centres. The roads are so constructed and interlinked as to enable one to go from one place to the other in minimum time. In the absence of such arrangement business suffers. This also multiplies wasteful expenditure and the liability to accident increases. Besides, land transport, river and aerial transport are also under the authority of town planners. In big towns the traffic is controlled automatically by the electric light and electronic control.

(2) Control of Land use. The second important duty of the Town Planning Authority (T.P.A.) is to regulate the use of land. The unplanned and disorderly use of land gives rise to slums and the problems of traffic control. The T.P.A. also determines the height and design of the houses.

(3) Slum-Clearance. The clearance of slums and prevention of slums is also an important function of T.P.A.

(4) Provision of low-rent Housing. It is also the job of T.P.A. to make provision for the availability of low rent houses.

(5) Zoning. In order to avoid pollution the cities are divided into zones and it is seen that the zones for houses and zones for industries are as far removed as possible from each other. Besides, shopping complexes must be within the zones.

(6) Provision of Utilities. The provision of fresh water, electricity and cooking gas is the duty of T.P.A.

(7) Disposal of Garbage. The disposal of garbage in a manner that there is no pollution is the job of T.P.A.

(8) Parking Places. In big towns unless parking places are provided, traffic control is not possible.

(9) Development of Residential Colonies. By making residential colonies in cities the T.P.A. tries to bring people together. By living together they meet and form association to promote friendship and neighbourliness.

Definition of slums

There is no general agreement on the definition of a 'slum'. Some writers regard it as a special type of disorganized area; others treat the terms 'slums' and 'blighted area' synonymous. Still others believe that slums also can be found in rural areas which is, however, a debatable proposition.

Slums may be characterised as areas of substandard housing within a city. A slum is an inhabited uninhabitable habitation. A slum is an area of dilapidated houses which are in the act of destruction. Slums exist either in the zone in transition or around factories or in congested districts. Poverty constitutes the main characteristic of slum dwellers. Multi-Family dwellings are a typical feature of slums and sometimes two or more families live in a single room. Self sustenance and struggle for survival is the main feature of slum life. Basic facilities like adequate air, water, lighting and other sanitary facilities are wanting. Slums are usually areas of filth and marsh which are the breeding places of disease carrying germs. Slums act as cover for hide-outs for all sorts of crimes and vices like gambling which prevail and live upon the city population. Slums are an area of constant conflicts, family desertion and evictions. A person is left on his own to look after himself. Educational and recreational facilities are conspicuous by their absence. Thus a slum mocks upon all forms of settled life. Juvenile delinquency and mal-socialization of more or less orphan juveniles of the slum society whose parents have not enough in their hands is a curse of the slums upon city life. Thus a slum is a half destructed area of worn-out buildings which provides housing facilities to the city's poor and needy. Congestion and lack of privacy are the concommitant of a slum culture.

Kinds of Slums

There are three main types of slums in our cities. These are:

(a) *Original Slum*. This is an area which forms the very beginning, consisted of unsuitable buildings. These are usually areas around an old factory or mining site which is now given up or is the zone in transition. These sections are beyond recovery as they consist of age old structures and they need to be razed in order to be eradicated e.g. the Mexican Slum in U.S.A.

(b) *Transitional Zone Slum*. The second type consists of slums created by the departure of middle and upper class families to other sections. Or it may be due to the starting of a new industry or due to congestion and subsequent deterioration of the living area. These types of slums are to be found in the transition zone of developing cities such as South End slum in Boston (U.S.A.). These are the areas which house vice and crime and where all sorts and shades of people live. In rehabilitation of this type of slums there is no need for wholesale demolition. Only delapildated structures must be replaced by housing projects. The remaining rehabilitation is mainly a matter of administration and community organization. But vested interests act as hindrances in the clearance of these slums.

(c) *The third and most unpleasant type of slum is mainly a phenomenon of transition*. Once the area around a main business district has become blighted, physical and social deterioration spreads rapidly. This type of slum looms with flophouses, one night accommodations for the destitute, houses of prostitution and speak easies. It is populated by transients, tramps, vagrants, chronic alcoholics, beggars, homeless men and habitual criminals. Its economic activities are carried out by the proprietors of saloons and pool rooms, fences, pawnbrokers, dope pedlars etc. This type of slum clearly defies rehabilitation. The proper remedy is better administration and stricter zoning laws.

Slums differ physically. Thus there are rooming house slums, tenement slums and slums of one family homes. Rooming house slums consist of structure where different rooms are let out for differet persons and families. Tenement slums consist of multistoreyed structures which house two or more families in a single dwelling. Rooming houses are let out on a temporary basis.

Slums of one family houses are very common which consist of typical small family structures.

Pathological Problems of Slums

Social pathology deals with the difficulties of adjustment with situations which hamper the fulfilment of social functions. Urban pathology investigates whether or not specific urban conditions create or promote social disorganization. Scientist argue that a city is a threat to social organization and many pathological features are the direct effects of urbanization. These are as follows:

(1) Death and disease. There is no doubt that the medieval city was an unhealthy place which supported all kinds of epidemics. But modern cities are cleaner and have better medical facilities to combat medical emergencies. Occupational hazards, motor accidents and suicide account for most of urban deaths. Specific urban diseases like syphillis and currhosis of liver result from urban factors of free sex and alcoholism. Some mental diseases are definitely town made. Nervous tension, psychopathy, various mental disorders and derangements result from the influence of peculiarly urban features of tension, anxiety, monopolistic competition etc.

Vices like drug addiction, gambling, prostitution and alcoholism are urban vices. In the absence of the protection of intimate groups, the urban man has to inevitably resort to these vices to get relaxation from unnecessary tensions and anxieties. These vices disorganize individuals, families and localities in an urban society. Drug addiction spoils the life of a youth and promotes dope peddling. Alcoholism is institutionalised into the patterns of professional city life. Prostitutes live and work in the area of transition and amusement centres. Gambling is a form of personal disorganisation and promotes the growth of racketeering.

Every modern city has its ecological crime area i.e. the zone in transition. White collar crime is internalised into the city culture. Juvenile delinquency develops largely in urban areas because of the structure of its social life and conflicting value patterns.

Slums are a major factor in urban pathology. It affects the physical and mental health of the urban community. It is a constant eye-sore and area of social disorganization. It is an inhabited uninhabitable habitation. Economic differentiation is the chief factor for its development. It is a congested area of poor housing. It prevents both public and private decency. It results in personal and family disorganization. It is a area which houses the criminal and the delinquent urban pathology is the result of loose social control and the lack of a stable value system. Health hazard remains a typical slum problem. Further, the slum affects the physical and mental health of its neighbourhood. It is the reservoir and hiding ground for all urban vices such as gambling, dope peddling, prostitution and so on. It promotes the lawlessness and social disorganization of the city. It is a disorganized residential area.

Slum clearance is a costly affair and faces the fury of slum dwellers when asked to vacate their slums. Slums increase with the increase in size of the city and its population and with the growth of factories. The existence of slums reflects upon the urban community's inability to provide proper housing to all its inhabitants and poor town planning. However, slum clearance and the creation of a social consciousness among slum dwellers about the harms of the existence of a slum is the duty of every town.

URBAN RECONSTRUCTION

The essential aim of urban planning is to promote the most effective spatial arrangement and social patterns of the components of a metropolis. The master plan of a city gives a broad general picture of the projected spatial pattern of the city. Urban planning aims at providing the facilities such as stores, factories and residences, most suitable location to each function in a city, an efficient transportation network connecting the length and breadth of a city and city beautification.

The urban planner begins with a system of streets and pattern of transportation and location of the central business district. The typical plan for an industrial location is either near the central business district or along lines of heavy transportation and at "break-in transportation" and at the periphery or the nearby hinterland. New and interdependent industries are directed towards the periphery of a city. The major shopping centre and luxury goods stores must be at the city centre. Suburban shopping complexes must provide for the necessities of suburban-dwellers. Multifamily residences should be located close to busy centres of dominance or close to streets of transportation lines. Decent residential areas should be planned at a reasonable distance from the city centre and must contain facilities for worship, trade, education recreation etc.

Systematic planning on a scientific basis is of a recent date but pre-historical cities show a clearly discernible design. The royal palace and temple used to form the city centre towards which a system of streets leads from all directions. The early history of America is rich in examples of planned cities.

In physical planning Washington D. C. represents one of the earliest planned cities of modern world.

According to the garden city idea, factories and business houses should be located outside the city. Physical planning can be roughly divided into three main components viz. areas, communications and services. Proper planning determines what steps are necessary to serve the city as completely and economically as possible. Services concern with location of schools, parks, playgrounds, garbage collection and utilities.

URBAN LAND (CEILING AND REGULATION) ACT, 1976

The Urban Land (Ceiling and Regulation) Act, 1976 came into force on 17 February 1976. It applies to all states and union territories except Jammu and Kashmir, Kerala, Nagaland and Sikkim which have not adopted the Act so far. It also excludes Tamil Nadu which had enacted its own law in 1978.

The main objectives of the Act are: (i) to prevent the concentration of urban land in the hands of a few persons: (ii) to bring about an equitable distribution of existing large urban holdings; (iii) to regulate the construction of buildings on such land; and (iv) to use the excess vacant land to subserve the common good.

Even though the objectives of the Act have been appreciated, it has been criticised as being harsh, restrictive and posing problem in actual operation. It has also been felt that it has affected the building activities in the country. The state governments from time to time have requested for making amendments to the Act to make it more effective and workable.

On the basis of the suggestions received from state governments, experts, leading organisations and the recommendations made by the National Commission on Urbanisation, the Government of India have formulated several proposals for making amendments in the various provisions of the Act. These proposals had been discussed in the Chief Ministers' Conference held in New Delhi on 7 March, 1992. On the basis of views expressed by various states, the amendment proposals are being modified accordingly. The amendments are proposed to be brought before the Parliament very shortly.

INTEGRATED DEVELOPMENT OF SMALL AND MEDIUM TOWNS

The scheme of Integrated Development of Small and Medium Towns was started by the Central Government in 1979-80 to develop small and medium towns by directing increased investment to these towns for improvement of their economic and physical infrastructures and other essential facilities and services. It was also envisaged that this scheme will slow down the growth of the metropolitan cities and will also result in the balanced distribution of urban population by creating sufficient employment opportunities.

Under this Scheme, normally, towns with a population of one lakh and below as per 1971 census are considered for inclusion, preference being given to district headquarter towns followed by sub-divisional towns, *mandi* towns and other important growth centres. The selection of towns vests with the state governments/UTs. Central assistance of 50 per cent on matching basis was limited to Rs. 40 lakh or 50 per cent of the total approved cost of the project, whichever is less. However, during Seventh Five Year Plan, the maximum Central assistance had been increased from Rs. 40 lakh to Rs 46 lakh per town. Besides, Rs. 14 lakh for low cost sanitation was also provided to each town.

So far, 517 towns have been assisted during the course of the Sixth and Seventh Five Year Plans, 1990-91 and 1991-92, and a total amount of Rs. 176.17 crore has been released.

Housing Schemes in Operation

A fairly large number of housing schemes are in operation in the urban areas: (a) social housing scheme for different income groups, operated by the state and city level agencies with state budget support and loans from HUDCO, LIC and other financial institutions; (b) shelter upgradation scheme for the urban poor launched by the Centre in November 1989, under the Nehru Rozgar Yojna with objectives of shelter improvement and provision of employment for the poor where Rs. 1000 subsidy for household is given by the Government with HUDCO loan for cities with population between one to twenty lakh; (c) Central scheme of footpath dwellers' night shelter a partially subsidised shelter scheme for identified target groups; (d) Housing scheme for weavers and bidi workers — Central grant scheme of the Ministry of Labour (bidi workers) and Textiles (Weavers) supplemented by the HUDCO loan: (e) ownership housing scheme under the Central Government Employees Group Insurance Fund operated with the HUDCO loan; (f) Working Women's condo minium scheme funded by HUDCO for the benefit of single-working women: (g) sites and services and slum upgradation schemes operated with the assistance of the World Bank and financial institutions for home improvement; (h) land acquisition development and shelter with HNB refinance and schemes under the state plans; (i) city level infrastructure development scheme funded by HUDCO; (j) environmental improvement of urban slums under minimum needs programme-state sector; (k) schemes for house improvement and repair. The Maharashtra Government operates a major scheme for building, repairs and reconstruction in Bombay under a statutory scheme; (l) schemes taken up by cooperatives of different income groups as well as scheduled castes and scheduled tribes with the help of apex federations and loans from LIC, HUDCO and scheduled banks; (m) rental housing schemes for employees by the Central and state Government, public sector autonomous agencies, private enterprises including house building advances on concessional terms; and (n) centrally sponsored schemes of urban basic services for the poor to be implemented in convergence with NRY, EIUS, Nutrition and Health Care programmes.

NEHRU ROZGAR YOJANA

The Nehru Rozgar Yojana has been designed to provide employment to the urban unemployed and under-employed poor. The employment contemplated is of two types : one relates to the setting up of self-employment ventures and the other type relates to provision of wage employment through the creation of socially and economically useful assets and shelter upgradation programmes in urban areas.

The programme has three schemes : (i) scheme for setting up micro enterprises and providing training and infrastructure support for urban poor beneficiaries. This scheme is operative in all urban settlements; (ii) scheme of wage employment for creation of socially and economically useful public assets in the jurisdiction of urban local bodies. This scheme is applicable in (a) towns with less than 20,000 population and (b) towns with population from 20,000 to one lakh, (iii) scheme of employment through housing and shelter upgradation in low income neighbourhoods mainly for the urban poor and economically weaker sections and training and infrastructure support for promotion of construction skills among beneficiaries. This scheme is applicable in settlements with population between one lakh and twenty lakh.

While the target group of the Yojana is urban poor, women beneficiaries and beneficiaries belonging to scheduled castes and scheduled tribes will consitute special target groups. The main achievements of the scheme for the period ending December 1992 are as such (i) Scheme of Urban Micro Enterprises (SUME) : Subsidy to the tune of Rs. 127 crore and institutional finance (in the form of bank loans) to the tune of Rs. 381 crore (approximately) i.e., three times of the subsidy have been sanctioned to the beneficiaries since the inception of the Yojana in 1989. Under the Training and Infrastructure Support component, 1.50 lakh beneficiaries have been trained/are undergoing training for skill upgradation; (ii) Scheme of Urban Wage Employment (SUWE) : Under this scheme, the states/UTs have reported expenditure of Rs. 213 crore till 31 December 1994 on creation of public assets in low income neighbourhoods and 380 lakh mandays of wage employment has been generated for the urban poor; (iii) Scheme of Housing and Shelter Upgradation (SHASU) : HUDCO has sanctioned schemes from various states/union territories worth Rs. 292 crore (subsidy of Rs. 55 crore and loans upto Rs. 237 crore) involving upgradation of more than 7.27 lakh dwelling units till 31 December 1994.

Central Public Works Department

The Central Public Works Department (CPWD) is the official agency of the Government of India for construction and maintenance of all Central government buildings except those of the railways, communication, atomic energy, defence services and All India Radio. The spectrum of the activities of the CPWD is very wide, ranging from the selection of site, architectual, structural and landscape planning, design, execution, including budgeting, monitoring and quality control to completion and post-completion maintenance. Contract management and defending arbitration cases are also done by the CPWD. The CPWD handles a wide-range of projects like housing and commercial complexes, educational institutions, hospitals, workshops, factories, food-grain storage, structures, airports, roads, bridges, sports complexes, mints, electronic complexes, National Library and Parliament Library etc.

In recent times, the CPWD has been engaged in providing border fencing, flood lighting and roads along the sensitive Indo-Pak and Indo-Bangladesh borders. The work is being enacted under very severe and hostile conditions and yet keeping up to the tight time schedules laid down by the Ministry of Home Affairs. The CPWD has gained considerable expertise in the study of restoration and rehabilitation of structures damaged by natural disasters. A study on the nature of the Uttarkashi (UP) earthquake and its effect on structures in the area has been conducted.

CONSTRUCTION AGENCIES

National Buildings Construction Corporation

National Buildings Construction Corporation (NBCC) was incorporated in 1960. It is one of the premier construction corporations which is actively engaged in execution of sophisticated construction/turnkey contracts, both at home and abroad. Its projects are put on network system. It has to its credit several important projects including major industrial structures, power stations, cement plants, fertilizers plants and refineries, tall RCC chimneys, bridges fly-overs, air-ports, luxury hotel complexes, water treatment plants and marine jobs, etc. It also provides consultancy services.

Hindustan Prefab Limited

The Hindustan Prefab Limited (earlier known as Hindustan Housing Factory), New Delhi, became a fully-owned Government company in 1955. It is engaged in production of pre-stressed concrete electric poles and railway sleepers. The company also manufactures wooden joinery items and prefab/ general construction works. Quality of wooden joinery items viz., doors and window shutters manufactured by the company, is the best in the country. Pre-fabricated components for industrial structures have not only effected saving in steel and resulted in quicker construction but also reduced construction cost to some extent.

ROLE OF URBAN SOCIOLOGISTS

It is said that many of the social evils of our urban society like the prevalence of vices amidst respectable areas of a city, the prevalent social tensions, etc., are the result of the lack of a proper sociological approach to the problem. Social planning forms a necessary part of a programme of urban reconstruction and occupies as much importance in the physical planning of zones since the socio-cultural aspect of a people play an important role in shaping their attitudes and in the promotion of a healthy social life. It is also argued that the traits of urbanization when developed to their extreme, act as impeders of healthy social life.

The sociologist has much to say in man power planning and in the construction of residential suburbs. Man power planning is a wider concept which includes the balancing of the supply of man power resources to its need. Here it is the sociologist who can detect the socio-cultural factors which are promoting a heavy rush of people to certain jobs while restricting people from taking certain other occupations. Thus the sociologist can say clearly why a shoe making factory cannot thrive in a brahmin dominated area. Again, it is the sociologist who can analyse the socio-cultural factors behind mass exodus such as rural unemployment or attractions of city life. It is the sociologist who can analyse and explain the causes of congestion and its effect in creating social tensions and conflicts. It is again the sociologist who can analyse the consequences of increased anonymity such as relative freedom and promotion of the growth of vices etc. The physical planner may accept the growth of slums around a factory as a natural factor. It is the sociologist who analyses their socio-cultural causes like poor income, the value of constant attachment to kith and kin etc. He analyses the social consequences of their growth amidst a city and their influence upon the morals of city dwellers. He can analyse the social factors of congestion and lack of privacy which is causing law and order problems in a congested area of household such as lack of proper care of children and their entry into life of juvenile delinquency. He can analyse the consequences of over-crowding in all places including buses, schools, shops etc., which result in lack of individual attention and constant quarrels and conflicts. He can analyse the causes of urban poverty and its consequences like poor housing, over-crowding, increasing of crime, vice, cheating, etc. It is he who can understand the tension of an urban student or youth who is constantly exposed to alternative and contradictory value orientations to attain his goals. He can analyse the factors of urban unemployment and its consequences on urban social life such as increase in crime, unrest, law and order problems etc. He can explain the excessive growth of vices as a means of livelihood to the needy and an outlet for pent up tensions of the mechanised life of the urbanite in the absence of healthy means of entertainment. He alone can explain the hostility encountered by an unfortunate low class dweller in a middle class neighbourhood or a negro dweller in a white neighbourhood or a harijan in a caste hindu locality. It is he who can explain the ill effects of the existence of a bar attached hotel or a cabaret in a commercial or residential area upon the minds of the youth or the existence of prostitution in an urban community upon family life.

Thus, it is the sociologist who can analyse the factors behind urban personal relations which have developed social unrest and disorganization. He alone can explain that the basic factor behind all these anomalies is the destruction of primary social relations and values. Hence the sociologist has the main role in social planning which aims at establishing healthy social relations and well adjusted life among urbanites. He can fix the number of people among whom a relatively intimate and normal social relations are possible. He explains that healthy urban social life is possible only through the development of small healthy areas in various parts of a city. In fact, healthy urban social life can be developed only by allowing for the fuller development of the concept of neighbourhood in residential suburbs and by encouraging the development of associations of various types like sports clubs, cultural associations, etc., which provide healthy leisure time pursuit for the urbanite.

QUESTIONS FOR EXERCISE

1. Write short note on Urban Planning.
2. "Planning aims at the optimum use of resources and the rational integration of community life" Discuss in relation to town Planning.
3. Discuss the need and importance of Urban Planning in India.
4. Define slum. Describe the kinds of slums that we have in our cities.
5. What are the pathological problems of cities ? Examine the problem of slums in detail.
6. What is town planning ? Discuss the ecological features of urban planning with examples.
7. Discuss the role of urban Sociologist in urban Reconstruction.

28

Welfare of Urban Backward Classes

Department of Women and Child Development in the Ministry of Human Resource Development is responsible for formulating policies and programmes for women and children besides coordinating, guiding and promoting the activities of both governmental and non-governmental organisations working for the welfare and development of women and children. The major thrust of the programmes of the department is towards ensuring the well-being of children and women, particularly those of the weaker sections of society and for raising the status of women and bringing them into the mainstream of development. The Department is comprised of the Nutrition and Child Development Bureau and the Women's Development Bureau. While the Nutrition and Child Development Bureau is responsible for the overall development of children, the Women's Bureau works to improve the lot of women. The National Institute of Public Cooperation and Child Development (NIPCCD), a society registered under the Societies Registration Act 1860, functions under the department. Its activities include research and evaluation studies, organisation and conduct of training programmes for programme functionaries, organisation of workshops/seminars and conferences in the area of women and child development. NIPCCD is also responsible for the training of functionaries of the department's most significant programme, the Integrated Child Development Service (ICDS). The Central Social Welfare Board (CSWB) which is a registered body under the Indian Companies Act of 1956, works as an apex body to promote voluntary action in the field of women and child development by extending financial support to various non-governmental organisations in the country. It reaches even to the grass root level organisations through its state boards.

CHILD DEVELOPMENT

Integrated Child Development Services

Following the adoption of the National Policy for Children in 1974, the scheme of Integrated Child Development Services (ICDS) was initiated in 1975 as a Centrally sponsored scheme. The scheme provides a package of services namely: (i) supplementary nutrition; (ii) immunization; (iii) health check-up; (iv) health referral; (v) pre-school non-formal education; and (vi) health and nutrition education for mothers. The target group consists of children in the age group 0-6 years and pregnant and lactating mothers.

The number of projects (Centrally sponsored) sanctioned as on 31 March 1995 stood at 3,397 and 194 state sector projects (rural/tribal blocks and urban blocks). 21.6 million (children and mothers) are receiving supplementary nutrition, while about 10.1 million children are receiving re-school stimulation under the scheme. The integrated package of services as mentioned above is delivered through the focal points of Anganwadis in which sanctioned number is over 3.9 lakh. Several evaluation studies have brought out that ICDS is currently fulfilling a major national need and there has been a decline in infant mortality rates and birth rates, better health and immunisation coverage and larger acceptance of family planning in ICDS areas.

In 1994-95, the financial provision for ICDS was Rs. 433.99 crore. This account for all components on projects expenditure except the nutritional component, which is funded by the state governments. For nutrition component, apart from state government's contribution, food aid is also available from Cooperative for American Relief Everywhere (CARE), World Food Programme (WFP) and through the erstwhile Centrally sponsored Wheat Based Nutrition Programme. A beginning was made to institutionlize a special set of interventions for adolescent girls through ICDS infrastructure. These interventions for adolescent girls were sanctioned in 507 ICDS projects. The services provided include health and nurtition cover, functional literacy and upgradation and improvement of home-base skills.

World Bank Assisted ICDS Projects

The Centrally-sponsored, World Bank assisted ICDS projects sanctioned during 1990-91 for predominantly tribal areas of Andhra Pradesh and Orissa, continued its operation during 1992-93. The project provides additional inputs for women's income generation. Women's Integrated Learning of Life (WILL), services for adolescent girls, strengthening of health components, experimentation with nutritional rehabilitation centres and therapeutic food, construction of anganwadi buildings and godowns-cum-CDPO's offices on a selective basis and enhanced inputs in the spheres of communications, training, project management, equipment, monitoring, evaluation, etc. Another World Bank assisted ICDS-II project, for certain areas of Bihar and Madhya Pradesh is being launched.

Training of ICDS Functionaries

The effective delivery of the package of services envisaged under the significant programme of ICDS depends on proper training and orientation of the functionaries at all levels. Accordingly, a comprehensive programme for the training of ICDS functionaries has been undertaken concurrently by this department. The National Institute of Public Cooperation and Child Development (NIPCCD), other selected training institutions and voluntary organisations recognised by the state governments have been involved in the training of ICDS functionaries namely, the anganwadi workers and helpers (the glass-root level functionaries of the ICDS scheme) supervisors and the child development project officers (CDPOs). There are 290 anganwadi workers training centres (AWTCs) for imparting training (job course as well as refresher course) to anganwadi workers/helpers and 20 middle level training centres (MLTCs) for imparting training (job course as well as refresher course) to supervisors. The job course training and refresher training to the CDPOs is given by NIPCCD and its three regional centres located at Bangalore, Lucknow and Guwahati.

Balsevika Training Programme

With the rapid expansion of welfare schemes in the country such as the Integrated Child Development Services Scheme the demand for the grassroot level functionaries is on the rise. The Balsevika Training Programme was started in 1961-62 to meet the requirement of the trained personnel for the institutions implementing welfare programmes for the pre-school children. The Programme is being run by the Indian Council for Child Welfare (ICCW) with cent per cent grant assistance. There are at present 25 *Balsevika* training institutes (BSTIs) in the country, each conducts this training course of 11 months duration for 50 trainees.

The syllabus of the Balsevika training programme covers the fields of nutrition, health, education and pre-school education and social work. Since the inception of the Balsevika Training Programme, a total number of 34,398 Balsevikas have been trained till March 1995.

Creches/Day-Centres for Children

Under the scheme, the services available to the children include sleeping and day-care facilities, supplementary nutrition, immunization, medicines, entertainment and weekly medical check-ups. It is being implemented by the Central Social Welfare Board through voluntary social welfare organisations and by Indian Council for Child Welfare and *Bhartiya Adimjati Sevāk Sangh* all over the country. During 1992-93, assistance was continued to be provided to support the existing 12,470 creche units.

Early Childhood Education (ECE)

ECE has been designed to improve the children's communication (language) and cognitive (social, emotional, intellectual and personality development) skills as preparation for entry into primary schools. The programme is in implementation in the nine educationally backward states of Andhra Pradesh, Assam, Bihar, Jammu and Kashmir, Madhya Pradesh, Orissa, Rajasthan, Uttar Pradesh and West Bengal and at present 4, 365 ECE centres are functioning in these states with over 1.53 lakh children beneficiaries.

Special Nutrition Programme (SNP)

This programme was launched in 1970-71 for children below six years of age and for expectant and nursing mothers. Under the programme, supplementary feeding is given for 300 days a year to the beneficiaries. Every child receives

300 calories and 8-10 gm of protein and every expectant and nursing mother 500 calories and 20-25 gm of protein per day. The programme is in the state sector.

Wheat Based Nutrition Programme (WBNP)

The Wheat Based Nutrition Programme is being implemented in 16 states and three union territories to cover about 31 lakh beneficiaries in ICDS areas. The programme has been transferred to the state sector with effect from 1 April 1992.

Infant Milk Substitutes, Feeding Bottles and Infant Foods Act, 1992

The Infant Milk Substitutes Bill, 1992 regulating the production and supply of breast milk substitutes, for the promotion of breast feeding was passed recently in Parliament.

National Plan of Action for Children

India reaffirmed its commitment to the cause of children, keeping in with the pledges made in the World Summit for Children by drawing up for implementation a decodal National Plan of Action for Children. The Plan identifies quantifiable goals to be achieved by 2000 AD in the spheres of health, nutrition, education and related areas.

Balwadi Nutrition Programme

Balwadi Nutrition Programme (BNP) is being implemented since 1970-71 through the Central Social Welfare Board and four national level voluntary organisations. About 5,600 *Balwadis* are being run by these five agencies to implement the programme. About 2.29 lakh children in the age group of 3-5 years are covered under this programme. Apart from nutritional supplementation, the balwadis look after the social and emotional development of children.

National Awards for Child Welfare

National Awards for Child Welfare were instituted in the year 1979, the International Year of the Child, as state's recognition for the voluntary action for the cause of child welfare. Five awards are given to institutions and three awards to individuals annually for the best work done in the field of child welfare. The award carries a cash prize of rupees two lakh and a citation for the awardee institution and Rs. 30,000 and a citation for the individual awardee.

United Nation's International Children Emergency Fund (UNICEF)

Department of Women and Child Development is the nodal department for UNICEF assistance in the country. UNICEF assistance has been available for the programmes which has focus on children. The programme areas, included the integrated child development services, urban basic services, women development, health, nutrition, education, water supply and sanitation.

WOMEN DEVELOPMENT

The Constitution of India guarantees equal rights and opportunities for both men and women. Towards this, efforts are being made through development planning to raise the status of women besides mainstreaming them into the process of national development on par with men. The programmes for the development of women include employment and income generation programmes, welfare and support services and programmes to create awareness generation, etc.

Hostels for Working Women

The scheme seeks to provide cheap and safe accommodation for working women belonging to low income group. The scheme was modified in 1980 to provide assistance for day-care centres for children attached to working women hostels. An outlay of rupees six crore has been made for 1994-95 to sanction 53 additional hostels to provide accommodation to 4,592 working women. Since inception of the scheme 740 hostels with an intake capacity of 49,507 women with day care facilities to 6,852 children in 264 hostels have been established.

Employment and Income Generating Training Production Units

The NORAD (Norwegian Agency for International Development) assisted programme started during 1982-83 to train women belonging to weaker sections of the society and to provide them employment on a sustained basis. The programme is implemented through public sector undertakings/corporations/autonomous bodies/voluntary organisations. Under this, training is imparted to women in selected non-traditional trades such as electronics, watch manufacturing/assembly, printing and binding, handlooms, weaving and spinning, garment making, etc. A budget provision of Rs. 4 crore was made for the year 1992-93. So far, about 300 projects have been sanctioned to benefit over 26,000 women.

Condensed Courses of Education and Vocational Training for Women

This programme is implemented by the Central Social Welfare Board (CSWB) through voluntary organisations. Under this programme, women in the age group 18-30 years who have had some schooling, are coached for 2-3 years to enable them to appear at different levels of examinations like middle school/secondary school/matriculation. The component of vocational training was added to this programme during 1975. During 1992-93, a provision of Rs. 8 crore was made for conducting 1,200 courses. During the year 1992-93, 893 courses to cover 22,375 women beneficiaries have been sanctioned till 31 January 1993.

Socio-Economic Programme

Under this programme, the Central Social Welfare Board gives financial assistance to voluntary organisations for undertaking wide variety of incomegenerating activities and provide opportunities for work and wages to needy women belonging to the category of poor and the downtrodden, widows, destitutes, disabled, etc., particularly from economically backward and underdeveloped areas. Small industrial units, handlooms and handicrafts units, dairy units and other animal husbandary programmes like piggery, goat rearing, ship breeding, poultry units and also self employment units are set up under this programme. A new thrust has been given identifying new sector of income-generating projects. Under this scheme, 3,642 women have been benefited till 31 January 1993 during the year 1992-93.

Support to Training-cum-Employment Programme

This Programme of Support to Training-cum-Employment for Women (STEP) living below poverty line, was launched in 1987 to strengthen and improve the skills and employment opportunites in traditional sectors where majority of women are already working. The sectors include agriculture, animal husbandary, dairying, fisheries, handlooms, handicraft, cottage and village industries and sericulture. The focus is mainly on marginalised and assetless women from households of wage labourers, unpaid female workers, marginal labourers, female-headed households and other dispossessed groups in order to integrate them into the mainstream of development. Since, the inception of the programme, about 81,000 women have been benefited.

Women Development Corporations

The Scheme for setting up of Women Development Corporations (WDCs) was formulated in 1986-87. These corporations are expected to play a catalytic role in identifying the women entrepreneurs; provide technical consultancy services; facilitate availability of credit; promote marketing of products; promote and strengthen women's cooperatives; arrange technical facilities, etc. So far, the corporations have been set up in the states of Andhra Pradesh, Goa, Haryana, Himachal Pradesh, Jammu and Kashmir, Karnataka, Kerala, Madhya Pradesh, Maharashtra, Meghalaya, Punjab, Tamil Nadu, Uttar Pradesh, West Bengal and in the Union Territory of Chandigarh. The scheme has been transferred to the state sector during 1992-93.

Short Stay Homes for Women and Girls

Governments give grant-in-aid to voluntary organisations/institutes to assist/run short stay homes for women and girls. The scheme was started in 1969 with the objective of providing temporary shelter and rehabilitation to those women and girls who are in social and moral danger due to family problems, mental strain, social ostracism, exploitation or other causes. Each home at a time accommodates 20-30 inmates. There are 294 short stay homes sanctioned in different states/union territories.

Awareness Generation Projects for Rural and Poor Women

This programme is implemented by the Central Social Welfare Board through voluntary organisations. Under it, awareness generation camps are conducted for the rural and poor women. The number of participants in each camp is 25 women. Since, the inception of the programme, over 4,000 projects have been sanctioned benefiting about one lakh women.

Education Work for Prevention of Atrocities Against Women

Assistance is given under the programme to the organisations for education work for the prevention of atrocities against women through propaganda/publicity and research work of related issues.

Information and Mass Education

Public awareness about social problems and consequent efforts to bring the desired behavioural changes are envisaged to be achieved through the use of mass-media including electronic, print, traditional media and outdoor publicity, utilising the outlets of Information and Broadcasting Ministry which include AIR, Doordarshan, Field Publicity, DAVP, Song and Drama Division, etc. Voluntary organisations and related institutions are also involved in creating public awareness about social evils and public perceptions towards child care, health, nutrition as well as women's development. Documentary films, TV coverage with a focus on the girl child, women's issues and social problems like dowry, etc., are also being made to sensitize the public and project positive image of the girl child.

Rehabilitation of Women in Distress

The major objective of the scheme is to rehabilitate destitute women and their dependent children through vocational training and residential care and make them economically independent. The expenditure is shared among the Central Government, the state governments and the voluntary agencies in ratio of 45:45:10. A provision of Rs. 15 lakh has been made during the year 1992-93. This Centrally sponsored scheme has been transferred from 1 April 1992 to the state sector.

National Commission for Women (NCW)

A National Commission for Women was set up on 31 January 1992 to monitor the matters relating to constitutional and legal safeguards provided for women to monitor the implementation of legislations made to protect the rights of women, review the existing legislations concerning women and suggest amendments, wherever necessary and look into the complaints and take *suo-moto* notice of cases involving deprivation of the rights of women. The Commission has since started its activities.

National Plan of Action for the SAARC Decade of the Girl Child (1991-2000 A.D.)

In fulfilment of the commitment made by the Heads of the Governments/States/SAARC countries at Male in 1990, the Department had prepared a National Plan of Action for the SAARC Decade of the Girl Child. This Plan of Action draws its inspiration from both the National Policy for Children (1974) and the National Plan of Action for Children (1992). The girl child, being an integral part of the target group of children, she will derive the fullest possible benefit from the general plan of action. However, her gender-specific needs and requirements will be taken care of by this Plan of Action.

WELFARE OF THE DISABLED

According to the estimates of the World Health Organisation (WHO), 10 per cent of the population in the world has one or more physical or mental disabilities. In a sample survey conducted in 1981 by the National Sample Survey Organisation of India, the total number of disabled persons in the country may be about 120 lakh who suffer from locomotor, speech, hearing and visual disabilities. No precise estimate in respect of mental retardation is available. However, studies undertaken by research organisations have indicated the extent of mentally handicapped persons between 2 to 2.5 per cent of the population. The Ministry of Welfare continued to implement special programmes for the early detection, education, training and rehabilitation of various categories of disabled persons.

Rehabilitation Council

Rehabilitation Council, an apex body to enforce uniform standards in training of professionals in the field of rehabilitation of the handicapped in the country has been set up as an autonomous body during 1992-93. The council prescribes minimum standards of education and training of professionals; recognises certain institutions for conducting training programmes leading to degrees or diplomas. The council also recognises foreign degrees or diplomas or certificates on reciprocal basis and maintains Central Rehabilitation Register of persons who are allowed to practise or seek employment in rehabilitation services for the handicapped.

Rehabilitation Council has finalised the standardisation of 43 courses. The Council is also organising the joint entrance examination on all India basis for the course in physiotherapy, occupational therapy, prosthetic and orthotic engineering and diploma in mental retardation in respect of institutions under the control of the Minstry of Welfare. The Council has been converted into a statutory body through the Act of Parliament. The Act has received the assent of the President of India on 1 September 1992.

Prohibition and Drug Abuse

In keeping with its nodal responsibility for drug abuse prevention, the Ministry of Welfare has been sponsoring a variety of research studies on the subject through major academic and research institutions. Recently, a nationwide project covering 33 cities and drug prone areas was commissioned by the Ministry to ascertain the nature and extent of the problem, to delineate the major socio-economic factors contributing to it, to identify areas and population groups affected or susceptible to it, and to assess adequacy or otherwise of the available services. Though, the studies were based on the perceptions of informed persons and affected individuals, the findings thereof provided some important clues for a better understanding of the problem and of its ill effects on the individual, the family and the society at large.

Article 47 of the Constitution enjoins that the state shall endeavour to bring about prohibition of consumption except for medicinal purposes, of intoxicating drinks and drugs which are injurious to health. Responsibility for fulfilling the Constitutional obligation in regard to prohibition rests largely with the state governments. The Centre has, however been continuously making efforts to educate people about ill effects of drinking through mass media and also encouraging voluntary organisations through grants for educative publicity.

During 1992-93, there has been spectacular expansion of drug couselling and de-addiction services to cover more beneficiaries. As against 111 couselling centres during the last year, the number has increased to 145. Similarly, as against 49 de-addiction centres last year, the number has increased to 84. The number of after-care centres has increased to 14 from 10 as compared to previous year. Inspite of financial constrains the number of all the services in the field of de-addiction has been expanded.

WELFARE OF THE AGED

The problems of the aged are acquiring larger dimensions and complexity due to the fact that the number of aged is on increase. According to 1981 census, the population of the aged persons (60+) was 4.45 crore. It is estimated to have increased to 5.48 crore in 1991. The proportion of the old people to the population has increased from 6.2 per cent in 1981 to 6.5 per cent in 1991. This may go upto 7.6 per cent by 2000 A.D.

Article 41 of the Constitution enjoins on the State to make effective provision within the limits of its economic capacity and development for public assistance in case of old age. Government is assisting voluntary organisations to establish old age homes and day care centres in providing diverse services to the aged. It is also making all efforts to provide and enlarge old age pension scheme implemented by different states and union territory administrations.

For the first time, a new scheme under Central sector has been launched by the Ministry for the welfare of the elderly people. The scheme is to be implemented through voluntary organisations and provides services like foster-care, day-care, old age homes, mobile medicare, etc. An amount of Rs. 10 crore has been provided under the scheme during the current Five Year Plan. The response to the scheme all over India continues to be overwhelming.

Department of Pension and Pensioners' Welfare

The Department of Pension and Pensioners' Welfare was set up in March 1985. Its responsibilities include formulation of policy and co-ordination of matters relating to the retirement benefits of all Central Government employees. The department has also provided an integrated approach to matters relating to post-retirement benefits.

A revised integrated pension structure was introduced on 1 January 1986 based on the recommendations of the Fourth Central Pay Commission. Pension for full qualifying service of 33 years is now uniformly calculated at 50 per cent of average emoluments drawn during the ten months preceding retirement. Benefit of the revised formula has also been extended to pre 1 January 1986 retirees and their pensions have also been improved upon. Minimum pension/

family pension is now, Rs. 375 per month. Pension structure for pre 1 January 1986 retirees as well as those retiring on or after 1 January 1986 is now linked to average Consumer Price Index (CP1) 608 (1960 as base) and a system for grant of relief against inflation beyond CPI 608 has been introduced. Provisions relating to retirement gratuity/death gratuity and family pension have also been improved upon. Procedure for sanction and disbursement of pension has been streamlined. Central Pension Accounting Officer (CPAO) has been set up from I January 1990. Action commences 24 to 30 months in advance of the date of retirement to ensure that retirement benefits are paid from the very date of retirement.

The revised procedure eliminates a number of intermediate agencies. The format of the pension payment order has been revised to indicate full particulars of service which go into the calculation of retirement benefits. The pension payment order also includes details regarding family pension; based on these details, payment of family pension is commenced by disbursing officers without requiring fresh sanctions from administrative authorities.

The Department of Pension and Pensioners' Welfare also plays a useful role in the redressal of pensioners' grievances. Pensioners' grievances received in this department are taken up with the respective ministries for appropriate remedial action. Qualified officers in this department also attend to pensioners' grievances in person; pensioners can meet the concerned officer on any working day between 4 PM and 5 PM without prior appointment. Pension *Adalats* are also held by the Ministry of Railways, Department of Posts, Department of Telecommunication and Ministry of Defence at places where there is a large concentration of Central Government pensioners in order to sort out pensioners' grievances on the spot.

Research and Publication

On research side, about 15 new studies have been sponsored to evaluate on going programmes of the Ministry in the field of handicapped, drug abuse, ageing, etc. About five conferences/workshops have been funded on various subjects dealt by the ministry. Translation of Encyclopaedia of Social Work in Hindi is in progress and likely to be completed shortly. In addition, six new publications are likely to be brought out by the Planning. Research, Evaluation and Monitoring Division (PREM) of the ministry, namely: Social Work Education Facilities in India, Summary of Research Reports, compilation of Social Welfare Statistics, Directory of Voluntary Organisations, A pocket book on Social Welfare and Development, etc.

QUESTIONS FOR EXERCISE

1. Describe Governmental efforts of child development in India.
2. Evaluate Women Development programme in India.
3. Write short note on the following in Indian context :
   (i) Welfare of the Disabled.
   (ii) Welfare of the Aged.

Bibliography

Alam, S. Manzoor, *Metropolitan, Hyderabad and Its Region*, Asia Publishing House, Bombay, 1972.

Chandra, Subhash, *Social Participation in Urban Neighbourhood,* National Publishers, New Delhi, 1977.

Doshi, Harihar, *Traditional Neighbourhood in a Modern City,* Abhinav Publications, New Delhi, 1974.

Dwyer, D.J., *People and Housing in Third World Cities.* Longmans, London, 1975.

Ferriera, J.V. and S.S. Jha (eds.), *The Outlook Tower : Essays on Urbanization in Memory of Patrick Gaddes,* Popular Prakashan Bombay, 1976.

Geoffery, K. Payne, *Urban Housing in the Third World,* Robert Maclehouse and Company Limited, 1977.

Ginsburg, Norton, "On Planning and Modernization in India", in Allen G. Noble and Ashok K. Dutt (Eds), *Indian Urbanization and Planning,* Mc Graw Hill Publishing Company Ltd., New Delhi, 1977.

Gupta, K. Surendra, "Economic Aspects of Urbanization" in *The Indian Journal of Social Work.* Vol. xxxvi, Nos. 384 Oct. '75 and Jan. '76.

Jakobson, Leo and Ved Prakash, "Urbanization in India. The Need for Normative Regional Development" in Allen G. Noble and Ashok K. Dutt (eds) *op.cit.*

Kulakarni, M.G., "Spatial Distribution : Some Characteristics in Aurangabad City" in Ferriera J.V. and Jha, S.S. (Eds.), *op.cit.*

Mishra, R.P. (ed), *Million-Cities of India,* Vikas Publishing House Pvt. Ltd., 1978.

Nangia, Sudesh, *Delhi Metropolitan Region : A Study in Settlement Geography,* K.B. Publications, New Delhi, 1976.

Narain, Vatsala, "Demographic Aspects of Urbanization" in *The Indian Journal of Social Work*, 1976, Vol, XXXVI Nos. 3 and 4 Oct. 1975 and Jan. 1976.

Nobal, Allen G. and K. Dutt (ed.), *Indian Urbanization and Planning : Vehicles of Modernization.* McGraw Hill Publishing Company Limited, New Delhi, 1977.

Singh, Andrea Menefer, *Neighbourhood and Social Networks in Urban India,* Marwah, New Delhi, 1976.

Singh, Harihar, *Kanpur, : A Study in Urban Geography,* Davis Printing Agency. Banaras, 1972.

Sinha, Pradip, *Calcutta In Urban History,* Firma K.L.M. Private Ltd., 1978.

Venkatarayappa, K.N., "Social Life of An Urban Community" in Ferriera J.V. and Jha S.S. (Eds.), *op. cit.*